Texas Promulgated Contracts Practice:

1st Edition

Performance Programs Company

Stephen Mettling
Ryan Mettling
Dan Hamilton

Material in this book is not intended to represent legal advice and should not be so construed. Readers should consult legal counsel for advice regarding points of law.

6810 190th Street East, Bradenton, FL 34211
info@performanceprogramscompany.com
www.performanceprogramscompany.com

ISBN: 978-1965482599

Texas Promulgated Contracts Practice

Table of Contents

PREFACE

Welcome to Texas Promulgated Contracts Practice published by Performance Programs Company. This course is one of the six required 30-hour prelicense education courses that every candidate for a Texas real estate salesperson license must complete before sitting for the state licensing examination administered by the Texas Real Estate Commission (TREC). Together, the six courses total 180 hours of qualifying education and are designed to give new licensees a thorough foundation in the law, ethics, and professional practice of Texas real estate.

About This Course

Contracts are the instruments through which every real estate transaction is created, modified, and concluded. A licensee who cannot read a contract carefully, complete a form correctly, explain provisions clearly to clients, and recognize when something is wrong before it becomes a problem will not serve clients well regardless of how skilled that licensee is in every other dimension of practice. This course treats contract law not as an abstract legal subject but as the practical core of professional real estate work in Texas.

The text is organized into nine chapters that build understanding progressively, beginning with the legal principles and Texas regulatory framework that govern real estate contracts, moving through the promulgated forms that licensees use every day, and ending with a hands-on workshop in which you complete those forms from realistic transaction facts.

Topics Covered

The opening chapters establish the foundation. You will study the origins of Texas real estate regulation, the essential elements and classifications of a valid contract, and the rules that govern how contracts are formed, performed, modified, and terminated. You will also study the Texas Real Estate License Act and TREC rules, the role of the Broker-Lawyer Committee in drafting promulgated forms, the antitrust limits on broker conduct, and the line between permissible brokerage activity and the unauthorized practice of law.

The heart of the course is the promulgated forms themselves. Several chapters work through the One to Four Family Residential Contract (Form 20-19) paragraph by paragraph, along with the financing addenda that accompany it, the earnest money and termination option, title insurance, the survey, and the property condition and seller disclosure notices. The course then examines the five other promulgated sale contracts, the temporary residential leases, and the addenda, amendment, and notice forms that licensees use to address situations the main contract does not cover.

A later chapter addresses other matters that surround the transaction, including the elements of fraud, the current broker compensation environment and the antitrust principles that apply to it, and the federal Fair Housing Act. The course closes with a Form Application Workshop, where you complete TREC forms from three realistic transactions and check your work against the completed answer forms.

How to Use This Text

Each chapter opens with a set of learning objectives and closes with a Snapshot Review summarizing the key rules, definitions, and principles introduced in that chapter. These summaries are designed for focused review and exam preparation.

This text presents approximately two hundred pages of instruction covering Texas contract law, the promulgated forms, and the practice of completing those forms correctly. Because this is a course about the forms themselves, the complete current set of TREC promulgated contracts, addenda, the amendment, and the related notices and disclosures is reproduced at the back of the book for ready reference.

You are encouraged to keep that forms section open beside each chapter, to locate every paragraph and provision as it is discussed, and to read the actual language of each form rather than relying on description alone. Becoming comfortable navigating the promulgated forms in their published layout is one of the central goals of this course, and having the forms reproduced here lets you study and practice on the same documents you will use in daily practice.

About the Authors

For nearly fifty years, Stephen Mettling has been actively engaged in real estate education. Beginning with Dearborn in 1972, then called Real Estate Education Company, Mr. Mettling managed the company's textbook division and author acquisitions. Subsequently he built up the company's real estate school division which eventually became the country's largest real estate, insurance and securities school network in the country. In 1978, Mr. Mettling founded Performance Programs Company.

Ryan Mettling, partner and publisher of Performance Programs, is an experienced online curriculum designer, author, and course developer.

Dan Hamilton is recognized nationally as a real estate author, educator and broker. During a Texas career spanning over 25 years, he has owned and operated many brokerages and received numerous professional awards and honors. Dan has operated his own school of real estate and currently teaches courses throughout the state. He has served on the board of the national Real Estate Educators Association (REEA) and as President of the Texas Real Estate Teachers Association (TRETA).

CHAPTER 1:
TEXAS CONTRACT LAW OVERVIEW

Chapter Overview

This chapter provides an in-depth introduction to Texas contract law as it applies to real estate practice. The material covers the origins of real estate regulation in Texas, the essential elements that make a contract valid, the classifications of contracts, and the rules that govern how contracts are formed, performed, modified, and terminated. Special emphasis is placed on the promulgated contract forms published by the Texas Real Estate Commission, the role of the Texas Real Estate Broker-Lawyer Committee, the boundaries of permissible licensee conduct, and the current addenda and amendment forms in use. Students will also examine dispute resolution options, seller disclosure obligations, and the proper use of the TREC Amendment to Contract.

Learning Objectives

Upon completing Chapter 1, the student will be able to:

1. Trace the history of Texas real estate regulation from the 1930s through the establishment of the Texas Real Estate Commission and explain TREC's current authority to promulgate and require the use of contract forms.
2. Identify and explain the four essential elements of a valid contract and apply each element to residential real estate transactions in Texas.
3. Distinguish among valid, void, voidable, and unenforceable contracts and explain the practical significance of each classification for real estate licensees.
4. Compare express, implied, executed, executory, bilateral, and unilateral contracts and give real estate examples of each type.
5. Explain the Texas Statute of Frauds and Recording Acts, identify which agreements must be in writing to be enforceable, and apply those requirements to common real estate scenarios.
6. Describe the rights and remedies available to a buyer or seller when the other party breaches a contract, including specific performance, specific damages, and termination with release of earnest money.
7. Explain the proper use of the TREC Amendment to Contract (Form 39-11) and describe how addenda are incorporated into a promulgated contract.
8. Distinguish among mediation, arbitration, and litigation as methods of dispute resolution, and explain the concepts of reasonable time and time is of the essence as they apply to contractual deadlines.

Contents

- Consideration
- Legal Objective
- Contract Classifications
- The Texas Statute of Frauds and Recording Acts
- Time in Contracts: Reasonable Time and Time Is of the Essence
- Contract Performance and Interpretation
- Assignment, Novation, and Discharge
- Breach of Contract and Remedies
- Mediation, Arbitration, and Litigation
- Seller Disclosures and Closing Obligations
- Contract Amendments and Addenda

The Origins of Texas Real Estate Regulation

Before the 1930s, real estate in Texas was largely unregulated. Anyone could call themselves a real estate broker, negotiate transactions, and draft agreements without any licensing requirement, educational standard, or government oversight. Brokers routinely prepared written contracts for buyers and sellers, a practice that placed them in the role of attorneys even though they had no legal training. Because attorneys hold the exclusive authority to draft legal documents, this created both a professional and legal problem that the legislature would eventually address.

In 1939 the Texas Legislature passed the Real Estate Dealer's License Act (REDLA), which for the first time required real estate agents to obtain a state license before practicing. The Secretary of State administered the act from its passage until 1949, when the Texas Real Estate Commission (TREC) was created and assumed those responsibilities. At the same time, the name of the governing statute was changed to the Texas Real Estate License Act (TRELA), the name by which it is still commonly known today.

TREC is the state agency that licenses and regulates real estate brokers and sales agents in Texas. Its authority extends to real estate brokerage, appraisal, inspection, home warranty, and timeshare interest providers. The Commission is composed of nine members appointed by the governor: six must be active brokers with at least five years of licensed experience, and three must be members of the general public with no financial interest in the real estate industry. TREC holds full rule-making authority, and its rules carry the force of law.

One of TREC's most significant responsibilities is the promulgation of standard contract forms for use in residential real estate transactions. Promulgated forms are forms that have been officially adopted by TREC and that license holders are required to use when negotiating contracts for the sale, exchange, option, lease, or rental of any interest in real property. The Texas Administrative Code (TAC) Chapter 537 reinforces this requirement and identifies limited exceptions to it.

The Texas Real Estate Broker-Lawyer Committee is the body that drafts and recommends contract forms to TREC for promulgation. The Committee has thirteen members: six appointed by TREC (who must be active real estate brokers), six appointed by the State Bar of Texas (who must be licensed attorneys), and one member of the public appointed by the governor. When the Committee completes a form or revision, it submits the form to TREC for review and approval. TREC typically allows licensees two to three months to study and become familiar with a newly promulgated form before its use becomes mandatory.

As of July 2026, the current promulgated sale contracts in Texas are the One to Four Family Residential Contract (Resale) (Form 20-19), the Residential Condominium Contract (Resale) (Form 30-18), the

Unimproved Property Contract (Form 9-18), the Farm and Ranch Contract (Form 25-17), the New Home Contract (Completed Construction) (Form 24-20), and the New Home Contract (Incomplete Construction) (Form 23-20). All six of these contracts were updated effective July 1st, 2026. Each form is available on the TREC website at trec.texas.gov.

TREC does not promulgate listing agreements, buyer representation agreements, property management contracts, forms for commercial property, or residential leases other than the two temporary residential lease forms used in connection with a sale. Those forms are the Seller's Temporary Residential Lease (Form 15-7) and the Buyer's Temporary Residential Lease (Form 16-7), both of which were updated effective January 5, 2026. For other types of agreements, license holders should direct clients to an attorney or a real estate trade association.

The Right to Fill In Contracts

When TRELA was enacted, it resolved the tension between real estate practice and the unauthorized practice of law by drawing a clear line. TREC regulates licensees who act in a third-party capacity, meaning those who represent buyers or sellers rather than acting as a principal in the transaction. A licensee acting as a principal (buying or selling property for themselves) is not subject to the promulgated form requirement in the same way.

The law permits a license holder to fill in the blanks of TREC-promulgated forms on behalf of clients, and doing so does not constitute the unauthorized practice of law. The key is that the license holder is completing a form that has already been drafted by attorneys on the Broker-Lawyer Committee. The licensee's role is to accurately insert the facts of the transaction into the spaces provided, not to create legal language or modify the form's terms.

Unauthorized practice of law covers two activities: constructing legal documents and giving legal advice or opinions about the legal effect of a document. A license holder may explain what a contract provision says but may not offer a legal opinion about what it means or how a court would interpret it. The Special Provisions paragraph in the promulgated contracts is the only designated place where a licensee may add factual statements and business details that are specific to the transaction and not otherwise addressed in the form. It is not a space for legal clauses or language that grants rights or remedies.

A license holder who drafts legal instruments, gives legal opinions, or advises clients on title validity outside of these limits risks TREC disciplinary action and may face charges of unauthorized practice of law. License holders must never alter a promulgated form's printed language, cross out provisions without the direction of the parties, or add language that creates legal rights beyond those stated in the form. If a client needs legal advice, the licensee's proper response is to refer that client to a licensed attorney.

Exceptions to the requirement to use promulgated forms exist but are narrow. A license holder acting as a principal in a transaction, a government agency requiring its own form, a property owner or the owner's attorney preparing the form, and situations where no promulgated form exists and an attorney or the Broker-Lawyer Committee has prepared a suitable form are all recognized exceptions under TAC Chapter 537.

The Four Elements of a Valid Contract

A contract is a voluntary agreement between legally competent parties to perform or refrain from performing some legal act, supported by legal consideration. This definition contains the four essential elements that every valid contract must have: agreement (mutual assent), consideration, competent parties, and a legal objective. If any one of these elements is missing, the contract is not valid.

Importantly, the elements do not need to be listed in a specific order, and no single element takes priority over the others.

Contracts are a fundamental part of everyday life. When a person buys a cup of coffee, boards a bus, or downloads an application on a phone, a contract has been formed. In real estate, the stakes are considerably higher, but the underlying principles are the same. Contract law in common law countries rests on the principle expressed in the Latin phrase pacta sunt servanda, which translates loosely as agreements are to be kept.

A contract must not be trifling, indeterminate, impossible, or illegal. Contracts may generally be created in writing, orally, or even by conduct, but a contract for the purchase of real estate must be in writing to be enforceable in Texas. Notice that the requirement of a written instrument is not itself one of the four essential elements. It is a separate requirement imposed by the Texas Statute of Frauds, which is addressed in a later section of this chapter.

To illustrate the four elements with a simple example: when a customer buys a donut at a bakery, the purchase is a voluntary agreement (the customer wanted to buy and the clerk wanted to sell), between competent parties (both are adults capable of making the decision), for a legal objective (the sale of food is lawful), supported by consideration (the customer paid money and received the donut in return). All four elements are present, making the exchange a binding contract even though no written document was signed.

Competent Parties

For a contract to be valid, all parties must be legally competent to enter into it. In the context of real estate, both the buyer and the seller must be of legal age and must have sufficient mental capacity to understand what they are agreeing to. In Texas, the age of majority is 18. A person who is under 18 may nonetheless have legal capacity to contract if they are or have been married, if they are serving in the military, or if a court has formally granted them emancipated status. Adult status acquired through marriage is not lost even if the marriage ends in divorce before the person turns 18.

A competent party is most easily understood by describing what a competent person is not. A person is not competent if they have been declared legally insane by a court, if they are under the influence of drugs or alcohol to the point that they cannot understand the nature and effect of the agreement, or if their mental development is insufficient to allow them to make independent decisions and appreciate the consequences of their actions.

Temporary incompetence is a recognized legal concept. A person who was intoxicated at the time of signing may later argue that they lacked capacity when the contract was executed. However, this is harder to prove than permanent incompetence because the person is typically sober long before any court hearing takes place. Courts will also consider whether the person acted in accordance with the contract after regaining capacity. If a buyer, for example, signed a contract while intoxicated and then spent the next three weeks applying for a mortgage, a court would likely find that the buyer ratified the contract through those subsequent actions and is therefore bound by it.

A license holder should never attempt to make an independent judgment about whether a person is mentally competent to sign a contract. If a licensee refuses to present an offer on the grounds that the potential buyer appears to be under the influence, the licensee could be found in violation of the Federal Fair Housing Act or could be breaching fiduciary duties owed to a client. If there is a genuine concern, the broker should be consulted immediately and, if necessary, the matter referred to legal counsel.

Competency Illustrated

Consider the following situation. A new home builder in Colleyville held an open house on a Sunday. A woman came in alone, viewed the home, and offered to pay the full asking price of $890,000 in cash without any negotiation. She agreed to close in fourteen days and gave the builder the business card of her financial advisor. A written contract was signed by both parties that same day. The next morning the builder contacted the financial advisor, who confirmed that the woman had more than sufficient funds but had been declared legally insane by a court. She had a guardian and frequently visited properties on weekends to write contracts she had no legal capacity to form. The financial advisor declined to proceed. The contract was void because one party lacked legal capacity from the outset.

There is little the builder could have done to prevent this. Requiring a mental health evaluation from every prospective buyer before accepting an offer is not practical and could expose the builder to a discrimination claim. The builder's best recourse was to continue marketing the property. The lesson for licensees is that they cannot always screen for legal capacity, but they can document every transaction thoroughly and consult their broker the moment a capacity concern arises.

Mutual Assent

Mutual assent means that all parties to the contract have agreed to all of the terms. Both words matter here. Agreement must be to all the terms, not just most of them, and it must come from all the parties, not just some of them. If a property is held by twelve heirs in an estate, all twelve must agree before a valid contract exists. If even one term remains unresolved, there is no contract, only a continuing negotiation.

In practice, mutual assent arises through the process of offer and acceptance. A buyer typically makes an offer in writing, and the seller decides whether to accept, reject, or counter that offer. If the seller counters, the original offer is extinguished, and the buyer now holds a new offer to accept, reject, or counter in turn. This process continues until either every term is agreed upon or one of the parties walks away. Courts examining whether a contract exists ask whether a reasonable person in the position of each party would have understood that a binding agreement had been reached.

A court's primary goal when interpreting a contract is to determine and give effect to the intent of the parties as expressed in the written document. In Seagull Energy E&P, Inc. v. Eland Energy, Inc., 207 S.W.3d 342 (Tex. 2006), the Texas Supreme Court stated that the objective is to ascertain what the parties meant from the language they actually used. This is why precision in drafting matters so much. A contract that is internally inconsistent or ambiguous may be unenforceable. As the Texas Supreme Court observed in Heritage Resources, Inc. v. NationsBank, 939 S.W.2d 118 (Tex. 1996), a contract is ambiguous when its meaning is uncertain and doubtful or is reasonably susceptible to more than one interpretation. When a contract is that unclear, the best practice is to start over, draft a new agreement with clear language, and obtain fresh signatures from all parties.

For mutual assent to be valid, acceptance must be free and voluntary. A contract that was obtained by misrepresentation (an error in a material fact), fraud (an intentional misrepresentation), duress (the use of force), menace (a threat of violence), or undue influence (the use of position or power to overcome another person's free will) is not the product of genuine assent. Additionally, there must be mutuality of obligation, meaning both parties are bound to perform. Neither party should be in a position to tower over the other during negotiations.

Neatness and clarity in contract drafting are professional obligations, not merely stylistic preferences. When a contract is confusing, it creates risk for both parties and for the licensees involved. The proper course is to prepare a clean, complete document and obtain signatures on that version, while retaining all prior drafts in the transaction file.

Consideration

Consideration is the element of a contract that requires something of value to change hands between the parties. Without consideration, an agreement is merely a gift, and courts will generally not enforce it. In real estate, consideration is almost always money exchanged for property, but the law recognizes a broader range of exchanges. A house traded for another house, a car exchanged for a parcel of land, or any other thing of value can satisfy the consideration requirement.

Texas law recognizes two types of consideration. Valuable consideration is something with objective monetary value. Cash is the most common form, but anything with market value qualifies. Good consideration refers to love and affection, the type of consideration present when a parent transfers property to a child as a gift. Good consideration is legally sufficient to support a contract, but it is much more difficult to prove in court than valuable consideration because it is inherently subjective. Gratuitous consideration, meaning a promise to give something for nothing in return, will not be enforced by the courts.

In Texas real estate transactions, it is rare for a buyer to have cash immediately available and equally rare for a seller to have a deed ready to deliver on the day the contract is signed. The buyer will need time to obtain financing, and the seller will need time to clear title through a title company or attorney. Each party therefore signs the contract with a promise: the buyer promises to pay the agreed price, and the seller promises to convey the property. These mutual promises constitute consideration and make the contract binding even though actual performance is weeks or months away. Courts require reasonable proof that the transaction benefited both parties.

Consideration must be present-oriented, not a compensation for something already done. In the English case Eastwood v. Kenyon, a guardian borrowed money to educate and raise a young girl. When she later married, her husband promised to repay the loan. The court refused to enforce that promise because the guardian's actions had already been completed before the husband made his promise. Past performance cannot serve as consideration for a new promise. Similarly, a promise to do something one is already legally obligated to do (such as obeying the law) provides no consideration for a new agreement, as established in Collins v. Godefroy.

Legal Objective

The final essential element is that the contract must have a lawful purpose. An agreement formed for an illegal objective or one that violates public policy is void from the start. Courts will not enforce a contract whose purpose is to accomplish something the law prohibits.

A straightforward example is a buyer who wants to purchase property near the Texas-Mexico border in order to use it as a base for smuggling contraband. Even if neither party mentions the illegal purpose in the written contract, the agreement cannot be enforced because its true objective is criminal. A more common example in practice involves zoning. If a buyer enters into a contract to purchase land for commercial development, but the land is zoned exclusively for single-family residential use and there is no realistic prospect of a zoning change through the governmental approval process, the contract's purpose is contrary to public policy and may be unenforceable.

The requirement of a legal objective is closely related to the concept of a void contract. When the objective of a contract is illegal at the time of formation or becomes illegal due to a change in law after formation, the contract is void.

Contract Classifications

Valid, Void, Voidable, and Unenforceable

A valid contract is one that is legally binding and enforceable by a court. All four essential elements are present, every term has been completely agreed upon, the parties are competent adults, nothing in the agreement is illegal or contrary to public policy, and the contract is expressed with sufficient clarity that a court can determine exactly what each party is required to do. The terms of a valid contract must be definite and certain. As the courts have noted, it would be unjust to compel performance of a contract whose terms are so vague that the court cannot determine what performance it is ordering.

A void contract is one that has no legal force or effect. It is treated as though it never existed. Common causes of a void contract include a missing essential element (such as no consideration), terms that are illegal or that have become illegal due to a change in law, or a party who has been declared legally incompetent by a court. Because a void contract never legally existed, it cannot be made valid by ratification, and no breach of contract claim can be based on it. A court action to declare the contract void is not required, though wise licensees will always document such situations in writing.

A voidable contract is one that is potentially valid but that can be set aside by one or more of the parties under certain circumstances. If a party was underage at the time of signing, or if evidence later emerges that a party lacked mental capacity even though that had not been formally adjudicated, the contract may be voidable at the option of the affected party. Contracts obtained through coercion, threats, false statements, undue influence, misrepresentation, or fraud are voidable by the victim of that conduct. The fundamental distinction between void and voidable is that a voidable contract can be legal and enforceable depending on how the parties choose to treat it, while a void contract was never legal at all.

An unenforceable contract is one that the courts will not compel the parties to perform, even though it might otherwise appear valid. If both parties voluntarily perform all of their obligations, the agreement will be honored. But if one party refuses to perform, the other party cannot sue to force compliance. The most common example in real estate is an oral listing agreement. If a broker finds a ready, willing, and able buyer but the seller refuses to pay the commission, the broker has no legal recourse because TREC rules require that any agreement obligating a party to pay a commission must be in writing to support a lawsuit.

Express and Implied Contracts

An express contract is one in which the terms are stated clearly and precisely, leaving no room for interpretation through the parties' conduct or unstated assumptions. Although a verbal agreement can technically be express if its terms are specific and unambiguous, written contracts are far more reliable as express agreements because the written word provides an objective record that any outside party (including a judge) can examine and interpret. The difficulty with verbal express contracts is that meaning is conveyed not only by words but also by tone, body language, and context, none of which are preserved in a document.

An implied contract is one in which the agreement is inferred from the actions of the parties rather than from explicit words. When one party reasonably expects certain conduct from the other based on their interactions, and the other party behaves in a way that confirms those expectations, an implied contract may exist even without any formal agreement. Many legal disputes arise from implied contracts because one party believed the other had committed to a certain course of action, while the other party did not share that understanding.

Executed and Executory Contracts

In real estate, the term executed is used in two related but distinct senses. In the most common usage, a contract is executed when all parties have signed and initialed every page and counterpart, meaning the negotiation is complete and the parties are bound. In the stricter legal sense, a contract is executed when all of its promises have been fully performed. In most residential transactions, that moment arrives at the closing table when the buyer delivers the purchase funds and the seller delivers the deed.

From the moment the parties reach agreement on every term through the date of closing, the contract is executory, meaning that obligations remain to be fulfilled. The buyer still needs to obtain financing, the seller still needs to clear title, inspections must be completed, and any agreed repairs must be made. All of these promises keep the contract open. Only when every obligation has been met and the transaction closes does the contract become fully executed in the legal sense.

Bilateral and Unilateral Contracts

A bilateral contract is one in which both parties make promises to each other and both have rights and obligations under the agreement. The prefix bi means two, and in a bilateral contract both sides are bound. Nearly every real estate sale contract is bilateral. The buyer promises to pay the agreed price, the buyer promises to obtain financing and pay for any agreed survey, and the buyer promises to close on the agreed date. The seller promises to convey the property, to make any agreed repairs, and to deliver clear title by closing. Each promise creates a corresponding right in the other party and an obligation in the promising party. If either party fails to perform any term, the other party may seek a remedy.

A unilateral contract is one in which only one party makes a promise, and the other party is not obligated to act but, if they do act, the promising party must perform. A reward poster is a classic example: the owner promises to pay anyone who finds a lost item, but no one is required to look. In real estate, a listing agreement between a seller and a broker is traditionally characterized as unilateral. The seller promises to pay a commission if the broker produces a ready, willing, and able buyer. The broker makes no promise to find a buyer, but if the broker does perform and a qualified buyer is produced, the seller is obligated to pay. Option contracts, feasibility study agreements, and similar arrangements are also examples of unilateral contracts in real estate practice.

The Texas Statute of Frauds and Recording Acts

The Texas Statute of Frauds requires that all documents involving the transfer of an interest in real property from one person to another must be in writing to be enforceable. This includes contracts for the sale of real estate, mortgages, deeds of trust, and easements. Leases for a term longer than one year must also be in writing. Note that one year and one day is considered longer than one year for this purpose.

The Statute of Frauds does not prohibit verbal contracts. It renders certain verbal agreements unenforceable. Suppose a landlord verbally agrees to lease a property for five years. The tenant pays rent for the first six months with no dispute, and then announces that they will be vacating at the end of the following month. The landlord cannot enforce the five-year term because the lease was not in writing. The tenant's verbal commitment is unenforceable even though both parties originally understood their agreement.

The Texas Recording Acts require that any claim, interest, or ownership in real property be recorded in the public records of the county where the property is located. Recording provides constructive notice to the world, meaning that anyone who later seeks to buy, lease, or mortgage the property is charged with knowledge of all recorded interests. This system of public records protects buyers, lenders, and other parties by making prior claims discoverable through a title search.

Time in Contracts: Reasonable Time and Time Is of the Essence

When a contract does not specify a deadline for performance, the courts apply a standard of reasonable time. Reasonable time is the amount of time that is fairly necessary, given the circumstances, for a party to do what the contract requires. It is determined by reference to trade practice, custom, and the specific facts of the situation. A court's finding of whether a delay was reasonable or unreasonable depends on the totality of the circumstances, including any expectations about timing that were expressed between the parties even if not written into the contract.

Time is of the essence is a phrase used in contracts to establish that strict compliance with stated deadlines is required. When this language appears in a contract, missing a deadline constitutes a material breach that may allow the non-breaching party to terminate the agreement and seek remedies. Without this specific language, courts in many states, including Texas, generally do not treat timing as essential and may allow some latitude for minor delays that do not harm the other party.

Even when a time is of the essence clause is present, courts sometimes give the breaching party an opportunity to cure the missed deadline or may disregard the clause entirely if enforcing it would be inequitable given the circumstances. In Foundation Development Corp. v. Loehmann's, Inc., the tenant received a demand for payment of common area maintenance charges with a ten-day cure period specified in the lease. The tenant mailed payment that arrived twelve days after the tenant received the demand. The landlord filed suit on the eleventh day. Both the trial court and the appellate court found in favor of the tenant, concluding that the breach was trivial and that the parties still had agreement even after the technical deadline passed. The time is of the essence clause was not held sufficient to justify termination under those circumstances.

The lesson for Texas real estate licensees is direct and important. A licensee should never add the words time is of the essence to a TREC promulgated contract without the explicit written direction of the parties. Adding such language unilaterally could constitute the unauthorized practice of law, because doing so introduces a legal consequence (the right to terminate upon a missed deadline) beyond what the form itself provides. TREC's position is that the promulgated contracts operate on a reasonable time standard, and modifications to that standard must come from the parties themselves.

Contract Performance and Interpretation

Performance is the fulfillment of one's obligations under a contract according to its terms. When both parties have fully performed all of their promises, the contract is said to have been executed and the parties are discharged from further liability. Until that point, the contract remains executory and each party retains enforceable rights against the other.

Courts in Texas have moved away from requiring the literal performance of every word in a contract toward requiring performance of the true meaning and intent of the parties. Part performance, meaning the completion of some but not all of what a party agreed to do, may be sufficient to entitle that party to partial recovery in appropriate circumstances. Specific performance is an equitable remedy by which a court orders a party to carry out the terms of the contract as agreed, rather than simply paying damages. Courts grant specific performance most often in real estate transactions because land is considered unique and monetary damages may be inadequate to compensate a buyer who loses the right to purchase a specific property.

The Four Corners Doctrine

When a dispute arises over the meaning of a contract provision, Texas courts apply the Four Corners Doctrine. Under this rule, the judge interprets any disputed clause in the context of the entire document, not in isolation. No single phrase will be pulled out and given a meaning that contradicts the agreement as a whole. The goal is to determine what a reasonable person would understand the contract to mean when reading it from beginning to end.

The Parol Evidence Rule

Closely related to the Four Corners Doctrine is the parol evidence rule. This common law principle prevents a party to a written contract from introducing oral evidence of prior negotiations or agreements to contradict or supplement the written terms of a contract that appears complete on its face. The reasoning is that the parties have chosen to express their final agreement in writing and, by doing so, have left behind any prior discussions or commitments that were not included in the document.

Consider a situation in which a seller verbally promised during negotiations to paint the house before closing, but that promise was never included in the written contract. Under the parol evidence rule, the buyer cannot later ask a court to order the seller to paint the house, because the verbal promise is outside the written agreement. The contract as signed represents the full scope of the parties' obligations.

The parol evidence rule reinforces why licensees must ensure that every material agreement between the parties is put in writing at the time of contract. A verbal side agreement, however clearly understood by both parties, will not survive a legal dispute if it was not captured in the written document. A practical illustration: if a buyer and seller conduct an extended verbal negotiation and ultimately agree verbally on a price of $235,000, but the licensees forget to change the written offer and both parties sign a contract showing $200,000, a court applying the parol evidence rule would most likely enforce the written price of $200,000. The licensees would bear the consequences of the error. This is why every counteroffer and every change to the price or terms of a transaction must be reflected in a signed written document.

Assignment, Novation, and Discharge

Assignment

Assignment occurs when one of the parties to a contract transfers their rights and obligations under that contract to a third party. A common real estate example involves a buyer who wishes to take title in the name of a trust or family LLC rather than in their personal name. The buyer may enter into the purchase contract individually and then assign their rights to the entity before closing. Assignment is also used by law enforcement personnel and others who need to keep their names out of the public property records for safety reasons.

Novation

Novation occurs when the original parties to a contract agree to replace that contract with a new one. In a real estate transaction, novation might be appropriate when a home inspection reveals significant issues that lead to such extensive renegotiation that the original document is no longer a clear expression of the parties' agreement. Rather than layering amendment upon amendment on an increasingly confusing document, the parties may choose to set aside the original contract and execute a new one. With novation, the parties remain the same but the agreement is entirely replaced.

Discharge of a Contract

A contract may be discharged, meaning terminated and the parties released from their obligations, in several ways. The most common is full performance: when both parties have done everything they promised, the contract is discharged. A contract may also be discharged by mutual agreement, as when both the buyer and seller decide not to proceed and agree in writing to release each other from their obligations. Fraud by either party is grounds for discharge. A legal impossibility, such as a buyer discovering that a zoning classification makes their intended use of the property illegal with no prospect of a variance, may also discharge a contract. Finally, a court may order discharge in certain circumstances, such as when a minor reaches the age of majority and elects to void a contract they entered into while underage.

Breach of Contract and Remedies

A breach of contract occurs when one party fails to perform an obligation required by the agreement. In real estate, breaches most commonly take the form of a buyer who refuses to close, a seller who backs out after accepting an offer, or either party failing to meet a contractual deadline. It is important to understand that only a court can make the final determination of whether a breach has occurred. A licensee should never advise a client that the other party is in breach or recommend a course of action based on that judgment. The proper guidance to give a client who believes the other party has breached is to consult an attorney and, simultaneously, to notify the broker.

When a breach occurs, the non-breaching party has three primary remedies available.

Specific performance is the remedy by which the non-breaching party asks a court to order the breaching party to carry out the terms of the contract as written. In residential sales, specific performance is most often sought by a buyer whose seller has refused to convey the property. Courts will grant specific performance in real estate cases more readily than in other types of contracts because real property is considered unique. However, courts are less likely to order a buyer to purchase a home than to order a seller to sell one, because compelling someone to borrow money and purchase real estate against their will may be seen as inequitable.

Specific damages is the remedy by which the non-breaching party seeks monetary compensation for the actual losses caused by the breach. The injured party, typically through an attorney, presents evidence of their out-of-pocket losses, which may include marketing expenses, appraisal and inspection fees paid in anticipation of closing, carrying costs during the period the property was under contract, and in some cases damages for emotional distress. A court then determines the amount that is fair and reasonable under the circumstances.

Termination with release of earnest money is the third option and is often the most practical in residential transactions. Either party may choose to terminate the contract rather than pursue litigation. Termination requires that the earnest money deposited with the escrow agent be released to the appropriate party. The parties may agree that one party receives all of the earnest money, or they may agree to split it. Once the earnest money is released and the contract is terminated, neither party retains any further rights against the other arising from that contract. This means that a seller who accepts the earnest money as their remedy cannot later sue for additional damages, because the release of the earnest money constituted full settlement of the dispute.

Equitable title is the interest in a property that the buyer acquires when a purchase contract is executed. The seller retains legal title until the deed is delivered at closing, but the buyer's equitable interest in the property means that the seller cannot freely convey the property to another party during the contract period. This concept is relevant to the termination process because releasing the earnest money and terminating the contract extinguishes the buyer's equitable interest, freeing the seller to relist the property.

Mediation, Arbitration, and Litigation

When a dispute arises between a buyer and a seller, the parties have several avenues for resolution before or in lieu of going to court. The appropriate path depends on the nature and severity of the dispute, the willingness of the parties to communicate, and the terms of any dispute resolution provisions in the contract.

Open Discussion

The first and least adversarial option is simply for the parties to sit down with their brokers and discuss the problem. Many disputes stem from misunderstandings that can be resolved once both sides have had an opportunity to explain their perspectives. Brokers are trained in dispute resolution and can facilitate this conversation. Licensees should not attempt to resolve a significant dispute without involving the broker, both because brokers may be able to defuse the situation and because poorly handled direct negotiations can escalate tensions. The broker must be careful not to make the situation worse by taking an overly aggressive position on behalf of one party.

Mediation

If direct discussion does not resolve the dispute, mediation is the next step. In mediation, a neutral third party called a mediator facilitates a conversation between the parties with the goal of helping them reach a voluntary settlement. The mediator does not impose a decision. Mediation is non-binding in the sense that either party may walk away without having reached a settlement and may still pursue court action afterward. In fact, many Texas courts require parties to attempt mediation before proceeding to trial, because a successful mediation frees court resources for cases that cannot be resolved any other way.

There are no state licensing requirements for mediators in Texas, but a mediator appointed by a court or a governmental body must have at least forty classroom hours of approved training in dispute resolution techniques. For disputes involving parent-child matters, an additional twenty-four hours of training in family dynamics, child development, and family law is required. The Texas Mediator Credentialing Association maintains a voluntary credentialing program for practicing mediators.

Arbitration

Arbitration is a more formal process in which a neutral arbitrator (or a panel of arbitrators) hears evidence and arguments from both sides and then issues a binding decision. Unlike mediation, the arbitrator's ruling is final and generally cannot be appealed or replaced by a court judgment. Texas does not have a state licensing requirement for arbitrators, but professional arbitrators typically hold law degrees or advanced degrees in law, public policy, or a related field, and many have completed additional training through organizations such as the American Arbitration Association. Gaining practical experience through internships at community dispute resolution centers is a common path into the field.

Litigation

Litigation is the formal process of resolving a dispute through the court system. It involves filing a lawsuit, conducting discovery, presenting evidence, and obtaining a judgment from a judge or jury. Litigation is almost always the most expensive and time-consuming dispute resolution option, typically requiring attorneys, expert witnesses, and extensive document production. For most residential real estate disputes, litigation is the option of last resort. Licensees should always encourage clients to exhaust other remedies before filing suit and to obtain qualified legal counsel before doing so.

Statutes of Limitations

A statute of limitations sets the maximum period of time within which a legal claim must be filed. Once the period expires, the right to sue is permanently lost. In Texas, the statute of limitations for written contracts is four years from the date the cause of action arises, and for oral contracts it is two years. Breach of contract and breach of fiduciary duty claims are both subject to the four-year limitation for written agreements. The statute of limitations for injury to personal property in Texas is two years. Under the Texas Business and Commerce Code, the parties to a contract for the sale of goods may agree to reduce the limitations period to as little as one year, but they may not extend it beyond the statutory period.

Seller Disclosures and Closing Obligations

Both the seller and the buyer carry disclosure and performance obligations that must be met for a real estate transaction to close properly. Understanding these obligations is an important part of a licensee's role in guiding clients through the transaction.

The seller's primary disclosure obligation is to complete the Seller's Disclosure Notice (TREC Form 55-1, effective May 28, 2026). This form is not a promulgated contract form but it meets the legal requirements for a seller to disclose the known condition of the property and any items that may be of concern to the buyer. The seller is also required to disclose the presence of any known environmental hazards that may affect future occupants, including asbestos, carbon monoxide, electromagnetic fields, groundwater contamination, lead-based paint, mold, PCBs, radon gas, underground storage tanks, urea formaldehyde, and waste disposal sites. The seller should also disclose the known presence of any endangered species of animals or plants on the property.

At closing, the seller must deliver the deed that conveys the property to the buyer. This typically also means providing either an abstract of title or a title insurance policy showing clear, marketable title. The seller must provide a release of the lien that was paid off during the closing and deliver any other documents necessary to transfer clear title to the buyer.

The buyer's obligations at closing include delivering the balance of the funds needed to complete the purchase. These funds come from the buyer's down payment and any loan proceeds from the lending institution. The buyer must also have a hazard insurance policy in effect for at least one year from the closing date to protect both the buyer and the lender against loss from fire, storm, or other covered events. A survey of the property must also be obtained by the buyer or, if agreed in the contract, provided by the seller, to satisfy the requirements of the lender.

Contract Amendments and Addenda

The Role of Addenda

Addenda are supplemental forms attached to a promulgated contract at the time of execution to address circumstances not covered by the main contract form. Each addendum must be referenced in paragraph 22 of the primary contract (in most promulgated forms) by checking the appropriate box. If the applicable addendum is not listed among the choices, the licensee should enter its name on the line provided for additional items and check that box. Failure to reference an addendum in paragraph 22 creates a risk that the addendum will be overlooked or treated as not part of the agreement, potentially exposing the licensee to liability.

The decision to attach an addendum must come from the client, not the licensee. A licensee should not include an addendum simply because they think it would be useful. The addendum should reflect the specific needs and desires of the party the licensee represents. Each TREC addendum addresses a distinct set of circumstances, and licensees must become familiar with when each one is appropriate. Examples include the Third Party Financing Addendum (Form 40-11) for transactions involving conventional, FHA, or VA financing; the Seller Financing Addendum (Form 26-8) when the seller is providing a note; the Back-Up Contract Addendum (Form 11-9) when the property is already under contract; the Short Sale Addendum (Form 45-2) when the sale proceeds will not satisfy the existing mortgage; and the Addendum for Property Subject to Mandatory Membership in a Property Owners Association (Form 36-11) for HOA properties.

The Amendment to Contract

When both parties to an existing contract agree to change one or more of its terms after it has been executed, the proper vehicle is the TREC Amendment to Contract (Form 39-11, effective July 1, 2026). An amendment does not replace the original contract. It modifies only the specific provisions identified in the amendment. If the changes required are so extensive that the original document has become confusing or internally inconsistent, the parties should consider writing an entirely new contract rather than layering multiple amendments on the old one. Courts have found contracts unenforceable when too many amendments, cross-outs, and handwritten changes made the document's meaning impossible to determine. All amendments must be in writing and signed by both parties to comply with the Statute of Frauds.

The Amendment to Contract identifies the property by street address and city from the original contract. Its provisions address the following categories of changes. Paragraph 1 handles adjustments to the sales price structure, including the down payment (1A), the loan amount (1B), and the total sales price (1C). Remember that the down payment plus the loan amount must always equal the sales price, so a change in one typically requires a corresponding adjustment to at least one other. Paragraph 2 documents agreed repairs that the seller will complete as a condition of closing, and is most commonly used after a home inspection report has been received. Paragraph 3 changes the closing date when circumstances such as pending repairs, the buyer's need to exit a lease, or a lender's request for additional time require more time than the original contract allows. The closing date may be extended more than once by successive amendments if both parties agree. The date entered must be a specific calendar date; a licensee must never write a phrase such as at lender's discretion in this space, as that would be imprecise language with legal consequences and would likely be considered unauthorized practice of law.

Paragraph 4 adjusts the seller's contribution to the buyer's closing costs as originally set out in paragraph 12 of the residential contract, and must state the new amount as a specific dollar figure, not a percentage. Paragraph 5 addresses repairs required by the lender's appraiser on VA or FHA loans and refers to the repair provisions in paragraph 7E of the residential contract. An itemized list of repairs should be attached, and the amendment should show the total dollar amount each party has agreed to pay. Paragraph 6 extends or adjusts the buyer's termination option period from Paragraph 5B of the residential contract when the buyer needs additional time to complete inspections or receive an engineer's report. Extending the option period may also require a corresponding extension of the closing date. The seller is not required to agree to an extension of the option period. Paragraph 7 allows the buyer to waive the unrestricted right to terminate for which the option fee was paid, effectively declaring the contract final. Paragraph 8 extends the financing approval deadline from the Third Party Financing Addendum when the buyer has switched lenders or needs additional time for the loan process. Paragraph 9 modifies the Special Provisions paragraph of the original contract to add, remove, or change items of personal property to be included in or excluded from the sale, or to adjust other factual details originally stated there.

The amendment must be signed by both the buyer and seller with the date entered under each signature. When multiple amendments have been executed in a single transaction, numbering them sequentially and maintaining all of them together with the original contract in the transaction file is essential for a clear record.

Changes to a contract that are made before the contract is signed are technically modifications, not amendments. If the parties handwrite a change into a printed contract form before signing, both parties must initial the change. Most digital contract platforms used in Texas do not allow direct modification of the printed language, which is why the Amendment to Contract form is so important for post-execution changes.

Chapter 1: Snapshot Review

The following review summarizes the key rules and concepts from Chapter 1.

Origins of Texas Real Estate Regulation

- The Real Estate Dealer's License Act (REDLA) was enacted in 1939 and required real estate agents to obtain licenses for the first time; it was administered by the Secretary of State until 1949
- The Texas Real Estate Commission (TREC) assumed administration in 1949 and the governing statute was renamed the Texas Real Estate License Act (TRELA)
- TREC is composed of nine members: six active brokers with at least five years of licensed experience and three public members with no financial interest in real estate
- TREC promulgates standard contract forms that license holders are required to use when negotiating contracts for the sale, exchange, option, lease, or rental of real property
- The Texas Real Estate Broker-Lawyer Committee has thirteen members (six brokers, six attorneys, one public member) and drafts promulgated forms for TREC's adoption
- TREC typically provides two to three months for licensees to become familiar with a newly promulgated form before its use becomes mandatory

Current Promulgated Contract Forms (Effective July 1st, 2026)

- One to Four Family Residential Contract (Resale) -- Form 20-19
- Residential Condominium Contract (Resale) -- Form 30-18
- Unimproved Property Contract -- Form 9-18
- Farm and Ranch Contract -- Form 25-17
- New Home Contract (Completed Construction) -- Form 24-20
- New Home Contract (Incomplete Construction) -- Form 23-20
- Seller's Temporary Residential Lease -- Form 15-7 (effective January 5, 2026)
- Buyer's Temporary Residential Lease -- Form 16-7 (effective January 5, 2026)

The Right to Fill In Contracts and Unauthorized Practice of Law

- TREC regulates licensees acting in a third-party capacity; a licensee acting as a principal is treated differently
- Filling in the blanks of a TREC-promulgated form is not the unauthorized practice of law
- Unauthorized practice of law includes constructing legal documents and giving legal opinions about the effect of a document
- The Special Provisions paragraph is the only place to add factual statements and business details not addressed elsewhere in the form
- A licensee must never alter promulgated form language, cross out provisions without the direction of the parties, or add language creating legal rights beyond those stated in the form
- TAC Chapter 537 exceptions: licensee acting as principal, government agency form required, form prepared by property owner or owner's attorney, or no promulgated form exists and an attorney or the Broker-Lawyer Committee prepared the form

The Four Elements of a Valid Contract

- Agreement (mutual assent): all parties have agreed to all terms
- Consideration: something of value is exchanged
- Competent parties: all parties are of legal age and mentally capable

- Legal objective: the purpose of the contract is lawful and not contrary to public policy
- All four elements must be present; the absence of any one renders the contract invalid
- A written contract is not an essential element but is required by the Statute of Frauds for real estate transactions

Competent Parties

- In Texas, the age of majority is 18; exceptions apply for those who are married, serving in the military, or emancipated by court order
- Incompetence may be permanent (declared by a court) or temporary (intoxication or drug impairment at the time of signing)
- A licensee may not independently determine that a person is incompetent and refuse to present an offer on that basis

Mutual Assent

- Mutual assent requires agreement to all terms by all parties; a single unresolved term means there is no contract
- Offer and acceptance is the standard mechanism; a counteroffer extinguishes the original offer
- Acceptance is not valid if obtained by misrepresentation, fraud, duress, menace, or undue influence
- A contract is ambiguous when its meaning is uncertain or reasonably susceptible to more than one interpretation; an ambiguous contract should be rewritten

Consideration

- Valuable consideration is something of objective monetary value; good consideration is love and affection; gratuitous consideration is not enforceable
- In Texas, a promise to perform is sufficient consideration; parties are bound by their mutual promises even before the actual exchange occurs
- Past consideration (something already done before the promise was made) is not valid consideration for a new promise

Contract Classifications

- Valid: all elements present, terms definite and certain, legally binding and enforceable
- Void: no legal force or effect; treated as if it never existed; cannot be ratified; no breach claim may arise from it
- Voidable: can be set aside by one of the parties; causes include minority, incapacity, fraud, duress, misrepresentation, and undue influence
- Unenforceable: courts will not compel performance; oral listing agreements are a common real estate example
- Express: terms are stated clearly; Implied: terms are inferred from conduct
- Executed: all obligations have been fully performed; Executory: obligations remain to be fulfilled
- Bilateral: both parties make promises and bear obligations; virtually all real estate sale contracts are bilateral
- Unilateral: only one party makes a promise; listing agreements and option contracts are examples

Texas Statute of Frauds and Recording Acts

- All transfers of interests in real property must be in writing to be enforceable

- Leases for more than one year must be in writing; one year and one day qualifies as more than one year
- The Statute of Frauds makes certain verbal agreements unenforceable; it does not make them criminal
- The Recording Acts require all claims and interests in real property to be recorded in the county public records

Time in Contracts

- Reasonable time applies when no deadline is specified; courts determine reasonableness based on circumstances and trade practice
- Time is of the essence is specific contract language that makes strict deadline compliance a material obligation
- A licensee must never add time is of the essence language to a TREC promulgated contract without explicit direction from the parties; doing so may constitute unauthorized practice of law

Contract Performance and Interpretation

- Performance is the fulfillment of all contractual obligations; courts require performance of the true intent of the parties
- Specific performance is an equitable remedy ordering a party to carry out the contract as written; available in real estate because land is unique
- Four Corners Doctrine: disputed provisions are interpreted in the context of the whole document, not in isolation
- Parol Evidence Rule: oral evidence of prior negotiations may not be used to contradict a written contract that appears complete
- Every counteroffer and agreed change must be documented in writing at the time it is made

Assignment, Novation, and Discharge

- Assignment transfers a party's rights under a contract to a third party
- Novation replaces the original contract with a new agreement while keeping the same parties
- Discharge releases the parties from their obligations; may occur by full performance, mutual agreement, legal impossibility, fraud, or court order

Breach of Contract and Remedies

- Only a court can determine whether a breach has occurred; licensees must not make that judgment for clients
- The three remedies for breach are: specific performance, specific damages, and termination with release of earnest money
- Once the earnest money is released as a remedy, no further claims for additional damages may be pursued
- Equitable title is the buyer's interest in a property from the time of contract execution until closing; it is extinguished when the earnest money is released and the contract terminated

Mediation, Arbitration, and Litigation

- Open discussion with brokers present should be the first step in any dispute
- Mediation is non-binding; a neutral mediator facilitates a voluntary settlement; either party may still pursue litigation if mediation fails
- Arbitration is binding; the arbitrator's decision replaces any court action

- Litigation is the most costly and time-consuming option and should be a last resort
- Statute of limitations for written contracts in Texas: four years; for oral contracts: two years

Seller Disclosures and Closing Obligations

- Sellers must complete the Seller's Disclosure Notice (Form 55-1) disclosing the known condition of the property
- Required environmental disclosures include asbestos, lead-based paint, mold, radon, underground storage tanks, and other known hazards
- At closing the seller delivers the deed, clears all liens, and provides title documentation
- At closing the buyer delivers all purchase funds, provides evidence of hazard insurance, and satisfies the lender's survey requirement

Contract Amendments and Addenda

- Addenda are attached at the time of contract execution; each must be referenced in paragraph 22 of the main promulgated contract
- The licensee's decision to attach an addendum must reflect the client's wishes, not the licensee's own preferences
- The Amendment to Contract (Form 39-11) is used to modify an executed contract; it does not replace the original agreement
- Amendment paragraph 3 requires a specific calendar date for any closing date extension; writing at lender's discretion is not permitted
- Amendment paragraph 4 requires closing cost contributions in dollar amounts, not percentages
- All amendments must be in writing and signed by all parties; amendments should be numbered and kept with the original contract
- Pre-signature handwritten changes to a printed contract are modifications, not amendments, and must be initialed by all parties

Chapter 1 Quiz: Texas Contract Law Overview

1. The Texas Real Estate Commission assumed administration of real estate licensing from the Secretary of State in what year?

a. 1939
b. 1949
c. 1956
d. 1968

2. How many total members serve on the Texas Real Estate Broker-Lawyer Committee?

a. 9
b. 10
c. 11
d. 13

3. Which of the following is NOT one of the four essential elements of a valid contract?

a. A written document
b. Consideration
c. Competent parties
d. Legal objective

4. A contract that is treated as though it never existed because it is missing an essential element is best described as what type of contract?

a. Voidable
b. Unenforceable
c. Void
d. Executory

5. Under the Texas Statute of Frauds, which of the following must be in writing to be enforceable?

a. A lease for exactly one year
b. A contract for the sale of real estate
c. An agreement to pay a finder's fee
d. A month-to-month rental agreement

6. Which type of consideration is defined as love and affection between the parties?

a. Good consideration
b. Valuable consideration
c. Past consideration
d. Gratuitous consideration

7. When a contract contains a time is of the essence clause, what is the legal effect of a party missing a stated deadline?

a. The escrow agent releases the earnest money immediately to the non-breaching party
b. The licensee bears personal financial liability for the missed deadline
c. The contract automatically renews with a new closing date
d. A material breach occurs that may allow the non-breaching party to terminate the contract

8. The rule that prevents a party from introducing evidence of prior oral negotiations to contradict a written contract that appears complete on its face is called what?

a. The Four Corners Doctrine
b. The Statute of Frauds
c. The Parol Evidence Rule
d. The Recording Act

9. A buyer accepts earnest money as the full remedy after a seller breaches a purchase contract. Which statement correctly describes the legal result?

a. The buyer retains the right to sue the seller for additional damages at a later date
b. Both parties are released from any further obligation under that contract
c. The seller must still complete any required repairs before the transaction terminates
d. The buyer may relist the property and recover any difference in the eventual sales price

10. A traditional residential listing agreement is best described as which type of contract?

a. Bilateral, because both the broker and the seller make promises to each other
b. Executed, because the seller has already signed the listing form
c. Void, because it is subject to the Texas Statute of Frauds
d. Unilateral, because only the seller makes a promise to pay if the broker produces a qualified buyer

11. In Texas, what is the minimum age at which a person is generally considered a competent party who is able to enter into a real estate contract?

a. 18
b. 16
c. 21
d. 17

12. When a licensee uses the TREC Amendment to Contract (Form 39-11) to extend the closing date, what must the licensee enter in the applicable blank?

a. The phrase "at lender's discretion" to provide scheduling flexibility
b. The number of additional days the parties need before closing
c. A specific calendar date
d. The initials of both the buyer and the seller

CHAPTER 2
TEXAS LAWS, RULES AND REGULATIONS

Chapter Overview

Texas has a comprehensive body of law that governs real estate practice and the professionals who engage in it. The Texas Real Estate License Act is the foundational statute, but it is supported by an extensive set of commission rules, anti-trust requirements, and the promulgation process administered by the Texas Real Estate Commission. Understanding these laws is not merely a matter of compliance. It is a matter of protecting clients, preserving a license, and avoiding the serious consequences that arise when a licensee crosses the line into the unauthorized practice of law. This chapter examines the rules governing the use of promulgated contract forms, the limits of what licensees may and may not do when working with contracts, and the step-by-step process by which an offer becomes a binding contract.

Learning Objectives

Upon completing Chapter 2, the student will be able to:

1. Identify the primary Texas laws and commission rules that govern a real estate licensee's use of contract forms and explain the consequences of non-compliance.
2. Define the unauthorized practice of law in the context of real estate and describe the specific acts that constitute a violation for license holders.
3. Explain the exceptions to the requirement to use TREC promulgated forms and apply those exceptions correctly to realistic transaction scenarios.
4. Describe the composition and role of the Texas Real Estate Broker-Lawyer Committee and explain how promulgated forms are created, revised, and made mandatory.
5. Distinguish between a unilateral mistake and a mutual mistake in a contract and identify the remedies available to the parties in each situation.
6. List the best practices a license holder should follow when completing a promulgated contract form to avoid errors and protect all parties to a transaction.
7. Explain the four options available to a seller upon receiving an offer and describe the process by which an offer becomes a binding contract under Texas law.

Contents

- Anti-Trust Compliance
- Presenting Offers and Multiple Offers
- When an Offer Becomes a Contract

The Texas Real Estate License Act and Contract Form Rules

The Texas Real Estate License Act, commonly known as TRELA, is the foundational law governing real estate professionals in Texas. Among its most important provisions are the rules relating to contract forms. TRELA gives the Texas Real Estate Commission the authority to adopt rules requiring license holders to use contract forms prepared by the Texas Real Estate Broker-Lawyer Committee and adopted by the commission. The result is a system of promulgated forms that licensees are generally required to use and may not freely substitute with forms of their own creation.

TRELA also establishes a clear limit on this requirement. The commission may not prohibit a license holder from using a contract form for the sale, exchange, option, or lease of an interest in real property if that form was prepared by the property owner, or if it was prepared by an attorney and required by the property owner. This exception exists because the commission's regulatory authority is triggered only when a licensee is acting in a third-party capacity, meaning as an agent for a buyer or seller. The commission does not directly govern buyers and sellers themselves. When a licensee is acting as a principal in a transaction, buying or selling property for themselves, the promulgated form requirement does not apply in the same way.

Listing contract forms adopted by the commission must include a provision informing the parties that real estate commissions are negotiable. Where appropriate, they must also include a provision explaining the availability of Texas coastal natural hazards information important to coastal residents. These are not optional disclosures. They are mandatory elements of any commission-adopted listing contract form.

Under Section 1101.652 of the Texas Occupations Code, the commission may suspend or revoke a license or take other disciplinary action if a license holder fails to use a contract form required by the commission. The state legislature regards proper form usage as sufficiently important to the protection of the public that non-compliance carries the risk of losing the right to practice entirely. Licensees should check the TREC website regularly and verify that they are using the current version of any form before proceeding with a transaction.

The Unauthorized Practice of Law

One of the most serious compliance obligations a Texas real estate license holder carries is the duty to avoid the unauthorized practice of law. Real estate transactions involve legal documents with binding consequences, and it is easy for a licensee acting in good faith to stray into territory that only a licensed attorney may occupy. Understanding exactly where that line falls is essential to protecting both the client and the license.

Under TRELA and TREC rules, a licensee may not practice law. More specifically, a licensee may not offer, give, or attempt to give legal advice, directly or indirectly. This prohibition extends to giving advice or opinions about the legal effect of any contracts or instruments that may affect title to real estate. A licensee may not give opinions about the status or validity of title to real estate. And a licensee must never attempt to prevent or discourage, in any manner, a principal to a real estate transaction from consulting an attorney. If anything, best practice points in the opposite direction: licensees should actively encourage clients to seek legal counsel whenever a question arises that goes beyond the plain facts of the transaction.

There is one recognized exception. If a licensee is also a licensed attorney in the state of Texas, that person may practice law. However, acting as both broker and attorney in the same transaction creates an inherent conflict of interest, and all parties to the transaction must be made fully aware that the individual is serving in both capacities.

What Licensees May Do

The existence of these prohibitions does not mean that licensees must remain silent about the documents they are helping clients complete. A licensee is both permitted and required to disclose to principals all pertinent facts within the licensee's knowledge, including facts that might affect the status of or title to real estate. The licensee should state those facts clearly and factually. If a client asks for an opinion about the legal meaning or effect of a contract term, the appropriate response is to explain what the provision says in plain language and to strongly recommend that the client consult an attorney for any legal interpretation.

A licensee may not undertake to draw or prepare documents that fix or define the legal rights of the principals to a real estate transaction. This prohibition becomes most relevant in practice when a client asks the licensee to add language to the Special Provisions paragraph of a contract that goes beyond factual statements and business details. If a client wants a clause that creates, modifies, or surrenders a legal right, that language must be drafted by an attorney, not inserted by the licensee. Attempting to craft such language, even with the best of intentions, is a violation of TRELA and puts both the client and the licensee at risk.

A licensee must also advise the principals, before they sign, that the instrument they are about to execute is binding on them. There is no automatic rescission period for a real estate purchase contract in Texas. Once both parties have signed and the other side has been notified of acceptance, a binding contract exists. Clients who are excited, nervous, or under financial pressure may not read every paragraph carefully. The licensee has an affirmative duty to make sure that the parties understand, in plain terms, that what they are signing will bind them to all of the obligations it contains.

Employing an Attorney

A licensee may not employ, directly or indirectly, a lawyer to represent any principal to a real estate transaction in which the licensee is acting as an agent, nor may the licensee pay for such representation. A licensee may hire and pay a lawyer to represent only the licensee in a real estate transaction, including the preparation of contract, agreement, or other legal instruments to be executed by the principals. The distinction matters because the moment a licensee begins hiring attorneys to work on behalf of clients, the licensee is crossing into territory that compromises the independence of both the legal and brokerage relationships.

Limits on Licensee Authority

TREC rules specify in detail what a licensee may and may not do when filling in a promulgated contract form. When negotiating real estate transactions, the licensee may fill in forms using exclusively forms that have been approved and promulgated by the commission or forms that are otherwise permitted by the rules. The licensee may fill in the blanks. That is the full extent of the license holder's authority to modify the printed text of a form.

A licensee may not add to or strike language from a promulgated form except under specific and limited conditions. The licensee may add factual statements and business details that the principals have requested, and may strike language only at the direction of the principals and only to the extent necessary to conform the instrument to the parties' intent. If a seller or buyer directs a licensee to strike a paragraph, the licensee may do so because the instruction comes from the principal. If the licensee believes the change could materially affect the transaction, the licensee should obtain written confirmation from the client that the client, not the licensee, directed the change. The agent on the other side of the transaction should inform their own client of the modification and recommend that an attorney review the document before proceeding.

A licensee may not add to a promulgated contract form any factual statements or business details for which a separate promulgated addendum, lease, or other form already exists for mandatory use. If there is a TREC promulgated form that addresses the situation, the licensee must use that form rather than attempting to handle the matter within the Special Provisions paragraph. For example, if a buyer's purchase is contingent on the sale of the buyer's existing home, the licensee must use the Addendum for Sale of Other Property by Buyer (Form 10-6) rather than describing the contingency in the Special Provisions paragraph. Using the wrong vehicle for this information is a violation of the commission rules.

A licensee may explain to the principals the meaning of the factual statements and business details contained in a contract form as long as the licensee does not offer or give legal advice. There is an important practical distinction here: explaining what a provision says is permissible; telling a client whether to accept, reject, or modify a provision on legal grounds is not.

Contract Mistakes and Remedies

A mistake in a contract is an error in the meaning of words, laws, or facts that causes one or both parties to enter into the agreement without fully understanding the outcomes or responsibilities it implies. Texas courts recognize two categories of contract mistake, and the distinction between them determines what remedy, if any, is available.

Unilateral Mistake

A unilateral mistake occurs when only one party to the contract is mistaken about a material term or the subject matter of the agreement. The other party either understands the true situation or should have known about the error. Because only one side is mistaken, this type of error can create an unfair advantage in bargaining power. If a contract was entered into on the basis of a unilateral mistake, a court will typically offer one of two remedies.

The first remedy is rescission. Contract rescission cancels the agreement entirely and restores both parties to the position they were in before the contract was executed. Rescission is available only when the non-mistaken party knew, or should have known, about the other party's mistake. The second remedy is reformation. Contract reformation rewrites the written agreement to reflect the parties' original understanding. Reformation is available only when one party was not aware that the written contract did not accurately reflect the actual agreement the parties reached.

The distinction is significant in practice. If the non-mistaken party knew about the error and said nothing, rescission is the likely outcome. If the non-mistaken party was genuinely unaware of the discrepancy, the court can reform the contract to correct it without canceling the entire agreement.

Mutual Mistake

A mutual mistake occurs when both parties to the contract share an erroneous belief about a material fact at the time of contracting. Consider the following scenario: a buyer and seller negotiate and execute a contract for the sale of a home, with closing scheduled in two weeks. One week before closing, the house is completely destroyed by a tornado and the seller has no insurance and no ability to restore the property to its previous condition. Because the entire contract was premised on the existence and condition of a specific house, and that house no longer exists, the buyer cannot be compelled to proceed. The subject matter of the contract has ceased to exist, making the original agreement impossible to perform. This is a mutual mistake, and it provides grounds to set aside the contract. TREC addresses this type of situation in the Casualty Loss paragraph of the One to Four Family Residential Contract (Form 20-19, effective July 1, 2026), which sets out the rights and obligations of the parties if the property is damaged or destroyed before closing.

Best Practices for Completing Contracts

Even when a licensee uses the correct form and stays within the boundaries of permissible activity, errors in the mechanics of completing a contract can create serious problems for clients and for the licensee. The following practices represent the professional standard for contract completion.

Contracts should be kept neat and legible. Sloppy, difficult-to-read documents invite disputes about what was agreed. All blanks in the form should be filled in accurately and completely. Leaving blanks unfilled can create ambiguity about the parties' intent or suggest that important terms were never addressed. Full legal names, not nicknames or abbreviated versions, should be used for all parties to the contract. Using incorrect or incomplete names can affect the enforceability of the agreement and create title problems at closing.

All numbers and figures should be double-checked before the contract is presented or signed. Mathematical errors in a purchase price, loan amount, or closing cost contribution can have consequences that are difficult and expensive to correct after the fact. All dates must be verified as well. A wrong closing date, an expired option period, or an incorrect financing deadline can trigger defaults or disputes that the parties never intended.

Clients should initial each page of the contract and any changes made to its terms, and should sign the signature page. Initialing confirms that each party reviewed the entire document and that any modifications were agreed upon. Each party should receive a copy of the executed contract as promptly as possible, and the licensee should obtain an original, meaning a version with original signatures, for the transaction file.

All addenda that are part of the agreement must be attached to the contract and referenced in the appropriate paragraph. Failing to attach a referenced addendum, or failing to reference an attached addendum, can create uncertainty about whether the addendum is actually part of the binding agreement. The legal description of the property must be double-checked carefully. An incorrect or incomplete legal description is one of the most common causes of title problems and can affect the validity of the deed delivered at closing.

The licensee's role is to explain the contract to the clients, not to interpret its legal ramifications. A licensee should not promise that a contract accomplishes any particular legal outcome. Real estate contracts put the desires of the parties regarding the sale of real property in writing. For anything beyond that, the client should be directed to an attorney. Finally, a licensee should never accept a poorly written or improperly completed contract from another real estate professional without raising the concern. Overlooking another agent's errors puts everyone involved, including the licensee's own client, at risk.

The Broker-Lawyer Committee

The Texas Real Estate Commission has the authority to form committees to assist in carrying out the business of regulating real estate practice. One of its most important standing committees is the Broker-Lawyer Committee, whose purpose is to draft and revise contract forms and other documents for use by licensees throughout the state.

The committee is composed of six real estate brokers appointed by the Texas Real Estate Commission and six attorneys appointed by the president of the State Bar of Texas. A thirteenth member, a representative of the general public, is appointed by the governor. This structure reflects the compromise that produced the committee in the first place: rather than litigating the question of whether broker-assisted contract preparation constituted the unauthorized practice of law, the State Bar and the real estate industry agreed to collaborate on a system of standardized forms that licensees could use without legal risk to themselves or their clients.

When a need arises for a new form or a revision to an existing one, the Broker-Lawyer Committee develops the language. The committee's recommendations go to the TREC board of directors, which has the final authority to approve and promulgate any form. A form becomes promulgated, meaning formally adopted and mandated by the commission, only after the board has approved it. Until that happens, the form may be available for voluntary trial use but is not required.

Promulgated Forms: Use, Reproduction, and Updates

Once the commission promulgates a form, that form is the one licensees must use for the kind of transaction it addresses. Working with an outdated contract or form is a violation of TREC rules. The commission does not excuse mistakes arising from the use of a superseded form. Prudent license holders monitor TREC communications, read real estate trade publications, and visit the TREC website regularly to stay current with form changes.

TREC promulgated forms may be reproduced only from specific approved sources. Acceptable sources include numbered copies obtained from the commission in printed or electronic format, printed copies made from commission copies, legible photocopies of those copies, or output from computer-driven printers that meet specific technical requirements. Software programs used to produce contract forms must not allow the user direct access to the text of the form. The software may permit the user only to insert language in blanks or to strike through language at the direction of the parties. The typefaces, text, number of pages, spacing, blank lengths, borders, and page layout must all appear identical to the commission's printed copies. The name and address of the software developer must appear legibly at the bottom of each page in a type size of no less than six and no more than ten points.

Forms approved or promulgated by the commission must also be reproduced on the same paper size used by the commission. The only additions permitted are the business name or logo of a broker, organization, or printer appearing at the top of the form outside the border, and the broker's name inserted in any blank provided for that purpose.

The current TREC promulgated sale contracts are the One to Four Family Residential Contract (Resale) (Form 20-19), the Unimproved Property Contract (Form 9-18), the New Home Contract (Incomplete Construction) (Form 23-20), the New Home Contract (Completed Construction) (Form 24-20), the Farm and Ranch Contract (Form 25-17), and the Residential Condominium Contract (Resale) (Form 30-18). All six were updated effective July 1, 2026. TREC does not promulgate listing agreements, buyer representation agreements, or property management contracts. For those, brokers typically use forms from the Texas REALTORS, forms created by an attorney, or forms developed by the broker's office. Salespeople use whichever forms their broker provides for these purposes.

Exceptions to Using Promulgated Forms

Section 537.11 of the Texas Administrative Code sets out the rule that a real estate licensee must use only TREC promulgated forms when negotiating contracts binding the sale, exchange, option, lease, or rental of any interest in real property. The rule also identifies four recognized exceptions.

The first exception applies when the licensee is functioning solely as a principal in the transaction, not as an agent. TREC governs licensees only when they act as a third party representing others. When a licensee is buying or selling property for themselves, they are acting as a principal and may use forms of their own choosing. A licensee who purchases a listed property as a personal investment, for example, is a buyer, not an agent, and the commission's form requirements do not apply in the same way. However, the licensee must disclose to all parties that they hold a Texas real estate license.

The second exception applies when an agency of the United States government requires a different form to be used. In these transactions the U.S. government is effectively acting as a principal, and the licensee has the right to fill in the government's form as directed.

The third exception applies when a contract form has been prepared by a principal to the transaction or prepared by an attorney and required by a principal. This situation arises most commonly when a licensee represents a buyer purchasing a home from a builder whose company uses its own attorney-prepared contract forms. It can also arise when an investor, a land developer, or a commercial property owner has their own preferred forms. In all of these cases the principal's direction to use a specific form gives the licensee the right to complete it. Licensees working with builder contracts should always advise buyer clients to have an attorney review the document before signing. Builder contracts are drafted by the builder's attorneys and may favor the builder's interests in ways that a TREC form, which is designed to be neutral between the parties, would not.

The fourth exception applies when no standard TREC form exists for the type of transaction involved, and the licensee uses a form prepared by a Texas-licensed attorney and approved by that attorney for the particular kind of transaction, or a form prepared by the Broker-Lawyer Committee and made available for trial use by licensees with the commission's consent. This situation is uncommon because TREC has promulgated forms for most standard residential transaction types. If a licensee believes no applicable form exists, the safe course is to seek additional guidance, check the TREC website, and consult the broker before using a non-promulgated form.

A Practical Illustration

Consider the following scenario. A real estate broker who is not an attorney helps a buyer purchase a home using a TREC promulgated form from 2019 that has since been superseded. The broker makes several hand-written modifications to bring the contract in line with current practices. In this situation, the broker has committed two separate violations: using an outdated form and modifying the printed text without the direction of the parties. Both violations expose the broker to disciplinary action by TREC.

If the same broker had used a current but non-promulgated form when a promulgated form was available, that would also be a violation. If the broker were a licensed Texas attorney, using a non-promulgated form would be permissible because the attorney exception applies, though the broker-attorney would need to disclose both roles to all parties. If the broker were purchasing the property for personal use as a principal, the use of a non-promulgated form would be permitted under the principal exception, and the broker would be required to disclose their license status.

Addenda and Voluntary Use of New Forms

A licensee may not add to a promulgated contract form any factual statements or business details for which the commission has promulgated a separate addendum, lease, or other form for mandatory use. The existence of a promulgated addendum addressing a particular circumstance means that the licensee must use that addendum. Attempting to address the same subject within the Special Provisions paragraph of the main contract when a dedicated form exists is a violation of the rules and may expose the licensee to disciplinary action.

There is a process by which newly created or revised forms become mandatory. When the Broker-Lawyer Committee completes a new or revised form, the commission may release it for voluntary use during a transition period. During this window, licensees may use either the old form or the new form. Licensees may also use forms that have been approved by the commission but not yet made mandatory. Once the commission formally promulgates a form and sets an effective date, the new form becomes mandatory on that date and the previous version is retired.

This transition process gives licensees time to become familiar with changes and to offer feedback about any practical difficulties. Licensees who encounter unusual circumstances during the transition period, or in any transaction where standard forms may not fully address the situation, should advise the parties to consult an attorney before executing any instrument. For example, if a buyer wishes to lease a property for one year before purchasing it, and no promulgated TREC form exists for that specific arrangement, the parties will need an attorney to draft documents that address their agreement. The licensee's role in this situation is to recognize the limitation and make the referral, not to improvise a solution within the forms available.

Anti-Trust Compliance

Real estate licensees operating in Texas must be aware that their conduct in the marketplace is subject not only to TRELA and TREC rules but also to federal anti-trust law. The Sherman Anti-Trust Act prohibits agreements among competitors that restrain trade or fix prices. TRELA mirrors this principle by making commissions negotiable and by making clear that no agreement among brokers to set, fix, or coordinate commission rates is permissible.

Price Fixing

Price fixing occurs when two or more real estate brokers conspire to charge the same commission rate or fee. In a competitive marketplace, individual brokers set their own rates based on the services they provide and the market conditions they face. When brokers coordinate to eliminate that competition by agreeing to charge identical or minimum rates, they harm consumers and violate federal law. A listing agreement must inform the parties that commissions are negotiable, and every licensee must understand that this is not a formality. It is a legal requirement rooted in anti-trust policy.

Boycotting

Boycotting is the active exclusion of a third person or group from participating in free commerce. In a real estate context, boycotting occurs when two or more brokerages agree, as a group, to refuse to show or sell each other's listings or to exclude a competitor from participation in cooperative transactions. Like price fixing, this conduct eliminates competition and harms the public.

Allocation of Customers

Allocation of customers is the division of the marketplace among competing brokers based on location, income level, or any other factor that limits competition. An example would be two brokers in a small community agreeing that buyers and sellers in one geographic area will be exclusively served by one broker and that the other broker will not compete for that business. This arrangement, however informal, is a restraint of trade and is prohibited.

Any of these anti-competitive practices can result in federal prosecution, substantial civil penalties, and the loss of a real estate license. Licensees who are approached with any suggestion of coordinating fees, dividing markets, or excluding competitors should refuse and report the conversation to their broker.

Presenting Offers and Multiple Offers

The buying process begins when a licensee and a buyer have identified a property and the buyer is ready to make an offer. The licensee sits down with the buyer, discusses the terms the buyer wants to propose, and goes through the promulgated contract form paragraph by paragraph. Every blank is filled in. Once the contract is complete, the licensee reviews it again with the buyer before asking the buyer to sign. Any addenda applicable to the transaction are attached at this stage, along with any cover letter that explains the buyer's position, loan approval status, or serious intent. At this point the document is an offer, not yet a contract.

Agency relationships must be clearly understood before the offer is presented. The licensee presenting the offer must know whether they represent the seller, the buyer, both parties as an intermediary, or neither party as a transaction coordinator. The manner in which the offer is presented and the duties owed to each party depend entirely on the agency relationship in place.

Once the offer is delivered to the seller or the listing agent, the seller, with the guidance of the listing agent, must evaluate it and decide how to respond. The listing agent's job at this stage is important. The agent should approach every offer with the understanding that it may represent the buyer's best position. Minor deficiencies in an offer should not automatically trigger a counteroffer when acceptance would accomplish the seller's goals. The agent is a third party whose role is to advise, but the decision belongs to the seller.

The Seller's Four Options

When a seller receives an offer, four responses are available.

The first option is acceptance. If the seller accepts all of the terms of the offer without modification, the offer becomes a contract. Acceptance must be absolute, meaning the seller agrees to every term, not just most of them. Once the seller has accepted, that acceptance must be communicated back to the buyer or the buyer's agent. Failure to communicate acceptance promptly creates uncertainty about whether a contract exists. A telephone call or text to the other agent constitutes notification, and a signed contract should follow as quickly as possible.

The second option is rejection. If the seller rejects the offer, both parties are free to move on. The seller may consider other offers and the buyer may look at other properties or submit a new offer on the same one. Rejection of any single term is a rejection of the entire offer. The seller cannot reject one provision while accepting others unless that action takes the form of a counteroffer.

The third option is a counteroffer. If the seller wants to change one or more terms of the original offer, the seller responds with a counteroffer. A counteroffer is not a modification of the buyer's offer. It is a new offer made by the seller to the buyer. The buyer's original offer is terminated the moment the seller responds with a counteroffer. If the buyer then rejects the seller's counteroffer, the seller cannot go back and accept the buyer's original offer because that offer no longer exists.

The fourth option is to fail to act. A seller may choose not to respond to an offer immediately. The buyer retains the right to withdraw the offer at any time before the seller's acceptance is communicated. A seller who waits too long risks losing the buyer entirely, particularly in a competitive market where the buyer is considering multiple properties.

Multiple Offers

In a competitive market with limited inventory, a seller may receive more than one offer on the same property. The listing agent must handle this situation carefully, ensuring that the seller understands all options and that all buyers are treated fairly. The listing agent should disclose to all parties the existence of multiple offers (without disclosing the specific terms of competing offers unless directed by the seller) and should advise the seller on how to respond. Buyers in a multiple-offer situation may be given the opportunity to submit their highest and best offer before the seller makes a decision. All offers and counteroffers must be in writing.

When an Offer Becomes a Contract

An offer becomes a contract only when all of the following have occurred: the seller (or buyer, in the case of a counteroffer) has agreed to every term of the offer, all parties have signed, and the acceptance has been communicated to the other side. Each of these three elements is required. An unsigned acceptance is not binding. A signed acceptance that has not been communicated leaves open the possibility that the offering party withdrew the offer before learning of the acceptance.

Communication of acceptance should occur as promptly as possible. In a competitive market, even a brief delay can give a buyer time to withdraw an offer or to accept another seller's counteroffer. When acceptance occurs, the licensee should communicate by every reasonable means simultaneously: by telephone call, text message, and email. A signed copy of the executed contract should be delivered to all parties no later than the following business day. An original, meaning a version that bears original signatures from all parties, should be provided as soon as practicable. Electronic signatures are valid under Texas law as long as both parties have agreed to use them.

When the last required signature or initial has been placed on the document by the final party to sign, and that signature has been communicated to the other side, the contract becomes effective. One of the licensees will then fill in the effective date blank in the contract. From that point forward, all of the deadlines and obligations in the contract begin to run. The earnest money must be delivered, the option fee must be paid if a termination option was negotiated, financing applications must be submitted, and the process of preparing for the closing formally begins.

These transactions involve real people with real financial stakes and real emotions. A buyer purchasing a home is often making the largest financial commitment of their life. A seller may be leaving a home they have lived in for decades. The licensees in the middle of this process carry a professional responsibility to manage the negotiation with care, communicate promptly and accurately, and keep every aspect of the agreement documented in writing. The moment a licensee begins cutting corners on documentation, relying on verbal understandings, or allowing verbal negotiations to outrun the written record, the foundation of a binding agreement is at risk.

Chapter 2: Snapshot Review

The following review summarizes the key rules and concepts from Chapter 2.

The Texas Real Estate License Act and Contract Form Rules

- TRELA authorizes the commission to require license holders to use contract forms prepared by the Broker-Lawyer Committee and adopted by TREC
- The commission may not prohibit use of a form prepared by the property owner or prepared by an attorney and required by the property owner
- TREC governs licensees acting as agents in third-party capacity; it does not directly regulate buyers and sellers as principals
- Listing contract forms must state that commissions are negotiable and, where applicable, must address Texas coastal natural hazards disclosures
- Failure to use a commission-required contract form may result in suspension or revocation of a license under Section 1101.652

The Unauthorized Practice of Law

- A licensee may not practice law, give legal advice or opinions, advise on the legal effect of instruments affecting title, give title validity opinions, or discourage a principal from consulting an attorney
- A licensee may and must disclose pertinent facts to principals, but must state facts only and not give legal opinions
- A licensee may not draft documents that fix or define the legal rights of principals to a transaction
- A licensee must advise principals that the document they are about to sign is binding; there is no automatic rescission period for real estate contracts in Texas
- A licensee may not hire or pay an attorney to represent a principal; the licensee may only hire an attorney to represent the licensee
- A licensee who is also a licensed Texas attorney may practice law but must disclose both roles and address the conflict of interest

Limits on Licensee Authority When Using Forms

- A licensee may fill in the blanks of a promulgated form only; the licensee may not add language or strike language from the form except at the direction of the principals
- Additions must be factual statements and business details; language creating legal rights must be drafted by an attorney
- If a TREC addendum exists for a particular circumstance, the licensee must use that addendum rather than addressing the matter in Special Provisions
- A licensee may explain what a contract provision says but must not interpret its legal effect or tell a client whether to accept, reject, or modify a term on legal grounds

Contract Mistakes and Remedies

- A unilateral mistake is an error held by only one party to the contract; the other party either knew or should have known about it
- Rescission (cancellation of the contract) is available when the non-mistaken party knew or should have known of the error
- Reformation (rewriting the contract to reflect the actual agreement) is available when the non-mistaken party was unaware of the discrepancy

- A mutual mistake occurs when both parties share an erroneous belief about a material fact; TREC's Casualty Loss paragraph in Form 20-19 addresses situations where the subject property is damaged or destroyed before closing

Best Practices for Completing Contracts

- Keep contracts neat and legible; fill in all blanks accurately
- Use full legal names for all parties; double-check all figures, dates, and the legal description
- Have clients initial each page and any changes; deliver copies promptly and obtain original signatures for the file
- Attach all addenda and reference them in the contract; verify that the current version of every form is being used
- Explain the contract to clients but do not interpret legal ramifications; refer legal questions to an attorney
- Do not accept poorly completed contracts from other licensees without raising the issue

The Broker-Lawyer Committee

- The committee consists of six real estate brokers appointed by TREC, six attorneys appointed by the president of the State Bar of Texas, and one public member appointed by the governor
- The committee drafts and revises contract forms; the TREC board of directors has final authority to approve and promulgate forms
- A form is promulgated, and therefore mandatory, only after the TREC board approves it

Promulgated Forms: Use, Reproduction, and Updates

- Current promulgated contracts (effective July 1, 2026): Form 20-19 (One to Four Family Residential Resale), Form 9-18 (Unimproved Property), Form 23-20 (New Home Incomplete Construction), Form 24-20 (New Home Completed Construction), Form 25-17 (Farm and Ranch), Form 30-18 (Residential Condominium Resale)
- TREC does not promulgate listing agreements, buyer representation agreements, or property management contracts; brokers obtain those from TAR, local boards, or attorneys
- Forms may be reproduced only from TREC-approved sources; software must replicate the form's typeface, spacing, page count, and layout exactly
- Using an outdated contract form is a violation of TREC rules; licensees must check the TREC website regularly for current versions

Exceptions to Using Promulgated Forms

- Licensee acting as a principal (buyer or seller) for themselves, not as an agent
- U.S. government agency requires a different form
- A principal to the transaction or an attorney hired by a principal has prepared and requires use of a different form
- No standard TREC form exists for the transaction type and the licensee uses a form prepared and approved by a Texas-licensed attorney or the Broker-Lawyer Committee with TREC's consent
- When using a non-promulgated builder or investor form, the licensee should strongly advise buyer clients to have an attorney review the document before signing

Addenda and Voluntary Use of New Forms

- If a promulgated addendum exists for a specific circumstance, it must be used; the Special Provisions paragraph is not a substitute for a mandatory addendum

- New or revised forms may be released for voluntary use during a transition period; either the old or new form may be used until the new form becomes mandatory
- Unusual circumstances that standard forms do not address require referral to an attorney before any instrument is executed

Anti-Trust Compliance

- The Sherman Anti-Trust Act and TRELA both prohibit anti-competitive conduct among real estate brokers
- Price fixing is when two or more brokers agree to charge the same commission rate; it eliminates competition and is prohibited
- Boycotting is when brokers collectively refuse to do business with a competitor or show another firm's listings
- Allocation of customers is when brokers divide the marketplace by geography, income, or other factors to eliminate competition
- Any of these practices can result in federal prosecution, civil penalties, and loss of a real estate license

Presenting Offers and the Seller's Four Options

- A completed and signed offer is an offer only, not a contract, until the seller accepts and communicates that acceptance
- All addenda must be attached to the offer at the time of presentation; agency relationships must be established before presenting
- Acceptance: seller agrees to all terms and communicates acceptance; the offer becomes a binding contract
- Rejection: seller declines; both parties are free to move on; rejection of one term is rejection of the entire offer
- Counteroffer: seller proposes changed terms; this is a new offer from the seller; the buyer's original offer is terminated and cannot be revived
- Failure to act: seller takes no action; buyer retains the right to withdraw the offer at any time before acceptance is communicated
- All offers and counteroffers must be in writing

When an Offer Becomes a Contract

- An offer becomes a contract only when all parties have agreed to every term, all have signed, and acceptance has been communicated to the other side
- Communication of acceptance should be immediate: by telephone, text, and email; a signed copy must follow promptly
- Electronic signatures are valid in Texas when both parties agree to use them
- The effective date of the contract is entered by a licensee after acceptance is communicated; all contractual deadlines run from that date
- Every negotiation and agreed change must be documented in writing; verbal understandings do not create enforceable contractual obligations

Chapter 2 Quiz: Texas Laws, Rules and Regulations

1. What statement must all Texas listing contract forms include regarding broker compensation?

a. The commission rate is set by the Texas Real Estate Commission
b. Real estate commissions are negotiable
c. The maximum commission rate allowed by Texas law is six percent
d. The commission is split equally between the listing and buyer's broker

2. Which of the following actions constitutes the unauthorized practice of law for a Texas real estate licensee?

a. Explaining what a contract provision says in plain language to a client
b. Disclosing a known material defect in the property to a prospective buyer
c. Filling in the blanks of a TREC promulgated contract form on behalf of a client
d. Giving a client an opinion about the legal effect of a contract term

3. What is the correct legal term for the remedy that cancels a contract entirely and restores both parties to the position each held before the contract was executed?

a. Rescission
b. Reformation
c. Novation
d. Specific performance

4. The Texas Real Estate Broker-Lawyer Committee includes six real estate brokers, six attorneys, and one public member. Who appoints the public member to the committee?

a. The president of the State Bar of Texas
b. The Texas Real Estate Commission board of directors
c. The governor of Texas
d. The Texas Legislature

5. When a seller responds to a buyer's offer by proposing different terms, what is the legal effect on the buyer's original offer?

a. The original offer is held in suspension until the parties resolve the counteroffer
b. The original offer is terminated and cannot be revived by either party
c. The original offer remains open for the buyer to accept at any time during negotiations
d. The original offer automatically becomes part of the counteroffer by default

6. Which of the following is a recognized exception to the requirement that a licensee use a TREC promulgated form?

a. The licensee believes the promulgated form does not adequately favor the buyer's interests
b. The transaction involves commercial property with a value over one million dollars
c. The licensee has held an active license for more than ten years
d. The licensee is acting as a principal in the transaction, buying or selling property for himself or herself

7. When two or more competing real estate brokers agree to charge the same commission rate, this conduct is known as what?

a. Price fixing
b. Boycotting
c. Allocation of customers
d. Market restraint

8. Under Texas law, at what point does an offer become a binding contract?

a. When the seller signs the contract and returns it to the listing agent
b. When the buyer delivers earnest money to the escrow agent
c. When all parties have signed and acceptance has been communicated to the other side
d. When the option fee is delivered to the seller

9. A licensee discovers that another real estate professional has submitted a poorly completed offer on a contract form with several blanks left empty. What is the appropriate professional response?

a. Accept the contract as submitted in order to avoid conflict with the other agent
b. Raise the concern directly with the other licensee rather than overlooking the errors
c. Add corrections directly to the contract and initial each change on behalf of the clients
d. Present the incomplete contract to the client and note the deficiencies in the Special Provisions paragraph

10. A buyer and a seller both believe a property includes a large storage building, but a survey reveals the building sits entirely on the adjacent lot. Both parties are mistaken about the same material fact. This situation is an example of which type of contract mistake?

a. Unilateral mistake
b. Reformation error
c. Legal impossibility
d. Mutual mistake

CHAPTER 3
PARTIES, PROPERTY AND FINANCING

Chapter Overview

This chapter walks through the first eight paragraphs of the One to Four Family Residential Contract (Resale), TREC Form 20-19 (effective July 1, 2026), the most frequently used promulgated contract in Texas real estate practice, and then examines the four primary financing addenda that accompany it. Each paragraph of the contract is examined in detail so that a license holder can fill out the form accurately, understand why each provision exists, and recognize the common mistakes that result in disciplinary action or financial liability. A realistic scenario is provided throughout the chapter to allow the student to work through the contract in a practical context. The chapter then addresses the Third Party Financing Addendum (Form 40-11), the Loan Assumption Addendum (Form 41-3), the Seller Financing Addendum (Form 26-8), and the Addendum for Release of Liability on Assumed Loan and/or Restoration of Seller's VA Entitlement (Form 12-3), all in their current versions.

Learning Objectives

Upon completing Chapter 3, the student will be able to:

1. Explain the TREC form numbering system and identify the distinguishing features printed at the top of Form 20-19 that define its appropriate use.
2. Correctly complete Paragraphs 1 and 2 of Form 20-19, including the identification of parties, the legal description, improvements, accessories, exclusions, and reservations.
3. Complete Paragraphs 3 and 4 of Form 20-19, including the cash portion, financing amount, total sales price, and any lease disclosures that apply to the property.
4. Explain the earnest money and termination option provisions of Paragraph 5, including delivery deadlines, the consequences of missed deadlines, and how the option fee is handled at closing.
5. Navigate Paragraph 6 of Form 20-19, including the title policy, the title commitment, survey options, buyer's objection rights, and all required title notices.
6. Complete Paragraphs 7 and 8 of Form 20-19, covering access and inspections, the Seller's Disclosure Notice, lead-based paint requirements, property condition acceptance, lender-required repairs, environmental matters, residential service contracts, and broker disclosures.
7. Explain when and how to complete the Third Party Financing Addendum (Form 40-11), including all seven financing types, the Buyer Approval and Property Approval provisions, and the FHA/VA required provision.
8. Describe the purpose and structure of the Loan Assumption Addendum (Form 41-3), the Seller Financing Addendum (Form 26-8), and the Release of Liability Addendum (Form 12-3), and explain the key provisions and risks associated with each.

Contents

- Paragraph 2: Property
- Paragraph 3: Sales Price
- Paragraph 4: Leases
- Paragraph 5: Earnest Money and Termination Option
- Paragraph 6: Title Policy and Survey
- Paragraph 7: Property Condition
- Paragraph 8: Brokers and Sales Agents
- Third Party Financing Addendum (Form 40-11)
- Loan Assumption Addendum (Form 41-3)
- Seller Financing Addendum (Form 26-8)
- Addendum for Release of Liability on Assumed Loan and/or Restoration of Seller's VA Entitlement (Form 12-3)

How TREC Numbering Works

Every TREC promulgated form carries a number that identifies the form and tracks its revision history. The One to Four Family Residential Contract (Resale) is Form 20-19. The first number, 20, identifies the document itself. The second number, 19, shows how many times the form has been revised since it was first promulgated. The first version of this contract was Form 20-1, and each subsequent revision increased the number to the right of the hyphen by one. The current version, Form 20-19, was revised effective July 1, 2026 and is the mandatory form for all covered transactions as of that date.

The form number and revision number appear in the lower right corner of each page of the contract. A license holder can visit trec.texas.gov to compare the number on any form in the office against the number of the currently promulgated version. Using a superseded form is a violation of TREC rules, and the commission does not make exceptions for honest mistakes. Checking the TREC website before beginning a transaction is a simple habit that eliminates this risk entirely.

The top of the first page of Form 20-19 carries several important notices that define the contract's appropriate use. The title 'One to Four Family' means the contract may be used only for properties with one, two, three, or four residential units. It may not be used for apartment complexes or any property with five or more units. The word 'Residential' means it is not appropriate for commercial transactions, which are typically handled by attorney-prepared documents. The notation '(Resale)' means the contract applies to existing construction, not new homes under construction or newly completed builder homes, for which TREC provides separate forms (Forms 23-20 and 24-20). The notice 'Not For Use For Condominium Transactions' is explicit: a separate form exists for condominium resales (Form 30-18). The Equal Housing Opportunity logo in the upper left corner reflects the obligation that applies to every transaction.

Every page of Form 20-19 except the first carries a space at the top for the property address. This is not a formality. If pages from two separate contracts become mixed during a transaction, the address at the top of each page allows any page to be correctly identified and restored to the right file. The bottom of each page also requires the initials of all parties, confirming that every page was reviewed before signing.

Transaction Scenario

The following scenario is used throughout this chapter to illustrate how each paragraph of Form 20-19 is completed. Read the scenario carefully before working through the contract. You may wish to print or download a copy of Form 20-19 from trec.texas.gov to follow along.

The Property and Transaction Terms

Property address: 1126 Casper Drive, Ghost Town, Texas 78110

Legal description: Lot 12, Block 16, Unit 2, Dreamland Estates, Ghost Town, Montague County, Texas

Sales price: $240,000

Down payment: 10% ($24,000)

Financing: Conventional loan through a local lending institution ($216,000)

Earnest money: $500 initial deposit plus $1,000 additional earnest money delivered within 3 days after the Effective Date

Escrow agent: Grant County Abstract, 110 S. Main, Ghost Town, Texas 78110

Termination option: 10-day option period; option fee of $200 credited to the Sales Price at closing

Title policy: Seller pays for the owner's title policy; Grant County Abstract is the title company

Survey: Seller provides existing survey and T-47 affidavit within 5 days after the Effective Date; if the title company or lender rejects the survey, Seller pays for a new one; standard exception amended to read 'shortages in area' at Seller's expense

Title objection period: 3 days after Buyer receives the title commitment, Exception Documents, and survey

Declared use: Residential; Buyer intends to operate an internet business from home

HOA: Property is subject to mandatory HOA membership

Agreed repairs: Seller to replace screen on the sliding glass door to the backyard prior to closing

Seller's Disclosure Notice: Already provided to Buyers before the offer

Residential service contract: Not required

Lead-based paint disclosure: Not required; property was built in 2009

Exclusions: Living room curtains (Seller is removing them)

Inclusions (non-standard): Propane barbecue grill in the backyard

Seller's contribution to Buyer's expenses: $1,000 toward closing costs

Closing date: May 25 of the current year

Possession: Upon closing and funding

Effective date: April 24 of the current year

Commission: 8% total, split evenly between the two brokerage offices

The Buyers

Names: Joe Johnson and Judy Johnson, husband and wife

Current address: 6217 Bumpy Road, Obnoxious, Texas 78210

Phone/Fax: 512-678-9898

Email: J&J@homeinternet.com

Buyer's agent: Bobby Brown, Texas Finest Real Estate Company, 3003 Hwy 12, Ghost Town, TX 78110

Buyer's broker license: 0430441
Agent phone: 813-625-8893
Agent email: BBrown@TxFinest.com

The Seller
Name: Kitty Gillespie, a single person
Property address: 1126 Casper Drive, Ghost Town, Texas 78110 (currently occupied by Seller)
Cell phone: 813-401-8282
Email: KG@email.com
Seller's agent: Tammy Thompson, Better Than the Best Realty, 1 Best Blvd., Ghost Town, Texas 78110
Seller's agent license: 0334187
Seller's agent phone: 813-666-1949
Seller's agent email: tammy@best.re.com
Listing broker: Vernon Best, license number 0234582, phone 813-666-1313
Co-op commission offered: 3% to the Other Broker

Paragraph 1: Parties

Paragraph 1 identifies the parties to the contract by name. This is where the seller's name and the buyer's name are written. The goal is to identify each party precisely enough that the title company can locate that person's records and confirm their legal authority to sell or purchase the property. The more complete the name information, the faster the title search proceeds.

Texas law requires only a first initial or first name and a last name to create a valid contract. In practice, however, providing full legal names, including middle names or initials, gives the title company the information it needs to run a thorough search for liens, judgments, and other encumbrances that might affect the transaction. Some offices also note the marital status of each party on the name line.

Marital status is important for title purposes. If the seller is married, the spouse may have rights in the property even if only one name is on the deed. In Texas, homestead property may not be conveyed without the signature of both spouses. After the seller's name, adding a brief status notation such as 'a married person' or 'a single person' helps the title company immediately identify whether spousal involvement will be required. Do not go beyond the name and status on the parties line. Adding any information about what happens to a party's interest upon death, for example, would be drafting a legal document, which is unauthorized practice of law. Estate planning belongs in a will, not in a purchase contract.

In the scenario, Kitty Gillespie is a single person. The seller line should read: Kitty Gillespie, a single person. The buyers are Joe Johnson and Judy Johnson, who are married to each other. The buyer line should reflect their names and their marital relationship.

One important professional reminder: never rely solely on what a client tells you about their marital status. Confirming this information through the title company's search process is part of the transaction. If there is any uncertainty, the broker and, if necessary, an attorney should be consulted before the contract is executed.

Paragraph 2: Property

Paragraph 2 defines what is being sold. It is divided into five sub-sections covering the land, improvements, accessories, exclusions, and reservations. Together these sub-sections answer the question: exactly what will the buyer own when this transaction closes?

Land

Paragraph 2A calls for the legal description of the property. A legal description is the official, recorded identification of a parcel of real estate. The most common format in a subdivided residential neighborhood is a lot and block description: Lot 12, Block 16, Unit 2, Dreamland Estates, Ghost Town, Montague County, Texas. When filling in this section, the licensee should copy the legal description exactly as it appears in the current deed or the county appraisal records. The street address is also entered here and on the top of every subsequent page, but the street address alone is never sufficient as a legal description in a real estate contract.

Some properties, particularly rural tracts or older urban parcels, use a metes and bounds description that is too long to fit in the space provided. In that case, the licensee notes in the blank that a full legal description is attached as an exhibit to the contract and then attaches that exhibit. The legal description in the exhibit must be identical to the one in the official public records.

Improvements

Paragraph 2B lists the improvements and permanently installed built-in items that convey with the property. This list is intentional and comprehensive. It includes equipment and appliances, valances, screens, shutters, awnings, wall-to-wall carpeting, mirrors, ceiling fans, attic fans, mailboxes, television antennas, mounts and brackets for televisions and speakers, heating and air-conditioning units, security and fire detection equipment, wiring, plumbing and lighting fixtures, chandeliers, water softener systems, kitchen equipment, garage door openers, cleaning equipment, generators, shrubbery, landscaping, outdoor cooking equipment, and all other property permanently attached to the described real property.

The list includes the qualifying phrase 'if any' after the first line. This means a licensee should never mark through or delete items from this list just because the property does not have them. The 'if any' language already accounts for the absence of a listed item. Striking items from the printed contract language is a modification of the form and may constitute unauthorized practice of law unless directed by the parties. If a particular item shown in the house might be confused by a buyer as being included when the seller intends to take it, the appropriate remedy is to list that item in Paragraph 2D as an exclusion, not to alter Paragraph 2B.

A common and entirely avoidable dispute involves personal property that a buyer assumes will remain because it is attached to the house. Consider an ornate ceiling fan. Because it is physically attached, a buyer viewing the home will naturally assume it stays. If the seller plans to take it, the licensee listing the property should identify this before the first showing. The seller should remove the item before any buyer sees it. Once a buyer has seen and formed an attachment to a fixture, a dispute over that item is almost inevitable. Burying an exclusion note in the MLS is not a reliable substitute for physical removal before marketing begins.

Accessories

Paragraph 2C lists accessories that convey with the property. These are items that are associated with the property but are not permanently installed. The list includes window air conditioning units, stoves, fireplace screens, curtains and rods, blinds, window shades, draperies and rods, door keys, mailbox keys, above-ground pools, swimming pool equipment and maintenance accessories, artificial fireplace logs, security systems that are not fixtures, and controls for garage doors, entry gates, and other improvements and accessories. The definition of 'controls' now includes the seller's transferable rights to software and applications used to access and control improvements or accessories, and hardware used solely to control improvements or accessories. This reflects the increasing prevalence of smart home technology in residential properties.

Just as with Paragraph 2B, a licensee should not mark through items in Paragraph 2C simply because the property does not have them. The 'if any' language in the paragraph header covers their absence.

Exclusions

Paragraph 2D is where the seller lists items that are being removed from the property and will not convey to the buyer. The seller must remove these items before delivery of possession. Exclusions listed here are not part of the sale, and the buyer cannot claim them at closing.

In the scenario, Kitty Gillespie is taking the living room curtains when she moves out. Curtains are listed in Paragraph 2C as accessories, which means they would ordinarily convey with the property. To make clear that they are not included in this sale, they must be listed in Paragraph 2D. Any item the seller plans to remove that would otherwise be understood to convey should be identified here. Paragraph 2D is the correct vehicle for seller exclusions, not the Special Provisions paragraph.

Reservations and the Propane Grill

Paragraph 2E provides space for any reservation by the seller of oil, gas, or other minerals, water, timber, or other interests, to be made in accordance with an attached addendum. Standard residential transactions typically do not involve mineral reservations, so this paragraph is usually left blank. When a mineral reservation is intended, the Addendum for Reservation of Oil, Gas and Other Minerals (Form 44-3) must be attached.

In the scenario, Kitty Gillespie has agreed to leave the propane barbecue grill in the backyard. A freestanding propane grill is personal property and is not automatically included in the sale. Since the scenario calls for it to convey, it should be addressed through the Non-Realty Items Addendum (Form 57-0, effective September 3, 2025) or noted in the Special Provisions paragraph as a factual business detail. The correct approach is to use the Non-Realty Items Addendum because TREC has promulgated that form specifically for the transfer of personal property items between the parties.

Paragraph 3: Sales Price

Paragraph 3 is where the financial terms of the offer are expressed. It has three lines that must always balance: the cash portion (3A), the sum of all financing (3B), and the total sales price (3C). The mathematical relationship is fixed: 3A plus 3B must equal 3C. Any counteroffer that changes the sales price will require all three lines to be recalculated and updated.

Paragraph 3A is the cash portion of the sales price payable by the buyer at closing. In the scenario, the buyers are making a 10% down payment on a $240,000 purchase, which means $24,000 is the cash portion. The contract itself clarifies that 'cash portion' does not include proceeds from borrowing of any kind or from selling other real property except as disclosed in the contract.

Paragraph 3B is the sum of all financing and requires a checkbox indicating which addendum describes the financing. The choices are the Third Party Financing Addendum (Form 40-11), the Loan Assumption Addendum (Form 41-3), and the Seller Financing Addendum (Form 26-8). In the scenario, the buyers are obtaining a conventional loan through a local lender, so the Third Party Financing Addendum applies and its box should be checked. The loan amount is $216,000 ($240,000 minus $24,000). A licensee who does not check the financing addendum box correctly leaves the contract without a clear description of how the sale will be funded.

Paragraph 3C is the total sales price: $240,000 in the scenario. Dollar amounts are always used in these blanks. Percentages are never appropriate in Paragraph 3. A buyer whose loan amount changes will require a contract amendment that adjusts all three figures to maintain the correct mathematical relationship.

If a seller is willing to provide owner financing, Paragraph 3B is still used for the loan amount, but the Seller Financing Addendum (Form 26-8) is checked and attached rather than the Third Party Financing Addendum. If the buyer is assuming the seller's existing loan, the Loan Assumption Addendum (Form 41-3) applies. Each addendum spells out the detailed terms of its respective financing arrangement. The main contract form captures only the dollar amounts; the addendum captures the terms.

Paragraph 4: Leases

Paragraph 4 is a disclosure and restriction paragraph regarding existing leases affecting the property. It begins with a statement that, except as disclosed in the contract, the seller is not aware of any leases affecting the property. After the Effective Date, the seller may not, without the buyer's written consent, create a new lease, amend any existing lease, or convey any interest in the property. This protects the buyer from a seller who might attempt to encumber the property with a new tenant or lock in unfavorable lease terms after the purchase contract is already in place.

Paragraph 4 has three checkboxes. Paragraph 4A is checked when the property is subject to one or more residential leases, requiring the Addendum Regarding Residential Leases (Form 51-1) to be attached. Paragraph 4B is checked when fixtures on the property are subject to one or more fixture leases, such as for solar panels, a propane tank, a water softener system, or a security system, in which case the Addendum Regarding Fixture Leases (Form 52-1) must be attached. These fixture lease situations have become increasingly common as more homeowners have acquired equipment through lease rather than purchase arrangements. A buyer who does not know about an existing fixture lease on, for example, solar panels may be unpleasantly surprised to discover that those panels do not convey free and clear.

Paragraph 4C is checked when the property is subject to a natural resource lease (oil and gas, mineral, geothermal, water, wind, or other natural resource). The seller must either have already provided copies of the leases to the buyer (box 4C(1)) or must deliver them within three days after the Effective Date (box 4C(2)). If delivery is delayed, the buyer may terminate the contract within the number of days specified in the blank after receiving the leases, and the earnest money will be refunded.

In the scenario, the property has no residential, fixture, or natural resource leases, so none of the boxes in Paragraph 4 are checked. However, before leaving this paragraph blank, a licensee should confirm with the seller that there are no leased appliances, no leased security systems, no solar panel leases, and no active mineral or surface leases on the property. If any such agreement exists and is not disclosed, the buyer may have grounds for a claim after closing.

Paragraph 5: Earnest Money and Termination Option

Paragraph 5 is one of the most operationally critical paragraphs in the contract because it establishes several hard deadlines where time is strictly of the essence. Missing any of these deadlines has immediate, automatic consequences.

Delivery of Earnest Money and Option Fee

Within three days after the Effective Date, the buyer must deliver two separate amounts to the escrow agent: the earnest money and the option fee. Both are made payable to the escrow agent and may be paid separately or combined in a single payment. In the scenario, the earnest money is $500 and the Option Fee is $200. The escrow agent is Grant County Abstract, located at 110 S. Main, Ghost Town, Texas 78110.

The scenario also calls for an additional $1,000 in earnest money to be delivered within three days after the Effective Date, which the licensee enters in the additional earnest money blank in Paragraph 5A(1). Paragraph 5A(3) establishes the order in which amounts received are applied: first to the Option Fee, then to the earnest money, and then to the additional earnest money.

If the last day to deliver the earnest money or Option Fee falls on a Saturday, Sunday, or Legal Holiday (Legal Holiday is defined by the Texas Government Code), the delivery deadline is automatically extended to the end of the next business day. This extension is built into the contract; no amendment is needed.

The Option Fee is handled differently from earnest money in an important respect. The buyer authorizes the escrow agent to release the Option Fee to the seller at any time without further notice, and the buyer releases the escrow agent from liability for delivering it. This means the Option Fee goes directly to the seller and is not subject to the dispute and demand procedures that govern earnest money. At closing, if the sale proceeds, the Option Fee is credited to the sales price.

The Termination Option

For the payment of the Option Fee, the seller grants the buyer the unrestricted right to terminate the contract for any reason during the Option Period. The Option Period in the scenario is 10 days. The buyer may terminate by giving written notice to the seller by 5:00 p.m. local time (at the location of the property) on or before the last day of the Option Period.

If the buyer terminates during the Option Period, the Option Fee is not refunded. However, the earnest money is refunded to the buyer. This is the key distinction: the Option Fee is what the buyer paid for the right to back out, and the seller keeps it as compensation for taking the property off the market during the option period. The earnest money, which is a deposit demonstrating the buyer's good faith intention to close, comes back to the buyer because the buyer exercised a contractual right rather than defaulting.

The practical purpose of the termination option is to give the buyer a window during which inspections can be completed. The buyer can hire a licensed inspector, review the inspection report, develop a repair request, and either negotiate repairs or decide to walk away, all without owing the seller anything more than the Option Fee. A license holder for the buyer must monitor the option period carefully. If the seller is slow to respond to repair requests and the option period is about to expire, the buyer must either terminate, extend the option by amendment, or accept the property's current condition. A verbal agreement to extend the option is not binding. All extensions must be documented in a signed written amendment.

Consequences of Late Delivery

Paragraph 5 imposes strict consequences for failing to deliver either the earnest money or the Option Fee within the required time. If the buyer fails to deliver the earnest money on time, the seller may terminate the contract or pursue the remedies available under Paragraph 15 (Default), or both, by providing written notice to the buyer before the buyer actually delivers the earnest money. If the buyer fails to deliver the Option Fee on time, or if no dollar amount was stated for the Option Fee, the buyer simply does not have the unrestricted right to terminate under the termination option. The buyer remains bound to the contract and may only exit through one of the other contingency provisions, if any apply.

The time provisions in Paragraph 5 are strict. The contract states explicitly: 'Time is of the essence for this paragraph and strict compliance with the time for performance is required.' This language means that a 5:00 p.m. deadline on a given day is precisely that. There is no grace period, and a buyer who misses the termination deadline by even a few minutes may lose the right to terminate.

Paragraph 6: Title Policy and Survey

Paragraph 6 is the longest paragraph in Form 20-19 and addresses one of the most legally significant aspects of any real estate transaction: the state of the title and the physical boundaries of the property. A license holder who understands Paragraph 6 in detail can guide clients through the title review process confidently and avoid the most common sources of disputes and transaction failures.

The Title Policy

Paragraph 6A requires the seller to furnish to the buyer an owner's title insurance policy (the Title Policy) issued by the named title company. The policy is written in the amount of the sales price and is dated at or after closing. A checkbox determines which party pays for the policy. In the scenario, the seller is paying for the title policy, so the seller's box is checked. The title company is Grant County Abstract.

The title policy insures the buyer against loss under its provisions, subject to the promulgated exclusions and a list of standard exceptions. The standard exceptions include restrictive covenants common to the platted subdivision, the standard printed exception for standby fees, taxes and assessments, liens created as part of the financing described in Paragraph 3, utility easements from the subdivision dedication, reservations or exceptions otherwise permitted by the contract or approved by the buyer in writing, the standard exception as to marital rights, and the standard exception as to waters, tidelands, beaches, streams, and related matters.

The eighth item in the standard exception list addresses discrepancies, conflicts, shortages in area or boundary lines, encroachments, protrusions, or overlapping improvements. This exception is a checkbox decision. If neither box is marked, the exception remains in the policy as written, meaning the title company will not insure against these matters. If the buyer wants coverage for boundary-related issues and the parties agree, the second checkbox is marked, and the exception is amended to read 'shortages in area' only. This endorsement costs approximately 5% of the title policy premium and must be paid by the party identified in the blank next to the checkbox. In the scenario, the standard exception is to be amended to read 'shortages in area' at the seller's expense, so the second checkbox is marked and the seller's box is checked. This endorsement provides the buyer with additional title coverage for area shortages that might be revealed by the survey.

A note on RESPA: Under Section 9 of the Real Estate Settlement Procedures Act (12 U.S.C. Section 2608), a seller may not require a buyer to purchase a title policy from a specific title company as a condition of the sale. A seller violation can result in liability to the buyer in an amount equal to three times the charges for the title insurance. However, when the seller is paying for the buyer's title policy, the seller does have the right to select the title company that will issue it. The distinction is between a seller who is paying for the policy (and may therefore choose the provider) and a seller who attempts to dictate the buyer's choice of company when the buyer is paying for their own coverage.

The Title Commitment

Paragraph 6B establishes the timeline for the title commitment. Within 20 days after the title company receives a copy of the contract, the seller must furnish to the buyer a commitment for title insurance (the Commitment) and, at the buyer's expense, legible copies of restrictive covenants and documents evidencing exceptions in the Commitment, other than the standard printed exceptions (the Exception Documents). The seller authorizes the title company to deliver these documents directly to the buyer at the buyer's address shown in Paragraph 21.

If the Commitment and Exception Documents are not delivered within the required time, the delivery period is automatically extended up to 15 days or three days before the Closing Date, whichever is earlier. If delivery still does not occur within the extended period, the buyer may terminate the contract and the earnest money is refunded.

The title commitment is a preliminary document issued before closing that describes what the title policy will show. It discloses existing liens, easements, restrictions, and other encumbrances that affect the title. Reviewing the commitment promptly is essential because the buyer's right to object to title issues is tied to the date of delivery.

The Survey

Paragraph 6C addresses who will obtain the survey and how it will be handled. A survey in this context is a formal measurement and documentation of the property by a registered professional land surveyor acceptable to both the title company and the buyer's lender. Three checkboxes offer distinct approaches.

The first option (6C(1)) requires the seller to furnish the existing survey and a Residential Real Property Affidavit or Declaration promulgated by the Texas Department of Insurance (commonly known as the T-47 Affidavit or T-47.1 Declaration) within a specified number of days after the Effective Date. The affidavit is a signed statement by the seller certifying that no changes have been made to the property since the existing survey was prepared that would affect the accuracy of the survey. If the seller fails to deliver both the existing survey and the affidavit or declaration within the required time, the buyer may obtain a new survey at the seller's expense no later than three days before the Closing Date. If the title company or the buyer's lender does not accept the existing survey, the buyer obtains a new survey at the expense of whichever party is identified in the adjacent checkbox.

In the scenario, the seller is providing the existing survey and T-47 affidavit within five days after the Effective Date. If the title company or lender rejects the survey, the seller pays for a new one. The first option checkbox (6C(1)) is selected, the number of days is five, and the seller's box for the expense of a replacement survey is checked.

The second option (6C(2)) has the buyer obtaining a new survey at the buyer's expense within a specified number of days. The third option (6C(3)) requires the seller to furnish a brand new survey at the seller's expense within a specified number of days. The choice depends on the parties' agreement and the nature of the property.

A listing agent should address the survey before the property goes on the market. The seller should locate any existing survey and confirm its accuracy. If the seller cannot locate a survey, the buyer's options under 6C(2) or the seller's obligation under 6C(3) should be factored into the listing strategy from the start.

Objections to Title

Paragraph 6D gives the buyer the right to object in writing to defects, exceptions, or encumbrances to title that are disclosed on the survey or in the title commitment, or that would prohibit a specific use of the property that the buyer has declared in the paragraph. The buyer's declared use in the scenario is residential operation of an internet business, which should be entered in the blank for the use or activity that must not be prohibited. If the title review reveals a restriction that would prevent that use, the buyer may object.

The buyer must make any objections by the earlier of the Closing Date or the number of days specified in the paragraph after receiving the Commitment, Exception Documents, and survey. In the scenario, the buyer has three days to object after receiving those materials. Failure to object within the allowed time constitutes a waiver of the buyer's right to object, except that requirements in Schedule C of the Commitment (which are conditions the buyer must meet rather than title defects) are never waived by inaction.

If the buyer objects in writing, the seller has 15 days (the Cure Period) to address the objections. The Closing Date automatically extends as necessary to accommodate the Cure Period. If the seller cannot cure the objections within the Cure Period, the buyer may, within five days after the Cure Period ends, either terminate the contract and recover the earnest money or waive the objections and proceed to closing. If the buyer does not terminate within that five-day window, the buyer is deemed to have waived the objections.

Title Notices

Paragraph 6E contains twelve required notices. Most of them alert the buyer to specific legal conditions or disclosure obligations that may apply depending on the location and characteristics of the property. A licensee should review each notice carefully and ensure that all applicable disclosures have been made and any required addenda have been attached.

The first notice (6E(1)) reminds the buyer to have the title commitment reviewed by an attorney or to obtain a title policy. The second notice (6E(2)) addresses mandatory property owner association membership. If the property is subject to a mandatory HOA, the buyer must be informed of the obligation to pay assessments and of the association's right to foreclose if assessments are not paid. In the scenario, the buyers are interested in the HOA, so this box is checked. Because the HOA is mandatory, the TREC promulgated Addendum for Property Subject to Mandatory Membership in a Property Owners Association (Form 36-11) should be attached.

The third notice (6E(3)) addresses statutory tax districts such as Municipal Utility Districts (MUDs), which are privately operated water and sewer providers that can charge fees outside of city oversight. If the property is in a MUD, the seller must deliver and the buyer must sign the statutory notice before final execution of the contract. The fourth notice (6E(4)) requires a notice when the property abuts tidally influenced waters of the state. The fifth notice (6E(5)) informs buyers of properties outside city limits that the property may be subject to future annexation by a municipality.

The sixth notice (6E(6)) alerts buyers in certificated utility service areas that special costs or a construction period may be required before water or sewer service is available. The seventh notice (6E(7)) requires attachment of a notice when the property is in a public improvement district (PID), which is an area where improvements are being funded through special assessments on property owners. The eighth notice (6E(8)) addresses private transfer fees. A private transfer fee created after September 1, 2011 is not binding or enforceable under Texas law. Fees created on or before that date may still be valid if the required notice was properly filed in the county records and re-filed every three years. The disclosure requirement in Paragraph 6E(8) ensures the buyer is informed if such an obligation exists.

The ninth notice (6E(9)) requires a notice for properties in a propane gas system service area, informing buyers of potential special charges and fees. The tenth notice (6E(10)) applies to properties adjoining a lake or reservoir with a storage capacity of at least 5,000 acre-feet at normal operating level: the buyer must be notified that water levels fluctuate. The eleventh notice (6E(11)) requires the seller to provide any certificate of mold damage remediation issued within the five years preceding the sale if the property has been remediated for mold.

In the scenario, only the HOA notice in 6E(2) applies. The 'is' box for mandatory HOA membership is checked. The appropriate addendum (Form 36-11) is attached and referenced in Paragraph 22.

Paragraph 7: Property Condition

Access, Inspections and Utilities

Paragraph 7A requires the seller to allow the buyer and the buyer's agents reasonable access to the property for inspections. The inspectors must be either licensed by TREC or otherwise permitted by law to make inspections. The seller must immediately cause existing utilities to be turned on and must keep them on throughout the contract period, at the seller's expense. Utilities must be active for inspections to be meaningful: inspectors cannot properly evaluate plumbing without water pressure, cannot assess electrical systems without power, and cannot test heating or cooling systems without gas or electricity.

Hydrostatic testing of the sewer system is addressed separately. If the buyer wants to authorize hydrostatic testing, the seller must agree to it in writing. The addendum for authorizing hydrostatic testing (Form 48-1) should be used for this purpose.

Seller's Disclosure Notice

Paragraph 7B addresses the Seller's Disclosure Notice (SDN), which is a written statement by the seller describing the known condition of the property, its systems, and any known defects. The SDN is required under Section 5.008 of the Texas Property Code for most residential resale transactions. One of three boxes must be checked.

Paragraph 7B(1) is checked when the buyer has already received the SDN before making the offer. In the scenario, the seller has already provided the SDN to the buyers, so 7B(1) is the correct choice. This is the preferred situation because it means the buyer made the offer with full knowledge of the disclosed condition of the property.

Paragraph 7B(2) is checked when the buyer has not yet received the SDN. The seller then has a specified number of days after the Effective Date to deliver it. If the seller delivers the notice late or not at all, the buyer may terminate the contract at any time before closing and recover the earnest money. If the seller does deliver the notice, the buyer has seven days after receipt to terminate the contract for any reason and recover the earnest money. This provision gives the buyer a second look after receiving the disclosure.

Paragraph 7B(3) is checked only when the seller is legally exempt from the SDN requirement under the Texas Property Code. Exemptions are narrow and include estate sales, foreclosures, and certain other circumstances specifically listed in the statute. Checking 7B(3) when an exemption does not apply could expose the licensee and the seller to serious liability. A licensee should always verify the applicable exemption before selecting this option.

Best practice is always to obtain the SDN before the property is listed, provide it to potential buyers before they submit offers, and ensure 7B(1) is checked in every contract where this is possible. Avoiding the 7B(2) route eliminates the buyer's second termination window and removes a significant source of post-contract uncertainty.

Lead-Based Paint Disclosure

Paragraph 7C requires compliance with federal lead-based paint disclosure laws for any residential dwelling constructed prior to 1978. If the property was built before 1978, the seller must provide the buyer with the federally required lead-based paint disclosure pamphlet and an opportunity to conduct a lead-based paint inspection before the offer becomes a contract. The TREC-promulgated Addendum for Seller's Disclosure of Information on Lead-Based Paint and Lead-Based Paint Hazards (Form 56-0) must be attached to any contract for a pre-1978 property. In the scenario, the property was built in 2009, so the lead-based paint disclosure is not required and Paragraph 7C does not require action.

Acceptance of Property Condition

Paragraph 7D addresses whether the buyer is accepting the property in its current condition. The paragraph defines 'As Is' as the present condition of the property with any and all defects and without warranty, except for the warranties of title and the warranties in the contract itself. Accepting a property 'As Is' does not prevent the buyer from inspecting it under Paragraph 7A, negotiating repairs in a subsequent amendment, or exercising the termination option. It means only that the seller is making no representations about condition beyond what the disclosure documents state.

Two checkboxes are available. If box 7D(1) is selected, the buyer accepts the property As Is with no specific repair conditions. If box 7D(2) is selected, the buyer accepts the property As Is provided the seller completes identified repairs before closing. The form's own instruction cautions against inserting general phrases such as 'subject to inspections' in the 7D(2) space. Only specific, clearly identified repairs are permissible. In the scenario, the seller has agreed to replace the screen on the sliding glass door to the backyard. This is a specific, identifiable repair, so box 7D(2) is selected and the repair is entered in the space provided.

Vague language in Paragraph 7D(2) creates serious problems. Consider a contract that reads 'repairs are to be completed and approved by the buyers.' This phrase gives the buyer unlimited discretion to reject any repair regardless of quality, effectively transforming the bilateral contract into a unilateral one in which the buyer holds all the rights. A licensee who inserts such language has altered the fundamental legal character of the contract and has likely crossed into unauthorized practice of law. If a client insists on such language, the licensee must document in writing that the client was advised against it.

Lender-Required Repairs and Treatments

Paragraph 7E addresses repairs that the buyer's lender requires as a condition of approving the loan. These repairs may be identified after an appraisal. Unless the parties have agreed otherwise in writing, neither party is obligated to pay for lender-required repairs, including treatment for wood-destroying insects. If both parties decline to pay for the required repairs, the contract terminates and the earnest money is refunded. If the cost of lender-required repairs exceeds 5% of the sales price, the buyer may terminate and recover the earnest money regardless of the parties' other agreements.

Completion of Repairs and Treatments

Paragraph 7F requires the seller to complete all agreed repairs before the Closing Date and to obtain any required permits. Repairs must be performed by licensed professionals or by those commercially engaged in the applicable trade. The seller must provide the buyer with documentation from the repair person showing the scope of work and confirmation of payment. The seller must also arrange, at the seller's expense, for transfer of any transferable warranties on the work to the buyer at closing.

If the seller fails to complete agreed repairs before the Closing Date, the buyer may exercise remedies under Paragraph 15 (Default) or extend the Closing Date by up to five days to give the seller additional time. A license holder representing the buyer must verify before closing that all agreed repairs have been completed, not assume they have been. Arriving at closing and discovering incomplete repairs creates a situation that is far more difficult to resolve than one caught in advance.

Environmental Matters

Paragraph 7G informs the buyer that the presence of wetlands, toxic substances such as asbestos or chemical wastes, or the presence of a threatened or endangered species or its habitat may affect the buyer's intended use of the property. If the buyer has concerns about any of these issues, the Environmental Assessment, Threatened or Endangered Species and Wetlands Addendum (Form 28-2) should be attached. That addendum gives the buyer a specified period to conduct formal environmental assessments by qualified inspectors and provides a termination right if an adverse report is received.

Residential Service Contracts

Paragraph 7H allows the parties to address a residential service contract (sometimes called a home warranty). A residential service contract is an optional insurance-style policy covering major home systems and appliances for a period of time after closing. If the buyer purchases a residential service contract, the seller may agree to reimburse the buyer at closing up to a specified dollar amount. If the seller is providing this benefit, the amount must be entered in the blank provided. If no residential service contract is involved, the blank is left empty or zero is entered. In the scenario, no residential service contract is required.

Seller's Disclosure About Groundwater and Surface Water Rights

The seller must disclose whether the buyer has received or will receive the Seller's Water Disclosure or that the seller is not required to provide the disclosure. Access to surface water (water on the surface of the property) or groundwater (water under the surface of the property) may be regulated, restricted or prohibited. Failure for the seller (if the seller is aware of the water situation) to provide such notice will allow the buyer to terminate the contract. This groundwater and surface water rights disclosure was added to the residential contract as Paragraph 7(I), effective July 1, 2026.

Paragraph 8: Broker and Sales Agent Disclosure

Paragraph 8 is a broker or sales agent disclosure paragraph. Texas law requires a real estate broker or sales agent who is a party to a transaction, or who is acting on behalf of certain related parties (including a spouse, parent, child, business entity in which the agent owns more than 10%, or a trust in which the agent serves as trustee or is a beneficiary), to notify the other party in writing before entering into a contract of sale. If any of these relationships apply, the disclosure is made in the space provided in Paragraph 8. If no such relationship exists, the blank is left empty.

For the scenario, the broker information page should reflect the following: for the Other Broker (buyer's side), Bobby Brown of Texas Finest Real Estate Company, license number 0430441, address 3003 Hwy 12, Ghost Town, TX 78110, phone 813-625-8893, email BBrown@TxFinest.com; for the Listing Broker, Vernon Best of Better Than the Best Realty, license number 0234582, address 1 Best Blvd., Ghost Town, TX 78110, phone 813-666-1313; the listing associate is Tammy Thompson, license number 0334187, phone 813-666-1949, email tammy@best.re.com.

Third Party Financing Addendum (Form 40-11)

The Third Party Financing Addendum (Form 40-11, effective January 3, 2025) is used in any transaction where the buyer is obtaining a loan from a lender other than the seller. It is the addendum attached to the contract when the Third Party Financing Addendum box is checked in Paragraph 3B of Form 20-19. The addendum is not used when the seller is carrying the note, when the buyer is paying all cash, or when the parties are exchanging properties with no financing involved.

The addendum begins with a property address line followed by the core financing description and duty to apply. The buyer is required to apply promptly for all financing described in the addendum and to make every reasonable effort to obtain approval, including furnishing all information and documents the lender requires. A buyer who deliberately fails to cooperate with the lender's requests in order to manufacture a reason to exit the contract would be in breach of this obligation.

Types of Financing

Form 40-11 now offers seven financing categories, each with its own checkbox. Conventional financing (A) covers standard first and second mortgage loans. The licensee enters the principal amount, the loan term in years, the maximum interest rate for the first stated number of years, and the maximum Origination Charges as a percentage of the loan as shown on the buyer's Loan Estimate. If the buyer is using two conventional loans simultaneously, both paragraphs A(1) and A(2) are completed.

Texas Veterans Loan (B) is for loans from the Texas Veterans Land Board. The loan amount and term in years are entered; the interest rate is established by the Board rather than negotiated and is not entered in the form.

FHA Insured Financing (C) requires entry of the FHA Section number identifying the loan program, the loan amount (excluding any financed mortgage insurance premium), the minimum amortization term, the maximum interest rate, and the maximum Origination Charges. The standard FHA program for a purchase with a low down payment is a Section 203(b) loan. The 203(k) program is for buyers who want to finance both the purchase price and the cost of rehabilitation or renovation in a single loan.

VA Guaranteed Financing (D) applies when the buyer has VA loan eligibility. The loan amount is entered excluding the VA Funding Fee, which is the fee the VA charges to guarantee the loan. The term, interest rate, and origination charge limit are also entered. The Funding Fee may be financed into the loan separately from the base loan amount shown in the addendum.

USDA Guaranteed Financing (E) is new in the current form and covers loans guaranteed by the United States Department of Agriculture for eligible rural and suburban properties. The structure mirrors the FHA and VA paragraphs: loan amount excluding any financed Funding Fee, term, interest rate cap, and origination charge limit.

Reverse Mortgage Financing (F) covers Home Equity Conversion Mortgage loans, which allow eligible borrowers to convert home equity into loan proceeds. The original principal amount excluding financed costs, the interest rate cap, and the origination charge limit are entered. A checkbox indicates whether the reverse mortgage will or will not be FHA insured.

Other Financing (G) covers any loan type not described in categories A through F, identifying the lender by name. The principal amount, term, interest rate cap, and origination charge limit are entered. A checkbox also allows the buyer to waive or retain the right to terminate under Paragraph 2B of the addendum for this particular loan.

Approval of Financing

Paragraph 2 of Form 40-11 addresses the approval process and contains a critical reminder that time is of the essence and strict compliance with all deadlines is required.

Paragraph 2A covers Buyer Approval, which is the lender's determination that the buyer has satisfied all of the lender's requirements related to the buyer's assets, income, and credit history. One of two boxes must be checked. If the first box is selected, the contract is contingent on Buyer Approval and the buyer must obtain it within the stated number of days after the Effective Date. If the buyer cannot obtain Buyer Approval within that period, the buyer may terminate by providing the seller both a written notice of termination and a copy of a written statement from the lender explaining the reason(s) for denial. The earnest money is then refunded. If the buyer does not terminate within the stated period, the contract is no longer contingent on Buyer Approval. If the second box is selected, the contract is not contingent on Buyer Approval at all, and the buyer is bound to close even if financing cannot be obtained.

Paragraph 2B covers Property Approval, which is the lender's determination that the property itself satisfies the lender's underwriting requirements, including appraisal, insurability, and any lender-required repairs. If the lender determines that the property does not qualify, the buyer may terminate no later than the third day before the Closing Date by giving the seller both written notice of termination and a written statement from the lender. If the buyer does not terminate within this window, Property Approval is deemed to have been obtained.

Security, FHA/VA Provision, and Authorization

Paragraph 3 states that if required by the buyer's lender, each note must be secured by vendor's and deed of trust liens. Paragraph 4 contains the FHA and VA required provision, which states that the buyer is not obligated to complete the purchase or forfeit earnest money unless a written appraisal statement reflecting an appraised value of not less than the stated amount has been provided in accordance with HUD/FHA or VA requirements. The buyer retains the option to proceed regardless of the appraised value. For VA loans, if the buyer elects to close at a price above the VA's established reasonable value, the buyer must pay the difference in cash from a source that is not borrowed funds (unless VA approves the borrowing). The estimated appraised value for FHA and VA purposes is entered in the blank in Paragraph 4.

Paragraph 5 contains authorization provisions. Paragraph 5A authorizes the buyer's lender to provide status updates on the loan to the seller or the seller's representatives. Paragraph 5B authorizes the lender, title company, and escrow agent to disclose and furnish copies of closing disclosures and settlement statements to the brokers and sales agents identified in the Broker Information section of the contract.

Loan Assumption Addendum (Form 41-3)

The Loan Assumption Addendum (Form 41-3, effective November 7, 2022) is used when the buyer is assuming one or more of the seller's existing loans rather than obtaining new financing. In this arrangement, the title to the property transfers to the buyer, but the existing promissory note and deed of trust remain in place and the buyer takes over the payment obligation. The Loan Assumption Addendum box is checked in Paragraph 3B of Form 20-19 when this structure applies.

Loan assumptions are less common in the current market than they once were because most loan documents written over the past several decades contain a due on sale clause, also known as an alienation clause, that gives the lender the right to declare the entire unpaid balance immediately due and payable when the property is transferred. However, when interest rates are significantly higher than the rate on an existing loan, assumption can be financially attractive to a buyer. The interest spread between the assumed rate and the current market rate needs to be meaningful enough to justify the effort. A second reason a buyer might pursue assumption is that the existing note has been substantially paid down, reducing the principal balance the buyer must carry.

Credit Documentation and Buyer Approval

Paragraph A requires the buyer to deliver specified credit documentation to the seller within a stated number of days after the Effective Date. The documentation may include a credit report, verification of employment and salary, verification of funds on deposit, a current financial statement, and any additional items the parties agree to. A common practice is to check the available checkbox and write 'Loan Assumption Package' in the blank, directing the buyer to obtain whatever documentation the specific lender requires for its assumption process. The buyer also authorizes any credit reporting agency to furnish copies of the buyer's credit reports to the seller and the noteholder at the buyer's expense.

Paragraph B addresses what happens based on the buyer's credit. If the buyer fails to deliver the required documentation on time, the seller may terminate at any time before all the documentation has been furnished, and the earnest money goes to the seller. If the documentation is delivered but the seller finds the buyer's credit unacceptable, the seller may terminate within seven days after the delivery deadline or the actual delivery date, whichever is later, and the earnest money is refunded to the buyer. If the seller does not act within that seven-day period, the seller is deemed to have approved the buyer's creditworthiness.

Assumption Details, Terms, and Noteholder Consent

Paragraph C identifies each loan to be assumed by lender name, current unpaid principal balance, and current total monthly payment (including principal, interest, and any reserve deposits). Two lines are provided for a first and second lien loan. Within seven days after the Effective Date, the seller must deliver to the buyer copies of the notes, the deeds of trust, and the most recent loan statements from the lender. Reviewing these documents is essential for the buyer to understand exactly what is being assumed.

The unpaid balance of any assumed loan rarely matches the original estimate exactly at closing because the seller continues making payments during the contract period. The addendum addresses this variance: either the cash payable at closing or the sales price will be adjusted by the amount of the difference. If the total principal balance of all assumed loans varies by more than the stated threshold at closing, either party may terminate and the earnest money is refunded, unless the other party elects to pay the excess variance.

Paragraph D gives the buyer the right to terminate if the noteholder imposes conditions beyond those contemplated in the contract. Specifically, the buyer may terminate if the noteholder requires an assumption fee exceeding the stated cap for the first or second lien, if the noteholder increases the interest rate above the stated maximum, or if the noteholder requires any other modification of the loan documents. These provisions protect the buyer from being forced to accept terms materially different from those anticipated when the contract was signed.

Paragraph E addresses the noteholder's consent to the assumption. If the noteholder fails to consent, either party may terminate and the earnest money is refunded to the buyer. The Due on Sale Notice at the end of the form is a critical reminder that the existing note or deed of trust may contain a provision allowing the noteholder to declare the note immediately due and payable if the noteholder refuses to consent to the sale. License holders should ensure both parties have read and understood this notice before proceeding.

Seller's Continuing Liability and Escrow

Paragraph F addresses an important risk for sellers in assumption transactions. Unless the seller is released from liability on the assumed note, the seller remains financially responsible if the buyer later defaults. To protect against this, the seller should use the Addendum for Release of Liability on Assumed Loan and/or Restoration of Seller's VA Entitlement (Form 12-3) whenever release is desired. If the seller is not released, a vendor's lien and deed of trust to secure the assumption will be required at closing. This lien is automatically released when the noteholder delivers an executed release.

Paragraph G requires the seller to transfer any existing tax and insurance escrow account to the buyer at closing without any deficiency. The escrow account typically holds funds accumulated by the seller through monthly mortgage payments for the purpose of paying property taxes, casualty insurance premiums, and mortgage insurance premiums when they come due. The buyer reimburses the seller for the balance in the transferred account, typically at closing as part of the settlement.

Seller Financing Addendum (Form 26-8)

The Seller Financing Addendum (Form 26-8, effective November 7, 2022) is used when the seller agrees to carry a promissory note for the buyer covering all or any portion of the sales price. Seller financing is available when the seller owns the property free and clear, or in some cases when the seller's existing lender permits a subordinate seller-carried note. The property itself serves as collateral for the note through a deed of trust. The Seller Financing Addendum box is checked in Paragraph 3B of Form 20-19 when this structure applies.

The form carries a prominent caution at the top: agreements for seller financing can be complicated and may be subject to laws regulating loans. Both parties are advised to consult an attorney and a financial professional before signing. TREC rules prohibit real estate brokers and sales agents from giving legal advice, and a licensee who attempts to draft the note or deed of trust provisions outside the addendum is in violation of those rules. The note and deed of trust that implement seller financing are attorney-prepared documents; the addendum identifies the key terms that will govern those documents.

Credit Documentation and Buyer Approval

Paragraph A requires the buyer to deliver credit documentation to the seller within a stated number of days after the Effective Date. The same categories apply as in the Loan Assumption Addendum: credit report, employment and salary verification, verification of financial institution deposits, current financial statement, and any additional items the parties specify. The buyer authorizes credit reporting agencies to provide copies of the buyer's credit reports to the seller at the buyer's expense.

Paragraph B establishes the same credit approval framework as in the Loan Assumption Addendum. Failure to deliver credit documentation on time allows the seller to terminate, with the earnest money going to the seller. If documentation is delivered but the seller finds the credit unacceptable, the seller may terminate within seven days and the earnest money is refunded. If the seller does not act within the seven-day window, buyer approval is deemed granted.

The Promissory Note

Paragraph C describes the promissory note. The note amount corresponds to the financing amount in Paragraph 3B of the main contract. The interest rate, which is negotiated between the buyer and seller, is entered in the second blank. The note carries a late fee of 5% of any installment not paid within ten days of its due date, and any matured unpaid amounts bear interest at 18% per annum or the highest lawful rate, whichever is less. The buyer may prepay the note in whole or in part at any time without penalty, with any prepayments applied to the last maturing installments of principal first.

Three payment structures are available. Paragraph C(1) is checked for a single lump sum payment, with the due date and interest payment frequency specified. This structure may be used in short-term seller financing arrangements. Paragraph C(2) is the most commonly used option, providing for monthly installments that include or are added to interest, continuing for a stated number of months after which the remaining balance is due. Paragraph C(3) is for interest-only payments for an initial period followed by regular amortizing installments, useful when the buyer needs lower initial payments before transitioning to full principal and interest payments.

The Deed of Trust

Paragraph D describes key provisions that will be included in the deed of trust securing the note.

Paragraph D(1) governs property transfers during the term of the note. Two options are available. If Paragraph D(1)(a) is checked, consent is not required: the buyer may sell, convey, or lease the property without the seller's approval, provided any subsequent buyer assumes the note. If Paragraph D(1)(b) is checked, the seller's prior written consent is required before the property is sold, conveyed, leased for a period longer than three years, leased with an option to purchase, or otherwise transferred, including through any contract for deed. If the buyer transfers without the required consent, the seller may declare the entire balance of the note immediately due and payable. Note that in either case, the buyer's personal liability on the note continues unless the seller executes a release of liability.

Paragraph D(2) addresses casualty insurance. A checkbox election determines whether the deed of trust will require the buyer to obtain casualty insurance naming the seller as a mortgagee loss payee. A seller who has a significant note outstanding will typically want to be named as a loss payee so that insurance proceeds can be applied to the note balance if the property is damaged or destroyed.

Paragraph D(3) addresses tax and insurance escrow. If Paragraph D(3)(a) is selected, no escrow is required; the buyer must simply provide the seller with annual proof that property taxes have been paid before they become delinquent and annual proof of any required casualty insurance. If Paragraph D(3)(b) is selected, the buyer deposits a pro rata portion of the estimated annual taxes and required insurance premiums with each loan payment. The seller must provide the buyer with annual accounting of the escrow account, pay taxes and insurance premiums in a timely manner to the extent funds are available, and hold the escrow balance in a separate account. The parties also choose whether escrow will be serviced by a third-party servicer and which party pays the cost of that service.

Paragraph D(4) provides that any default under a lien superior to the seller's deed of trust will also constitute a default under the seller's deed of trust. This protects the seller from a situation where the buyer falls behind on a senior loan while continuing to pay the seller's note.

Addendum for Release of Liability on Assumed Loan and/or Restoration of Seller's VA Entitlement (Form 12-3)

Form 12-3 (effective December 5, 2011) is the tool by which a seller who allows the buyer to assume an existing loan can seek to be released from continuing personal liability on that loan after closing. It is used in conjunction with the Loan Assumption Addendum and should be attached any time an assumption is involved and the seller wants protection from future liability.

The need for this form arises because in many loan assumptions the original borrower, the seller, remains liable to the lender even after the buyer has taken over the payments. If the buyer later defaults, the lender may pursue the original seller for the deficiency. Form 12-3 puts in motion the formal process by which the lender agrees to release the seller.

Release of Seller's Liability

Paragraph A requires both the seller and the buyer to apply for release of the seller's liability within a stated number of days after the Effective Date. This application may be made to a conventional lender, to the VA and the VA-backed lender, or to the FHA and the FHA-backed lender, depending on the type of loan being assumed. Both parties must furnish all information and documents the lender requires.

If the release has not been approved by the Closing Date, one of two boxes must be checked. The first option (A(1)) terminates the contract and refunds the earnest money to the buyer. The second option (A(2)) permits closing to proceed even without release approval, meaning the seller accepts the risk that their liability will continue beyond the closing date.

Restoration of Seller's VA Entitlement

Paragraph B addresses the additional concern that applies specifically when the seller obtained the original loan using VA loan benefits. When a VA loan is assumed by a buyer who is not a veteran or who does not substitute their own VA entitlement, the seller's VA entitlement remains encumbered and cannot be used to obtain another VA-guaranteed loan until it is restored.

Paragraph B follows the same structure as Paragraph A: the seller and buyer apply for restoration within a stated number of days, and if restoration has not been approved by the Closing Date, the parties choose between termination (B(1)) or proceeding without restoration (B(2)). The VA will restore the seller's entitlement only if the buyer is a veteran with sufficient unused VA entitlement who is otherwise qualified for VA financing. When both release of liability and restoration of VA entitlement are desired, both Paragraphs A and B must be completed.

The seller is responsible for the cost of securing the release and restoration. The seller's deed must contain any loan assumption clause required by the relevant lender. License holders should ensure that sellers in assumption transactions understand the importance of Form 12-3 and the risk of continuing liability before closing proceeds without a confirmed release.

Chapter 3: Snapshot Review

The following review summarizes the key rules and concepts from Chapter 3.

TREC Form Numbering and Form 20-19 Basics

- The number to the left of the hyphen identifies the form type; the number to the right tracks the revision count (Form 20-19 has been revised 19 times)
- The current version of Form 20-19 became effective July 1, 2026 and is the mandatory form for all covered resale transactions as of that date
- Form 20-19 is for one-to-four family residential resale only; it may not be used for condominiums, new construction, or commercial transactions
- Every page except the first requires the property address at the top and the initials of all parties at the bottom
- Using a superseded form is a TREC rule violation; licensees should verify form currency at trec.texas.gov before every transaction

Paragraph 1: Parties

- Full legal names and marital status should be provided for all parties to facilitate the title search
- Texas law requires at minimum a first initial or first name and last name, but more information is always better for the title company
- Do not add anything beyond name and marital status to the parties line; anything further could constitute unauthorized practice of law
- Do not assume marital status; if there is uncertainty, consult the broker or refer the parties to an attorney

Paragraph 2: Property

- The legal description in Paragraph 2A must match the recorded description exactly; the street address alone is never sufficient
- If the legal description is a metes and bounds description too long for the blank, use an attached exhibit and reference it in 2A
- Do not strike through items in Paragraphs 2B or 2C that are not present on the property; the 'if any' language in the paragraph already addresses their absence
- Items the seller is keeping must be listed in Paragraph 2D as exclusions; personal property items the buyer wants included should be addressed in the Non-Realty Items Addendum (Form 57-0)
- Ceiling fans, light fixtures, and other attached items that the seller plans to remove should be physically removed before the property is marketed, not merely noted in the MLS
- Smart device controls, software, and applications are now part of the accessories definition in Paragraph 2C; sellers must transfer access credentials and terminate their own device connections at possession

Paragraph 3: Sales Price

- 3A (cash portion) + 3B (financing) = 3C (sales price); these three amounts must always balance
- Always use dollar amounts in Paragraph 3; percentages are never appropriate
- Check the correct financing addendum box in 3B: Third Party Financing Addendum (Form 40-11), Loan Assumption Addendum (Form 41-3), or Seller Financing Addendum (Form 26-8)
- Any counteroffer changing the sales price requires all three figures in Paragraph 3 to be updated

Paragraph 4: Leases

- After the Effective Date, the seller may not create a new lease, amend an existing lease, or convey any interest in the property without the buyer's written consent
- Paragraph 4A is checked when residential leases exist; Form 51-1 must be attached
- Paragraph 4B is checked when fixture leases exist (solar panels, propane tanks, water softeners, security systems, etc.); Form 52-1 must be attached
- Paragraph 4C is checked when natural resource leases (oil, gas, minerals, water, wind, etc.) exist; the seller must deliver copies within 3 days after the Effective Date if not already provided

Paragraph 5: Earnest Money and Termination Option

- Earnest money and Option Fee must both be delivered to the escrow agent within 3 days after the Effective Date; both may be combined in one payment
- The Option Fee is released directly to the seller and is not refunded even if the buyer terminates; earnest money is refunded to the buyer if the buyer terminates during the Option Period
- If no Option Fee amount is stated, or if the Option Fee is not delivered on time, the buyer has no unrestricted right to terminate
- Time is of the essence for Paragraph 5; notice of termination must be delivered by 5:00 p.m. local time on the last day of the Option Period
- If the earnest money delivery deadline falls on a Saturday, Sunday, or legal holiday, it is automatically extended to the next business day
- If the buyer fails to deliver earnest money on time, the seller may terminate or pursue default remedies before the buyer actually delivers the funds

Paragraph 6: Title Policy and Survey

- The parties negotiate who pays for the owner's title policy; the seller who pays for it has the right to select the title company, but no seller may require a buyer to use a specific title company for the buyer's lender's policy under RESPA
- The standard exception for discrepancies, conflicts, and encroachments may be amended to read 'shortages in area' only; the cost of this endorsement is approximately 5% of the title policy premium
- The title commitment must be delivered within 20 days after the title company receives the contract; if late, an automatic extension of up to 15 days applies
- The three survey options are: (1) seller furnishes existing survey and T-47 affidavit or T-47.1 declaration; (2) buyer obtains new survey at buyer's expense; (3) seller furnishes new survey at seller's expense
- The T-47 Affidavit (or T-47.1 Declaration) is a statement by the seller that no changes have been made to the property that would affect the survey
- Buyer has a specified number of days after receiving the commitment, Exception Documents, and survey to object in writing to title issues; failure to object is a waiver
- Title Notices in 6E include 12 disclosure requirements: abstract/title policy advisory, mandatory HOA, statutory tax districts, tide waters, annexation, certificated utility service area, public improvement districts, private transfer fees, propane gas service area, water level fluctuations, certificate of mold remediation, and other required notices
- Mandatory HOA properties require the Addendum for Property Subject to Mandatory Membership in a Property Owners Association (Form 36-11)
- Private transfer fees created after September 1, 2011 are void; fees created before that date may be valid if properly noticed and re-filed every 3 years

Paragraph 7: Property Condition

- Seller must permit buyer access at reasonable times and must keep utilities on throughout the contract period at seller's expense
- Hydrostatic testing of the sewer system requires separate written authorization from the seller; use Addendum Form 48-1
- Paragraph 7B has three options: (1) buyer has already received the SDN (preferred); (2) buyer has not received the SDN and has 7 days to terminate after it is delivered; (3) seller is legally exempt from the SDN requirement
- Properties built before 1978 require the federal lead-based paint disclosure and Form 56-0 (Lead-Based Paint Addendum)
- Paragraph 7D(1) is for pure As Is acceptance; 7D(2) is for As Is with specific identified repairs; vague language such as 'subject to inspections' is prohibited
- Neither party is required to pay for lender-required repairs; if both decline, the contract terminates; if lender-required repairs exceed 5% of the sales price, the buyer may terminate
- Agreed repairs must be completed before closing by licensed professionals; the seller provides documentation and transfers any warranties to the buyer
- Environmental concerns (wetlands, asbestos, contamination, endangered species) may require Form 28-2; a residential service contract reimbursement is entered as a dollar amount in 7H

Paragraph 8: Broker and Sales Agent Disclosure

- Paragraph 8 requires written disclosure when a broker or sales agent is a party to the transaction or acting on behalf of a related party (spouse, parent, child, business entity with more than 10% ownership, or trust)
- Detailed broker and sales agent information, license numbers, and contact details are entered on the Broker Information pages (pages 10 and 11 of Form 20-19), not within the contract body

Third Party Financing Addendum (Form 40-11)

- Form 40-11 (effective January 3, 2025) is used any time the buyer is obtaining a loan from a third-party lender; it is not used for seller financing, cash purchases, or straight property exchanges
- Seven financing types are available: Conventional (A), Texas Veterans Loan (B), FHA Insured (C), VA Guaranteed (D), USDA Guaranteed (E), Reverse Mortgage (F), and Other Financing (G)
- Buyer Approval under Paragraph 2A: check the first box to make the contract contingent on Buyer Approval and enter the number of days; check the second box if the contract will not be contingent on Buyer Approval
- If the contract is subject to Buyer Approval and the buyer cannot obtain it, the buyer must give written notice and a written statement from the lender stating the reason(s) within the specified days; the earnest money is refunded
- Property Approval under Paragraph 2B: if the lender determines the property does not satisfy underwriting requirements, the buyer may terminate no later than the third day before the Closing Date with written notice and a lender statement; earnest money is refunded
- Time is of the essence for all approval deadlines in Form 40-11
- Paragraph 3 requires that each loan be secured by vendor's and deed of trust liens if required by the lender
- Paragraph 4 contains the FHA/VA required provision: the buyer is not obligated to complete purchase unless given a written appraisal statement at the value specified; the buyer may elect to proceed regardless of appraised value

- Paragraph 5A authorizes the buyer's lender to provide approval status updates to the seller; Paragraph 5B authorizes the lender, title company, and escrow agent to share closing disclosures and settlement statements with the parties' brokers and sales agents
- Origination Charges are referenced to the Buyer's Loan Estimate and limited by the percentage entered in the form; this protects the buyer from excessive lender fees
- Buyers should be prequalified by a lender before making an offer to ensure the financing terms entered in the addendum are realistic and achievable

Loan Assumption Addendum (Form 41-3)

- Form 41-3 (effective November 7, 2022) is used when the buyer will assume the seller's existing loan; it is used alongside the Loan Assumption box checked in Paragraph 3B of the main contract
- Paragraph A requires the buyer to deliver specified credit documentation to the seller within a stated number of days; common practice is to check the box for 'Loan Assumption Package' and let the lender define the required documents
- If the buyer delivers the credit documentation and the seller finds the buyer's credit unacceptable, the seller may terminate within 7 days after the delivery deadline or actual delivery, whichever is later; the earnest money is refunded
- If the seller does not terminate within the 7-day window, the seller is deemed to have approved the buyer's creditworthiness
- Paragraph C documents the existing loan(s) to be assumed; two lines are provided for first and second lien loans; the current unpaid balance, monthly payment amount, and lender name are entered for each
- Within 7 days after the Effective Date, the seller must deliver to the buyer copies of the notes to be assumed, the deeds of trust, and the most recent loan statements from the lender
- If the actual unpaid principal balance at closing varies from the stated balance, the cash payable at closing or the sales price is adjusted; if the variance exceeds the stated threshold, either party may terminate and the earnest money is refunded
- Paragraph D allows the buyer to terminate if the noteholder requires an assumption fee above the stated cap, an interest rate increase above the stated maximum, or any other modification of the loan documents
- Paragraph E provides that either party may terminate if the noteholder refuses to consent to the assumption; earnest money is refunded to the buyer
- Paragraph F: unless the seller is released from liability on the assumed note, a vendor's lien and deed of trust to secure assumption will be required; the vendor's lien is automatically released when the noteholder delivers an executed release
- Paragraph G requires the seller to transfer any tax and insurance escrow account to the buyer at closing without deficiency; the buyer reimburses the seller for the transferred balance
- The Due on Sale Notice at the end of the form warns both parties that the existing note or deed of trust may contain a provision allowing the noteholder to declare the entire note due and payable upon conveyance
- Buyers should review the original note and deed of trust before signing; sellers should consider using Form 12-3 to obtain a release of continuing liability

Seller Financing Addendum (Form 26-8)

- Form 26-8 (effective November 7, 2022) is used when the seller carries a promissory note for the buyer for all or any portion of the sales price; the form carries a prominent notice to consult an attorney and a financial professional before signing
- Paragraph A requires the buyer to deliver credit documentation to the seller within a specified number of days; the seller uses this information to evaluate whether to approve the financing
- If credit documentation is not delivered on time, the seller may terminate and receive the earnest money; if documentation is delivered and the seller finds the buyer's credit unacceptable, the seller may terminate within 7 days and the earnest money is refunded to the buyer
- If the seller does not terminate within the allowed time, the seller is deemed to have approved the buyer's creditworthiness
- Paragraph C describes the promissory note: dollar amount, interest rate, late fee of 5% of any installment not paid within 10 days, and matured unpaid amounts bearing interest at 18% per annum or the highest lawful rate; the buyer may prepay without penalty
- Three payment structures are available in Paragraph C: (1) a single lump sum payment; (2) monthly installments including or plus interest; (3) interest-only installments for a stated period followed by regular installments
- Paragraph D(1) addresses whether property transfers require the seller's consent; if consent is not required, a subsequent buyer may assume the note; if consent is required, transferring the property without consent allows the seller to call the entire note due
- Paragraph D(2) requires a checkbox election on casualty insurance: the deed of trust will or will not require the buyer to obtain casualty insurance naming the seller as a mortgagee loss payee
- Paragraph D(3) addresses tax and insurance escrow: either no escrow is required (buyer provides annual proof of payment directly) or escrow payments are made to the seller with each installment; if escrow is required, the seller provides annual accounting, pays taxes and insurance timely, and holds the escrow in a separate account
- Paragraph D(4) provides that any default under a lien superior to the seller's lien will also constitute a default under the seller's deed of trust
- The seller should be advised to have an attorney prepare the note and deed of trust; these are complex legal documents and a licensee may not draft them

Addendum for Release of Liability on Assumed Loan and/or Restoration of Seller's VA Entitlement (Form 12-3)

- Form 12-3 (effective December 5, 2011) is used whenever a buyer is assuming the seller's loan and the seller wants to be released from continuing liability on that loan after closing
- Paragraph A requires the seller and buyer to apply for release of the seller's liability within a stated number of days after the Effective Date; both parties must furnish all required information and documents
- If the release has not been approved by the Closing Date, the parties check one of two boxes: (A(1)) the contract terminates and earnest money is refunded to the buyer, or (A(2)) the failure to obtain release will not delay closing and the seller remains liable
- Paragraph B is for restoration of the seller's VA entitlement and is used only when the seller obtained the original loan using VA benefits; the same approval/no-delay checkbox structure applies
- The VA notice on Form 12-3 states that VA will not restore the seller's entitlement unless the buyer is a veteran with sufficient unused VA entitlement who is otherwise qualified

- When the seller is a VA loan holder who wants both release of liability and restoration of entitlement, both Paragraphs A and B must be completed
- The seller pays the cost of securing the release and restoration; the seller's deed will contain any loan assumption clause required by the relevant lender (FHA, VA, or conventional)

Chapter 3 Quiz: Parties, Property and Financing

1. In the TREC form numbering system, what does the number to the right of the hyphen in Form 20-19 represent?

a. The year in which the form was first promulgated
b. The total number of paragraphs contained in the form
c. The total number of pages in the form
d. The number of times the form has been revised since it was first issued

2. A licensee taking a listing discovers that the seller plans to remove an ornate chandelier before closing. What is the most appropriate action for the licensee to take?

a. Ask the seller to remove the chandelier before any buyer views the property
b. Note the exclusion only in the MLS remarks field
c. Strike through the word chandeliers in Paragraph 2B with the seller's initials
d. Describe the exclusion in the Special Provisions paragraph of the contract

3. In the chapter scenario, the sales price is $240,000 and the buyer makes a 10% down payment with conventional financing for the remainder. Which of the following correctly shows the figures that belong in Paragraphs 3A, 3B, and 3C?

a. 3A = $216,000; 3B = $24,000; 3C = $240,000
b. 3A = $240,000; 3B = $216,000; 3C = $24,000
c. 3A = $24,000; 3B = $216,000; 3C = $240,000
d. 3A = $24,000; 3B = $240,000; 3C = $264,000

4. A buyer is purchasing a home that has solar panels on the roof covered by an existing lease agreement. Which paragraph of Form 20-19 must be checked and which addendum must be attached?

a. Paragraph 4A, with the Addendum Regarding Residential Leases (Form 51-1) attached
b. Paragraph 4B, with the Addendum Regarding Fixture Leases (Form 52-1) attached
c. Paragraph 4C, with the Addendum for Reservation of Oil, Gas and Other Minerals (Form 44-3) attached
d. Paragraph 2E, with the Non-Realty Items Addendum (Form 57-0) attached

5. Under Paragraph 5 of Form 20-19, what happens to the Option Fee if the buyer exercises the right to terminate during the Option Period?

a. It is refunded to the buyer along with the earnest money
b. It is divided equally between the buyer and the seller
c. It is held by the escrow agent until both parties agree on its distribution
d. It is retained by the seller and is not refundable to the buyer under any circumstances

6. Under Paragraph 5 of Form 20-19, within how many days after the Effective Date must the buyer deliver both the earnest money and the Option Fee to the escrow agent?

a. 3 days
b. 5 days
c. 7 days
d. 10 days

7. Under Paragraph 6B of Form 20-19, within how many days after the title company receives a copy of the contract must the seller furnish the buyer with the title commitment and exception documents?

a. 10 days
b. 15 days
c. 20 days
d. 30 days

8. In the chapter scenario, the seller agrees to provide the existing survey and a T-47 affidavit within five days after the Effective Date. If the title company or the lender rejects the existing survey, who is responsible for the cost of obtaining a new survey under the agreed terms?

a. The buyer
b. The seller
c. The parties share the cost equally
d. The title company

9. A buyer objects in writing to items disclosed in the title commitment. How many days does the seller then have to address those objections during what the contract calls the Cure Period?

a. 5 days
b. 7 days
c. 10 days
d. 15 days

10. Under Paragraph 6E of Form 20-19, when a property is subject to mandatory HOA membership, which TREC form must be attached to the contract?

a. Form 36-11, Addendum for Property Subject to Mandatory Membership in a Property Owners Association
b. Form 37-5, Subdivision Information Including Resale Certificate
c. Form 47-0, Addendum for Property in a Propane Gas System Service Area
d. Form 52-1, Addendum Regarding Fixture Leases

11. In the chapter scenario, the seller provided the Seller's Disclosure Notice to the buyers before they submitted the offer. Which box in Paragraph 7B of Form 20-19 is the correct choice?

a. 7B(2), because the seller delivered the notice prior to the Effective Date
b. 7B(3), because the seller is exempt from the notice requirement for this property
c. 7B(1), because the buyer already received the notice before making the offer
d. 7B(2), because the notice was not delivered as part of the executed contract

12. Under Paragraph 7E of Form 20-19, if the cost of lender-required repairs exceeds what threshold as a percentage of the sales price, does the buyer have the right to terminate the contract and recover the earnest money?

a. 3%

b. 5%

c. 7%

d. 10%

13. The Third Party Financing Addendum (Form 40-11) is NOT appropriate for which of the following transactions?

a. A buyer who is purchasing the property entirely in cash with no financing of any kind

b. A buyer who is obtaining a conventional mortgage through a local lending institution

c. A buyer who qualifies for and is using VA guaranteed financing

d. A buyer who is applying for a USDA guaranteed loan for a rural property

14. Under the Seller Financing Addendum (Form 26-8), what late fee applies if the buyer fails to make a scheduled payment within ten days of the due date?

a. 2% of the installment amount

b. 3% of the installment amount

c. 4% of the installment amount

d. 5% of the installment amount

15. A seller who used VA benefits to obtain the original loan wants both release of personal liability on the assumed loan AND restoration of VA entitlement. How must Form 12-3 be completed to accomplish both goals?

a. Complete only Paragraph A, which covers both release of liability and VA entitlement restoration

b. Complete only Paragraph B, because VA entitlement restoration automatically releases seller liability

c. Complete both Paragraphs A and B, because each paragraph addresses a separate and distinct purpose

d. Attach a separate attorney-drafted addendum in addition to Form 12-3

CHAPTER 4
COVENANTS, COMMITMENTS AND NOTICES

Chapter Overview

Real estate transactions are built on a network of financial commitments, legal covenants, and disclosure notices that protect every party involved. This chapter examines the foundational elements that give a real estate contract its legal and practical substance beyond the basic agreement on price. Beginning with earnest money and the termination option, the chapter moves through title insurance and its two distinct policy forms, the survey systems used to describe and locate real property, and the Notice to Prospective Buyer (Form 58-0). The chapter then addresses property condition disclosures in depth, including the Seller's Disclosure Notice (Form 55-1, effective May 28, 2026), the federal lead-based paint disclosure requirements, and the Environmental Assessment addendum (Form 28-2). It concludes with a practical guide to the professionals who protect all parties in a transaction and the Disclosure of Relationship with Residential Service Company (Form RSC-4, effective June 11, 2023).

Learning Objectives

Upon completing Chapter 4, the student will be able to:

1. Explain the two legal purposes of earnest money in a real estate contract and distinguish earnest money from consideration.
2. Describe the termination option in Paragraph 5 of Form 20-19, including the option fee, the option period, and the difference between a residential termination option and a standalone option to purchase.
3. Distinguish between an owner's title insurance policy and a mortgagee's title insurance policy, explain the terms 'good and marketable title' and 'free and clear,' and describe the role of the title officer and title attorney.
4. Explain the purpose and structure of a title commitment, identify the four Schedules of the commitment, and describe the role of endorsements.
5. Compare the metes and bounds, rectangular government survey, and lot and block survey systems and explain which system is most commonly used in Texas residential transactions.
6. Explain when and how to use the Notice to Prospective Buyer (Form 58-0) and identify the circumstances that make this form especially important.
7. Describe the purpose, structure, and 11 sections of the Seller's Disclosure Notice (Form 55-1), identify the transactions exempt from the notice requirement, and explain the liability implications of incomplete disclosure.
8. Explain the federal lead-based paint disclosure requirements, identify the components of the Lead-Based Paint Addendum (Form 56-0), and describe the buyer's inspection rights under that addendum.
9. Describe the purpose and use of the Environmental Assessment, Threatened or Endangered Species, and Wetlands Addendum (Form 28-2) and explain how inspectors, appraisers, surveyors, and structural engineers protect the parties to a transaction.
10. Explain when the Disclosure of Relationship with Residential Service Company (Form RSC-4) is required, describe what a residential service contract covers, and identify the prohibitions that apply to a licensee recommending such coverage.

Contents

Earnest Money: Purpose and Legal Effect

One of the most common misconceptions among new license holders is that earnest money constitutes the consideration of a real estate contract. It does not. Consideration in a real estate contract is the mutual exchange of promises: the buyer promises to pay the agreed price, and the seller promises to convey the property. Earnest money is simply a term of the contract, a deposit negotiated by the parties and governed by the contract's provisions. A contract with zero earnest money, if the buyer and seller both agree to that amount, is still a valid and binding contract as long as all other essential elements are present.

In practice, earnest money is almost always included, and one to two percent of the sales price is a common range, though the amount is entirely negotiable. When the transaction closes successfully, the earnest money is applied first to the buyer's cash down payment, then to the buyer's closing expenses, with any excess refunded to the buyer. The earnest money serves two distinct legal purposes that make it valuable to both parties.

Good Faith Money

The first purpose of earnest money is to demonstrate the buyer's good faith. By depositing money with the escrow agent, the buyer is communicating that the offer is serious and that the buyer intends to follow through. A seller who receives an offer with no earnest money is reasonably skeptical about the buyer's commitment, because the buyer has nothing at risk if the deal falls apart. An appropriate earnest money deposit signals that the buyer is not merely testing the market. In most termination scenarios where the buyer terminates through a contractual right (such as the termination option or a financing contingency), the earnest money is refunded to the buyer, meaning the buyer typically does not lose the deposit unless they breach the contract without a valid basis for termination.

Liquidated Damages

The second purpose of earnest money is to serve as liquidated damages. Liquidated damages are an amount of compensation that the parties agree in advance will be paid in the event of a default. In the context of a residential real estate contract, calculating the actual damages a seller suffers when a buyer walks away can be difficult: lost marketing time, carrying costs, the difference in ultimate sales price, emotional distress, and other factors are genuinely hard for a court to quantify precisely. By including earnest money in the contract, the parties have essentially pre-agreed that this amount represents a fair measure of the seller's damages if the buyer defaults.

Under Paragraph 15 (Default) of Form 20-19, if the buyer fails to comply with the contract, the seller may either enforce specific performance (pursue a court order requiring the buyer to close) or terminate the contract and receive the earnest money as liquidated damages. If the seller accepts the earnest money as liquidated damages, both parties are released from the contract and the seller may not pursue additional damages. The same logic applies in the reverse: if the seller defaults, the buyer may enforce specific performance or terminate and receive the earnest money back. Earnest money therefore provides a practical, cost-effective way to resolve a breach without always going to court.

Options: Termination Rights and Standalone Options

The word option is used in two distinct ways in Texas real estate practice, and understanding both uses is essential for every license holder.

The Residential Termination Option

The most common use of the term option in residential practice refers to the unrestricted right to terminate in Paragraph 5B of Form 20-19. In exchange for payment of an Option Fee to the seller, the seller grants the buyer the right to terminate the contract for any reason during the Option Period, which begins on the Effective Date and runs for the number of days the parties negotiate. The buyer must deliver the Option Fee to the escrow agent within three days after the Effective Date. The escrow agent releases the Option Fee directly to the seller without further instruction.

If the buyer exercises the right to terminate during the Option Period, the buyer delivers written notice to the seller by 5:00 p.m. local time on or before the last day of the Option Period. The Option Fee is not refunded, but the earnest money is returned to the buyer. If the buyer does not terminate within the Option Period, the termination right expires and the buyer is committed to proceeding under the remaining contractual provisions.

The primary practical use of the termination option is to allow the buyer time to have the property professionally inspected. The inspection gives the buyer objective, documented information about the property's condition. The buyer can then decide to proceed without requesting any repairs, negotiate specific repairs through an amendment, or terminate the contract if the inspection reveals conditions the buyer finds unacceptable. A license holder for the buyer must closely monitor the option period deadline. Allowing the option period to expire without a clear written direction from the buyer, whether to proceed, extend the option by amendment, or terminate, leaves the buyer exposed and the licensee potentially liable.

Standalone Options to Purchase

The second use of the term option is as a standalone agreement that gives one party the right to purchase a specific property at an agreed price within a stated period of time. This type of option is common in commercial and investment real estate. An investor who believes a parcel of land will appreciate significantly might pay the owner a fee to hold the property off the market for, say, two years, during which the investor has the exclusive right to complete the purchase at the pre-agreed price. If the investor chooses not to exercise the option, the owner retains the option fee as compensation for keeping the property off the market during that period.

A standalone option to purchase is a unilateral contract: only the property owner is bound to perform if the option is exercised, and the buyer is not obligated to buy at all. The buyer holds all the rights; the seller holds all the obligations. Option contracts, feasibility study agreements, and right-of-first-refusal arrangements all function on this unilateral framework. Buyers exercise standalone options when it is economically advantageous to do so.

Title Insurance

The title process in a residential transaction is primarily a seller-side obligation. The seller must demonstrate to the buyer that the seller has the legal right to sell the property as agreed, and that the buyer will receive clear ownership once the deed is delivered. The mechanism through which this demonstration occurs is the issuance of a title insurance policy. The transaction almost always closes at the title company, which serves as the neutral third party administering the transaction.

Title insurance protects ownership interests in real property. Real estate has historically been regarded as one of the most valuable forms of property, and many special laws exist to protect ownership rights in land and everything attached to it. When a buyer purchases property, the seller's rights in the property are strong, but so are the rights of the seller's heirs, creditors, prior lienholders, government agencies, homeowners associations, and contractors who may have performed work. Some of these claims may not be obvious from a visual inspection of the property. A title search uncovers these matters, and title insurance protects the buyer if hidden problems emerge after closing.

A title search investigates the chain of ownership recorded in the county's public records and discloses unpaid taxes, mortgages, judgments against prior owners, easements, court orders, and any other recorded documents that may affect the ownership of the property. Finding and reporting these defects is the first benefit a title insurance policy provides: it tells the parties what problems exist so they can be corrected before closing.

Protection Against Hidden Risks

The second benefit of title insurance is protection against claims that cannot be discovered by examining the public records. Even after a thorough title search, certain threats to ownership can remain hidden. Examples include forgeries in the chain of title, documents executed by persons who lacked legal capacity at the time, confusion caused by similar names in the records, clerical errors in recorded instruments, and undisclosed heirs of prior owners who may assert a claim against the property years after closing. Title insurance covers these hidden risks. If a covered claim is made against the insured title, the title company is obligated to defend the title in court at the company's expense and to pay the cost of settling any valid claim in order to preserve the insured party's ownership. Unlike most forms of insurance, the owner's title insurance policy requires only a single premium paid at closing. No annual premiums are required, and the policy remains in force as long as the original insured party owns the property.

Two Types of Title Policy

There are two distinct types of title insurance policies used in real estate transactions, and a license holder must understand both.

The Owner's Policy of Title Insurance is issued to the buyer (the new owner) of real property. It insures that the title is good and marketable, meaning the property can be sold and ownership can be transferred without interference from undisclosed claims. The Owner's Policy protects the buyer against defects that were not disclosed on the title commitment. In Form 20-19, who pays for the Owner's Policy is negotiated between the parties and identified in Paragraph 6A with a checkbox.

The Mortgagee's Policy of Title Insurance is issued to the lender, not to the buyer. It insures the lender's security interest in the property against the same categories of defects. If the buyer pays cash for a property with no lender involved, there is no Mortgagee's Policy because there is no lender to insure. A critical point that license holders must understand: the Mortgagee's Policy does not protect the buyer. A buyer who relies on the lender's title policy for protection is unprotected. The buyer must have an Owner's Policy to be insured. This is why TREC requires license holders to advise buyers in writing to obtain either a title policy or to have an abstract examined by an attorney.

Good and Marketable vs. Free and Clear

Two phrases appear regularly in title discussions, and using them incorrectly can create liability for a license holder.

A title that is good and marketable is one that can be transferred to a buyer. The property may have encumbrances such as utility easements, restrictive covenants, or other recorded matters, but those encumbrances do not prevent the property from being sold. A title company can issue a title policy on a property with encumbrances by noting them as exceptions in the policy. The buyer then has full information and can decide whether to accept the title with those exceptions. License holders should use the phrase good and marketable title when describing property that can be sold, even if encumbrances exist.

A title that is free and clear is one that can be transferred and has no encumbrances of any kind. In practice, virtually every piece of real property in Texas has at least one utility easement, which is a recorded encumbrance. Telling a buyer that a property is free and clear when a utility easement exists is factually inaccurate. If a license holder makes this statement and the buyer later discovers an encumbrance and suffers a loss as a result, the licensee may be liable for clearing the problem or compensating the buyer. In casual conversation, agents often say free and clear to mean that the seller has no outstanding mortgage. That meaning is acceptable in that context, but the phrase should never be used to describe the state of the title as a whole.

The Title Officer and Title Attorney

The title officer, also known as the closer, is the professional at the title company who coordinates and executes the closing. In Texas, the title officer is typically a neutral third party who ensures that all conditions of the transaction have been met, manages the flow of documents and funds, calculates prorations and settlement charges, and oversees the actual transfer of the deed. Title officers do not represent either the buyer or the seller; their role is to facilitate a clean transfer of title and the correct disbursement of funds.

The title attorney is a licensed attorney whose role is to prepare the legal instruments needed to complete the transfer of title. Documents such as the deed, the promissory note, and the deed of trust must be prepared by or under the supervision of an attorney. These attorneys are not advocates for either party but serve the transaction itself by ensuring the legal documents are properly drafted and executed.

The Title Commitment and Endorsements

Before closing, the buyer needs to know the current state of the title. Since the buyer does not yet own the property, the title company issues a title commitment, sometimes called a commitment for title insurance, to provide that information. The commitment looks substantially like the title policy itself, but it is a preliminary instrument, not the final insurance policy. It tells the buyer what title exceptions will appear in the policy and what requirements must be met before the policy can be issued. The commitment is not a guarantee of title; it is a disclosure of the conditions under which title insurance will be issued.

Under Paragraph 6B of Form 20-19, the title company must deliver the commitment within 20 days after receiving a copy of the contract. A commitment is issued only when the title company has a bona fide order for a policy to be issued within 90 days from the effective date of the commitment. There is no charge to the buyer for the commitment itself. The seller is responsible for providing the commitment to the buyer.

The Four Schedules of a Title Commitment

All title commitments in Texas follow the same standardized format, regulated by the Texas Department of Insurance. They consist of four schedules.

Schedule A sets out the basic facts of the transaction: the effective date of the commitment, the names of the parties to be insured, the sales price, the loan amount if applicable, the type of interest being conveyed (fee simple, leasehold, etc.), the names of the current title holders as of the commitment date, and the full legal description of the property.

Schedule B discloses everything in the public record that affects the title of the property. This includes deed restrictions applicable to the subdivision, recorded easements, oil and gas reservations, existing liens, property owners association covenants, ad valorem tax status, and any other recorded instrument that limits or encumbers ownership. Schedule B defines the scope of the title policy's coverage by identifying what the policy will not insure against. Reviewing Schedule B carefully is one of the most important steps in the title review process.

Schedule C identifies the requirements that must be satisfied before the title policy can be issued. Common Schedule C requirements include payoff and release of existing mortgage liens, delivery of a properly executed deed, resolution of any open judgments against the seller, and satisfaction of other conditions that must be cleared before the title is considered marketable. These are not waivable by the buyer; they are conditions the seller must meet.

Schedule D discloses the officers of the title company and the underwriter, and provides the premium schedule showing the charges for the title policy and endorsements and who will benefit from those premiums. This disclosure is required under Texas regulations.

Endorsements

An endorsement is an addition to a title policy that expands or modifies the standard coverage. Each endorsement addresses a specific type of risk or circumstance and adds to the cost of the title policy. The cost of each endorsement is set by the Texas Department of Insurance and is not negotiable between the title company and the consumer. Some lenders require certain endorsements as a condition of funding a loan. For example, the survey endorsement that amends the standard exception for discrepancies and shortages to read only 'shortages in area' (as addressed in Paragraph 6A(8) of Form 20-19) is one of the most common endorsements in residential transactions and costs approximately 5% of the title policy premium. Real estate license holders are rarely involved in selecting or recommending endorsements. Those decisions come from the lender, the title company, or an attorney. A license holder who does not understand what an endorsement covers should direct the question to the title company rather than guessing.

Survey Systems and Legal Descriptions

A survey is a professional analysis of a parcel of real property that measures and documents its boundaries, total area, elevations, and location relative to surrounding properties and recorded references. Surveys in Texas are regulated by the Texas Board of Professional Land Surveying, and all surveys used in real estate transactions must be prepared and sealed by a Registered Professional Land Surveyor.

Metes and Bounds

The metes and bounds system is one of the oldest methods of describing land. In this system, the boundaries of a parcel are described in sequence starting from a fixed reference point called a point of beginning (also referred to as a place of beginning or point of commencement). From the point of beginning, the description traces each boundary line of the parcel by direction and distance, returning to the starting point when the description is complete. The words metes and bounds come from old English: metes means measure and bounds means boundary.

A monument is any permanent physical feature used as a point of reference in a metes and bounds description. Monuments may be natural features such as large rocks, old trees, creek confluences, or road intersections, or they may be artificial markers such as iron pins, concrete monuments, or other surveyor-placed objects. Because a metes and bounds description must precisely identify every line and angle in the parcel's perimeter, these descriptions can be quite lengthy for irregular-shaped parcels. A metes and bounds survey must produce a closed area: the directions of all boundary lines must trace a complete loop that returns to the point of beginning. Metes and bounds descriptions are common for rural property and older urban parcels.

The Rectangular Government Survey System

Beginning in 1785, the federal government adopted the rectangular survey system (also called the government survey system) for describing and organizing publicly owned lands. This system divides land into a grid of squares measured from two intersecting reference lines: a Principal Meridian running north and south, and a Base Line running east and west. The land is divided into six-mile-wide strips called ranges running parallel to the Principal Meridian, and six-mile-wide strips called township tiers running parallel to the Base Line. Where range lines and township lines intersect, they form six-mile-square units called townships, each containing 36 square miles or 23,040 acres.

Each township is divided into 36 one-mile-square sections, each containing approximately 640 acres. Sections can be further subdivided into halves, quarters, and smaller fractions for more precise descriptions. The rectangular survey system is used in many parts of the United States and in rural areas of Texas, but because of the curvature of the earth, mathematical corrections must be made periodically as the grid extends over long distances.

The Lot and Block System

The lot and block system is the most widely used survey method in Texas residential real estate and in developed areas generally. When a tract of land is subdivided for development, a licensed surveyor prepares a plat of the subdivision showing every lot, its dimensions, its number, the block in which it sits, streets and right-of-ways, easements, and other relevant features. The plat is reviewed for compliance with local development standards covering minimum lot size, street access and width, setback requirements, utility provisions, drainage regulations, open space, and building codes. Once the plat is approved by the appropriate government authority, it is filed in the real property records of the county where the land is located.

After the plat is recorded, each parcel in the subdivision can be described simply by its lot and block number within the named subdivision: for example, Lot 12, Block 16, Unit 2, Dreamland Estates, Ghost Town, Montague County, Texas. This is far shorter and easier to communicate than a metes and bounds description of the same parcel. Texas courts have held that once a subdivision plat is recorded, the recorded plat description will prevail over a competing metes and bounds description if the two conflict. It is a misdemeanor to describe a tract of land by lot and block number if the plat for that subdivision has not been formally recorded in the applicable county.

License holders should always verify the correct legal description of a property before completing a contract. Copying a description from a prior MLS listing or from a tax record without verifying it against the current deed or plat introduces the risk of perpetuating an error. An incorrect legal description in a contract creates title problems that can delay or derail a closing.

Notice to Prospective Buyer (Form 58-0)

Section 1101.555 of the Texas Occupations Code requires a license holder, when an offer to purchase real estate is signed, to advise each buyer in writing that the buyer should either have an abstract of title examined by an attorney of the buyer's own choice or be furnished with or obtain a title insurance policy. Form 58-0 (effective November 7, 2022) is the TREC-approved form for delivering this notice.

In most transactions involving a lender, the lender independently requires a title search and a title insurance policy (the Mortgagee's Policy) as a condition of funding the loan. In those situations, the title search occurs as a matter of course, and buyers naturally receive the benefit of that process even if they have not specifically requested it. The Notice to Prospective Buyer is most critical in transactions where there is no lender, specifically cash purchases and owner-financed transactions. In these cases, no third party is requiring a title search, and without the form being provided and acknowledged, a buyer might close on a property without any examination of its title history.

Form 58-0 is brief and direct. It states the address of the property, advises the buyer to have an abstract examined by an attorney of the buyer's choice or to obtain a title insurance policy, and notes two additional disclosure obligations: if the property is in a utility district, the buyer must receive and sign the statutory MUD notice; and if the property is in a public improvement district, the seller must provide the required written notice under Section 5.014 of the Texas Property Code. The form is dated and signed by the brokerage company name and the broker or sales agent. The buyer then signs to acknowledge receipt of the notice.

Notice that the seller does not sign Form 58-0. This is a disclosure from the licensee to the buyer, not an agreement between the buyer and seller. The licensee should retain the original signed form in the transaction file and provide a copy to the buyer. A prudent designated broker will not allow a licensee to proceed with a residential transaction, whether or not a lender is involved, without ensuring that title insurance has been obtained or that the abstract has been reviewed. If a buyer insists on closing without a title policy for any reason, the designated broker should be consulted immediately, and Form 58-0 should be provided and acknowledged before any offer is signed.

Form 58-0 is approved but not promulgated by TREC. The notation 'approved' rather than 'promulgated' means the form is strongly recommended and meets TREC's requirements, but its use is not required in every transaction in the same mandatory way that promulgated contracts are required. The form's own footnote clarifies that it is intended for use when a contract of sale has not been promulgated by TREC, but the underlying advisory obligation to inform buyers about title protection exists in every transaction regardless of which form is used.

Seller's Disclosure Notice (Form 55-1)

The Seller's Disclosure Notice (Form 55-1, effective May 28, 2026) is the document by which a seller discloses to a prospective buyer everything the seller knows about the condition of the property and the existence of features, systems, and circumstances that may affect the buyer's decision. The form replaces the prior version known as OP-H. It is prepared under Section 5.008 of the Texas Property Code, which requires sellers of residential real property to furnish the notice to buyers before an earnest money contract is signed. The notice is a disclosure of the seller's knowledge as of the date signed; it is explicitly not a warranty and is not a substitute for an inspection.

The license holder should provide the blank form to the seller at the time the listing is obtained. The seller, not the licensee, must complete the form. If the licensee fills out the form, the licensee risks checking off incorrect information and misrepresenting the property's condition to the buyer, which creates both disciplinary and financial liability. The completed notice should be made available to every buyer who expresses interest in the property, and in many MLS systems it can be uploaded to the listing for direct access.

Structure of Form 55-1

Form 55-1 covers eleven categories of information across four pages.

Section 1 is a comprehensive inventory checklist of features and systems the property may or may not have. It includes ranges, ovens, dishwashers, security systems, fire detection equipment, smoke detectors with hearing-impaired capability, carbon monoxide alarms, ceiling fans, HVAC systems, plumbing and sewer connections, pools and spas, fireplaces and chimneys, garage door openers, water heaters, roof type and approximate age, and many other items. For each item, the seller writes Y (yes, present), N (no, not present), or U (unknown). The seller is then asked whether any of the listed items are not in working condition, have known defects, or are in need of repair.

Section 2 asks whether smoke detectors are installed in accordance with Chapter 766 of the Texas Health and Safety Code, which requires working detectors in one-family and two-family dwellings installed per local building code requirements. Section 3 is a yes/no/unknown checklist of known defects or malfunctions in interior walls, ceilings, floors, exterior walls, doors, windows, the roof, the foundation and slab, sidewalks, walls and fences, driveways, plumbing and sewers, electrical systems, lighting fixtures, and other structural components.

Section 4 asks about specific conditions the seller may be aware of, including active termites or wood-destroying insects, termite or wood rot damage needing repair, previous termite treatment or damage, improper drainage, water damage not due to flooding, landfill or soil movement or fault lines, previous structural or roof repair, hazardous or toxic waste, asbestos components, urea-formaldehyde insulation, radon gas, lead-based paint, aluminum wiring, previous fires, unplatted easements, subsurface structures or pits, and previous use of the premises for methamphetamine manufacture.

Sections 5 through 9 cover additional condition items and special environmental concerns. Section 5 asks generally whether the seller is aware of any item, equipment, or system in need of repair. Sections 6, 7, and 8 address flood-related disclosures in detail, including whether the property is in a 100-year floodplain (Special Flood Hazard Area) or 500-year floodplain (Moderate Flood Hazard Area), whether there has been previous flooding from a reservoir breach or emergency release, whether there has been previous water penetration from a natural flood event, whether the seller has ever filed a flood insurance claim with any provider including the NFIP, and whether the seller has received FEMA or SBA assistance for flood damage.

Section 9 covers room additions, structural modifications, or repairs made without permits or not in compliance with building codes; homeowners association fees and assessments; any common area co-owned in undivided interest; notices of violations of deed restrictions or government ordinances; lawsuits affecting the property; any condition materially affecting physical health or safety; rainwater harvesting systems larger than 500 gallons using public water as an auxiliary source; and any portion of the property in a groundwater conservation or subsidence district.

Additions to Paragraph 9 arise out of the directive from the Sunset Commission that the seller provide additional information that could impact a property's value or desirability. In response to this directive, TREC has added information relating to insurance, private roads on or adjoining the property that the buyer would be responsible for maintaining, the existence of aboveground storage tanks, and whether a property is located in a conservation easement.

Section 10 contains a notice that coastal properties seaward of the Gulf Intracoastal Waterway or within 1,000 feet of the mean high tide may be subject to the Open Beaches Act or the Dune Protection Act and may require a beachfront construction certificate or dune protection permit for repairs or improvements.

Section 11 contains a notice that the property may be near a military installation affected by high noise or air installation compatible use zones, with references to publicly available studies.

After all sections are completed, both sellers and both buyers (if applicable) sign and date the notice. The buyer's signature confirms receipt. The notice is then incorporated into the transaction file and referenced in Paragraph 7B of the sales contract.

Transactions Exempt from the Seller's Disclosure Notice

Section 5.008 of the Texas Property Code exempts certain transactions from the notice requirement. The seller is not required to provide the formal notice when the property transfer occurs by court order or foreclosure sale; when a trustee in bankruptcy transfers the property; when a deed is made from a trust in connection with a release of lien or a trustee's deed for the benefit of a beneficiary; when a lender acquires the property through a power of sale clause, a court-ordered foreclosure, or a deed in lieu of foreclosure; when an executor of an estate or a guardian is transferring the property; when a co-owner transfers their interest to another co-owner; when a transfer is made to a spouse or close family member; when the transfer results from a divorce proceeding; when the transfer is to or from a governmental entity; when a builder sells a new home for the first time; or when the transfer involves no more than 5% of the value of the property.

Even in exempt transactions, sellers are not relieved of their common law and DTPA obligations to disclose known material defects that affect the property. The exemption removes the requirement to use the formal Form 55-1, but a seller who knowingly conceals a material defect in an exempt transaction remains liable for that concealment.

Liability Implications

A seller who completes the Seller's Disclosure Notice honestly and provides it to the buyer before the contract is signed has taken the most important step available to reduce their legal exposure. A seller cannot disclose what they genuinely do not know. Courts generally find that a seller who made complete and honest disclosures and gave the buyer an opportunity to inspect the property has satisfied their legal obligation. A seller who answers 'No' on the notice to a condition they actually know about, and who takes steps to conceal the evidence of that condition, faces significant liability. In one well-known scenario, buyers who removed wall paneling in a home they had occupied for five years discovered evidence of a prior fire that the sellers had covered up. The court dismissed the case against the real estate agent because a reasonable person inspecting the property would not have discovered the concealed fire, but held the sellers liable because they had answered 'No' next to Previous Fires on the disclosure and had physically hidden the evidence.

Lead-Based Paint Disclosure (Form 56-0)

Federal law requires the disclosure of lead-based paint hazards in residential dwellings built before 1978. The Lead-Based Paint Disclosure and Acknowledgment form (Form 56-0) promulgated by TREC is the vehicle through which this disclosure is made in Texas residential transactions. Until 1978 the government permitted lead to be used as an additive in paint; the heavy metal properties of lead make it particularly dangerous to developing children and can cause severe neurological damage. Although most homeowners today simply assume that pre-1978 paint may contain lead and accept that condition, the disclosure requirement ensures that buyers are formally informed of the potential hazard.

Form 56-0 is attached to the contract when the property was built before 1978. In the scenario used throughout Chapter 3, the property was built in 2009, so the form is not required. For any property constructed before 1978, the form must be used.

Completing Form 56-0

The form is divided into several sections covering the seller's knowledge, any available documentation, the buyer's election, and the licensee's obligations.

The seller's knowledge section requires the seller to check one of two boxes: either the seller has knowledge of lead-based paint and lead-based paint hazards in the property (in which case the seller describes that knowledge, such as by referencing a prior inspection report), or the seller has no knowledge of such conditions. The documentation section asks whether the seller has records or reports available pertaining to lead-based paint conditions; if so, the seller identifies those documents and provides copies to the buyer.

The buyer's election section requires the buyer to make a choice. The buyer may accept the property in its current condition with acknowledgment of the potential presence of lead-based paint. Alternatively, the buyer may elect to have the property inspected for lead-based paint within ten days of the Effective Date. If the buyer chooses to inspect and receives an inspection report, the buyer then has until the fourteenth day after the Effective Date to terminate the contract based on the inspection results.

The acknowledgment section identifies the obligations of the license holder, which include: providing the buyer with the EPA pamphlet titled 'Protect Your Family from Lead in Your Home'; completing the addendum; disclosing any knowledge the licensee has of lead-based paint or lead-based paint hazards in the property; delivering all available records and reports pertaining to lead-based paint in the property to the buyer; providing the buyer a period of up to ten days for an inspection; and retaining a completed copy of the addendum for at least three years following the sale. All parties, including the sellers, buyers, and licensees, sign and date the form.

Environmental Assessment Addendum (Form 28-2)

The Environmental Assessment, Threatened or Endangered Species, and Wetlands Addendum (Form 28-2, effective December 5, 2011) is used when a buyer has concerns about the environmental condition of a property or about the presence of protected species or regulated wetlands that might restrict its use. This addendum is listed in Paragraph 22 (Agreement of Parties) of Form 20-19, which means it applies to residential as well as rural transactions. It should not be thought of as a form reserved only for farm and ranch contracts.

Each of the three paragraphs in Form 28-2 addresses a distinct category of concern, and the buyer or the buyer's agent checks the applicable paragraphs. In many transactions involving properties with environmental sensitivity, all three paragraphs are checked. The licensee representing the buyer should maintain a list of qualified environmental inspectors, wildlife biologists, and wetland specialists who can be engaged quickly when these concerns arise.

Environmental issues that may prompt use of Form 28-2 include the presence of mold, asbestos, radon gas, water contamination, electromagnetic fields, carbon monoxide sources, toxic waste sites, leaking underground storage tanks, and any other substance or condition that might affect the buyer's health or limit the intended use of the property. Threatened or endangered species or their habitats on a property can dramatically restrict what improvements may be made and in some cases require the owner to preserve portions of the land. Wetland designations under federal and state law restrict development, filling, and drainage in ways that can significantly affect a buyer's plans for the property.

The buyer is given a specified number of days, negotiated between the buyer and seller, to obtain formal assessments from qualified inspectors. If the buyer receives an adverse report on any of the three categories, the buyer may terminate the contract and provide a copy of the report to the seller. Sharing the report is significant: it gives the seller full documentation of the condition, which the seller is then obligated to disclose to any subsequent buyer. Because environmental assessments can be expensive and time-consuming, this form is sometimes underused relative to the potential risks it addresses. License holders should ensure that buyers with any environmental concerns are aware of Form 28-2 and its protections.

Professionals Who Protect the Parties

A network of licensed professionals exists to protect every party to a real estate transaction. License holders should always recommend, and in many cases insist, that appropriate professionals be engaged. Understanding why each professional is important helps license holders communicate the value of these services to clients and reduces the likelihood that either party will later claim they were not adequately informed.

Home Inspectors

Inspectors licensed by TREC examine residential properties and document their findings in a written inspection report. A thorough inspection covers structural elements, roofing, plumbing, electrical systems, HVAC systems, insulation, windows, and all visible components. Inspectors rarely identify hidden catastrophic damage in definitive terms; instead, they frequently recommend additional inspections by specialists such as roofers, structural engineers, or plumbers when evidence of potential problems is found. Even a report noting only minor issues is valuable because it establishes the documented condition of the property at the time of contract.

Inspections protect the buyer by ensuring they have objective, professional information about the condition of the property before they are committed to closing. They protect the seller by providing documented evidence of what was disclosed, reducing the risk of post-closing claims. They protect the license holders by demonstrating that the professionals involved did everything possible to give the consumer the information needed to make an informed decision. They protect the lender by ensuring that the property securing the loan does not have undisclosed material defects.

Appraisers

A licensed or certified real estate appraiser provides an independent estimate of a property's market value using one or more of the three recognized approaches: the cost approach, the sales comparison approach, and the income capitalization approach. Most lenders require an appraisal before funding a loan and will not lend on a property that does not appraise at the contract price.

Appraisals protect the seller from undervaluing a property in a rising market. They protect the buyer from overpaying for a property by an amount the market does not support. They protect the lender from funding a loan secured by a property whose value cannot support the debt if the lender must eventually sell the collateral. And they protect license holders from later claims that the professional's price guidance was incorrect or misleading.

Surveyors

A survey establishes where the boundary lines of a property actually are and identifies any encroachments, easements, or discrepancies between what is recorded and what exists on the ground. Buyers benefit from knowing exactly where their property ends and their neighbor's begins. The survey also identifies whether any improvements, such as fences, garages, or additions, encroach on a neighbor's land or on a recorded easement.

Surveyors protect the seller from being accused of misrepresenting the property's boundaries. They protect the lender from funding a loan on a property with boundary issues that could cloud the title if the property must later be resold. They protect the license holder by providing a professional document to reference if boundary questions arise after closing.

Structural Engineers

A structural engineer is a licensed professional who evaluates the structural integrity of a building, including its foundation, load-bearing walls, and other systems that bear the physical weight of the structure. When a home inspector finds evidence of potential foundation movement, settling, or cracking, a structural engineer is the appropriate specialist to determine whether a real problem exists, what caused it, and what remediation, if any, is required.

A critical caution applies here: buyers and sellers should not rely on the opinion of a foundation repair company to evaluate whether foundation work is necessary. A foundation company has a financial incentive to find problems because it profits from the work. A structural engineer, by contrast, is paid for an independent assessment and has no stake in the outcome. A structural engineer who determines that a foundation is sound can save a seller thousands of dollars in unnecessary repairs. An engineer who confirms a real problem gives the buyer the information needed to negotiate or decide whether to proceed. Lenders who suspect foundation issues will almost certainly require a structural engineering report before funding a loan.

Residential Service Contracts and Form RSC-4

A residential service contract, commonly known as a home warranty, is a product under which a licensed residential service company agrees, for a fee, to repair or replace certain specified equipment and systems in a property during a defined coverage period. Coverage typically applies to major systems such as plumbing, electrical, HVAC, and appliances, and is most commonly purchased for the first year following the sale. When a service call is needed, the homeowner pays a co-payment and the residential service company pays for parts and labor up to the policy limits. Residential service companies are licensed and regulated by TREC. Coverage terms, excluded items, and co-payment amounts vary among providers.

In Form 20-19, Paragraph 7H allows the parties to negotiate whether the seller will reimburse the buyer at closing for the cost of a residential service contract, up to a specified dollar amount. The choice of which company to use and what level of coverage to purchase lies entirely with the buyer. Neither the seller nor any licensee may condition the sale of the property on the buyer's purchase of a residential service contract from any specific company.

Disclosure of Relationship with Residential Service Company (Form RSC-4)

Form RSC-4 (effective June 11, 2023) is required whenever a license holder receives any form of compensation from a residential service company. The form must be provided to the buyer and seller at or before the time a contract is signed. The compensation that triggers the disclosure obligation does not have to be cash; any benefit, fee, or arrangement between the licensee and the residential service company must be disclosed.

There is an important distinction about what kind of compensation is permitted. A license holder may receive compensation from a residential service company for services provided to or on behalf of the company, such as collecting property data or coordinating service arrangements. That compensation must not be contingent upon a party to the transaction actually purchasing a contract or services from the company. A fee that is paid only when a client buys coverage is a kickback-style arrangement and is prohibited. The form itself identifies which licensees (the listing broker, the other broker, or both) have received or will receive payment from the company and confirms the nature of that compensation.

The form is not required in every transaction. If there is no residential service contract involved in the transaction, the form is not needed. If there is a residential service contract but the licensee is not receiving any compensation from the company providing it, the form is not required. If the other agent or broker is providing their own disclosure, a licensee may choose to provide the form as well for additional transparency. The form is only required when a licensee has a financial relationship with a specific residential service company that could potentially influence the recommendation being made to clients.

When recommending any service provider, whether a title company, lender, inspector, or residential service company, the license holder is legally and ethically obligated to disclose any financial relationship that might affect the recommendation. Any arrangement where a licensee receives finder's fees, referral bonuses, or other compensation from a provider must be disclosed to the client. The licensee should also ensure that receiving such fees does not violate the Real Estate Settlement Procedures Act or other applicable law. For disclosures involving relationships with providers other than residential service companies, the broker should have an attorney prepare appropriate disclosure forms rather than attempting to draft them independently.

Chapter 4: Snapshot Review

The following review summarizes the key rules and concepts from Chapter 4.

Earnest Money: Purpose and Legal Effect

- Earnest money is not the consideration of a real estate contract; consideration is the mutual exchange of promises between buyer and seller
- A contract with zero earnest money is still valid if all essential elements are present and both parties agree
- Earnest money serves two purposes: (1) it demonstrates the buyer's good faith, and (2) it serves as liquidated damages (pre-agreed compensation for a breach)
- Under Form 20-19 Paragraph 15, if the buyer defaults the seller may take the earnest money as liquidated damages; once accepted, no further damages may be pursued
- Typical earnest money is one to two percent of the sales price; at closing it is applied first to the down payment, then to buyer's closing costs

Options: Termination Rights and Standalone Options

- The residential termination option in Paragraph 5B of Form 20-19 gives the buyer the unrestricted right to terminate for any reason during the Option Period in exchange for the Option Fee
- The Option Fee must be delivered to the escrow agent within 3 days after the Effective Date; the escrow agent releases it directly to the seller without further instruction
- If the buyer terminates during the Option Period: Option Fee is not refunded; earnest money is refunded
- Notice of termination must be delivered by 5:00 p.m. local time on or before the last day of the Option Period; the right expires automatically at that deadline
- A standalone option to purchase is a unilateral contract giving a buyer the exclusive right to purchase at an agreed price within a stated period; only the seller is bound if the buyer elects to exercise

Title Insurance

- A title search uncovers unpaid taxes, mortgages, judgments, easements, and other recorded claims; title insurance then protects against hidden risks not discoverable through the public records
- The Owner's Policy insures the buyer against defects not disclosed on the title commitment; the Mortgagee's Policy insures the lender only -- it does NOT protect the buyer
- A buyer who relies on the lender's title policy has no title protection; an Owner's Policy is essential
- 'Good and marketable title' means the property can be sold even if encumbrances exist; 'free and clear' means no encumbrances of any kind, which is rare since virtually every property has at least a utility easement
- Do not use the phrase 'free and clear' when describing the title as a whole; reserve it only for confirming that no mortgage lien exists
- The title officer (closer) is a neutral facilitator who manages documents and funds; the title attorney prepares the deed and other legal instruments
- Owner's title insurance requires only a single premium paid at closing; no annual renewals are required

The Title Commitment and Endorsements

- The title commitment discloses the conditions under which title insurance will be issued; it is preliminary information, not a guarantee of title
- The title company must deliver the commitment within 20 days after receiving the contract; it is issued when the title company has a bona fide order for a policy to be issued within 90 days
- Schedule A: basic facts (parties, price, interest type, legal description)
- Schedule B: all recorded matters affecting the title (restrictions, easements, liens, etc.); defines what the policy will not insure against
- Schedule C: requirements that must be satisfied before a title policy will be issued; these cannot be waived by the buyer
- Schedule D: disclosure of title company officers, underwriter, and premium schedule
- Endorsements modify or expand the standard title policy coverage; costs are set by the Texas Department of Insurance and are not negotiable

Survey Systems and Legal Descriptions

- Metes and bounds describes land by direction and distance starting from a point of beginning, tracing the perimeter and returning to the starting point; common for rural and older urban parcels
- A monument is a fixed physical reference point used in a metes and bounds description
- The rectangular government survey system divides land into townships (6 miles square) and sections (1 mile square, 640 acres); used in rural areas and parts of Texas
- The lot and block system is used in subdivided urban and suburban areas; each parcel is identified by its lot number, block number, and named subdivision within a recorded plat
- Once a subdivision plat is recorded, the plat description prevails over a conflicting metes and bounds description; describing land by lot and block before the plat is recorded is a misdemeanor in Texas
- Always verify the legal description against the current deed or recorded plat before completing any contract

Notice to Prospective Buyer (Form 58-0)

- Texas law requires a license holder to advise each buyer in writing to have an abstract examined by an attorney or to obtain a title insurance policy; Form 58-0 is the TREC-approved vehicle for this notice
- Form 58-0 (effective November 7, 2022) replaces Form OP-C
- The form is most critical in cash and owner-financed transactions where no lender is requiring a title search
- The seller does not sign Form 58-0; the broker or sales agent and the buyer(s) sign; the licensee retains the original in the transaction file
- Form 58-0 is approved (not promulgated) by TREC; the underlying advisory obligation to buyers about title protection exists in every transaction

Seller's Disclosure Notice (Form 55-1)

- Form 55-1 (effective May 28, 2026) replaces Form OP-H; it is a disclosure of the seller's knowledge of property condition as of the date signed, not a warranty
- The seller completes the form; the licensee should never fill it out on the seller's behalf to avoid misrepresentation liability

- Form 55-1 covers 11 categories: inventory checklist of features/systems; smoke detector compliance; known defects in structural components; environmental and hazard conditions; flood disclosures; general repair needs; permits and code compliance; HOA information; lawsuits; health/safety conditions; and coastal/military proximity notices
- Flood disclosures are now detailed and extensive, requiring disclosure of floodplain location (100-year and 500-year), previous flood damage, FEMA/SBA assistance, and flood insurance claims
- Exemptions from the formal notice include court-ordered transfers, foreclosures, bankruptcy sales, trustee deeds, lender acquisitions, executor or guardian transfers, co-owner transfers, spousal/family transfers, divorce transfers, government transfers, new home builder first sales, and transfers of no more than 5% of value
- Exempt sellers still owe common law and DTPA duties to disclose known material defects
- Sellers who complete the notice honestly and allow buyer inspections generally satisfy their legal obligations; sellers who conceal known defects face significant liability

Lead-Based Paint Disclosure (Form 56-0)

- Federal law requires lead-based paint disclosure for all residential dwellings built before 1978; Form 56-0 (the Lead-Based Paint Addendum) is the TREC-promulgated form for this disclosure
- The seller discloses knowledge of lead-based paint conditions and provides any available documentation; the buyer then chooses to accept as-is or to conduct an inspection within 10 days of the Effective Date
- If the buyer inspects and receives a report, the buyer has until the 14th day after the Effective Date to terminate the contract based on the report
- The licensee must provide the EPA pamphlet 'Protect Your Family from Lead in Your Home,' complete the addendum, disclose any known lead conditions, and retain the completed form for at least 3 years after the sale

Environmental Assessment Addendum (Form 28-2)

- Form 28-2 is used when the buyer has concerns about environmental conditions, threatened or endangered species, or wetlands on the property; it applies to residential as well as rural transactions
- Environmental concerns covered include mold, asbestos, radon, water contamination, toxic waste, leaking underground storage tanks, and other hazardous conditions
- If the buyer receives an adverse environmental report, the buyer may terminate and provide a copy of the report to the seller, who must then disclose its contents to future buyers
- Licensees should maintain a list of qualified environmental specialists; this form is often underused relative to the protections it provides

Professionals Who Protect the Parties

- Home inspectors: protect buyers (condition information), sellers (documentation of disclosure), licensees (professional diligence), and lenders (collateral quality)
- Appraisers: protect sellers from undervaluing, buyers from overpaying, lenders from over-lending, and licensees from price guidance claims
- Surveyors: establish accurate boundary lines; protect sellers from misrepresentation claims, lenders from clouded title risk, and licensees from boundary disputes
- Structural engineers: evaluate foundation and structural integrity; buyers and sellers should never rely on a foundation repair company's assessment -- that company has a financial incentive to find problems

Residential Service Contracts and Form RSC-4

- A residential service contract (home warranty) covers repair or replacement of specified systems and appliances for a fee; the buyer pays a co-payment per service call; coverage terms vary by company
- Residential service companies are licensed and regulated by TREC
- Paragraph 7H of Form 20-19 allows the parties to negotiate seller reimbursement of the buyer's residential service contract cost up to a stated dollar amount
- Form RSC-4 (effective June 11, 2023) is required whenever a license holder receives any compensation from a residential service company; it must be provided before the contract is signed
- Permitted compensation: fees for services provided to or on behalf of the residential service company, as long as the fee is NOT contingent upon the client purchasing coverage
- The form is not required if there is no residential service contract in the transaction, or if the licensee receives no compensation from the company involved
- Neither the seller nor any licensee may condition the sale of the property on the buyer's purchase of a residential service contract from any specific company
- Any financial relationship between a licensee and any service provider must be disclosed; a broker should have an attorney prepare disclosure forms for provider relationships not covered by Form RSC-4

Chapter 4 Quiz: Covenants, Commitments and Notices

1. What are the two legal purposes that earnest money serves in a Texas real estate contract?

a. It serves as the consideration that makes the contract binding on both parties, and it confirms the buyer's financing approval

b. It represents the buyer's down payment held in trust until closing, and it guarantees the seller's right to accept backup offers

c. It demonstrates the buyer's good faith, and it serves as liquidated damages that are agreed upon in advance in the event of a default

d. It guarantees the buyer's unrestricted right to terminate the contract without penalty, and it secures the seller's obligation to close

2. Which of the following best describes a title that is described as good and marketable?

a. A title that can be transferred to a buyer even though certain encumbrances, such as utility easements, exist on the property

b. A title that has no encumbrances of any kind, including all utility easements and deed restrictions

c. A title that has been reviewed and certified by a licensed title attorney as completely defect-free

d. A title that is covered by both an owner's policy and a mortgagee's policy at the same time

3. A buyer purchases a home with a conventional loan and, after closing, discovers a previously undisclosed lien against the property. Which title insurance policy provides protection to the buyer in this situation?

a. The Mortgagee's Policy, because the lender's policy covers all title defects that arise after closing

b. Both the Owner's Policy and the Mortgagee's Policy, because they cover the same risks equally

c. Neither policy, because title insurance does not cover liens that are discovered after the closing date

d. The Owner's Policy, because it is issued to the buyer and insures against defects not disclosed on the title commitment

4. In a Texas title commitment, which Schedule identifies the specific requirements that must be satisfied before the title company will issue a title policy?

a. Schedule A

b. Schedule C

c. Schedule B

d. Schedule D

5. In which type of transaction is Form 58-0, the Notice to Prospective Buyer, considered most critical for protecting the buyer?

a. A cash purchase or an owner-financed transaction where no lender is independently requiring a title search

b. A transaction involving a property that has changed ownership more than three times in the past five years

c. Any transaction where the seller is providing a seller's disclosure notice for the first time

d. A new construction transaction where the property has no previous title search history

6. Who is responsible for completing the Seller's Disclosure Notice (Form 55-1)?

a. The listing agent, because the agent has professional knowledge of the property's condition and the applicable disclosure requirements

b. The buyer's agent, in order to ensure that the buyer receives unbiased and objective information about the property

c. The title company, as part of the standard closing preparation and document review process

d. The seller, because the form requires disclosure of the seller's actual knowledge of the property's condition

7. Under the survey system most widely used in Texas residential real estate, how is a property typically identified in its legal description?

a. By metes and bounds, starting from a designated point of beginning and tracing all boundary lines back to that same point

b. By township and section number within the federal rectangular government survey system

c. By lot number, block number, and the name of the recorded subdivision plat filed in the county records

d. By the property's tax parcel identification number as maintained by the county appraisal district

8. Federal law requires a lead-based paint disclosure for all residential dwellings constructed before what year?

a. 1968

b. 1978

c. 1990

d. 1986

9. What happens to a buyer's earnest money if the buyer exercises the unrestricted right to terminate the contract during the Option Period under Paragraph 5B of Form 20-19?

a. The earnest money is refunded to the buyer, and the seller retains the Option Fee as compensation for taking the property off the market

b. Both the earnest money and the Option Fee are retained by the seller as the agreed remedy for termination

c. Both the earnest money and the Option Fee are fully refunded to the buyer upon delivery of written notice

d. The earnest money is divided equally between the buyer and the seller, and the Option Fee is refunded to the buyer

10. A buyer who has concerns about mold contamination, asbestos, and the presence of wetlands on a rural property should attach which TREC addendum to the contract?

a. The Seller's Disclosure Notice (Form 55-1)

b. The Addendum for Property Subject to Mandatory Membership in a Property Owners Association (Form 36-11)

c. The Addendum for Coastal Area Property (Form 33-2)

d. The Environmental Assessment, Threatened or Endangered Species, and Wetlands Addendum (Form 28-2)

11. Under which circumstances is Form RSC-4, the Disclosure of Relationship with Residential Service Company, required?

a. Whenever a residential service contract is included as part of any real estate transaction in Texas

b. Whenever a license holder receives any form of compensation from a residential service company in connection with a transaction

c. Whenever a seller agrees to contribute money toward the buyer's purchase of a residential service contract

d. Whenever the buyer requests specific information about a residential service company from the licensee

12. A buyer who relies solely on the lender's Mortgagee's Policy for title protection has what level of actual coverage for title defects that arise after closing?

a. Full coverage for all title defects, because the Mortgagee's Policy protects all parties in the transaction

b. Partial coverage up to the loan amount, with the buyer personally responsible for any claim that exceeds that amount

c. No coverage, because the Mortgagee's Policy is issued to and protects the lender only, not the buyer

d. Coverage equal to the Owner's Policy, because both policies insure against the same categories of title risk

---

CHAPTER 5
CLOSING, POSSESSION AND MORE

Chapter Overview

The closing of a real estate transaction is the culmination of every promise made in the contract. It is the moment when the deed is delivered, funds are transferred, and ownership changes hands. Getting to that moment cleanly and on time depends on preparation that begins at the listing appointment, continues through the contract period, and reaches its conclusion when the parties sign the closing documents. This chapter examines the practical steps that lead to a smooth closing, the proper use of the Special Provisions paragraph, and the two promulgated temporary residential lease forms that TREC provides for situations where possession does not transfer on the same day as closing. The Seller's Temporary Residential Lease (Form 15-7) and the Buyer's Temporary Residential Lease (Form 16-7), both effective November 3, 2025, are covered paragraph by paragraph so that license holders can complete them accurately and understand the rights and obligations they create.

Learning Objectives

Upon completing Chapter 5, the student will bc able to:

1. Identify the closing preparation questions a license holder should ask at a listing appointment and explain how early gathering of this information leads to a smoother closing.
2. Describe the appropriate uses of the Special Provisions paragraph in Form 20-19 and explain the risks and boundaries that apply when completing it.
3. Explain when the Seller's Temporary Residential Lease (Form 15-7) is required, identify the parties and their roles, and correctly complete each paragraph of the form.
4. Explain when the Buyer's Temporary Residential Lease (Form 16-7) is appropriate, identify the key differences between it and the Seller's Temporary Lease, and correctly complete each paragraph of the form.

Contents

- Preparing for a Smooth Closing
- Special Provisions: Paragraph 11 of Form 20-19
- When Possession and Closing Do Not Align
- Seller's Temporary Residential Lease (Form 15-7)
- Buyer's Temporary Residential Lease (Form 16-7)

Preparing for a Smooth Closing

The closing date in a residential transaction is both an obligation and a deadline. Missing it creates costs for both parties and may trigger default provisions. The best time to begin preparing for a smooth closing is at the listing appointment, long before any offer has been received. A license holder who asks the right questions early gives the title company, the lender, and everyone else in the transaction the information they need to do their work without last-minute surprises.

There is a practical wisdom in trying to close early rather than close late. The longer a transaction remains open, the more opportunities arise for something to go wrong. Interest rates may change in a direction the buyer finds unfavorable. The seller may reconsider the price if market conditions shift. Title issues may surface and require time to resolve. Lender conditions may stack up. A transaction that could close in 30 days but drags on for 60 creates unnecessary exposure for both parties and for the license holders involved.

Questions to Ask at the Listing Appointment

The following questions should be asked and answered when a property is listed. Each answer has a direct bearing on how the transaction will proceed at closing, and waiting until a contract is in place to gather this information is too late.

Who are all parties with an ownership interest in the property? Every person who holds title must sign the deed at closing. If the seller is not sure who is on the deed, the title company needs to know immediately so a title search can confirm the current ownership.

What is the marital status of the seller? In Texas, homestead property cannot be conveyed without the signature of both spouses, even if only one spouse is on the deed. If the seller is married, the seller's spouse will be required to sign the deed regardless of whether the spouse's name appears in the title chain.

If the seller is divorced, did the divorce occur before or after the purchase of this property? A divorce that took place after the property was acquired may have created rights or obligations in the other spouse, or may have conveyed the property entirely to one party. The title company needs this information to ensure the chain of title is clear.

Has the seller been widowed since acquiring the property? If the seller's spouse has died since the property was purchased, probate proceedings or an affidavit of heirship may be required to establish that the surviving spouse or heirs have clear authority to sell.

Is the property a homestead? Homestead property carries additional protections under Texas law. Both spouses must sign the deed conveying a homestead regardless of how title is held, and certain transactions affecting homestead property have additional requirements.

Who holds the first and second liens on the property, and are the payments current? The title company will require payoff letters from all lienholders. If payments are delinquent, additional funds may be required at closing to bring the account current, and the seller needs to know this in advance.

Are there mineral rights associated with the property, and does the seller intend to retain them? If the seller wishes to reserve mineral rights, the Addendum for Reservation of Oil, Gas and Other Minerals (Form 44-3) must be attached to the contract.

Are property taxes current, or is there a delinquency? Delinquent taxes must be paid at or before closing. The title company will not close a transaction with outstanding ad valorem tax liens unless they are being satisfied from the proceeds.

If any prior liens have been paid off, has the release of lien been recorded? A paid-off loan that does not have a recorded release of lien still appears as a cloud on title. The title company will require a recorded release or will contact the prior lender to obtain one before insuring the title.

The answers to these questions put the title company, the lender, and the license holders in the best possible position to identify and resolve issues early. An issue discovered and resolved in the first week of a transaction is manageable. The same issue discovered on the day before closing can be catastrophic.

Special Provisions: Paragraph 11 of Form 20-19

Paragraph 11 of the One to Four Family Residential Contract (Form 20-19) is the Special Provisions paragraph. Its purpose is narrow and specific: it is a place to add factual statements and business details that are not addressed anywhere else in the contract. The paragraph itself now includes an explicit reminder printed in the form that real estate brokers and sales agents are prohibited from practicing law and shall not add to, delete, or modify any provision of the contract unless drafted by a party to the contract or a party's attorney.

Special Provisions is the paragraph that generates more disciplinary actions against license holders than any other single part of the contract. The problem is not that the paragraph is difficult to understand. The problem is that many license holders see a blank space and feel compelled to fill it with something, not realizing that what they write may exceed the limits of permissible brokerage activity. The discipline for writing something in Paragraph 11 that creates, modifies, or removes a legal right is the same as the discipline for any other form of unauthorized practice of law: it can cost a license holder their license.

The rule is straightforward. An informational item is a statement that completes a blank in the form, discloses a factual condition, or provides an instruction. Examples of appropriate entries include a statement that the buyer is a licensed real estate sales agent (a required disclosure to avoid a DTPA violation), a statement that the buyer requests a walkthrough of the property within a specified window before closing, or a reference to a separately attached agreement such as a Bill of Sale for personal property items being transferred. These are factual and operational; they do not create legal rights that are not already in the contract.

Examples of what does not belong in Paragraph 11 include language that purports to make the contract contingent on an event for which a promulgated addendum already exists (such as the sale of another property by the buyer or a financing contingency), language that alters the default provisions of the contract, and language that gives one party a right to approve or reject the other party's performance. In one instructive example from the original course material, a licensee wrote 'The repairs are to be completed and approved by the buyers.' That single phrase removed the bilateral character of the contract by giving the buyer unlimited discretion to reject any repair, effectively making the contract unilateral and the seller powerless to deliver performance that would satisfy the buyer. The licensee who wrote it had modified the contract in a legally significant way.

Before writing anything in Paragraph 11, the license holder should ask two questions. First, is there a promulgated addendum or another paragraph in the contract that already addresses this subject? If so, use that provision and leave Paragraph 11 blank. Second, does the language being considered create a legal right or remedy that is not already in the contract? If the answer to either question is yes, the client should be directed to an attorney. The broker should also review whatever the license holder intends to write in this paragraph before it is submitted. Brokers, in turn, should consult a real estate attorney when they encounter entries in Paragraph 11 that they are not certain are appropriate.

The Remaining Contract Paragraphs: 12 Through 23

Paragraphs 12 through 23 of Form 20-19 are largely pre-printed terms that the parties do not complete with transaction-specific entries the way they complete the earlier paragraphs. A license holder must still understand what each one does, both to answer client questions and to recognize the point at which a situation calls for a referral to an attorney. Several of these topics are also treated as broader concepts elsewhere in this course, and those cross-references are noted below.

Paragraph 12: Settlement and Other Expenses

Paragraph 12 allocates the expenses of closing between the parties. It lists the expenses the seller customarily pays, such as releasing existing liens and recording the releases, preparing the deed, and providing required tax statements or certificates, and it lists the expenses the buyer customarily pays, including loan-related expenses and other customary buyer costs. Paragraph 12A(1)(b) provides a blank for any amount the seller agrees to contribute toward the buyer's expenses other than brokerage compensation, and that amount must be stated as a specific dollar figure. Effective July 1, 2026, brokerage compensation is set out separately in a new Paragraph 12B: Paragraph 12B(1) states any amount the seller will pay toward the buyer's broker's compensation, and Paragraph 12B(2) states any amount the buyer will pay toward the seller's broker's compensation. Each of these amounts may be expressed either as a dollar figure or as a percentage of the sales price. Paragraph 12 also addresses expenses that a buyer is prohibited from paying under FHA, VA, or other governmental loan-program rules; in that situation the seller may pay those expenses, and if the amount required exceeds what the seller has agreed to pay, either party may terminate.

Paragraph 13: Prorations

Paragraph 13 provides that taxes, interest, maintenance fees, assessments, dues, and rents are prorated through the Closing Date. Because the year's property tax bill is often not final at closing, the paragraph also addresses what happens if taxes are later determined to differ from the amount prorated, for example when a change in exemptions or a reassessment alters the tax obligation after closing; the parties are to adjust the proration between themselves when the actual amounts become known. Rollback taxes, which can arise when land receiving an agricultural-use valuation is converted to another use, are handled in the Farm and Ranch and Unimproved Property contracts rather than here.

Paragraph 14: Casualty Loss

Paragraph 14 governs what happens if the property is damaged or destroyed between the effective date and closing. The seller is obligated to restore the property to its previous condition as soon as reasonably possible, but no later than the Closing Date. If the seller is unable to do so through no fault of the seller, the buyer has three choices: terminate the contract and receive a refund of the earnest money; extend the closing date by up to 15 days to allow the restoration to be completed; or accept the property in its damaged condition together with an assignment of any insurance proceeds and credit for the seller's deductible. A license holder should counsel the client to involve the insurance carrier promptly and, where significant damage is involved, an attorney.

Paragraph 15: Default

Paragraph 15 sets out the remedies available when a party fails to perform. If the buyer defaults, the seller may either terminate the contract and retain the earnest money as liquidated damages or pursue the other remedies the law allows. If the seller defaults, the buyer may either terminate and recover the earnest money or enforce the contract through specific performance. The legal principles behind these remedies, including liquidated damages and specific performance, are discussed in Chapter 1 under Breach of Contract and Remedies. Only a court can determine that a party has actually defaulted; a license holder should never advise a client that the other party is in default, but should instead direct the client to an attorney and notify the broker.

Paragraph 16: Mediation

Paragraph 16 contains a mediation provision that the parties may elect by checking the appropriate box, agreeing to submit disputes arising under the contract to mediation before resorting to litigation.

Paragraph 17: Attorney's Fees

Paragraph 17 provides that the prevailing party in any legal proceeding related to the contract is entitled to recover reasonable attorney's fees and all costs of the proceeding from the non-prevailing party. The practical effect is to discourage meritless claims, since a party who sues and does not prevail may be ordered to pay the other side's legal costs.

Paragraph 18: Escrow

Paragraph 18 governs the escrow agent's handling of the earnest money and option fee. It authorizes the escrow agent to hold the funds and to disburse them according to the contract, and it establishes the procedure that applies when a dispute arises over who is entitled to the money. If no closing occurs, the escrow agent may require a written release of liability, signed by the parties, before releasing the earnest money, and a party who wrongfully refuses to sign a release acceptable to the escrow agent may be liable to the other party. Consistent with this paragraph, the escrow agent's notices are effective when sent in compliance with the Notices paragraph.

Paragraph 19: Representations

Paragraph 19 provides that all covenants, representations, and warranties in the contract survive closing, meaning they remain enforceable after the transaction is completed. If any representation made by the seller is untrue on the Closing Date, the seller is in default. The paragraph also confirms that, unless the parties have agreed otherwise in writing, the seller may continue to show the property and may receive, negotiate, and accept back-up offers while the contract is pending.

Paragraph 20: Federal Tax Requirements

Paragraph 20 addresses the buyer's obligation, under the federal Foreign Investment in Real Property Tax Act (FIRPTA), to withhold a portion of the sales proceeds when the seller is a foreign person and to remit that amount to the Internal Revenue Service. FIRPTA is examined in detail in Chapter 8. Effective July 1, 2026, Paragraph 20 also includes a new Paragraph 20B addressing federal Financial Crimes Enforcement Network (FinCEN) reporting: it requires the parties to provide the escrow agent with the information needed to satisfy any governmental reporting requirements and requires the buyer to pay any charges associated with gathering and reporting that information.

Paragraph 21: Notices

Paragraph 21 establishes how the parties give one another notice under the contract and provides the blanks where each party's contact information is entered. Effective July 1, 2026, this paragraph was amended to clarify the acceptable methods of delivery and to provide that a notice is effective when sent to a party or that party's agent. The revised paragraph also adds more options for the buyer's, seller's, and agents' contact information, including a line for delivering a copy to each party's agent. Because nearly every deadline in the contract depends on proper notice, the license holder must confirm that the information in Paragraph 21 is complete and accurate; an incomplete Paragraph 21 is a common and consequential error.

Paragraph 22: Agreement of Parties

Paragraph 22 states that the contract contains the entire agreement of the parties and cannot be changed except by their written agreement, and it is where the parties identify the addenda that are made part of the contract. Effective July 1, 2026, all addenda and notices were consolidated into Paragraph 22 and reorganized into clearly labeled categories: Financial, Leases, Additional Tests and Reports, Statutory Disclosures and Notices, and Other. The individual promulgated addenda that may be attached here are covered in Chapter 7. The license holder must check the box for every addendum that applies and attach the corresponding form; an addendum that is referenced but not attached, or attached but not referenced, is a frequent source of disputes.

Paragraph 23: Consult an Attorney Before Signing

Paragraph 23 reminds the parties that TREC rules prohibit real estate brokers and sales agents from giving legal advice and urges each party to have the contract reviewed by an attorney before signing; it provides blanks for the buyer's and seller's attorney information. This is the final numbered paragraph of the contract. The standalone Termination Option that older versions of the form placed near the end has been combined into Paragraph 5 (Earnest Money and Termination Option), so the current contract concludes at Paragraph 23, followed by the signature blocks, the broker information section, and the receipts for the option fee and earnest money.

When Possession and Closing Do Not Align

In most residential transactions, possession of the property transfers on the same day the transaction closes and funds. This is the standard arrangement contemplated by Form 20-19, which provides in Paragraph 10A that the seller shall deliver possession upon closing and funding. However, there are circumstances where the parties need to separate the date of closing from the date of possession, and TREC has promulgated two forms to address each scenario.

The Seller's Temporary Residential Lease (Form 15-7) is used when the seller needs to remain in the property for a period of time after the closing has occurred. The seller has already conveyed title to the buyer but has not yet vacated. The buyer becomes the landlord and the seller becomes the tenant.

The Buyer's Temporary Residential Lease (Form 16-7) is used in the opposite situation: the buyer takes possession of the property before the closing has occurred. The title still belongs to the seller, who becomes the landlord, while the buyer moves in as the tenant.

Both forms carry TREC's notice that they may be used only when the period of the temporary occupancy does not exceed 90 days. If either party needs to occupy the property outside of these parameters, a full residential lease agreement must be used instead. These forms are addenda to a TREC promulgated contract form and may not be used as standalone lease agreements.

Before allowing a buyer to take early possession under Form 16-7, both the seller and the seller's agent should have a high degree of confidence that the transaction will close. Moving a buyer into a property before closing creates practical and legal complications if the transaction subsequently falls apart: the seller must then deal with removing an occupant in addition to dealing with the failed contract. The designated broker should always be consulted before early possession is granted.

A critical note from Form 20-19 itself: any possession by the buyer before closing or by the seller after closing that is not authorized by a written lease will establish a tenancy at sufferance relationship between the parties. A tenancy at sufferance provides minimal legal protection and creates uncertainty about insurance coverage and liability. It is not a substitute for one of the promulgated temporary lease forms. The forms are there for a reason, and using them is the only way to establish a clear legal framework for the transitional occupancy period.

Seller's Temporary Residential Lease (Form 15-7)

The Seller's Temporary Residential Lease (Form 15-7, effective November 3, 2025) is used when the seller needs to remain in the property after the closing date. The form replaces Form 15-6. Its header carries a clear notice: for use only when the seller occupies the property for no more than 90 days after the closing. Every paragraph of this form must be completed carefully, and the roles of the parties must be kept clear throughout.

Parties and Property

Paragraph 1 identifies the parties. In this arrangement the buyer from the purchase contract becomes the Landlord and the seller becomes the Tenant. This reversal of the familiar buyer-seller terminology is the single most common source of error when completing this form: many license holders instinctively write the names in the wrong blanks. Use the same names as they appear in Paragraph 1 of Form 20-19. Paragraph 2 identifies the property being leased, which is the same property described in the purchase contract. The full address including city, state, and zip code must be entered.

Term

Paragraph 3 sets the duration of the lease. The commencement date is fixed by the form itself: the lease begins on the date the sale closes and funds. The license holder enters only the termination date. This date must not be more than 90 days after the closing date. If the seller needs to remain longer than 90 days, this form may not be used and the parties must execute a full residential lease agreement instead.

Rental

Paragraph 4 requires a daily rental rate, not a monthly rate. The daily rate approach is used so that if the seller vacates early or if the lease ends on an irregular date, the calculation is straightforward. The full amount of rent for the entire anticipated lease term is paid at the time of funding, meaning it is collected at the closing table, not in monthly installments. If the seller closes on May 15 and the lease runs through May 31, the total rent for those 16 days (at whatever daily rate was agreed) is paid out of the seller's closing proceeds or by check at closing. The tenant will not receive a refund of rent if the lease terminates early because the seller chose to leave ahead of schedule or because the seller defaulted under the lease.

Deposit

Paragraph 5 addresses the security deposit. The deposit amount is also paid at the time of closing. The deposit protects the landlord (buyer) against damage to the property that occurs during the seller's occupancy after the sale. When the tenant surrenders possession, the landlord must return any unused portion of the deposit along with an itemized list of all deductions within 30 days after the tenant both surrenders possession and provides the landlord with written notice of the tenant's forwarding address. This 30-day period and the requirement for an itemized statement are legally significant: a landlord who wrongfully withholds a deposit may face liability under the Texas Property Code.

Utilities, Use, and Pets

Paragraph 6 addresses utilities. The most common arrangement is for the tenant (former seller) to continue paying the same utility accounts that were in service during the seller's ownership. The form allows exceptions to be written in if the parties agree that the landlord will cover certain utilities. Paragraph 7 restricts the tenant's use of the property to residential purposes only. The tenant may not assign the lease or sublet any portion of the property to a third party. Paragraph 8 governs pets. If the tenant has had pets on the property prior to the sale, those pets may be specified as permitted. Any restrictions on size, breed, or number should be written into the blank. If no pets are permitted, that restriction is entered here.

Condition, Alterations, and Special Provisions

Paragraph 9 addresses the condition of the property. When the tenant surrenders possession at the end of the lease, the property must be returned in the condition required under the purchase contract, meaning in the condition the seller warranted or agreed to deliver at closing, with allowance for normal wear and tear and any casualty loss. The buyer should conduct a final walkthrough of the property immediately before closing while they still have the ability to object to the condition as buyers. That walkthrough documents the baseline condition and gives the landlord a factual basis for evaluating whether any deductions from the security deposit are warranted when the tenant eventually moves out.

Paragraph 10 prohibits the tenant from making any alterations, additions, or improvements to the property without the landlord's prior written consent. If the tenant does obtain consent and makes improvements, those improvements become the property of the landlord. The tenant cannot remove them when vacating.

Paragraph 11 is the Special Provisions paragraph, the same concept as in Form 20-19. Anything written here must be a factual statement or an agreed business detail. The same prohibitions against unauthorized practice of law that apply in the main contract apply with equal force here.

Inspections, Laws, and Maintenance

Paragraph 12 gives the landlord the right to enter the property at reasonable times to inspect it. The tenant must provide the landlord with door keys and access codes for the property during the lease term. This is important because the buyer may need access to obtain measurements, arrange for moving logistics, or verify the condition before the tenant vacates. Paragraph 13 requires the tenant to comply with all laws, ordinances, and subdivision and homeowners association rules that apply to the property. Paragraph 14 makes the tenant responsible for all costs of repairing and maintaining the property during the lease period, including the yard, trees, and shrubs, except as otherwise provided by the Texas Property Code. The tenant must also promptly repair any damage caused directly or indirectly by the tenant or anyone else the tenant allows on the property.

Indemnity, Insurance, and Default

Paragraph 15 requires the tenant to indemnify the landlord against third-party claims for injury or property damage arising from the tenant's use or occupancy of the property. This includes any attorney's fees, costs, and expenses the landlord incurs as a result of such claims. Paragraph 16 addresses insurance and carries an important warning printed in all capital letters: possession of the property by the seller as tenant may change insurance policy coverage. Both the buyer and the seller should contact their respective insurance representatives immediately when this type of arrangement is contemplated. The buyer's homeowner's policy now covers a property occupied by a tenant, not by the owner, which may affect the terms of coverage. The seller may need to convert their existing coverage to a renter's policy.

Paragraph 17 covers default. If the tenant fails to perform any obligation under the lease and does not begin to cure that failure within the time specified after receiving written notice from the landlord, the tenant will be in default. For example, if the tenant is not maintaining the yard in a satisfactory condition, the landlord may give written notice, and if the tenant does not begin remedying the problem within the stated time period, default occurs and the landlord may pursue remedies.

Termination, Holdover, and Attorney's Fees

Paragraph 18 identifies the events that terminate the lease. Paragraph 19 addresses holdover: if the tenant remains in the property after the lease termination date, the landlord is not obligated to allow the tenancy to continue on any terms. The tenant must pay a daily damages amount specified in this paragraph for each day of possession after the termination date, in addition to any other remedies the landlord is entitled to pursue. The holdover rate is typically set higher than the regular daily rental rate to create a financial incentive for the tenant to vacate on time. Paragraph 20 provides that the prevailing party in any lawsuit relating to the lease is entitled to recover all costs and reasonable attorney's fees from the non-prevailing party.

Smoke Alarms, Security Devices, and Notices

Paragraph 21 addresses smoke alarms. Because the tenant was recently the owner and is familiar with the property and its systems, the tenant waives the landlord's obligation to inspect and repair smoke alarms. The tenant takes responsibility for ensuring that smoke alarms are in working order during the lease period.

Paragraph 22 provides that the Texas Property Code requirements relating to security devices, including requirements for door locks, deadbolts, and pin locks for sliding glass doors, do not apply to a residential lease for a term of 90 days or less. This waiver reflects the transitional nature of the arrangement and the fact that the tenant was the recent owner and is already familiar with the property's security configuration.

Paragraph 23 urges both parties to consult an attorney before signing. This reminder mirrors the Consult an Attorney paragraph in Form 20-19 and reinforces the obligation that license holders should be directing clients to legal counsel whenever there are legal questions about what they are signing.

Paragraph 24 provides space for the mailing addresses and contact information for both the landlord and the tenant. These blanks must be filled out completely. All notices under the lease are effective when mailed to, hand-delivered at, or transmitted by fax or electronic transmission to these addresses. A license holder should never enter their own address in the landlord or tenant lines on behalf of a client. The blanks are for the clients, and substituting the licensee's contact information creates liability by making the licensee responsible for receiving and transmitting legal notices on behalf of a party. Both the landlord and the tenant must sign the completed form.

Buyer's Temporary Residential Lease (Form 16-7)

The Buyer's Temporary Residential Lease (Form 16-7, effective November 3, 2025) is used when the buyer takes possession of the property before the closing occurs. The form replaces Form 16-6. Its header carries a notice mirroring the seller's form: for use only when the buyer occupies the property for no more than 90 days prior to the closing. In this arrangement, the seller retains title and becomes the Landlord, while the buyer moves in as the Tenant before the sale is complete.

The structure of Form 16-7 closely parallels Form 15-7, with 24 paragraphs covering the same subjects in the same sequence. The key conceptual differences reflect the inverted relationship between the parties: the buyer is the occupant before they own, and the seller is still the owner and bears certain continuing obligations related to the property during the pre-closing period.

Parties, Property, and Term

Paragraph 1 identifies the parties. In Form 16-7, the seller is the Landlord and the buyer is the Tenant. This is the opposite of the arrangement in Form 15-7. Paragraph 2 identifies the property, with the full address including city, state, and zip code. Paragraph 3 states that the term commences and terminates as specified in Paragraph 18, which governs the conditions under which the lease ends. This differs from Form 15-7, where the commencement date is fixed by the closing event.

Rental

Paragraph 4 of Form 16-7 operates somewhat differently from the comparable paragraph in Form 15-7. The daily rental rate is entered, and the buyer pays the full anticipated rental (from the commencement date through the Closing Date specified in Paragraph 9 of the purchase contract) at the start of the lease, when the buyer takes possession. If the actual term turns out to be longer or shorter than anticipated, any additional rent owed or any reimbursement due is settled at closing. Rent is not applied to the down payment, closing costs, or any other item covered by the purchase contract. The no-rental-credit provision is important because allowing rent to reduce the purchase price or closing costs could create complications with lender underwriting requirements.

Deposit, Utilities, and Use

Paragraph 5 of Form 16-7 requires the buyer to pay a deposit to secure performance under the lease. If the lease terminates before the Closing Date, the seller may use the deposit to satisfy any obligations the buyer has not performed. If the lease terminates because the sale closes and funds, the deposit is handled at the closing table as part of the settlement. In either case, if a refund is owed, the landlord must return any unused portion with an itemized statement of deductions within 30 days after the tenant surrenders possession and provides written notice of their forwarding address.

Paragraph 6 of Form 16-7 requires the buyer-tenant to pay all utility connections, deposits, and charges during the lease period, except as otherwise agreed. Note that this paragraph specifically mentions utility connections and deposits, recognizing that when a buyer moves into a property before closing, new utility accounts may need to be established. This is a broader requirement than the comparable paragraph in Form 15-7, where the seller simply continues paying accounts already in their name. Paragraph 7 restricts use to residential purposes only and prohibits assignment or subletting.

Pets and Condition

Paragraph 8 governs pets, subject to whatever the seller as landlord is willing to accept. Paragraph 9 addresses the condition of the property. When the buyer accepts possession before closing, the buyer takes the property in its present condition as improved by the landlord, meaning the seller is still expected to complete any repairs agreed upon in the purchase contract. If the lease is terminated before the closing occurs (if the sale does not close), the buyer must surrender the property in its present condition as improved by the landlord, excluding normal wear and tear and casualty losses. The buyer should conduct a careful walkthrough immediately before taking possession to document the baseline condition.

Alterations, Inspections, and Maintenance

Paragraph 10 prohibits the buyer-tenant from making any alterations without the seller-landlord's written consent. Paragraph 11 is the Special Provisions paragraph. Paragraph 12 gives the seller the right to enter the property at reasonable times to inspect it, and also to replace, repair, or complete improvements during the lease period. This additional authority reflects the fact that the seller may still be obligated to perform repairs under the purchase contract while the buyer is occupying the property. The tenant must provide the landlord with door keys and access codes. Paragraph 13 requires the tenant to comply with all applicable laws and subdivision rules.

Paragraph 14 of Form 16-7 is somewhat broader in scope than the comparable paragraph in Form 15-7. The buyer-tenant is responsible for all costs of repairing, replacing, and maintaining the property, including not only the yard, trees, and shrubs but also all equipment and appliances, unless otherwise required by the Texas Property Code. This is a broader maintenance obligation than the seller's form imposes because the buyer, as the future owner, has a greater stake in keeping the property in good condition. The tenant must also promptly repair any damage the tenant or anyone else the tenant allows on the property causes.

Indemnity, Insurance, Default, and Termination

Paragraph 15 requires the buyer-tenant to indemnify the seller-landlord from third-party claims arising from the tenant's occupancy. Paragraph 16 addresses insurance and carries the same capital-letter warning as the seller's form: possession of the property by the buyer as tenant may change insurance policy coverage. The seller should consult their insurance agent about whether the current homeowner's policy covers a property being occupied by a tenant before the sale closes. The buyer may need to obtain a renter's or tenant's policy to cover personal liability and personal property while they occupy the home before they own it.

Paragraph 17 covers default in the same terms as the seller's form: notice, opportunity to cure, and then default. Paragraph 18 defines when the lease terminates. The Buyer's Temporary Lease terminates upon the closing and funding of the purchase contract, upon default by either party, or upon any other event specified in the lease. This is the key structural difference from the Seller's Temporary Lease: the buyer's lease terminates when the purchase closes, not simply on a calendar date that is separate from and after the closing.

Holdover, Fees, Smoke Alarms, and Notices

Paragraph 19 addresses holdover. If the buyer remains in the property past the termination date without the seller's consent, no tenancy arises and the buyer must pay the daily damages amount specified in this paragraph for each day of continued possession. This amount should be set higher than the regular daily rental rate to provide a financial incentive for the buyer to close or vacate on time. Paragraph 20 provides that the prevailing party in any lease-related lawsuit recovers all costs and reasonable attorney's fees.

Paragraph 21 addresses smoke alarms. The landlord (seller) is not required to inspect or repair smoke alarms during the lease period; the tenant takes responsibility for them. Paragraph 22 waives the Texas Property Code requirements for security devices because the lease term is 90 days or less. Paragraph 23 urges both parties to consult an attorney before signing. Paragraph 24 provides spaces for the mailing addresses and contact information for both parties. As with Form 15-7, the licensee must never place their own contact information in the landlord or tenant blanks. These spaces are for the actual parties to the lease, and substituting a licensee's address creates liability that the license holder should not accept. Both the landlord and the tenant must sign the completed form.

Executory Contracts and the Limits of These Forms

TREC and Texas law take a very cautious approach to any arrangement in which a buyer occupies a property and pays a recurring consideration with an expectation of eventually becoming the owner at the end of a period of occupancy. This arrangement, sometimes called a lease with an option to purchase, a lease-purchase, or a contract for deed, is an executory contract and is subject to extensive regulation under Chapter 5 of the Texas Property Code. These protections exist because buyers in executory contract arrangements are particularly vulnerable to losing their accumulated payments and their occupancy if they miss a single payment or fail to meet some condition of the arrangement.

The Buyer's Temporary Residential Lease is not an executory contract vehicle. It is a bridge document for a specific and limited situation: a buyer who needs to occupy the property for a short period before a defined and pending closing date. If the parties are contemplating any arrangement where the buyer's path to ownership is uncertain, contingent on future performance, or extends beyond 90 days, both parties must be referred to an attorney before any documents are signed. This is not optional guidance; it is a fundamental obligation of any license holder who encounters such a situation.

Chapter 5: Snapshot Review

The following review summarizes the key rules and concepts from Chapter 5.

Preparing for a Smooth Closing

- Closing preparation should begin at the listing appointment, not when a contract is received
- Closing early is always preferable to closing late; longer transaction periods create more opportunities for problems to arise
- Key questions to ask at listing: all parties with ownership interests; marital status of seller; whether a divorce occurred before or after purchase; whether the seller has been widowed since acquisition; whether the property is homestead; identity of all lienholders and current payment status; mineral rights; delinquent tax status; whether released liens have been recorded
- Both spouses must sign the deed conveying Texas homestead property, even if only one spouse's name is on the deed
- Unrecorded releases of paid-off liens appear as clouds on title and must be resolved before closing

Special Provisions: Paragraph 11 of Form 20-19

- Special Provisions is for factual statements and business details only; it is the most frequent source of TREC disciplinary actions against license holders
- Form 20-19 now states explicitly in the paragraph itself that licensees shall not add to, delete, or modify any provision of the contract unless drafted by a party or a party's attorney
- Appropriate entries include: disclosure that the buyer is a licensed real estate agent; a request for a pre-closing walkthrough; a reference to an attached Bill of Sale for personal property
- Inappropriate entries include: contingency language for which a promulgated addendum exists; language that alters default provisions; language giving one party approval rights over the other's performance
- Before writing anything in Paragraph 11, confirm that no existing paragraph or addendum already addresses the subject; if the language creates a legal right, refer the client to an attorney
- The broker should review all Paragraph 11 entries before any offer is submitted; brokers with uncertainty should consult a real estate attorney

The Remaining Contract Paragraphs: 12 Through 23

- Paragraph 12 (Settlement and Other Expenses) allocates the expenses of closing; effective July 1, 2026, brokerage compensation is set in a new Paragraph 12B, with 12B(1) for the seller's contribution to the buyer's broker and 12B(2) for the buyer's contribution to the seller's broker, each stated as a dollar amount or a percentage, and the former Paragraph 8B was removed
- Paragraph 13 (Prorations) prorates taxes, interest, dues, assessments, and rents through the Closing Date; under Paragraph 14 (Casualty Loss), if pre-closing damage is not restored by the Closing Date the buyer may terminate for a refund, extend closing up to 15 days, or accept the property with an assignment of the insurance proceeds and the seller's deductible
- Paragraph 15 (Default), Paragraph 16 (Mediation), and Paragraph 17 (Attorney's Fees) supply the contract's remedies, the dispute-resolution election, and prevailing-party fee recovery; the underlying default and mediation concepts are detailed in Chapter 1
- Paragraph 18 (Escrow) allows the escrow agent to require a signed release of liability before releasing earnest money when no closing occurs; Paragraph 19 (Representations) provides that the seller's representations survive closing and that the seller is in default if a representation is untrue on the Closing Date

- Paragraph 20 covers FIRPTA withholding (detailed in Chapter 8) and, effective July 1, 2026, adds Paragraph 20B requiring the parties to give the escrow agent any governmental-reporting (FinCEN) information with the buyer paying the related charges; Paragraph 21 (Notices) now makes a notice effective when sent to a party or that party's agent; and Paragraph 22 (Agreement of Parties) groups the addenda into five categories: Financial, Leases, Additional Tests and Reports, Statutory Disclosures and Notices, and Other
- The contract ends at Paragraph 23 (Consult an Attorney Before Signing); the former standalone Termination Option is now part of Paragraph 5, so the current Form 20-19 has 23 numbered paragraphs

When Possession and Closing Do Not Align

- Paragraph 10A of Form 20-19 provides that possession transfers upon closing and funding unless a temporary residential lease applies
- Any possession by the buyer before closing or by the seller after closing without a written lease creates a tenancy at sufferance, which provides minimal legal protection and uncertain insurance coverage
- Form 15-7 is used when the seller remains after closing: buyer becomes Landlord, seller becomes Tenant
- Form 16-7 is used when the buyer takes possession before closing: seller becomes Landlord, buyer becomes Tenant
- Both forms are limited to 90 days; if a longer period is needed, a full residential lease agreement must be used
- Both forms are addenda to a promulgated contract and may not be used as standalone lease agreements
- Early buyer possession under Form 16-7 should always involve the knowledge and consent of the designated broker

Seller's Temporary Residential Lease (Form 15-7)

- Form 15-7, effective November 3, 2025, replaces Form 15-6
- Buyer = Landlord; Seller = Tenant; this role reversal is the most common error in completing the form
- Lease commences on the closing and funding date; termination date (no more than 90 days after closing) is entered by the licensee
- Rent is a per-day rate paid in full at the time of closing and funding; no refund if the tenant vacates early or defaults
- Security deposit is paid at closing; must be returned with itemized deductions within 30 days after tenant surrenders possession and provides a forwarding address
- Tenant pays utilities (usually continuing prior arrangements); residential use only; no assignment or subletting
- Tenant maintains the property including yard, trees, and shrubs; any alterations require landlord's written consent and become landlord's property
- Landlord may enter at reasonable times; tenant provides keys and access codes
- Paragraph 16 warning: seller's post-closing occupancy may change insurance coverage -- both parties must contact their insurance agents
- Holdover damages (Paragraph 19) should be set higher than the regular daily rental rate as an incentive to vacate on time

- Smoke alarm maintenance is the tenant's responsibility; security device requirements of the Texas Property Code are waived for leases of 90 days or less
- Paragraph 24 notices must contain the parties' own addresses; the licensee must never insert their own contact information in the landlord or tenant blanks

Buyer's Temporary Residential Lease (Form 16-7)

- Form 16-7, effective November 3, 2025, replaces Form 16-6
- Seller = Landlord; Buyer = Tenant; buyer occupies before closing, seller still holds title
- Lease term commences and terminates as specified in Paragraph 18; the lease terminates upon closing and funding or upon default
- Rent is a per-day rate; full anticipated rental is paid at commencement (when buyer takes possession), not at closing; adjustments for actual vs. anticipated term are settled at closing
- No portion of the rental may be applied to the down payment, closing costs, or any other item covered by the purchase contract
- Deposit is paid upfront; if the sale does not close, the seller may use the deposit against tenant obligations; refund within 30 days with itemized statement if applicable
- Paragraph 6 requires buyer to pay all utility connections, deposits, and charges -- broader than the comparable seller's form provision, reflecting that buyer may need new service accounts
- Paragraph 12 allows the seller to enter not only to inspect but also to replace, repair, or complete improvements during the lease period, since the seller may still have contractual repair obligations
- Paragraph 14 is broader than the seller's form: buyer responsible for all equipment and appliances in addition to yard, trees, and shrubs
- Paragraph 16 warning: buyer's occupancy before closing may change insurance policy coverage -- both parties must contact their insurance agents
- The Buyer's Temporary Lease is not a vehicle for executory contracts (lease-purchase, contract for deed, or lease with option to purchase); any such arrangement must be referred to an attorney
- Smoke alarm maintenance is the tenant's responsibility; security device requirements waived for 90-day leases; both parties urged to consult an attorney (Paragraph 23)
- Paragraph 24 notices must contain the parties' own contact information; licensees must not insert their own addresses on behalf of clients

Chapter 5 Quiz: Closing, Possession and More

1. In Texas, which of the following statements correctly describes the signature requirement for conveying homestead property?

a. Only the person whose name appears on the deed is required to sign the deed at closing
b. Both spouses must sign the deed, even if only one spouse's name appears on the deed or title
c. A homestead may be conveyed by one spouse alone if the property was purchased before the marriage began
d. The dual-signature requirement applies only to properties that have served as a homestead for more than five years

2. The Special Provisions paragraph in Form 20-19 generates more TREC disciplinary actions against license holders than any other paragraph. What is the primary reason this paragraph creates so many problems?

a. License holders often omit this paragraph entirely, leaving important transaction terms unaddressed
b. The paragraph requires separate written approval from all parties before any entry in it becomes valid
c. The Texas Real Estate Commission requires every license holder to complete this paragraph in full for every transaction
d. License holders often write language in this paragraph that creates, modifies, or removes legal rights, which constitutes unauthorized practice of law

3. A licensee plans to write the following in the Special Provisions paragraph of Form 20-19: "Buyer is a licensed Texas real estate sales agent." How should this entry be characterized?

a. Appropriate, because it is a factual disclosure that the buyer is required to make in order to avoid a DTPA violation
b. Inappropriate, because broker compensation arrangements must be addressed only in the broker information section of the contract
c. Inappropriate, because the entry discloses information that is protected by the buyer's right to privacy in the transaction
d. Appropriate only if the buyer is also acting as the principal in the transaction without any representation

4. What legal relationship arises between a buyer and a seller when the buyer takes possession of a property before closing without any written lease agreement in place?

a. A month-to-month tenancy that is governed automatically by the Texas Property Code
b. A tenancy in common, because both parties share interests in the property before the closing occurs
c. A tenancy at sufferance, which provides minimal legal protection for either party and creates uncertainty about insurance
d. A constructive trust, because the seller still holds legal title while the buyer occupies the property

5. Under Form 15-7, the Seller's Temporary Residential Lease, who serves as the Landlord?

a. The seller, because the seller is the party who remains in the property after the closing date
b. The listing broker, because the broker manages the property on behalf of the new owner during the lease period
c. The title company, because the title company holds the deed in trust until possession is fully transferred
d. The buyer, because the buyer holds title to the property after closing and funding have occurred

6. Under Form 15-7, the Seller's Temporary Residential Lease, at what point is the full rent for the entire anticipated lease term paid to the landlord?

a. On the first day of each calendar month following the closing date
b. At the time of closing and funding, as part of the closing and settlement process
c. Within three business days after the transaction closes and the deed is recorded
d. On the last day of the lease term, when the tenant surrenders possession of the property

7. What is the maximum number of days that either a Seller's Temporary Residential Lease (Form 15-7) or a Buyer's Temporary Residential Lease (Form 16-7) may cover?

a. 30 days
b. 60 days
c. 90 days
d. 120 days

8. Under Form 16-7, the Buyer's Temporary Residential Lease, when does the buyer pay the full anticipated rental amount, and how are any differences in the actual term resolved?

a. At the time the buyer takes possession when the lease commences, with any adjustments for actual versus anticipated term settled at closing
b. At the time of closing and funding, as part of the standard settlement statement process
c. In equal monthly installments paid to the seller throughout the duration of the lease period
d. Within three business days after the buyer takes possession and signs the lease form

9. Form 16-7, the Buyer's Temporary Residential Lease, imposes a maintenance obligation on the buyer-tenant that is broader than the obligation contained in Form 15-7. What additional maintenance responsibility does Form 16-7 include?

a. The buyer is responsible for maintaining the HOA common areas and amenities throughout the lease period
b. The buyer must obtain a professional inspection of all appliances and HVAC systems before taking possession
c. The buyer must maintain all structural systems at the standard required by the buyer's lender
d. The buyer is responsible for all equipment and appliances in addition to the yard, trees, and shrubs

10. A buyer and a seller agree that the buyer will move into a property, make recurring monthly payments to the seller, and then decide whether to purchase the property after three years. Which of the following statements correctly describes how a license holder should handle this arrangement?

a. This is a valid use of Form 16-7 as long as the buyer genuinely intends to purchase the property at the end of the period

b. This is an executory contract that requires referral to an attorney and cannot be handled using Form 16-7 or any other promulgated TREC form

c. This arrangement requires only the Buyer's Temporary Residential Lease and the Third Party Financing Addendum to be properly documented

d. This is permissible under Form 16-7 as long as the total occupancy in each period does not exceed 90 days per renewal

11. Effective July 1, 2026, Form 20-19 was revised so that a seller's agreement to contribute toward the buyer's broker's compensation is now stated in which provision?

a. Paragraph 8B, the Brokers' Fees paragraph

b. Paragraph 12A(1)(b), and only as a percentage of the sales price

c. Paragraph 12B(1), which may be stated as a dollar amount or a percentage of the sales price

d. Paragraph 17, Attorney's Fees

12. Under Paragraph 14 (Casualty Loss) of Form 20-19, if the property is damaged before closing and the seller is unable to restore it to its previous condition by the Closing Date through no fault of the seller, which of the following is NOT an option available to the buyer?

a. Terminate the contract and receive a refund of the earnest money

b. Extend the closing date by up to 15 days to allow the restoration to be completed

c. Accept the property in its damaged condition with an assignment of the insurance proceeds and credit for the seller's deductible

d. Require the seller to reduce the sales price by the full replacement cost of the damage

13. The July 1, 2026 revision to Paragraph 21 (Notices) of Form 20-19 clarified that a notice given under the contract is effective when it is:

a. received and acknowledged in writing by the other party

b. sent to a party or that party's agent by a method the paragraph permits

c. filed with the Texas Real Estate Commission

d. three days past the date it was mailed, regardless of actual delivery

14. A study guide a student found online lists 'Termination Option' as Paragraph 23 of the One to Four Family Residential Contract. In the current Form 20-19, where is the termination option actually located?

a. It remains a standalone Paragraph 23

b. It has been combined into Paragraph 5, Earnest Money and Termination Option

c. It is now found only in a separate promulgated addendum

d. It was removed from the contract entirely

CHAPTER 6
THE REMAINING PROMULGATED FORMS

Chapter Overview

The One to Four Family Residential Contract (Form 20-19) handles the vast majority of residential transactions in Texas, but the Texas Real Estate Commission promulgates five other sale contracts to address the full range of property types that licensees encounter. This chapter examines each of those forms in detail, using Form 20-19 as the baseline for comparison so that a license holder can quickly understand which provisions are shared and which are unique. The Residential Condominium Contract (Resale) (Form 30-18) and the Condominium Resale Certificate (Form 32-5) address the distinctive ownership structure of condominiums. The Farm and Ranch Contract (Form 25-17) and the Addendum for Reservation of Oil, Gas and Other Minerals (Form 44-3) cover rural properties and the complex question of mineral rights. The Unimproved Property Contract (Form 9-18) handles vacant lots in subdivided areas. And the two New Home contracts (Forms 24-20 and 23-20) address newly constructed and under-construction residential properties. All forms discussed in this chapter were updated effective July 1, 2026 unless noted otherwise.

Learning Objectives

Upon completing Chapter 6, the student will be able to:

1. Explain what a condominium is, identify the ownership interests a condominium buyer acquires, and describe the header notices on Form 30-18 that define its appropriate use.
2. Identify the provisions in Paragraph 2 of Form 30-18 that are unique to condominium transactions, including the Condominium Documents, the Resale Certificate, and the Right of First Refusal, and describe the buyer's termination rights under each.
3. Describe how the Title Policy paragraph in Form 30-18 differs from Form 20-19, including the absence of the survey provision and the modifications to the standard exception list.
4. Explain the unique provisions in Paragraphs 12, 13, and 14 of Form 30-18 relating to association fees, prorations, and casualty loss involving common elements.
5. Explain the purpose of the Condominium Resale Certificate (Form 32-5), identify who completes it, and describe the information covered in each of its sections.
6. Identify the provisions in the Farm and Ranch Contract (Form 25-17) that are unique to rural property transactions, including the property description, crop rights, the sales price adjustment for acreage variances, Surface Leases, and the Final Page broker compensation provisions.
7. Describe the purpose and structure of the Addendum for Reservation of Oil, Gas and Other Minerals (Form 44-3) and explain when it is required.
8. Identify the provisions in the Unimproved Property Contract (Form 9-18) that differ from Form 20-19, including the property description, the sales price adjustment clause, the absence of a Seller's Disclosure Notice, rollback taxes, and the unique seller disclosure paragraph.
9. Describe the key differences between the New Home Contract (Completed Construction) (Form 24-20) and Form 20-19, including the absence of a Seller's Disclosure Notice, the insulation disclosure, the additional seller disclosures, and the Chapter 27 buyer protections.
10. Identify the provisions unique to the New Home Contract (Incomplete Construction) (Form 23-20), including construction document references, buyer selections, commencement and

completion dates, and cost adjustments, and explain the practice of registering a client with a builder.

Contents

- Residential Condominium Contract (Form 30-18)
- Condominium Resale Certificate (Form 32-5)
- Farm and Ranch Contract (Form 25-17)
- Addendum for Reservation of Oil, Gas and Other Minerals (Form 44-3)
- Unimproved Property Contract (Form 9-18)
- New Home Contract (Completed Construction) (Form 24-20)
- New Home Contract (Incomplete Construction) (Form 23-20)
- Working with Builders

Residential Condominium Contract (Form 30-18)

A condominium is a form of real property ownership in which the buyer acquires an individual unit together with an undivided interest in the common elements of the project. In the strictest legal sense, a condominium owner owns the interior airspace of their unit, bounded essentially from wall paint to wall paint and from floor to ceiling. The exterior of the building, the hallways, the lobby, the parking areas, the recreation facilities, and other shared spaces are owned collectively by all unit owners as tenants-in-common through the condominium association. The association manages the common elements, enforces the rules of the project, and collects assessments from owners to fund operations and reserves.

Because the buyer will be bound by the governing documents of the association, a condominium buyer needs to understand how restrictive those rules are before signing a contract. Some associations permit owners to paint and customize interiors freely; others require written approval before any alteration, including hanging a picture. Reviewing the documents carefully before or immediately after signing is essential.

The Residential Condominium Contract (Resale) (Form 30-18, effective July 1, 2026) is a 10-page, 24-paragraph form that follows the same general sequence as Form 20-19 but is designed for this distinctive ownership structure. The header of the form carries a critical notice: Not For Use Where Seller Owns Fee Simple Title to Land Beneath Unit. If the seller owns the land as well as the structure, the parties own a fee simple interest and Form 20-19 is the correct form to use, not Form 30-18.

Paragraph 2: Property and Condominium Documents

Paragraph 2 of Form 30-18 is the most distinctively different paragraph in the form. Rather than describing a lot and block in a subdivision, Paragraph 2A(1) identifies the condominium unit by unit number, building number, project name, address, city, and county. It also states the unit's undivided interest in the common elements as designated by the Declaration, including any limited common elements specifically assigned to the unit (such as an assigned parking space or storage locker). Parking areas assigned to the unit are listed here. Paragraphs 2A(2) and 2A(3) cover improvements and accessories in essentially the same terms as Paragraphs 2B and 2C of Form 20-19, including the smart device controls provision. Paragraph 2A(4) is for exclusions.

Paragraph 2B addresses the Condominium Documents, which consist of the Declaration, Bylaws, and any Rules of the Association. These are the governing instruments of the project and contain the rules by which all owners must live. One of two boxes must be checked: either the buyer has already received the Documents, or the seller must deliver them within a stated number of days after the Effective Date. If delivery is delayed, the buyer may terminate the contract within seven days after receiving the Documents, and the earnest money is refunded. The buyer also retains any rights to terminate under Section 82.156 of the Texas Property Code.

Paragraph 2C addresses the Condominium Resale Certificate (discussed separately in the next section). The Certificate must be prepared at the seller's expense and must have been issued no more than three months before the date it is delivered to the buyer. It must contain at minimum the information required by Section 82.157 of the Texas Property Code. One of three boxes is checked: the buyer has received the Certificate; the seller will deliver it within a stated number of days (with the buyer retaining a seven-day termination right after receipt); or the buyer has received the seller's affidavit that the seller requested the Certificate from the Association but the Association failed to provide it, in which case both parties agree to waive the Certificate requirement.

Paragraph 2D addresses the right of first refusal. Some condominium declarations give the Association, or individual owners within the association, the right to match any accepted offer and purchase the unit before the contract buyer can close. If the Documents reveal such a right, the Effective Date of the contract is automatically amended to the date the buyer receives written certification from the Association that the right of refusal has been complied with and that all persons who could have exercised it have not or have waived their right to do so. If that certification is not received within the stated number of days after the Effective Date, or if the right of refusal is exercised by someone other than the buyer, the contract terminates and the earnest money is refunded.

Title Policy: No Survey Required

Paragraph 6 of Form 30-18 covers the title policy but omits the survey provision entirely. This is deliberate and correct. Because a condominium owner does not own the exterior of the building or the land beneath it, there is no exterior boundary to survey. The concept of a property survey as it applies to a house on a lot simply does not translate to condominium ownership. As a result, Form 30-18 has no Paragraph 6C for a survey, and what is numbered 6C in Form 20-19 (Objections) is renumbered 6C in the condominium contract as well, but covers only title commitment objections, not survey objections.

Paragraph 6A of Form 30-18 also differs from Form 20-19 in one important respect: the standard exception in item 6A(4) refers to the terms and provisions of the condominium Documents, including assessments and platted easements, rather than utility easements created by a subdivision plat. The Declaration, Bylaws, and Rules of the Association are by their nature exceptions to the title policy; the buyer takes ownership subject to those governing documents. The standard exception for discrepancies, conflicts, and encroachments in item 6A(8) appears in Form 30-18 but without the checkbox option to amend it to read only 'shortages in area' that appears in Form 20-19. Title Notices in Paragraph 6D mirror those in Form 20-19 but omit the HOA membership notice (since the condominium association structure replaces that), and include the same eleven notices covering statutory tax districts, tide waters, annexation, certificated utility service areas, public improvement districts, transfer fees, propane gas service areas, water level fluctuations, certificate of mold remediation, and required notices.

Unique Financial Provisions

Paragraph 12 of Form 30-18 adds Paragraph 12A(3), which does not appear in Form 20-19. This provision requires the buyer to pay all association fees, deposits, and reserve contributions resulting from the transfer of the property, up to a specified dollar amount stated in the contract. If the actual fees exceed that cap, the seller pays the excess. This paragraph does not apply to regular periodic maintenance fees and assessments that are prorated in Paragraph 13, nor to the costs associated with the Documents and Certificate addressed in Paragraph 2.

Paragraph 13 of Form 30-18 is the prorations paragraph and includes two condominium-specific provisions. First, cash reserves held in condominium assessment accounts for deferred maintenance or capital improvements will not be credited to the seller. These reserves belong to the association, not to the individual seller, and pass with ownership to the buyer. Second, any special condominium assessment that is due and unpaid at the time of closing is the obligation of the seller, not the buyer.

Paragraph 14 of Form 30-18 addresses casualty loss with greater complexity than Form 20-19, because a condominium involves two distinct categories of property: the unit itself (which the seller maintains) and the common elements (which the association maintains). For damage to the unit, the seller must restore it to its previous condition by the Closing Date or the buyer has the standard options of terminating, extending the closing period, or accepting the damaged condition with an assignment of insurance proceeds. For damage to common elements or limited common elements, the buyer has seven days from notice of the casualty to notify the seller in writing that the contract will terminate unless the buyer receives written confirmation from the Association that the damage will be restored at no cost to the buyer. If the confirmation is not provided within seven days of the seller's receipt of the buyer's notice, the buyer may terminate and recover the earnest money.

Addenda List Differences

Paragraph 22 of Form 30-18 lists the available addenda. Two that appear in Form 20-19 are absent from the condominium contract. The Addendum for Property Subject to Mandatory Membership in a Property Owners Association is not needed because the condominium association structure replaces a traditional HOA. The Addendum for Reservation of Oil, Gas and Other Minerals is not needed because a condominium unit owner holds no subsurface rights. However, Form 30-18 does include an addendum on its list that Form 20-19 does not list: the Addendum for Release of Liability on Assumption of FHA, VA, or Conventional Loan and Restoration of Seller's VA Entitlement. This addendum is available in any transaction but is specifically listed in the condominium form because assumption transactions arise in condominium sales. In Form 20-19, the same addendum would need to be entered in the 'Other' line of Paragraph 22.

Condominium Resale Certificate (Form 32-5)

The Condominium Resale Certificate (Form 32-5, effective November 25, 2024) is the document that tells a prospective buyer about the financial, physical, and legal condition of the condominium association as of the date of issuance. Texas law requires the Association, upon written request, to provide this certificate to a seller who is transferring a unit. The seller is responsible for obtaining the Certificate and bearing the cost of its preparation. A license holder should not complete the Certificate; it must be completed by the condominium association's board of directors or its managing agent.

The Certificate must be dated no more than three months before the date it is delivered to the buyer to ensure the information is current. Section 82.157 of the Texas Property Code specifies the minimum information the Certificate must contain. Boards and managers completing the Certificate must be thorough and accurate; failure to disclose assessments owed or covenant violations by the seller, for example, may prevent the association from pursuing those matters against the new owner. Incomplete or inaccurate information about the association's financial or legal condition can also prompt legal claims against the association and its management.

The Certificate consists of 16 items labeled A through P. Paragraph A states whether the Declaration contains a right of first refusal or other restraint on the transfer of the unit. If such a right exists, the Effective Date provision in Paragraph 2D of Form 30-18 is triggered. Paragraph B states the periodic common expense assessment for the unit. Paragraph C discloses whether any common expense or special assessment is due and unpaid by the seller to the Association, along with the dollar amount. Paragraph D identifies any other amounts owed by the seller to the Association. Paragraph E states the capital expenditures approved by the Association for the next twelve months. Paragraph F states the current reserves for capital expenditures.

Paragraph G confirms that the current operating budget and balance sheet of the Association are attached. Paragraph H states the amount of any unsatisfied judgments against the Association. Paragraph I discloses whether any suits are pending against the Association. Paragraph J states whether the Association provides insurance coverage and describes the coverage. Paragraphs K and L were updated in 2024 to conform to Section 82.157 of the Texas Property Code: Paragraph K addresses whether the Association has received notice of any building or health code violation, and Paragraph L addresses any pending improvements required by governmental authority. Paragraph M states the remaining term of any leasehold estate affecting the condominium. Paragraph N identifies the Association's managing agent. Paragraph O states the Association fees payable as a result of the transfer of the unit. Paragraph P states any required contribution to the capital reserves account.

A buyer who receives the Certificate and the Documents has the information needed to make an informed decision about whether to proceed with the purchase. A buyer who encounters an association with large unsatisfied judgments, substantial pending capital expenditures, inadequate reserves, or ongoing litigation has every right to exercise the termination right provided in Paragraph 2C of Form 30-18.

Farm and Ranch Contract (Form 25-17)

The Farm and Ranch Contract (Form 25-17, effective July 1, 2026) is designed for the sale of existing farms or ranches of any size, from a small country homestead to a working ranch of hundreds of thousands of acres. The form carries a notice that it is designed for sales of existing farms or ranches and is not for complex transactions. Rural real estate is a specialty, and license holders who wish to practice in this area should seek additional education and should understand the significant ways in which this contract differs from the residential forms.

Paragraph 2: Property Description

The legal description in Paragraph 2A of the Farm and Ranch Contract identifies the property by county or counties rather than by subdivision and lot. Ranch and farm properties are typically described by metes and bounds, abstract number, survey number, or reference to recorded deeds. A large ranch may span multiple counties and require an attached exhibit because the description is too lengthy for the contract form. Surveyors on farm and ranch properties face unique challenges: some properties have not been formally surveyed in generations, and in Texas many older surveys used the vara, a Spanish unit of measurement equal to approximately 33 and one-third inches. Varas appear in deeds and survey records as late as the mid-to-late twentieth century. Converting varas to feet requires dividing by 0.36; one acre equals approximately 5,645 square varas. These historical measurement systems create uncertainty in boundary locations and make accurate surveys both important and potentially expensive.

Paragraph 2B divides improvements into two categories: Farm and Ranch Improvements, which include windmills, tanks, barns, pens, fences, gates, sheds, outbuildings, and corrals; and Residential Improvements, which mirror the permanently installed built-in items list in Form 20-19. Paragraph 2C similarly divides accessories into Farm and Ranch Accessories (with specific checkboxes for portable buildings, hunting blinds, game feeders, livestock feeders and troughs, irrigation equipment, fuel tanks, submersible pumps, pressure tanks, corrals, gates, chutes, and other) and Residential Accessories, which track the residential contract list.

Paragraph 2D addresses crops and is a provision that surprises many first-time farm and ranch buyers. Unless the parties agree otherwise in writing, the seller retains the right to harvest all growing crops until delivery of possession. A buyer who assumes that crops on the property at the time of closing will convey with the land is mistaken; the contract allocates those crops to the seller by default. If the buyer wants the crops to convey, a specific written agreement to that effect must be incorporated into the contract.

Paragraph 2E covers exclusions and Paragraph 2F covers reservations of oil, gas, minerals, water, timber, and other interests through an attached addendum.

Paragraph 3D: Sales Price Adjustment for Acreage Variance

Paragraph 3D is unique to the Farm and Ranch Contract (and the Unimproved Property Contract) and addresses the possibility that the actual acreage of the property, as measured by a survey, differs from the acreage the seller quoted in the contract. The parties may agree in Paragraph 3D that the sales price will be adjusted based on the survey results. They specify a price per acre and agree that any difference between the quoted acreage and the surveyed acreage will be multiplied by that per-acre amount and added to or subtracted from the sales price. If the adjustment would be more than 10% of the sales price, either party may terminate the contract within a stated number of days after receiving the survey. If neither party terminates or if the variance is 10% or less, the adjustment is made to the cash portion, the financing amount, or proportionately to both, according to the box the parties check.

Paragraph 4: Leases

The Farm and Ranch Contract's Paragraph 4 is substantially broader than Form 20-19's lease provision. In addition to the restriction on creating new leases after the Effective Date, it includes two additional categories. Paragraph 4C covers Natural Resource Leases, which include oil and gas, mineral, geothermal (added in 2024 to reflect a Texas law change recognizing property owners' rights to geothermal energy), water, and other natural resource leases to which the seller is a party. The seller must either have already provided copies of these leases to the buyer or must do so within three days after the Effective Date, with the buyer retaining a termination right for a stated number of days after receiving them.

Paragraph 4D covers Surface Leases, meaning leases for the surface use of the property only. Examples include grazing leases, hunting leases, agricultural leases, recreational leases, wind leases, solar leases, and timber or forestry leases. Ranch properties commonly have hunting leases that allow a group of hunters to use the land during deer or quail season, or grazing leases under which someone else's cattle are being raised on the land. Some landowners use grazing arrangements specifically to maintain an agricultural exemption for property tax purposes. A buyer who does not know about existing surface leases may find the use and enjoyment of the property significantly constrained after closing. The seller must disclose all written and oral surface leases, and the buyer has a termination right if disclosure is delayed.

Title, Survey, and Unique Title Provisions

The Farm and Ranch Contract's title policy exceptions in Paragraph 6A differ from Form 20-19 because rural properties typically are not in platted subdivisions and do not carry the same subdivision-based restrictive covenants. The standard exception list in the Farm and Ranch Contract therefore does not include restrictive covenants common to a platted subdivision or utility easements from a subdivision dedication.

Paragraph 6C(4) is a survey option unique to the Farm and Ranch Contract: a box for 'no survey required.' This option is available when no lender is involved and the buyer is willing to close without a survey. Surveys of large acreage properties are expensive. The research required to locate boundaries on land that may not have been formally surveyed in decades, using historical records in multiple languages and measurement systems, is time-consuming and costly. A cash buyer may choose to waive the survey requirement after understanding the risks. Most lenders, however, will require a survey as a condition of funding.

Paragraph 6E provides space to list specific exceptions to title beyond the standard printed exceptions, such as a retained access easement across the property being sold. Paragraph 6F provides space to list surface lease exceptions. Paragraph 6G covers Title Notices and is similar to Form 20-19 but includes a notice about Texas Agricultural Development Districts (Paragraph 6G.7) rather than the mandatory HOA notice that appears in Form 20-19. An Agricultural Development District offers certain investment advantages, and the licensee should investigate whether the property is located in one and advise the buyer accordingly.

Property Condition and Government Programs

Paragraph 7A includes a note suggesting that the buyer confirm utility availability. Rural properties may not have access to city water, sewer, or electricity. The licensee should advise buyers to investigate whether utilities are available at the property line and, if not, whether it is financially feasible to drill a well or install other utility solutions.

While the Texas Property Code's seller's disclosure requirements apply to residential improvements on farm and ranch properties, many farm and ranch sellers are exempt from the formal Seller's Disclosure Notice for the land itself. Paragraph 7H of the Farm and Ranch Contract creates a specific disclosure obligation regardless of whether a formal SDN is required: the seller must disclose any known flooding or drainage issues, pending litigation or condemnation, environmental hazards, dump sites or landfills, underground storage tanks, wetlands, and endangered species or their habitats on the property.

Paragraph 7I mirrors Paragraph 7H on Form 20-19 and covers residential service contracts. Paragraph 7J is unique to the Farm and Ranch Contract: it requires the seller to disclose any government program agreements affecting the property, such as conservation easements, USDA program contracts, or other arrangements that bind the land. The seller must provide the buyer with documentation of any such programs, because they may affect how the buyer may use the property after closing.

Rollback Taxes and the Final Page

Paragraph 13 of the Farm and Ranch Contract includes the same rollback tax provision found in the Unimproved Property Contract (discussed in the next section). When land has been taxed at a preferential agricultural rate and changes use to residential or commercial development, the taxing authority may assess rollback taxes representing the difference between the taxes paid at the agricultural rate and what would have been owed at full market value. If a builder purchases a ranch and converts it to a residential subdivision, rollback taxes may be triggered. The contract identifies who bears this liability and ensures both parties understand the risk.

The final page of the Farm and Ranch Contract contains a section titled Broker Information and Agreement for Payment of Brokers' Fees, set off in its own box with separate signature lines. This section exists because farm and ranch transactions have historically been conducted without separate written listing agreements, and TREC rules require that any lawsuit for a commission must be supported by a written agreement signed by the person responsible to pay. If no separate written listing agreement or buyer representation agreement is in place, this section of the final page should be completed and signed.

The section carries a bold warning: Do not sign if there is a separate written agreement for payment of Brokers' fees. When a proper listing agreement or buyer representation agreement is already in place, the broker compensation section of the final page does not need to be signed.

Addendum for Reservation of Oil, Gas and Other Minerals (Form 44-3)

The Addendum for Reservation of Oil, Gas and Other Minerals (Form 44-3, effective February 1, 2023) is used when the seller intends to retain all or a portion of the mineral estate rather than conveying it to the buyer with the surface. In Texas, real property can be severed laterally: one person may own the surface of the land and an entirely different person may own the minerals beneath it. This severance can create significant complications for surface owners who may find that a mineral rights holder has the legal right to access the surface for drilling and production.

Paragraph A of the addendum defines the mineral estate, which includes oil, gas, and other minerals, along with any royalty interests under existing mineral leases. By checking the appropriate box, the seller specifies whether the entire mineral estate or only a specified interest is being reserved.

Paragraph B addresses surface rights connected to the mineral estate. If the seller retains mineral rights, the deed of trust and title documents must address whether the mineral owner retains rights of ingress and egress across the surface to access the minerals for drilling, production, and related activities. The seller specifies in Paragraph B what, if any, surface use rights are retained in connection with the mineral interest.

Paragraph C requires the seller to provide the buyer with copies of any existing mineral leases on the property. A buyer needs to know whether mineral activity is currently authorized on the land and what the terms of any existing lease are, including the royalty rate, the primary term, and any production history.

Because oil and gas law is a specialized area of Texas law with its own extensive body of statutes, case law, and regulatory structure, all parties in a transaction involving mineral rights should be advised to consult a licensed attorney before proceeding. The consequences of getting this wrong, whether by accidentally conveying mineral rights that the seller intended to keep or by failing to disclose an existing mineral lease, can be financially significant and legally complex.

Unimproved Property Contract (Form 9-18)

The Unimproved Property Contract (Form 9-18, effective July 1, 2026) is used for vacant lots in a subdivided area where no improvements have been placed on the property. It follows the same general paragraph sequence as Form 20-19 but omits or modifies provisions that apply only to improved residential properties. The form carries a notice that it is not for use in condominium transactions.

Paragraph 2: Property Description

Because there are no improvements, accessories, or exclusions, Paragraph 2 of the Unimproved Property Contract is a single paragraph that identifies the land by lot, block, subdivision, city, county, and address or attached exhibit. Any reservations for minerals, water, timber, or other interests are addressed within Paragraph 2 itself through a reference to an attached addendum, keeping the form compact.

Paragraph 3D: Sales Price Adjustment

Form 9-18 includes the same sales price adjustment provision as the Farm and Ranch Contract. Paragraph 3D allows the parties to agree that the sales price will be adjusted if the survey reveals an acreage variance. The structure is identical: the parties specify a per-acre price, a tolerance threshold, and the termination right if the variance exceeds 10%. This provision was added to the Unimproved Property Contract in the January 2025 form updates to align it with the Farm and Ranch Contract.

Paragraph 4: Natural Resource Leases

Paragraph 4B of Form 9-18 addresses Natural Resource Leases (oil and gas, mineral, geothermal, water, wind, and other natural resource leases). The seller states whether they are or are not a party to such a lease. If the seller is a party, one of two boxes is checked: either the seller has already delivered copies of all leases to the buyer, or the seller will provide them within three days of the Effective Date. If delivery is delayed, the buyer has a termination right for a stated number of days after receiving the leases.

Title and FEMA Flood Map Objection

Paragraph 6D of the Unimproved Property Contract (Objections) includes a provision not found in Form 20-19: the buyer may object if any portion of the property lies in a special flood hazard area as shown on the current FEMA flood insurance rate map. Flood plain location is particularly significant for vacant land buyers who plan to develop the property. If a buyer intended to build a residence but discovers that the entire parcel is in a Zone A or Zone V flood hazard area, the use they planned may be impossible or may require expensive flood insurance and elevated construction. The buyer has the right to object and terminate within the stated time period.

Paragraph 6E of the Unimproved Property Contract's Title Notices section includes all of the standard notices from Form 20-19 but adds a notice about Agricultural Development Districts (moved to Paragraph 6E.8 on the UPC, which pushed transfer fees to Paragraph 6E.9).

Property Condition

Paragraph 7 of the Unimproved Property Contract omits several provisions that exist in Form 20-19 because they apply only to improved property. There is no Seller's Disclosure Notice provision (the Texas Property Code does not require a formal disclosure notice for unimproved property, though the seller still has common law disclosure obligations for known material conditions). There is no provision for lender-required repairs or residential service contracts, both of which are irrelevant to vacant land.

The form does include Paragraph 7D, a seller disclosure provision unique to unimproved property. The seller must disclose any known flooding or inundation, any pending litigation or condemnation, any environmental hazards, any dump sites or landfills, any underground storage tanks, any wetlands, and any endangered species or their habitats on the property. These are the specific environmental and governmental concerns most likely to affect a buyer's ability to develop or use vacant land. Paragraph 7C of the UPC addresses environmental matters and directs buyers to use the Environmental Assessment addendum if they have concerns.

Rollback Taxes and Paragraph 13

Paragraph 13 of the Unimproved Property Contract includes a rollback tax provision. Agricultural property is taxed at a preferential lower rate. If the seller has been receiving an agricultural exemption on the land and the buyer subsequently changes the use to residential or commercial development, the taxing authority may demand back taxes at the full non-agricultural rate for up to several years. In addition, even if the seller changed the use before selling, the new buyer may inherit this liability. This provision ensures both parties understand who is responsible for any rollback taxes triggered by the transaction or by the subsequent use of the property.

Paragraph 22 of the Unimproved Property Contract omits three addenda that are listed in Form 20-19: the Loan Assumption Addendum, the Short Sale Addendum, and the Lead-Based Paint Addendum. The Loan Assumption Addendum is generally inappropriate for vacant land because most existing loans on raw land will not permit assumption on favorable terms. The Short Sale Addendum and Lead-Based Paint Addendum have no application to unimproved property.

New Home Contract (Completed Construction) (Form 24-20)

The New Home Contract (Completed Construction) (Form 24-20, effective July 1, 2026) is used for newly constructed homes where the construction is finished at the time of the contract. The form carries a notice that it is not for use in condominium transactions or for closings prior to completion of construction. TREC does not promulgate a form for new condominium construction.

This form is most commonly relevant when a small custom builder who constructs only a few homes per year needs a contract and does not have their own attorney-prepared forms. Most large production builders have their own contract forms, and license holders working with buyers in builder subdivisions will typically use those forms.

Paragraph 2: Property Description

Paragraph 2 of Form 24-20 is shorter and simpler than Paragraph 2 of Form 20-19. A builder who has never occupied the property has no items of personal property to exclude or retain, and there is typically no concern about the seller keeping an accessory. The description covers the lot, block, subdivision, city, county, and address, together with improvements, fixtures, and all other property located on the land. Reservations of minerals, water, timber, or other interests may be made through an attached addendum.

Paragraph 7: Property Condition

Paragraph 7 is where Form 24-20 diverges most significantly from Form 20-19. Because the Texas Property Code exempts builders selling new homes for the first time from the formal Seller's Disclosure Notice requirement, there is no SDN provision in the completed construction contract. In its place, the form includes provisions specific to new construction.

Paragraph 7C states that the seller is not making any general warranty about the property beyond what is in the contract. Any specific builder's warranty must be set out in a separate written document, not within the contract form itself. Any manufacturer's warranties on materials and equipment pass from the builder to the buyer.

Paragraph 7D contains the insulation disclosure, which exists because federal law (the Federal Trade Commission's R-value rule) requires new home sellers to disclose the thermal performance characteristics of the insulation installed in the structure. Either an attachment containing insulation specifications is identified (7D.1), or the insulation details are entered directly in the form, covering exterior walls, interior walls, ceiling, floor, and other insulated areas (7D.2).

Paragraph 7H is a seller disclosure provision specific to new construction, covering flooding and drainage issues, pending litigation or condemnation, environmental hazards, dump sites or landfills, wetlands, and endangered species. This provision ensures that a builder discloses known conditions about the site that would affect the buyer's use and enjoyment of the property, even though the formal SDN is not required.

Paragraph 7I mirrors the residential service contract provision in Form 20-19.

Rollback Taxes and Buyer Protections

Paragraph 13B of Form 24-20 addresses rollback taxes. A builder who purchased agricultural land to develop for residential construction may trigger rollback taxes when the land's use changes. These taxes can be substantial and must be addressed in the contract. The parties specify who bears this liability, and both sides need to understand that if the builder fails to pay rollback taxes, the new buyer may ultimately bear the financial consequences.

The final page of Form 24-20 includes a buyer notice related to the Texas Property Code Chapter 27, which gives a buyer who discovers a construction defect in a new home certain rights before filing suit. The buyer must give the builder written notice of the defect, and the builder has an opportunity to inspect, remedy, or make a settlement offer before litigation can proceed. This notice ensures new home buyers understand these statutory rights before they need to invoke them.

The January 2025 updates to Form 24-20 also added Paragraph 20B, which addresses obligations under the federal Agriculture Foreign Investment Disclosure Act when agricultural property is involved in the transaction. This addition reflects federal law requirements for reporting certain agricultural land transactions involving foreign persons.

New Home Contract (Incomplete Construction) (Form 23-20)

The New Home Contract (Incomplete Construction) (Form 23-20, effective July 1, 2026) is used when a buyer contracts to purchase a home that is still being built. The form is not for use in condominium transactions or for closings prior to completion. Its notice at the top makes clear that closing must not occur until construction is substantially complete.

This form is used less frequently than the completed construction contract. Most new homes are not sold until they are finished. The most common situation where Form 23-20 is needed is the speculation house (commonly called a spec house), a home that a builder is constructing on purchased land in the hope of selling it profitably once complete. If a buyer wants to be involved in the construction process, make selections for finishes and fixtures, or otherwise customize the home before it is finished, an agreement made before completion requires this form. The buyer's opportunity to influence the final product is one of the attractions of buying a spec house early in the construction process.

Paragraph 2 and Construction Documents

Paragraph 2 of Form 23-20 describes the property as including improvements, fixtures, and all other property described in the Construction Documents, rather than improvements already located on the land. The Construction Documents are the plans, specifications, and other documentation that define what is to be built. These documents govern the scope of construction and serve as the reference point for disputes about whether the finished home meets what was promised.

Paragraph 7: Construction-Specific Provisions

Paragraph 7 of Form 23-20 is substantially different from Form 24-20 because it addresses a home under construction rather than a finished one. Paragraph 7A provides that the builder is not required to keep all utilities on during construction since various systems may be incomplete and turning on utilities prematurely can create hazards or code violations. Paragraph 7B requires the seller to complete the property in accordance with the Construction Documents. If the finished home does not match the Construction Documents, the buyer has grounds to object.

Paragraph 7C addresses cost adjustments, which arise when changes are made to the construction plans during the building process. Change orders can increase or decrease the cost, and this paragraph provides the mechanism for adjusting the contract price accordingly. Paragraph 7D gives the buyer the right to make certain selections (such as carpet color, countertop material, appliance finishes, or fixture styles) within a stated number of days after the Effective Date if the Construction Documents provide for such choices. Failure to make selections within the deadline may bind the buyer to the builder's standard selections.

Paragraph 7E establishes the commencement and completion dates for construction. The commencement date is when the builder will begin active construction; the completion date is the target date for substantial completion. These dates are important because they tie into the Closing Date provisions. If the builder fails to complete construction by the agreed date, the buyer and seller must negotiate an extension or the buyer may have termination rights.

Form 23-20 omits the lender-required repairs provision that appears in Form 20-19 and Form 24-20. There is no lender funding the purchase during construction; financing for new construction typically is not secured until after the home is complete and ready for the buyer to occupy. For the same reason, the residential service contract provision is omitted from the incomplete construction contract, since a home warranty for a property that does not yet exist as a finished structure does not apply.

The Survey

Paragraph 6C of Form 23-20 states that the survey must be made after the Substantial Completion Date. This is the practical reality of construction surveys: a survey must show the location of improvements on the land, and the improvements cannot be mapped until they exist in their final form. An as-built survey is one of the final steps before closing.

Working with Builders

Most production builders in Texas use contract forms prepared by their own attorneys rather than TREC promulgated forms. Builder contracts are drafted to protect the builder's interests and may contain provisions that favor the builder in ways that a TREC-promulgated form, which is designed to be neutral, would not. A license holder working with a buyer at a builder's model home should never attempt to interpret or give legal opinions about the builder's contract. Buyers should be strongly advised to have an attorney review any builder contract before signing.

One of the most important practical steps a licensee can take when working with a buyer interested in new construction is to register the buyer with the builder before the first visit to any model home or sales office. Registration is the process of filling out a form provided by the builder that identifies the buyer as the licensee's client. Most builders honor client registrations and will pay the cooperating broker's commission even though the negotiations proceed through the builder's own sales representative. Failing to register a client before the first visit can result in the builder refusing to pay any commission if the buyer ultimately purchases directly, arguing that the sale was not the result of the licensee's efforts. Once a builder's sales representative meets a buyer independently, the opportunity to register that buyer as the licensee's client is typically lost. Most builders want to maintain productive relationships with real estate licensees and will honor properly submitted registrations.

The main practical reason for using TREC Form 24-20 rather than a builder's contract is when a small custom builder who constructs only a handful of homes per year does not have their own attorney-prepared forms. In that situation, the promulgated new home contract provides a neutral, well-understood framework for both parties.

Chapter 6: Snapshot Review

The following review summarizes the key rules and concepts from Chapter 6.

Residential Condominium Contract (Form 30-18)

- Form 30-18 (effective July 1, 2026) is for condominiums where the seller does NOT own fee simple title to the land beneath the unit; if the seller owns the land, Form 20-19 is correct
- Condominium ownership = individual unit airspace (from paint to paint, floor to ceiling) plus undivided interest in common elements
- Paragraph 2B: Condominium Documents (Declaration, Bylaws, Rules) -- buyer may terminate within 7 days of receipt if not previously received
- Paragraph 2C: Resale Certificate must be dated no more than 3 months before delivery to buyer; buyer may terminate within 7 days of receipt
- Paragraph 2D: Right of First Refusal -- if the Declaration contains such a right, the Effective Date is amended to the date the buyer receives the Association's certification that the right has been resolved
- No survey provision in Form 30-18; condominiums have no exterior boundaries to survey
- Paragraph 12A(3): Buyer pays association transfer fees up to a stated cap; seller pays excess (does not apply to prorated regular assessments or Document/Certificate costs)
- Paragraph 13: Cash reserves from regular condo assessments do not credit to seller; special assessments due at closing are seller's obligation
- Paragraph 14 Casualty Loss: Two categories -- damage to the unit (seller must restore) and damage to common elements (buyer has 7 days to notify seller of termination unless buyer gets Association written confirmation of restoration)
- Addenda list in Paragraph 22: omits HOA addendum and Minerals addendum (neither applies to condos); adds Addendum for Release of Liability on Assumed Loan

Condominium Resale Certificate (Form 32-5)

- Form 32-5 (effective November 25, 2024) is completed by the condominium association's board of directors or managing agent, not the license holder
- Required under Section 82.157 of the Texas Property Code; must be prepared at seller's expense no more than 3 months before delivery to buyer
- 16 items (A through P): right of first refusal; periodic assessment; unpaid special assessments; other amounts owed by seller; approved capital expenditures; reserves; operating budget (attached); judgments; pending suits; insurance; government violations; improvement disclosures; leasehold term; managing agent; transfer fees; capital reserve contribution
- Incomplete or inaccurate disclosure in the Certificate may prevent the Association from pursuing certain claims against the new owner

Farm and Ranch Contract (Form 25-17)

- Form 25-17 (effective July 1, 2026) is for existing farms or ranches of any size
- Legal description uses county-based or metes and bounds descriptions, not lot and block; complex descriptions require attached exhibits
- The vara is a historical Spanish unit of measurement (approximately 33 and one-third inches) that appears in older Texas survey records
- Paragraph 2B: Farm and Ranch Improvements (windmills, tanks, barns, pens, fences) separate from Residential Improvements

- Paragraph 2C: Farm and Ranch Accessories have specific checkboxes (hunting blinds, game feeders, irrigation equipment, fuel tanks, etc.)
- Paragraph 2D: Seller retains the right to harvest all growing crops until delivery of possession unless parties agree otherwise in writing
- Paragraph 3D: Sales price adjusts for acreage variance revealed by survey; if adjustment exceeds 10%, either party may terminate
- Paragraph 4C: Natural Resource Leases (including geothermal as of 2024 update); 4D: Surface Leases (grazing, hunting, wind, solar, etc.) -- all must be disclosed
- Paragraph 6C(4): No survey required option available for cash transactions
- Paragraph 6E adds exceptions to title; 6G.7 addresses Agricultural Development Districts
- Paragraph 7H: Seller disclosure for flooding, litigation, environmental hazards, dump sites, wetlands, endangered species
- Paragraph 7J: Government programs affecting the property must be disclosed and documented
- Paragraph 13: Rollback taxes -- when agricultural land changes use, back taxes at full rates may be assessed
- Final Page: Broker Information and Agreement for Payment of Brokers' Fees -- must be completed and signed if no separate written listing or buyer rep agreement exists; do not sign if a separate written agreement is already in place

Addendum for Reservation of Oil, Gas and Other Minerals (Form 44-3)

- Used when seller intends to retain all or part of the mineral estate rather than conveying it with the surface
- Paragraph A defines what is being reserved (mineral estate and royalties under existing leases)
- Paragraph B addresses the mineral owner's surface use rights for access, drilling, and production
- Paragraph C requires the seller to provide the buyer with copies of existing mineral leases
- All parties should consult a licensed attorney before proceeding with any mineral rights transaction

Unimproved Property Contract (Form 9-18)

- Form 9-18 (effective July 1, 2026) is for vacant lots in subdivided areas with no improvements; not for condominiums
- Paragraph 2: No sub-sections for improvements, accessories, or exclusions; includes reservations reference
- Paragraph 3D: Sales price adjustment for acreage variance (same structure as Farm and Ranch Contract -- added in January 2025 update)
- Paragraph 4B: Natural Resource Leases must be disclosed
- Paragraph 6D Objections: Buyer may object if any part of the property is in a FEMA special flood hazard area
- No Seller's Disclosure Notice provision; no lender-required repairs; no residential service contract
- Paragraph 7D: Seller disclosures for flooding, litigation, environmental hazards, dump sites, wetlands, endangered species
- Paragraph 13: Rollback taxes provision applies when land changes from agricultural to other use
- Paragraph 22 omits: Loan Assumption Addendum, Short Sale Addendum, Lead-Based Paint Addendum

New Home Contract (Completed Construction) (Form 24-20)

- Form 24-20 (effective July 1, 2026) is for newly constructed homes where construction is finished at time of contract; not for condominiums or pre-completion closings
- No Seller's Disclosure Notice -- Texas Property Code exempts builders selling new homes for the first time
- Paragraph 7C: No general warranty by seller; any builder warranty must be in a separate document; manufacturer warranties pass to buyer
- Paragraph 7D: Insulation disclosure required by federal law (FTC R-value rule) -- exterior walls, interior walls, ceiling, floor, and other areas
- Paragraph 7H: Additional seller disclosures for flooding, litigation, environmental hazards, dump sites, wetlands, endangered species
- Paragraph 13B: Rollback taxes apply when builder converts agricultural land to residential development
- Final page: Chapter 27 buyer notice -- buyer must give builder written notice of construction defects and allow opportunity to remedy before filing suit
- Paragraph 20B (added January 2025): Federal Agriculture Foreign Investment Disclosure Act obligations

New Home Contract (Incomplete Construction) (Form 23-20)

- Form 23-20 (effective July 1, 2026) is for homes still under construction; not for condominiums; closing may not occur prior to completion
- Most commonly used for spec house purchases where buyer contracts before construction is complete
- Paragraph 2 references the Construction Documents, which govern the scope of what must be built
- Paragraph 7B: Seller must complete the property in accordance with the Construction Documents
- Paragraph 7C: Cost adjustments (change orders) may increase or decrease the sales price
- Paragraph 7D: Buyer selections (carpet, countertops, fixtures) must be made within the stated number of days; missed deadlines may result in builder's standard selections
- Paragraph 7E: Construction commencement and completion dates are specified
- No lender-required repairs provision and no residential service contract -- home is not yet complete
- Survey must be made after the Substantial Completion Date (Paragraph 6C)
- Paragraphs 8 through 24 and final pages are the same as Form 24-20

Working with Builders

- Most production builders use attorney-prepared contract forms that may favor the builder; buyers should always consult an attorney before signing a builder's contract
- Registration is the process of identifying a buyer as the licensee's client before the buyer's first contact with the builder; failure to register before the initial visit may result in loss of commission
- Builders typically honor registrations and pay cooperating broker commissions if the buyer was properly registered before visiting
- TREC Form 24-20 is most useful for small custom builders who do not have their own attorney-prepared forms

Chapter 6 Quiz: The Remaining Promulgated Forms

1. A seller owns a dwelling and also holds fee simple title to the land beneath it. Which TREC promulgated contract form is appropriate for this transaction?

a. Form 30-18, because the property is a dwelling that the seller currently occupies

b. Form 30-18, because that form covers all types of single-family residential resales in Texas

c. Form 20-19, because the seller owns the land, making this a fee simple sale rather than a condominium transaction

d. Form 24-20, because any property sold by a seller who also owns the underlying land qualifies as new construction

2. Which phrase best describes what a condominium buyer actually owns after the sale closes?

a. The interior airspace of the unit from wall paint to wall paint and floor to ceiling, plus an undivided interest in the common elements of the project

b. The interior airspace of the unit and the parcel of land directly beneath it within a defined footprint

c. The entire floor of the building on which the unit is located, subject to shared maintenance responsibilities with other owners

d. The unit and a proportionate share of the entire building, including the roof and all exterior walls

3. Under Paragraph 2D of Form 30-18, if a condominium Declaration contains a right of first refusal in favor of the Association, what happens to the contract's Effective Date?

a. The Effective Date becomes void immediately and both parties must renegotiate the contract from the beginning

b. The Effective Date remains unchanged, but the closing date is automatically extended by 30 days

c. The Effective Date is moved to the date the Association formally waives its right of first refusal in a written resolution

d. The Effective Date is amended to the date the buyer receives the Association's written certification that the right of first refusal has been complied with or waived by all eligible parties

4. Who bears the responsibility for completing the Condominium Resale Certificate (Form 32-5)?

a. The listing agent, because the listing agent has the most complete knowledge of the property and the association's operations

b. The condominium association's board of directors or managing agent, not the license holder or the seller

c. The buyer's agent, in order to ensure that the information provided in the certificate is objective and unbiased

d. The title company, as part of the standard title search and commitment preparation process

5. Under the Farm and Ranch Contract (Form 25-17), what is the default rule regarding crops that are growing on the property at the time of closing?

a. All growing crops automatically convey to the buyer as part of the real property and may not be excluded from the sale

b. The buyer and the seller each receive a proportionate share of the crops based on the number of days each party holds title during the growing season

c. The seller retains the right to harvest all growing crops until delivery of possession, unless the parties specifically agree otherwise in writing

d. Growing crops are excluded from the transaction by default and must be listed in a separate Bill of Sale if the buyer wishes to acquire them

6. The vara is a historical unit of measurement that appears in older Texas survey records and property deeds. Which of the following correctly states the approximate length of one vara in Texas?

a. 33 and one-third inches

b. 36 inches, which is equal to one standard American yard

c. 42 inches, reflecting the Spanish measurement standard used throughout colonial Texas

d. 48 inches, which is equivalent to four standard linear feet

7. The Broker Information and Agreement for Payment of Brokers' Fees section on the final page of the Farm and Ranch Contract (Form 25-17) carries a bold warning. What does that warning instruct the parties to do?

a. Disclose any dual agency relationship to all parties before the broker compensation section is executed

b. Consult a licensed attorney before completing or signing any provision of the broker compensation section

c. Limit the broker's commission to the amount customarily charged in the county where the property is located

d. Not sign this section if a separate written agreement for payment of brokers' fees already exists between the parties

8. Which of the following provisions appears in the Unimproved Property Contract (Form 9-18) but does NOT appear in the One to Four Family Residential Contract (Form 20-19)?

a. The buyer's right to terminate the contract if the Seller's Disclosure Notice is not delivered within the required time

b. The buyer's right to object if any portion of the property is located in a FEMA special flood hazard area

c. The requirement to attach the Third Party Financing Addendum whenever the buyer obtains a mortgage loan

d. A provision allowing the seller to contribute a specified dollar amount toward the buyer's closing costs

9. The Addendum for Reservation of Oil, Gas and Other Minerals (Form 44-3) is required in which of the following situations?

a. Whenever a property is located in a rural county where active oil and gas production occurs nearby
b. Whenever the buyer wishes to include the mineral rights in the purchase along with the surface estate
c. Whenever the seller intends to retain all or any portion of the mineral estate rather than conveying it to the buyer
d. Whenever an existing mineral lease currently affects the property being sold, regardless of who retains the mineral estate

10. The New Home Contract (Completed Construction) (Form 24-20) includes an insulation disclosure provision. Which federal requirement does this provision satisfy?

a. The EPA's Residential Energy Audit Disclosure Rule, which requires all new home sellers to provide estimated annual energy usage figures
b. The HUD Energy Efficiency Standards, which require disclosure of utility costs paid during the prior 12 months
c. The Department of Energy's New Home Thermal Performance Act, which mandates specific insulation levels in all residential sales contracts
d. The Federal Trade Commission's R-value rule, which requires new home sellers to disclose the thermal performance characteristics of the insulation installed in the structure

11. What is the most common situation in which a licensee uses the New Home Contract (Incomplete Construction) (Form 23-20)?

a. When a buyer contracts to purchase a spec house that a builder is currently constructing before construction is complete
b. When a builder begins constructing a custom home for a specific buyer before the parties agree on a final sales price
c. When a buyer purchases a newly completed home and discovers construction defects requiring remediation before closing
d. When a buyer wishes to make structural changes to a completed new home before taking possession of the property

---

CHAPTER 7
PROMULGATED ADDENDA, NOTICES, AND OTHER FORMS

Chapter Overview

The TREC promulgated contracts are designed to handle the most common elements of a real estate transaction in a single document, but no single form can address every variation that the parties might encounter. A library of promulgated addenda, notice forms, and other TREC instruments exists precisely to fill those gaps, each designed for a specific purpose and each carrying its own obligations and protections. This chapter examines the forms that license holders encounter most frequently beyond the main contract forms.

Beginning with the Information About Brokerage Services form (IABS 1-2), which every consumer must receive early in their interaction with a license holder, the chapter moves through the Amendment to Contract (Form 39-11), the Non-Realty Items Addendum (Form 57-0), the HOA Addendum (Form 36-11), the Subdivision Information form (Form 37-5), the Addendum for Sale of Other Property by Buyer (Form 10-6), the Addendum for Back-Up Contract (Form 11-9), the Short Sale Addendum (Form 45-2), the Addendum for Reservation of Oil, Gas and Other Minerals (Form 44-3), the Addendum for Coastal Area Property (Form 33-2), and the Addendum for Property Located Seaward of the Gulf Intracoastal Waterway (Form 34-4).

The chapter then examines a broader set of specialized addenda and notice forms that license holders may encounter in particular transactions, including the Addendum Concerning Right to Terminate Due to Lender's Appraisal (Form 49-1), the Addendum Containing Notice of Obligation to Pay Improvement District Assessment (Form 53-0), the Addendum for Authorizing Hydrostatic Testing (Form 48-1), the Addendum for Property in a Propane Gas System Service Area (Form 47-0), the Addendum for Section 1031 Exchange (Form 60-0), the Addendum Regarding Fixture Leases (Form 52-1), and the Addendum Regarding Residential Leases (Form 51-1). The chapter further covers the Landlord's Floodplain and Flood Notice (Form 54-1), the Notice of Buyer's Termination of Contract (Form 38-8), the Notice of Seller's Termination of Contract (Form 50-0), the Notice to Purchaser of Special Taxing or Assessment District (Form 59-0), the Property Inspection Report (Form REI 7-6), the Notice Concerning Easements and Rights-of-Way (Form ERW 4-1), the Texas Real Estate Consumer Notice Concerning Hazards or Deficiencies (Form OP-I), and the Consumer Protection Notice (Form CN 1-5). Understanding when and how to use each of these forms is essential to complete and professional representation.

Learning Objectives

Upon completing Chapter 7, the student will be able to:

1. Explain the purpose and required content of the Information About Brokerage Services form (IABS 1-2), identify the circumstances that trigger its use, and describe the three primary types of agency relationships it discloses, including the updated written agreement requirements effective under Texas law.
2. Describe the purpose of the Non-Realty Items Addendum (Form 57-0), explain the seller's warranties and disclaimers under the form, and distinguish between personal property transferred through the addendum and the items listed in Paragraphs 2B and 2C of Form 20-19.

3. Explain the HOA Addendum (Form 36-11), the Subdivision Information form (Form 37-5), and how these two documents work together to protect a buyer purchasing into a mandatory property owners association.
4. Describe the purpose and key provisions of the Addendum for Sale of Other Property by Buyer (Form 10-6), including the contingency structure, the seller's right to continue marketing, the buyer's election to waive the contingency, and the additional earnest money requirement.
5. Explain the purpose and updated provisions of the Addendum for Back-Up Contract (Form 11-9), describe the sequence of events that move a back-up contract into the primary position, and identify the earnest money and option fee obligations it creates.
6. Describe the purpose and key provisions of the Short Sale Addendum (Form 45-2), and explain how it protects both the buyer and the seller in a transaction where the sales price is insufficient to satisfy existing liens.
7. Identify the purpose of the Addendum for Reservation of Oil, Gas and Other Minerals (Form 44-3), the Addendum for Coastal Area Property (Form 33-2), and the Addendum for Property Located Seaward of the Gulf Intracoastal Waterway (Form 34-4), and explain when each is required and how it differs from the others.
8. Explain the purpose and three election options of the Addendum Concerning Right to Terminate Due to Lender's Appraisal (Form 49-1), describe the consequences of a full Waiver, a Partial Waiver, and an Additional Right to Terminate, and identify the financing types for which the form is appropriate.
9. Describe the disclosure obligations created by the Addendum Containing Notice of Obligation to Pay Improvement District Assessment (Form 53-0), the Addendum for Property in a Propane Gas System Service Area (Form 47-0), the Notice to Purchaser of Special Taxing or Assessment District (Form 59-0), and the Landlord's Floodplain and Flood Notice (Form 54-1), and explain how each form notifies a buyer or tenant of conditions that materially affect a property.
10. Explain the proper completion and use of the Addendum for Authorizing Hydrostatic Testing (Form 48-1), the Addendum for Section 1031 Exchange (Form 60-0), the Addendum Regarding Fixture Leases (Form 52-1), and the Addendum Regarding Residential Leases (Form 51-1), and identify the risk allocations, delivery timelines, and party obligations each form establishes.
11. Identify the appropriate use of the Notice of Buyer's Termination of Contract (Form 38-8) and the Notice of Seller's Termination of Contract (Form 50-0), explain the contractual basis required for each termination option, and describe how these notices interact with the release of earnest money.
12. Describe the purpose and structure of the Property Inspection Report (Form REI 7-6), the Notice Concerning Easements and Rights-of-Way (Form ERW 4-1), the Texas Real Estate Consumer Notice Concerning Hazards or Deficiencies (Form OP-I), and the Consumer Protection Notice (Form CN 1-5), and explain the role of each in supporting consumer awareness and professional accountability.

Contents

- Addendum for Reservation of Oil, Gas and Other Minerals (Form 44-3)
- Coastal Area Addenda (Forms 33-2 and 34-4)
- Addendum Concerning Right to Terminate Due to Lender's Appraisal (Form 49-1)
- Addendum Containing Notice of Obligation to Pay Improvement District Assessment (Form 53-0)
- Addendum for Authorizing Hydrostatic Testing (Form 48-1)
- Addendum for Property in a Propane Gas System Service Area (Form 47-0)
- Addendum for Section 1031 Exchange (Form 60-0)
- Addendum Regarding Fixture Leases (Form 52-1)
- Addendum Regarding Residential Leases (Form 51-1)
- Landlord's Floodplain and Flood Notice (Form 54-1)
- Notice of Buyer's Termination of Contract (Form 38-8)
- Notice of Seller's Termination of Contract (Form 50-0)
- Notice to Purchaser of Special Taxing or Assessment District (Form 59-0)
- Property Inspection Report (Form REI 7-6)
- Notice Concerning Easements and Rights-of-Way (Form ERW 4-1)
- Texas Real Estate Consumer Notice Concerning Hazards or Deficiencies (Form OP-I)
- Consumer Protection Notice (Form CN 1-5)

Information About Brokerage Services (IABS 1-2)

The Information About Brokerage Services form (IABS 1-2, effective November 3, 2025) is a required consumer disclosure that every Texas real estate license holder must provide to prospective buyers, tenants, sellers, and landlords. It is not a contract; it creates no obligations between the parties. Its purpose is to ensure that every consumer who works with a Texas license holder understands the role that licensee can play in a transaction, the duties that licensee owes, and the type of representation that will apply.

The form is required to be provided at the first substantive communication with a prospective party to a transaction. It must be provided prior to showing residential property to an unrepresented buyer, and it must be provided before a written representation agreement is entered into. The form can be delivered in person, by email, or through a link posted prominently on the broker's website and advertising. The consumer acknowledges receipt by initialing the form, and the license holder retains the form in the transaction file.

What the IABS Discloses

The IABS form opens by explaining the two categories of real estate license holders in Texas. A broker is responsible for all brokerage activities, including acts performed by sales agents the broker sponsors. A sales agent must be sponsored by a broker and works with clients on behalf of the broker. This distinction is important because it establishes that the sales agent's authority flows from the broker: the client's legal relationship is ultimately with the broker, not the individual sales agent.

The form then states the broker's four minimum duties required by law when representing a client. The broker must put the interests of the client above all others, including the broker's own interests. The broker must inform the client of any material information about the property or transaction received by the broker. The broker must answer the client's questions and present any offer or counteroffer to or from the client. And the broker must treat all parties to a real estate transaction honestly and fairly. These duties apply in every client relationship regardless of the type of representation.

Written Agreements

A critically important update in Form IABS 1-2, reflecting both Senate Bill 1968 (effective January 1, 2026) and updated TREC rules, is the explicit statement that written agreements are required in certain situations. A license holder who performs brokerage activity for a prospective buyer of residential property must enter into a written agreement with the buyer before showing any residential property to the buyer, or, if no residential property will be shown, before presenting an offer on behalf of the buyer. This written agreement must contain specific information required by Texas law, including the amount or rate of compensation the broker will receive and how that amount is determined. The IABS itself cautions that even when a written agreement is not required, all agreements between the consumer and the broker should be in writing.

The form also addresses showing property to an unrepresented buyer without entering into a full representation agreement. A license holder may show a property to a buyer without representing that buyer only if the broker has not agreed with the buyer to represent them, is not otherwise acting as the buyer's agent at the time of showing, does not provide the buyer opinions or advice regarding the property or real estate transactions, and does not perform any other act of brokerage for the buyer. Before showing a residential property to an unrepresented prospective buyer, the license holder must enter into a written agreement. That agreement may not be exclusive and is limited to no more than 14 days.

Types of Representation

The IABS describes three forms of representation a license holder may provide. As agent for the owner (seller or landlord), the broker becomes the property owner's agent through an agreement, usually a written listing to sell or property management agreement. The owner's agent must inform the owner of any material information, including information disclosed to the agent by the buyer or buyer's agent. Owner's agent fees are negotiable and are not set by law.

As agent for the buyer or tenant, the broker becomes the buyer's or tenant's agent through an agreement to represent them, usually a written buyer representation agreement. The buyer's agent must inform the buyer of any material information about the property or transaction, including information disclosed by the seller or seller's agent. Buyer's and tenant's agent fees are also negotiable and are not set by law.

As intermediary, the broker acts between both parties to the transaction. The broker must first obtain the written agreement of each party. The written agreement must state who will pay the broker and must set forth the broker's obligations as intermediary in conspicuous bold or underlined print. An intermediary must treat all parties impartially and fairly. With the parties' written consent, the intermediary may appoint a different license holder associated with the broker to each party to communicate with, provide opinions and advice to, and carry out the instructions of each party. The intermediary must not disclose, without specific written authorization, that the owner will accept a price less than the asking price, that the buyer will pay a price greater than the written offer, or any other confidential information or information a party has specifically instructed the broker not to disclose.

The bottom of the IABS form contains the License Holder Contact Information section, where the sponsoring broker's name and license number, the designated broker of a licensed business entity, the licensed supervisor of the sales agent, and the sales agent's own name and license number are all entered. Email addresses and phone numbers are also included. The consumer initials the form and receives a copy. This section is essential: providing inaccurate or incomplete contact information in the IABS creates both regulatory and civil liability for the license holder.

Amendment to Contract (Form 39-11)

The Amendment to Contract (Form 39-11, effective July 1, 2026) is the instrument used to modify the terms of a contract that is already in place. No term of a promulgated contract can be changed after execution except through a signed written amendment agreed to by both buyer and seller. Verbal agreements to extend deadlines, change the sales price, add repairs, or modify any other term are not binding and create significant risk for both parties and their license holders.

The amendment form lists the most common modifications that arise during the contract period: changes to the sales price (with the three-line format matching Paragraph 3 of the main contract), additional repairs and treatments the seller agrees to perform, changes to the closing date, changes to the option period and option fee, changes to the deadline for the buyer to obtain financing approval, changes to the amount the seller will pay toward the buyer's closing costs, and the seller has the option to contribute to buyer's broker compensation in 12B(1), and the buyer now has the option to contribute to the seller's broker compensation in 12B(2). It also clarifies that 12A(1)(b) is only to be used for seller's contributions for buyer's expenses other than broker compensation and any other modification the parties agree to. The 'Other Modifications' section uses the same approach as Paragraph 11 of the main contract: only factual statements and business details that complete a blank, disclose factual information, or provide instructions are appropriate entries.

Every completed amendment must include the property address, must be signed and dated by both the buyer and the seller, and takes effect when executed by both parties. If a deadline has already passed, the amendment should be signed and dated before that deadline unless the parties agree to extend it retroactively in the amendment itself. License holders should monitor all dates in the contract carefully and prepare amendments promptly when circumstances require a change. A licensee who allows deadlines to pass without executing the appropriate amendment may leave the client without the protection the contract was designed to provide.

In the Other Modifications section a statement that real estate brokers and sales agents are prohibited from practicing law. Any change that creates a new legal right or obligation that is not contemplated by the form's pre-printed blanks must be drafted by a party to the contract or a party's attorney, not by the license holder.

Seller's Disclosure about Groundwater and Surface Water Rights (Form 61-0)

This form provides prospective buyers with information on groundwater and surface water rights associated with a property.

Paragraph 1. Defines certain terms for the benefit of those involved.

Paragraph 2. Asks the seller several questions (if the seller is aware) about the property including if the property is in a Groundwater District or has any wells on the property and any issues with a well.

Paragraph 3. Asks the seller about Surface Water rights associated with the property.

And the form ends with several Notices to Buyer and Seller

Non-Realty Items Addendum (Form 57-0)

The Non-Realty Items Addendum (Form 57-0, effective October 10, 2011) is a TREC-approved form for voluntary use that facilitates the transfer of personal property items from the seller to the buyer as part of a real estate sale. It supplements the items of personal property already addressed in Paragraphs 2B (improvements/accessories permanently installed and built-in) and 2C (related accessories) of Form 20-

19. When the buyer and seller agree to transfer personal property that is not covered by those paragraphs, Form 57-0 is the appropriate vehicle.

Examples of items commonly transferred through the Non-Realty Items Addendum include a freestanding propane barbecue grill, a pool table, outdoor patio furniture, a riding lawn mower, or a generator. These are items of personal property that the seller owns separately from the real property. Because they are not part of the real estate, their transfer requires separate documentation to protect both parties.

Paragraph A is where each item of personal property is specifically described. The form instructs the user to specify each item carefully, including description, model numbers, serial numbers, location, and other identifying information. Vague descriptions such as 'all items in the garage' are insufficient and create disputes. The more precise the description, the clearer the obligation. In exchange for the additional consideration stated in the paragraph (which may be a nominal amount), the seller agrees to convey the listed items to the buyer at closing.

Paragraph B contains the seller's warranty: the seller represents and warrants that the seller owns the personal property described in Paragraph A free and clear of all encumbrances. This means the seller is promising that there are no liens, security interests, or other claims against the personal property. A seller who has financed a piece of equipment or appliance through a retail credit agreement may have an encumbrance on that item that must be satisfied before it can be transferred. This warranty obligates the seller to deliver clean title to the personal property.

Paragraph C contains a significant disclaimer: the seller does not warrant or guarantee the condition or future performance of the personal property being conveyed. The buyer is accepting the personal property in whatever condition it is in at the time of transfer. This is in contrast to the seller's warranty of title to the real property in the main contract. The seller is guaranteeing ownership of the personal property but not its functionality. Buyers should inspect personal property items before the closing date and should understand that once the sale closes, the seller has no obligation to repair or replace items that malfunction.

Form 57-0 is approved rather than promulgated by TREC. Approved means TREC has reviewed the form and finds it acceptable for use, but its use is not mandatory. Some transactions may use other forms, such as a separate Bill of Sale prepared by an attorney, to accomplish the same purpose when large amounts or complex personal property are involved.

HOA Addendum and Subdivision Information (Forms 36-11 and 37-5)

When a property is subject to mandatory membership in a property owners association, the buyer has a right to receive information about the association's financial condition, rules, and obligations before being committed to purchasing into that community. Two forms work together to address this: the Addendum for Property Subject to Mandatory Membership in a Property Owners Association (Form 36-11) and the Subdivision Information, Including Resale Certificate for Property Subject to Mandatory Membership in a Property Owners' Association (Form 37-5). Both forms apply to traditional residential subdivisions with homeowners associations; neither is used for condominiums, which have their own separate forms (the condominium contract Form 30-18 and the Condominium Resale Certificate Form 32-5).

Form 36-11: The HOA Addendum

Form 36-11 (effective November 7, 2022) is the promulgated addendum that is checked in Paragraph 22 of Form 20-19 and attached to the contract whenever the property is subject to mandatory HOA membership. It is referenced by the HOA notice in Paragraph 6E(2) of the main contract.

Paragraph A defines Subdivision Information as a current copy of the restrictions applying to the subdivision and bylaws and rules of the Association, together with a resale certificate, as described by Section 207.003 of the Texas Property Code. The paragraph then establishes how the buyer receives this information. Three approaches are available. Under the first option, the seller delivers the Subdivision Information to the buyer, and the buyer may terminate the contract within three days after receiving it or before closing, whichever occurs first, with earnest money refunded. If the seller fails to deliver, the buyer may terminate at any time before closing. Under the second option, the buyer obtains the Subdivision Information directly from the Association at the buyer's expense, with the same three-day termination right after receipt. Under the third option, the buyer elects not to receive the Subdivision Information, waiving those review and termination rights.

Paragraph B addresses who pays the seller's obligations to the Association at the time of transfer. The seller pays all fees imposed by the Association in connection with the transfer of the property except for the amount negotiated and stated in Paragraph C. This includes transfer fees, move-in fees, and similar charges, but specifically excludes regular periodic maintenance fees, assessments, or dues that are prorated under Paragraph 13 of the main contract, and excludes the costs and fees associated with the Subdivision Information itself as provided in Paragraphs A and D.

Paragraph C identifies the amount the buyer will pay toward the Association fees associated with the transfer, up to the dollar amount stated. Any transfer-related Association fees in excess of that cap are the seller's responsibility. This paragraph requires a specific dollar amount. License holders who leave Paragraph C blank or enter an amount that does not reflect the actual fees expected should check with the title company about typical fees charged by the specific association before the contract is submitted.

Paragraph D is the authorization paragraph. The seller authorizes the Association to release and provide the Subdivision Information and any updated resale certificate to the buyer, the title company, or any broker in the transaction. If the buyer does not need the Subdivision Information or an updated resale certificate but the title company independently needs information from the Association (such as confirmation of dues status, special assessments, covenant violation status, or waiver of any right of first refusal), either the buyer or the seller, as checked by the parties, will pay the title company the cost of obtaining that information before the title company orders it.

Form 37-5: The Subdivision Information and Resale Certificate

Form 37-5 (effective February 10, 2014) is the voluntary-use form that the Association itself completes to deliver the required Subdivision Information to the buyer. Like the Condominium Resale Certificate (Form 32-5), this form is completed by the Association's board of directors or managing agent, not by the license holder or the seller. A license holder who attempts to complete the Association's certificate on behalf of the seller risks misrepresentation if any information is incorrect.

The resale certificate covers thirteen items labeled A through M. Paragraph A addresses whether the property is subject to a right of first refusal or other restraint in the restrictions that would limit the owner's right to transfer. Paragraph B states the current regular assessment for the property. Paragraph C discloses any special assessment due after the certificate is delivered. Paragraph D states the total amounts due and unpaid to the Association attributable to the property. Paragraph F states the reserves for capital expenditures. Paragraph G reports the total amount of any unsatisfied judgments against the Association. Paragraph H discloses whether any suits are pending in which the Association is a party, excluding suits regarding unpaid ad valorem taxes of individual members.

Paragraph I discloses whether the Association's board has actual knowledge of conditions on the property that violate the restrictions, bylaws, or rules. Paragraph J discloses whether the Association has received any notices from a governmental authority regarding health or building code violations with respect to the property or common areas. Paragraph K states the amount of any administrative transfer fee charged by the Association for a change of ownership. Paragraph L identifies the Association's managing agent. Paragraph M states whether the restrictions allow the Association to foreclose its lien on the property for failure to pay assessments. The certificate carries a prominent notice that the Subdivision Information may change at any time, and buyers should understand that the certificate reflects conditions as of the date it was prepared.

The form is accompanied by the restrictions applicable to the subdivision, the bylaws, the rules, and any other required documents. Buyers who take their three-day review period seriously and actually read these materials are in a far better position to understand the obligations and restrictions that will govern their use of the property. The right to terminate for three days after receipt of the Subdivision Information is a genuine consumer protection that disappears if the buyer does not act.

Addendum for Sale of Other Property by Buyer (Form 10-6)

The Addendum for Sale of Other Property by Buyer (Form 10-6, effective April 1, 2014) is used when the buyer cannot purchase the new property unless and until the buyer's existing property is sold and the proceeds from that sale are received. This type of transaction is commonly called a sale contingency. A buyer who has most of their equity tied up in their current home and cannot qualify for the new purchase without those proceeds needs this addendum to protect themselves if their existing property does not sell by the required date.

The Contingency Structure

Paragraph A establishes the contingency. The contract is contingent upon the buyer's receipt of the proceeds from the sale of the buyer's property at a specified address on or before a specified date. If the contingency is not satisfied (the buyer's property does not sell and fund by the deadline) and is not waived by the buyer, the contract terminates automatically on the deadline date and the earnest money is refunded to the buyer. Time is of the essence for all provisions of this addendum.

The seller does not have to simply wait passively during the contingency period. Paragraph B addresses what happens if the seller receives another written offer to purchase the property while the Form 10-6 contingency is in place. The seller must notify the buyer of the accepted offer and simultaneously notify the buyer that the seller requires the buyer to waive the contingency. The buyer then has a specified number of days (typically one day after the seller's notice) to waive the contingency or the contract terminates automatically and the earnest money is refunded to the buyer.

Waiving the Contingency

Paragraph C governs how the buyer waives the contingency. The buyer may only waive by taking two specific actions simultaneously: notifying the seller in writing of the waiver, and depositing a stated amount of additional earnest money with the escrow agent. Both steps are required. A written waiver without the additional earnest money deposit, or a deposit without a written notice, is not a valid waiver. The additional earnest money is intended to demonstrate that the buyer is genuinely committed to proceeding without the protection of the contingency.

Paragraph D addresses a specific situation that can arise after the buyer waives the contingency: the buyer's existing property still has not closed and funded by the closing date of the new purchase. If the buyer waives the contingency but then cannot close on the new purchase solely because the buyer's existing property has not sold, the buyer is not in default under the main contract as long as the buyer notifies the seller before the Closing Date. This gives the buyer one additional avenue to protect the earnest money if the sale of their property is still pending. However, this protection only applies if the non-closing is solely the result of not receiving the proceeds. If there are other reasons the buyer cannot close, the default provisions of the main contract apply.

The Sale of Other Property contingency is one of the less popular contract contingencies because sellers generally prefer not to accept offers that come with this condition attached. A seller who already has an interested buyer has reason to continue marketing the property until the contingency is resolved, which is exactly what Paragraph B of the addendum provides. License holders working with sellers should explain the contingency structure clearly and help the seller understand both the protection the addendum provides to the buyer and the seller's right to require a waiver if a better offer appears.

Addendum for Back-Up Contract (Form 11-9)

The Addendum for Back-Up Contract (Form 11-9, effective July 1, 2026) allows a buyer to enter into a contract on a property that is already under contract with a different buyer. The back-up buyer's contract is subordinate to the first contract; it does not obligate the seller to sell the property to the back-up buyer unless and until the first contract terminates. The first contract's termination causes the back-up contract to automatically move into the primary contract position.

This addendum was significantly updated in the January 2025 revisions to clarify the timing and payment of earnest money and the option fee for the back-up buyer. The revisions incorporate language similar to Paragraph 5 of the main contract and specifically address the timing and payment of any additional fees.

Structure of the Back-Up Agreement

The addendum identifies the address of the property, the name of the first contract buyer, and the date of the first contract. The back-up contract then states that the parties are entering into this contract knowing that a prior contract exists and that the back-up contract is subordinate to it. The back-up contract does not terminate the first contract and does not prevent the seller from performing the seller's obligations under the first contract.

While the first contract is in place, the earnest money and option fee provisions for the back-up contract are typically structured so that they must be delivered within a specified period after the Effective Date of the back-up contract. This timing mirrors the requirements of Paragraph 5 of the main contract. Time is of the essence for these deliveries, just as it is in the primary contract context.

The back-up contract automatically becomes the primary contract on the date the first contract terminates. From that point forward, all provisions of the back-up contract apply as if it were the original contract, and dates and deadlines begin to run from the date the back-up contract became primary. The seller is required to notify the back-up buyer promptly when the first contract terminates so that the back-up buyer can prepare to proceed. If the first contract does not terminate and closes successfully, the back-up contract terminates automatically.

A back-up position can be valuable when a buyer is highly motivated and willing to be in a holding pattern while the first contract plays out. From the seller's perspective, having a back-up contract means that if the first buyer terminates for any reason during the option period, a financing contingency, or any other provision, the seller immediately has a new buyer ready to proceed rather than having to start the marketing process over. Back-up contracts are most common in competitive markets where desirable properties attract multiple buyers quickly.

Seller's Notice to Buyer of Removal of Contingency Under Addendum for "Back-Up" Contract (Form 62-0)

This notice is voluntary. This form may be used to satisfy the notice required in Paragraph H of the Addendum for "Back-Up" Contract (TREC 11-9) to notify the buyer that the First Contract is terminated and the Back-Up Contract is now in the first position. The seller should indicate the date the notice of termination of the First Contract is delivered to the buyer, which becomes the amended effective date of the Back-Up Contract. Delivery of the notice should be in accordance with Paragraph 21 of the contract.

Short Sale Addendum (Form 45-2)

A short sale occurs when a seller owes more on a property than the property's current market value, and the lender or lenders holding the existing mortgages agree to accept less than the full amount owed as a condition of releasing their liens so that the property can be sold. The Short Sale Addendum (Form 45-2, effective April 1, 2021) is used in every transaction where the proceeds from the sale will be insufficient to pay all existing liens in full and the seller is therefore relying on noteholder consent to complete the sale.

Short sales are more complicated and time-consuming than conventional sales for several reasons. The lender's approval process takes time, often weeks or months. The lender may require its own appraisal or review of comparable sales. The lender may counter the offered price, require the buyer to contribute more, or impose other conditions. And there is no guarantee the lender will approve the transaction at all. Both buyer and seller enter a short sale with the understanding that significant uncertainty exists.

Key Provisions of Form 45-2

The addendum makes the entire transaction contingent on the noteholder's approval of the sale. The seller must make a prompt and diligent effort to obtain approval from all noteholders whose liens will not be fully paid from the sales proceeds. The seller must provide the buyer with written notice of any approvals or denials received and must keep the buyer informed of the status of the approval process.

If all required approvals are not obtained within a specified period, or if a noteholder's approval contains conditions that are not acceptable to the buyer or seller, either party may terminate the contract and the earnest money is refunded to the buyer. The addendum also addresses the specific termination notice requirements and the earnest money refund process.

The form includes a notice that short sales involve debt and tax consequences that neither the real estate licensees nor the Texas Real Estate Commission can advise on. Both the buyer and the seller should consult with attorneys, tax advisors, and financial professionals before proceeding. A seller facing a short sale may have income tax implications from the forgiven debt, and a license holder who attempts to provide guidance on these issues is outside the permissible scope of brokerage activity.

License holders should understand that working a short sale to completion requires patience, consistent follow-up with the lender, organized documentation, and clear communication with both parties. The listing broker is typically responsible for assembling and submitting the short sale package to the lender, which may include a hardship letter from the seller, a complete financial statement, tax returns, bank statements, payoff letters from all lienholders, and documentation of the buyer's offer.

Addendum for Reservation of Oil, Gas and Other Minerals (Form 44-3)

The Addendum for Reservation of Oil, Gas and Other Minerals (Form 44-3, effective February 1, 2023) is the instrument used when a seller intends to retain all or a portion of the mineral estate rather than conveying it with the surface of the property. This addendum was introduced in Chapter 6 in the context of the Farm and Ranch Contract, but it applies equally to any TREC-promulgated contract form when a mineral reservation is intended. It is listed in Paragraph 22 of Form 20-19 and may be attached to residential, unimproved property, and new home contracts as well as the farm and ranch form.

Paragraph A identifies the mineral estate being reserved, including any royalty interests under existing mineral leases. Paragraph B addresses surface rights: whether the mineral estate owner retains ingress and egress rights across the surface for access to the minerals. Paragraph C requires the seller to provide the buyer with copies of any existing mineral leases affecting the property.

Mineral rights transactions require the involvement of a licensed attorney. The legal consequences of severing the surface estate from the mineral estate, the implications of existing leases, and the rights of a mineral owner to use the surface for drilling and related activities are complex legal matters that a real estate license holder may not advise on. Any time a seller raises the subject of reserving mineral interests, the license holder should promptly direct both parties to consult attorneys before any agreement is made.

Coastal Area Addenda (Forms 33-2 and 34-4)

Texas has two distinct promulgated addenda for coastal properties, each addressing a different geographic situation. Both are required by specific provisions of the Texas Natural Resources Code and are referenced in the main contract forms through the Title Notices in Paragraph 6E. Understanding the difference between them is essential because confusing the two, or failing to attach the correct one, leaves the parties without the statutorily required disclosures.

Form 33-2: Addendum for Coastal Area Property

The Addendum for Coastal Area Property (Form 33-2, effective March 1, 2012) is required when the property being sold adjoins and shares a common boundary with the tidally influenced submerged lands of the state of Texas. This means the property's boundary touches the tidal zone, the area where the tides ebb and flow. Properties on bays, estuaries, lagoons, and the Gulf Coast shoreline that border the water itself fall into this category. The addendum is triggered by the Tide Waters notice in Paragraph 6E(4) of Form 20-19 and is listed in Paragraph 22.

The Coastal Area Property Addendum provides the notice required by Section 33.135 of the Texas Natural Resources Code. The core concern addressed by this addendum is the dynamic and legally uncertain nature of coastal boundaries. The shoreline between private property and state-owned submerged lands shifts over time due to erosion, accretion, and storm activity. The public's right of access to the beach under the Texas Open Beaches Act may also affect the property. The addendum informs the buyer that the boundary of the property on the water side may not be fixed and that public rights may exist on the coastal portion of the property even after purchase.

The addendum places specific obligations on the seller to disclose any known encroachments, public easements, or other conditions affecting the tidal boundary. It also reminds the buyer to obtain appropriate professional advice, including a survey and legal counsel, before proceeding. A license holder who sells coastal property without ensuring this addendum is attached when required may face both disciplinary and civil liability for the failure to make required disclosures.

Form 34-4: Addendum for Property Located Seaward of the Gulf Intracoastal Waterway

The Addendum for Property Located Seaward of the Gulf Intracoastal Waterway (Form 34-4, effective June 8, 2005) is required when the property is located seaward of (on the Gulf side of) the Gulf Intracoastal Waterway. This applies specifically to properties on the barrier islands and coastal strips that lie between the Gulf Intracoastal Waterway and the Gulf of Mexico, such as Padre Island, Galveston Island, and other barrier bar formations along the Texas coast.

Properties seaward of the Gulf Intracoastal Waterway face environmental risks that are both more extreme and more certain than properties that merely adjoin tidal waters. These properties are subject to the full force of Gulf storms without the protection of the mainland or the waterway itself. They may be subject to open beach easements under the Texas Open Beaches Act, dune protection requirements, restrictions on construction, and mandatory buyout programs after major storms. The physical boundary between the property and the Gulf can be dramatically altered or entirely eliminated by hurricane activity.

The distinction between Forms 33-2 and 34-4 is therefore geographic and risk-based. Form 33-2 applies to any Texas property that borders tidally influenced waters, which includes inland bays and estuaries far from the Gulf. Form 34-4 applies specifically and only to the narrow coastal strip seaward of the Gulf Intracoastal Waterway. A property on Galveston Bay on the north side of Galveston Island needs Form 33-2; a property on the south (Gulf-facing) side of Galveston Island needs Form 34-4. A property can potentially need both if it borders tidally influenced waters in a location that is also seaward of the waterway, in which case both addenda should be attached.

License holders who work in coastal Texas markets should be fully familiar with both addenda and with the physical geography of the areas they serve. The geographic line of the Gulf Intracoastal Waterway is clearly visible on maps and satellite imagery, and most title companies in coastal markets routinely identify which addendum is required for a given property. When in doubt, a call to the title company before the contract is written is far preferable to a situation where required disclosures are missing at closing.

Form 49-1: Addendum Concerning Right to Terminate Due to Lender's Appraisal

The Addendum Concerning Right to Terminate Due to Lender's Appraisal is a form promulgated by the Texas Real Estate Commission (TREC) that modifies the terms of the Third Party Financing Addendum attached to a residential real estate contract. This addendum is used exclusively in transactions involving conventional financing and is not appropriate for transactions involving FHA-insured or VA-guaranteed loans. Its purpose is to clarify, modify, or expand the buyer's rights with respect to terminating the contract when the lender's appraisal yields an opinion of value that does not meet the lender's underwriting requirements. Texas real estate licensed professionals should use this form when buyers and sellers wish to negotiate appraisal-related contingencies that differ from the default protections offered under Paragraph 2B of the Third Party Financing Addendum.

The opening section of the form requires the licensee to insert the street address and city of the property being sold. This identifying information should match the property description used throughout the contract and any related addenda to maintain consistency across all transaction documents. The licensee should confirm that the Third Party Financing Addendum is in fact attached to the contract before using this form, as it functions only in conjunction with that addendum.

Following the property identification, the form contains a confirming statement that the financing does not involve FHA or VA loans. The licensee must then check one - and only one - of the three boxes that follow. Selecting more than one option creates ambiguity and could render the addendum unenforceable. The decision regarding which box to check should be made by the buyer after consultation with the buyer's agent, and the seller's agent should review the selected option to ensure the seller understands the implications.

The first option is a full Waiver. By checking this box, the buyer surrenders the right to terminate the contract under Paragraph 2B of the Third Party Financing Addendum if Property Approval is not obtained because the appraised value falls short of the lender's underwriting requirements. Under this scenario, if the lender reduces the loan amount because of a low appraisal, the cash portion of the Sales Price increases by the corresponding amount the loan is reduced. The licensee should ensure the buyer understands that selecting this option means the buyer must come up with additional funds to close if the appraisal comes in low, or risk default. This option is often used in competitive markets where buyers want to strengthen their offers.

The second option is a Partial Waiver. The buyer waives the right to terminate only if the appraisal's opinion of value is equal to or greater than a specific dollar amount written into the blank provided. The licensee should confirm with the buyer the threshold value below which the buyer wishes to retain termination rights and insert that figure clearly in the blank. As with the full waiver, if the lender reduces the loan amount due to the appraisal, the cash portion of the Sales Price is increased by the amount of the reduction. This option provides a middle-ground approach, offering the seller some assurance while still protecting the buyer from a substantially low appraisal.

The third option creates an Additional Right to Terminate that supplements the buyer's existing rights under Paragraph 2B. The licensee must complete two blanks: the number of days after the Effective Date within which the buyer may exercise this additional termination right, and the dollar amount that represents the minimum acceptable appraised value. If the appraised value falls below the stated amount and the buyer delivers a copy of the appraisal to the seller within the specified number of days, the buyer may terminate the contract and receive a full refund of the earnest money. The licensee should coordinate the day count with the lender's expected appraisal timeline to ensure the buyer has adequate time to receive and review the appraisal report before the deadline expires.

In all instances, the licensee should ensure that the addendum is signed and dated by all parties, attached to the original contract, and distributed to the buyer, seller, lender, and title company. Careful completion of this addendum protects both parties and clearly establishes the appraisal-related rights and obligations governing the transaction.

Form 53-0 Addendum Containing Notice of Obligation to Pay Improvement District Assessment

The Texas Real Estate Commission (TREC) promulgates this addendum to provide buyers with formal notice that the property they are purchasing is located within a public improvement district (PID) and is subject to ongoing assessments. This addendum is attached to the contract when the property being sold lies within a designated improvement district created under either Subchapter A, Chapter 372, or Chapter 382 of the Texas Local Government Code. Texas real estate licensed professionals must complete this form accurately to ensure the buyer fully understands the financial obligations attached to the property before closing.

The opening section of the addendum requires the licensee to insert the name of the municipality or county levying the assessment, followed by the property address. The licensee should verify the proper governmental entity by reviewing the recorded service and assessment plan, the title commitment, or by contacting the taxing authority directly. The property address must match exactly what appears on the main contract and any other addenda to avoid inconsistencies that could delay closing or create future disputes.

In the next paragraph, the licensee identifies the specific governmental entity to which the buyer will owe assessments and references the District by its full legal name. The licensee must also indicate whether the District was created under Subchapter A, Chapter 372, Local Government Code, or under Chapter 382, Local Government Code. This determination should not be guessed; the licensee should obtain confirmation from the municipality or county, the developer, or the title company. Selecting the correct enabling statute is important because it identifies the legal framework governing the assessment, the buyer's obligations, and the rights of the District.

The all-capitalized notice paragraph is statutorily mandated language and must not be altered. It informs the buyer that an assessment has already been levied against the property, that the assessment may be paid in full at any time, and that if it is not paid in full, the balance becomes due in annual installments. The licensee should walk the buyer through this paragraph carefully, emphasizing that the annual installment amounts will fluctuate based on interest, collection costs, administrative costs, and delinquency costs. Buyers often confuse PID assessments with property taxes or HOA dues, so a clear explanation by the licensee helps prevent misunderstandings later.

Following the notice, the form requires the licensee to insert the name of the municipality or county where the buyer can obtain the exact amount of the assessment. The licensee should provide accurate contact information to the buyer, ideally including a department name, phone number, or website where assessment data is published. The next blank requires the name of the city council or county commissioners court that approves the annual service plan update. Once again, the licensee must verify the correct governing body, as the entity approving the plan may differ depending on whether the District was created by a municipality or a county.

The paragraph that follows directs the buyer to obtain additional information about the assessments, including amounts and due dates, from the named municipality or county. The licensee should fill in the same governmental entity identified earlier in the form to maintain consistency. Buyers should be encouraged to request and review the most recent service plan update before closing to understand the projected payment schedule.

The final substantive paragraph warns the buyer that failure to pay any assessment or annual installment may result in penalties, interest, a lien on the property, or foreclosure. The licensee should ensure the buyer recognizes the seriousness of these consequences, which mirror those associated with unpaid ad valorem taxes.

The form concludes with signature lines for both the seller and the buyer. The licensee should confirm that both parties sign and date the addendum at the same time as the main contract. A properly executed addendum becomes part of the binding agreement and provides documented evidence that the buyer received the statutorily required notice regarding the improvement district assessment obligations associated with the property.

Form 48-1: Addendum for Authorizing Hydrostatic Testing

The Addendum for Authorizing Hydrostatic Testing is a form promulgated by the Texas Real Estate Commission (TREC) that allows a buyer, with the seller's permission, to conduct a hydrostatic plumbing test on a property under contract. Hydrostatic testing is a specialized inspection procedure used to detect leaks in a property's sewer or drainage system by pressurizing the plumbing lines with water. Because this type of test can sometimes cause damage to older or compromised plumbing systems, the addendum provides a structured way for the parties to address authorization and allocate the risk of any resulting damage. Texas real estate licensed professionals should be familiar with how to complete this form correctly to protect the interests of their clients.

At the top of the form, the licensee must enter the street address and city of the property under contract. This information should match exactly what appears on the underlying purchase contract to avoid any ambiguity about which property the addendum applies to. The licensee should confirm the property address with the client before completing the form to ensure consistency across all transaction documents.

Just below the property identification, the form contains an advisory recommending that the parties consult a licensed plumber about the scope of hydrostatic testing and the risks associated with it before signing. While this is not a fillable section, the real estate professional should draw the client's attention to this notice and encourage them to follow the recommendation. Hydrostatic testing involves plugging the plumbing system and filling it with water under pressure, which can stress aging pipes and potentially cause leaks or breaks that did not previously exist. Both buyers and sellers should understand these risks before proceeding.

Paragraph A is the authorization paragraph, in which the seller agrees to allow the buyer, at the buyer's expense, to engage a licensed plumber to perform a hydrostatic plumbing test on the property. There is nothing for the licensee to fill in here, but it is important to confirm that both parties understand the cost responsibility. The buyer pays for the test itself, regardless of the outcome, and only a licensed plumber may perform it. The licensee should remind the buyer to obtain a written estimate from the plumber and to schedule the testing within the negotiated inspection or option period if applicable.

Paragraph B addresses the allocation of risk and provides three mutually exclusive options. The licensee must select only one of these by checking or marking the appropriate box, depending on what the parties have negotiated. Option (1) places liability for damages caused by the hydrostatic plumbing test on the seller. This option is typically more favorable to the buyer and may be appropriate when the seller has represented that the plumbing is in good condition. Option (2) places liability on the buyer, meaning the buyer is responsible for any damage caused by the test. This option is generally more favorable to the seller and is often requested when the property is older or when the seller is concerned about potential damage to fragile plumbing. Option (3) is a compromise position that places liability on the buyer but caps the buyer's exposure at a specified dollar amount, which the licensee must fill in on the blank line. When using Option (3), the licensee should ensure that the agreed-upon dollar amount is clearly written and that both parties understand any damages above that threshold would be the seller's responsibility.

At the bottom of the form, both the buyer and the seller must sign and date the addendum. The licensee should confirm that all parties to the underlying contract sign in the appropriate spaces and that the addendum is attached to and made part of the original purchase contract. Without proper signatures from all parties, the addendum will not be enforceable, and the buyer's authorization to conduct hydrostatic testing will not be valid under the terms of the transaction.

Form 47-0 Addendum for Property in a Propane Gas System Service Area

The Texas Real Estate Commission (TREC) Addendum for Property in a Propane Gas System Service Area is a disclosure document promulgated under Section 141.010 of the Texas Utilities Code. It is used when a property being sold falls within a designated propane gas system service area. The addendum's purpose is to inform the buyer that the property may be subject to special charges, fees, or service-related conditions associated with receiving propane gas service from the distribution system retailer authorized to operate within that area. Texas real estate licensed professionals should understand each section of this addendum and how to properly complete it to ensure compliance with state law and to protect both parties involved in the transaction.

The first section of the addendum is the property identification line, where the agent must enter the street address and city of the property being purchased. This information must match exactly what is referenced in the main contract for sale. Accuracy here is important because the addendum is tied directly to the property in question, and any inconsistency could create confusion or legal issues later in the transaction process. The licensed professional should double-check the property details against the contract and any title documents before completing this field.

The notice paragraph that follows is the substantive disclosure to the buyer. This paragraph does not require the agent to fill in any blanks, but it is important that the licensed professional review the contents with the buyer to ensure understanding. The notice explains that the property may be located within a propane gas system service area authorized under Chapter 141 of the Utilities Code, and that the buyer may be responsible for special costs or charges before receiving propane gas service. It also alerts the buyer that there may be a waiting period while lines or facilities are constructed to deliver service to the property. The agent should encourage the buyer to confirm whether the property is indeed within such a service area and to contact the distribution system retailer directly to learn about any associated costs and timelines. This level of due diligence helps the buyer make a fully informed decision before closing.

The next paragraph contains the buyer's acknowledgment that they have received the notice either at or before signing a binding contract for the purchase of the property, or at the closing. While there is no blank to complete in this paragraph, the licensed professional should ensure that the buyer is provided this addendum at the appropriate time during the transaction. Delivery of the notice is required by statute, and timing matters because the acknowledgment confirms that the buyer received the disclosure within the legally permitted window.

The following paragraph references Section 141.010(a) of the Utilities Code, which requires that a copy of the notice the distribution system retailer recorded in the real property records be attached to this addendum. The licensed professional should obtain this recorded notice and physically attach it to the addendum before presenting it to the buyer. Without the attached recorded notice, the addendum is incomplete and may not satisfy the statutory disclosure requirement. The note at the bottom of the form provides direction to the seller, indicating that the recorded notice can be obtained from the county clerk's office in the county where the property is located, or directly from the distribution system retailer. Real estate professionals representing the seller should assist their client in obtaining this recorded notice promptly so that it is available when the addendum is delivered to the buyer.

Finally, the form contains signature lines for both the buyer and the seller. The licensed professional should ensure that all parties to the transaction sign and date the addendum and that copies are distributed to everyone involved. Both signatures confirm acknowledgment of the disclosure and the inclusion of the recorded notice. Once executed, the addendum becomes part of the overall transaction record and demonstrates compliance with the disclosure requirements set forth under Texas law for properties located within propane gas system service areas.

Form 60-0: Addendum for Section 1031 Exchange

The Texas Real Estate Commission (TREC) Addendum for Section 1031 Exchange is a supplemental document attached to a primary contract of sale when one of the parties - either the buyer or the seller - intends to structure the transaction as a like-kind property exchange pursuant to Section 1031 of the Internal Revenue Code. This addendum serves to formally notify the opposing party of the intent to complete a 1031 exchange and to establish the framework under which both parties will cooperate to facilitate that exchange. Texas real estate licensed professionals must understand that this form does not, by itself, create or execute the 1031 exchange; rather, it confirms intent and outlines the parameters of cooperation between the parties involved in the underlying real estate transaction. The actual exchange must be coordinated through a qualified intermediary and structured in compliance with IRS regulations, which typically requires the involvement of a tax professional or attorney specializing in 1031 exchanges. Below is a paragraph-by-paragraph commentary on how the form should be completed.

The opening section of the addendum requires the licensee to enter the street address and city of the property that is the subject of the underlying contract. This information must match exactly what appears on the primary sales contract to which the addendum is attached. Any discrepancy between the property description on the addendum and the main contract could create ambiguity or enforcement issues later in the transaction. The licensee should double-check the property address for accuracy, including correct spelling of the street name and proper city designation, and ensure consistency throughout all transaction documents.

Paragraph A identifies which party intends to use the property to accomplish a like-kind exchange under Section 1031. The form provides two checkboxes - one for Seller and one for Buyer - and the licensee must mark only the box that corresponds to the party initiating the exchange. If the seller is selling the subject property as the relinquished property in a 1031 exchange, the Seller box should be checked. If the buyer is acquiring the subject property as the replacement property in their own 1031 exchange, the Buyer box should be checked. Only one party typically initiates the exchange, although in rare cases both parties may be conducting separate exchanges, in which case two addenda may be appropriate. The licensee should confirm with their client which role applies before marking the form, and they should not provide tax or legal advice regarding whether the transaction qualifies under Section 1031.

Paragraph B sets forth the cooperation obligations between the parties. It states that both parties will reasonably cooperate to accomplish the exchange, but it places two important limitations on that cooperation. First, the non-exchanging party will not incur any additional expense or liability as a result of the exchange. Second, the closing will not be delayed because of the exchange. This paragraph requires no input from the licensee, as it is pre-printed contractual language. However, the licensee should review this paragraph with their client to ensure understanding. The non-exchanging party should be reassured that they will not be financially burdened or exposed to additional risk, while the exchanging party should understand that they must structure their exchange in a manner that does not push back the agreed-upon closing date. Any costs associated with the qualified intermediary, exchange documentation, or assignment of the contract must be borne by the exchanging party.

The addendum concludes with signature lines for both Buyer and Seller. Both parties must sign the addendum to make it binding, and the licensee should ensure that signatures are obtained from all parties identified on the primary contract. Once executed, the addendum becomes part of the contract between the parties. The licensee should deliver fully executed copies to all parties, the title company, and the qualified intermediary handling the exchange, and should retain a copy for their transaction file in accordance with TREC record-keeping requirements.

Form 52-1 Addendum Regarding Fixture Leases

The Addendum Regarding Fixture Leases is a form promulgated by the Texas Real Estate Commission (TREC) used in conjunction with a residential real estate contract when the property contains fixtures that the seller leases rather than owns. This addendum allows the parties to address how those leased items, such as solar panels, propane tanks, water softeners, or security systems, will be handled at closing. Texas real estate licensed professionals should use this form whenever the seller has disclosed leased fixtures on the property and the buyer and seller need to clarify whether the buyer will assume the lease, whether the seller will remove the items, and how related costs will be allocated.

At the top of the form, the licensee must enter the street address and city of the subject property. This identifying information should match the property description used in the underlying contract to avoid any inconsistency between the documents.

Paragraph A requires the licensee to identify which fixtures on the property are leased. The form provides checkboxes for solar panels, propane tanks, water softener, and security system, along with a blank line to list any additional leased fixtures not covered by the preset options. Only the items that the seller has confirmed to be leased should be checked. The licensee should verify with the seller exactly which fixtures are subject to a fixture lease before completing this section, as accuracy here will determine how the rest of the form is filled in.

Subparagraph A(1) addresses which fixture leases the buyer agrees to assume at closing. The licensee should check only those leases the buyer has expressly agreed to take over. A dollar amount must be entered indicating the maximum amount the buyer will pay toward the cost of assuming or receiving an assignment of the leases, with the seller responsible for any remainder. This figure should reflect what the parties negotiated, and the licensee should confirm the amount with the buyer before completing this blank. Both parties also agree to execute any documents required by the lessor to complete the assumption or assignment.

Subparagraph A(2) deals with leased fixtures the buyer is not assuming. The licensee should check either "will" or "will not" to indicate whether the seller will remove those leased fixtures prior to closing. If the seller will remove them, the seller is responsible for repairing any resulting damage. The form also includes a notice reminding the parties that any leased fixture remaining on the property continues to be subject to the lessor's rights under the original lease.

Paragraph B addresses the delivery of the fixture leases to the buyer. The licensee should check the appropriate box. Box (1) confirms the buyer has already received copies of all assumed leases. Box (2) is checked when the buyer has not yet received copies, in which case the seller has five days after the Effective Date to provide them, and the buyer has a seven-day right to terminate the contract after receiving them, with a refund of earnest money. Box (3) is used to disclose any oral fixture leases, requiring the licensee to identify the lessee, rental amount, and term, either on the line provided or on an attached exhibit.

Paragraph C confirms that at closing there will be no liens or security interests against the leased fixtures other than those tied to leases the buyer agrees to assume. Any other encumbrances must be satisfied out of the sales proceeds at closing. No information needs to be filled in for this paragraph, but the licensee should make sure the parties understand the representation.

The form ends with a notice encouraging both buyer and seller to consult with the lessor and their attorneys regarding any assignment, assumption, or termination of the fixture leases. Both parties must sign and date the form. The licensee should ensure all signatures are obtained and that signed copies are distributed to all parties and retained in the transaction file.

Form 51-1: Addendum Regarding Residential Leases

The Addendum Regarding Residential Leases, promulgated by the Texas Real Estate Commission (TREC), is used when a property under contract is currently leased or may be subject to a lease at the time of closing. This addendum clarifies how existing or new Residential Leases will be treated during the transaction and protects both the buyer and the seller by establishing notice requirements, delivery obligations, and remedies if conditions surrounding the leases change. The Texas real estate licensed professional should walk the parties through each section carefully to confirm the proper handling of any lease arrangement tied to the property.

The opening section of the addendum identifies the property by street address and city. The licensed professional should ensure that the address matches exactly what appears on the contract to avoid any discrepancies. The form then defines "Residential Lease" broadly to include any lease of the property and any addendum, amendment, or move-in condition form, ensuring that all related lease documentation is captured under this addendum.

The form makes clear that the seller may not execute any new Residential Lease or amend an existing one without the buyer's written consent after the effective date. The licensed professional should remind the seller of this restriction so the seller does not inadvertently breach the contract. The parties must then choose between Paragraph A or Paragraph B - these options are mutually exclusive, and only one box should be checked.

Paragraph A addresses Termination of Residential Leases. By selecting this option, all Residential Leases must be terminated by closing, and the seller must deliver possession with no tenant or other party occupying the property. The licensed professional should remind the seller that this addendum itself does not terminate the lease; the seller must take separate legal steps and should consult an attorney before agreeing to this provision, as Texas law provides specific rights to tenants that may limit early termination.

Paragraph B addresses the Assignment and Assumption of Residential Leases, where the seller assigns and the buyer assumes the existing leases at closing. Subparagraph (1) addresses delivery of the leases. The licensed professional should determine whether the buyer has already received copies (option a) or has not yet received them (option b). If option (b) applies, the seller has 3 days after the effective date to provide copies, and the parties must fill in the number of days the buyer has to terminate the contract after receiving them. Option (c) is reserved for any oral leases, which must be described by tenant name, rental amount, and term, either in the blank provided or on an attached exhibit.

Subparagraph (2) requires the seller to transfer security deposits to the buyer at closing, as defined under §92.102 of the Texas Property Code. The buyer is then responsible for delivering a signed statement to each tenant acknowledging the acquisition and confirming the dollar amount of the security deposit. The licensed professional should make sure both parties understand these obligations and prepare the proper documentation in advance of closing.

Subparagraph (3) provides representations from the seller about each Residential Lease, including that the lease is in full force and effect, no tenant is in default, no rent has been prepaid, no offsets are owed, no claims are pending, and no side agreements exist. If any representation is inaccurate, the seller must explain the exception in the blank space provided or attach additional sheets. The licensed professional should encourage the seller to disclose any known issues fully to avoid disputes later.

Subparagraph (4) creates a continuing duty for the seller to notify the buyer if any statement in B(3) becomes untrue after the effective date. The seller has 7 days to cure, and if the issue remains unresolved, the buyer has 5 days afterward to terminate the contract and receive a refund of the earnest money. The closing date will be extended as needed to allow these notices and remedies to play out.

Finally, both the buyer and seller must sign the addendum at the bottom. The licensed professional should confirm signatures and dates and attach the addendum to the executed contract.

Form 54-1: Landlord's Floodplain and Flood Notice

The Landlord's Floodplain and Flood Notice, approved by the Texas Real Estate Commission (TREC), is a disclosure document that must accompany a residential lease agreement in Texas. The form is designed to inform prospective tenants about the flood risk associated with the rental dwelling, helping them make informed decisions about their housing and insurance needs. It is important to note that this form is not required when using a TREC Temporary Residential Lease. Texas real estate licensed professionals assisting landlords with residential rentals should ensure this notice is properly completed and delivered to tenants before lease execution.

The opening section of the form requires the licensee or landlord to identify the property by entering the complete street address and city of the dwelling being rented. Accuracy in this section is important, as it ties the disclosure directly to the specific property covered under the lease. The licensee should verify the address matches what appears on the corresponding residential lease agreement to avoid inconsistencies between documents.

Paragraph A addresses whether the landlord is aware that the dwelling is located within a 100-year floodplain. The licensee should assist the landlord in checking either the "is" or "is not" box based on the landlord's actual knowledge. The form includes a notice that if neither box is checked, the tenant should assume the property is located in a 100-year floodplain, which makes it especially important that one of the boxes be marked. The paragraph also reminds tenants that even properties outside a 100-year floodplain may still be susceptible to flooding and directs them to the Federal Emergency Management Agency (FEMA) flood map, which is available online and searchable by address at no cost. Additionally, this paragraph informs tenants that most tenant insurance policies do not cover flood-related damages, and tenants are encouraged to seek separate flood insurance coverage. Licensees should encourage landlords to consult the FEMA map before completing this paragraph to ensure their disclosure is accurate.

Paragraph B requires the landlord to disclose whether they are aware that the dwelling has flooded at least once within the last five years. The licensee should ensure the landlord checks either "is" or "is not" based on their honest knowledge of the property's flood history. This includes any flooding events the landlord may have personally observed, repaired, or been informed about by previous tenants or property managers. Failing to disclose known flooding could expose the landlord to legal consequences, so licensees should counsel landlords on the importance of full and truthful disclosure here.

Paragraph C provides the legal definitions used throughout the notice. Subsection (1) defines "100-year floodplain" as any area designated as a flood hazard area with a one percent or greater chance of flooding each year by FEMA under the National Flood Insurance Act of 1968. Subsection (2) defines "flooding" as a general or temporary condition of partial or complete inundation of a dwelling caused by the overflow of inland or tidal waters, the unusual and rapid accumulation of runoff or surface waters from an established water source such as a river, stream, or drainage ditch, or excessive rainfall. Subsection (3) defines "dwelling" as one or more rooms rented for use as a permanent residence under a single lease to one or more tenants. These definitions are pre-printed in the form and require no input from the licensee, but the licensee should be familiar with them and prepared to explain the terms to landlords or tenants if questions arise.

The form concludes with signature lines for both the landlord and the tenant. The licensee should ensure that all parties sign and date the document, with each party retaining a copy for their records. The signed notice should be attached to the residential lease agreement and kept in the transaction file. Proper execution of this form fulfills statutory disclosure requirements under Texas property code and supports transparency between landlord and tenant regarding flood risk.

Form 38-8: Notice of Buyer's Termination of Contract

The Notice of Buyer's Termination of Contract is a form promulgated by the Texas Real Estate Commission (TREC) that allows a buyer to formally notify a seller that they are exercising their right to terminate an existing real estate contract. This form is used after a sales contract has already been executed, and it identifies the specific contractual basis under which the buyer is choosing to walk away from the transaction. Texas real estate licensed professionals must complete this form accurately to ensure their client's termination is documented and aligns with the rights granted in the underlying contract.

At the top of the form, the licensee should fill in the property's street address and city to identify the contract being terminated. Next, the seller's name should be entered in the designated space following "BETWEEN THE UNDERSIGNED BUYER AND." These identifying details should match exactly what appears on the original sales contract to avoid any confusion regarding which agreement is being terminated.

Paragraph (1) addresses the buyer's unrestricted right to terminate under Paragraph 5 of the contract, commonly referred to as the option period. The licensee should select this option only when the buyer is terminating during the negotiated option period and has paid the option fee. This is typically the simplest basis for termination because no specific reason needs to be provided.

Paragraph (2) applies when the buyer cannot obtain Buyer Approval as described in the Third Party Financing Addendum. The licensee must confirm that the buyer has delivered the lender's written statement detailing the reasons for the denial to the seller before submitting this notice. Without that documentation, the termination under this paragraph may not be valid.

Paragraph (3) is selected when the property fails to meet Property Approval requirements outlined in the Third Party Financing Addendum. Similar to paragraph (2), the licensee should ensure the lender's written statement explaining the determination has been delivered to the seller along with this notice.

Paragraph (4) should be marked when the buyer elects to terminate under Paragraph A of the Addendum for Property Subject to Mandatory Membership in a Property Owners' Association. This typically occurs when the buyer reviews the subdivision information and decides not to proceed.

Paragraph (5) covers terminations under Paragraph 7B(2) related to the Seller's Disclosure Notice. The licensee should select this when the seller failed to provide the disclosure notice within the required time, allowing the buyer to terminate.

Paragraph (6) is used when the buyer terminates under Paragraph (3) of the Addendum Concerning Right to Terminate Due to Lender's Appraisal. The licensee should verify that a copy of the appraisal has been delivered to the seller, as this is a requirement for using this termination basis.

Paragraph (7) applies to terminations under Paragraph 6.D. of the standard contract or 6.C. of the Residential Condominium Contract, when timely objections to title issues were not cured by the end of the Cure Period. The licensee should make sure objections were properly raised within the contract's specified timeframes before selecting this option.

Paragraph (8) is a catch-all "Other" section where the licensee identifies any other paragraph number from the contract or addendum that provides grounds for termination. The specific paragraph reference should be written clearly to avoid disputes about the basis for termination.

The note reminds all parties that this notice does not constitute an election of remedies and that the release of earnest money is governed separately by the contract terms. Real estate licensees should advise their clients that completing this form does not automatically release earnest money funds; a separate Release of Earnest Money form is generally needed for that purpose.

Finally, the form must be signed by the buyer and delivered to the seller. The form also includes a reminder to consult an attorney before signing because TREC rules prohibit real estate license holders from giving legal advice. Licensees should encourage their clients to seek legal counsel when there is any uncertainty about the consequences of termination.

Form 50-0: Notice of Seller's Termination of Contract

The Notice of Seller's Termination of Contract is a form promulgated by the Texas Real Estate Commission (TREC) that allows a seller to formally notify a buyer that an existing real estate contract is being terminated. This form is used in specific circumstances permitted under the original sales contract and serves as written documentation of the seller's decision to end the agreement. Texas real estate licensed professionals should approach this form with attention to detail, as accurate completion protects the seller's interests while maintaining compliance with TREC regulations.

The opening section of the form requires identification of the property and the parties involved. The licensed professional should enter the complete street address and city of the property that is the subject of the terminated contract. This information must match exactly what appears on the original contract to prevent any confusion regarding which transaction is being terminated. Following this, the buyer's name should be entered in the designated space, again matching the name as it appears on the original sales contract. The seller's identification is established through the signature line at the bottom of the form, but the licensed professional should confirm that the seller signing the notice is the same party listed on the original contract.

The first reason for termination, listed as item (1), addresses a scenario where the buyer failed to deliver the earnest money within the timeframe required under Paragraph 5 of the contract. The licensed professional should only mark or rely upon this reason if the buyer genuinely failed to deposit the earnest money on time and the seller is providing this notice before the buyer cures the failure. Timing is significant here because once the buyer delivers the earnest money, even if late, the seller may lose the right to terminate under this provision. The licensed professional should verify the date the earnest money was due, confirm with the escrow agent or title company whether the funds were received, and document the timeline carefully before advising the seller to proceed under this paragraph.

The second reason for termination, identified as item (2), provides space for the seller to specify any other contractual basis for termination. The licensed professional should assist the seller in identifying the specific paragraph number of the contract or addendum that grants the right to terminate. Common examples might include failure to satisfy contingencies, default provisions, or specific performance issues outlined in addenda. The blank lines should be filled in with clear, factual language referencing the applicable paragraph and the circumstances triggering the termination right. Professionals should avoid editorial commentary or legal conclusions and instead stick to objective references to the contract language. If the seller is uncertain about the legal basis for termination, the licensed professional must direct the seller to consult an attorney rather than offering legal advice.

The note included on the form reminds users that this notice does not constitute an election of remedies and that the release of earnest money is governed by the contract itself. The licensed professional should explain to the seller that submitting this notice does not automatically resolve the question of who receives the earnest money. A separate release of earnest money form will likely be necessary, and disputes over the earnest money may need to be addressed through negotiation, mediation, or legal proceedings as outlined in the contract.

The final advisory directs all parties to consult an attorney before signing, as TREC rules prohibit license holders from giving legal advice. The licensed professional should reiterate this advisement to the seller and ensure the seller understands the consequences of terminating the contract. The signature blocks for the seller and buyer should be completed with the seller signing to authorize the termination notice and delivery being made to the buyer. The licensed professional should retain copies for transaction files and ensure that all parties, including the title company or escrow agent, receive copies of the executed notice in a timely manner to facilitate next steps in resolving the transaction.

Form 59-0: Notice to Purchaser of Special Taxing or Assessment District

This form, promulgated by the Texas Real Estate Commission (TREC), serves as a disclosure document that informs prospective purchasers when a property is located within a special taxing or assessment district. It is important to note at the outset that this form is not to be used for Public Improvement Districts (PIDs). Under Section 49.453 of the Texas Water Code, each district is required to make a notice form available to the public, either on the district's website or by another means. The Texas real estate licensed professional should always check with the district first to determine whether the district has its own promulgated form. If the district provides its own notice, that version should be used in place of this

TREC form. If not, the licensee should gather the necessary information directly from the district and use it to complete this form accurately.

At the top of the form, the licensee must enter the street address and city of the property being sold. This identifies the subject property covered by the disclosure.

In Paragraph 1, the licensee should insert the official name of the special district in which the property is located. This name must match exactly what the district uses in its public records to avoid confusion.

Paragraph 2 addresses the tax rate. The licensee must check only one box: either the box indicating the current rate of district property tax per $100 of assessed valuation, or the box indicating that the district has not yet imposed taxes, in which case the projected rate must be entered. This information should be obtained directly from the district.

Paragraph 3 covers assessments. Again, only one box should be checked. The licensee must indicate either the current rate of the district assessment per $100 of assessed valuation, the specific assessment amount on the property, or that the district has not yet imposed an assessment but has a projected rate or amount. The blanks should be filled in with the figures supplied by the district.

In Paragraph 4, the licensee must complete two subsections regarding bonds. Subsection A requires the total amounts of bonds approved by voters that are payable wholly or partly from property taxes or assessments, broken down by category: water, sewer, and drainage facilities; road facilities; parks and recreational facilities; and any other purpose, which must be specified. Subsection B requires the aggregate initial principal amounts of all such bonds issued, again broken down by the same categories. All figures should be confirmed with the district.

Paragraph 5 deals with standby fees. If the district has obtained approval from the Texas Commission on Environmental Quality to impose a standby fee, the licensee must enter the dollar amount. The paragraph also explains that unpaid standby fees become a personal obligation of the property owner at the time of imposition and create a lien on the property.

Paragraph 6 addresses location. The licensee should check only one box, if applicable, to indicate whether the district is located wholly or partly within the extraterritorial jurisdiction of a city, or wholly or partly within the corporate boundaries of a city. The name of the city must be entered in the appropriate blank.

Paragraph 7 concerns any strategic partnership agreement between the district and a municipality. If applicable, the licensee should check the box and enter the name of the city involved. This agreement may govern future annexation procedures.

In Paragraph 8, the licensee must check all applicable boxes to disclose the purpose of the district, including water, sewer, drainage, flood control, firefighting, road, parks and recreational, or other services that should be specified in the blank provided.

The form concludes with a notice advising the purchaser that the information disclosed is subject to change by the district at any time and that the purchaser should contact the district directly to verify current details. Both Seller and Buyer must sign the document to complete the disclosure process.

Form REI 7-6: Property Inspection Report

The Property Inspection Report Form (REI 7-6) is the standardized document promulgated by the Texas Real Estate Commission (TREC) that licensed real estate inspectors must use when performing a real estate inspection in Texas. The form serves as a written record of the inspector's visual survey and basic performance evaluation of a residential structure's systems and components at a specific point in time. Below is a summary of each section of the form and how the licensed real estate professional should approach completing it.

The Purpose of Inspection paragraph establishes the foundational understanding of what the inspection actually represents. The inspector should ensure that the client understands this is a visual survey only and reflects the property's general condition on the date of inspection. When delivering the report, the inspector should encourage the client to read the entire document carefully and offer to clarify any items or comments that are unclear. This sets the proper expectation regarding the limited scope of the inspection.

The Responsibility of the Inspector paragraph outlines what the inspector must and must not do under the TREC Standards of Practice (SOPs) found in 22 TAC 535.233. The inspector is required to use this specific form, inspect only components that are present, visible, and accessible, and mark each item as Inspected (I), Not Inspected (NI), Not Present (NP), or Deficient (D). When marking an item as Deficient, the inspector must explain the finding in the corresponding section of the report. The inspector should also remember they are not required to identify every potential hazard, operate decommissioned equipment, move furnishings, prioritize deficiencies, perform follow-up verification, or inspect optional systems unless agreed upon. Filling out this section accurately requires careful judgment to distinguish between minor cosmetic issues and conditions that materially affect performance or pose hazards.

The Responsibility of the Client paragraph clarifies that deficiencies noted in the report do not obligate any party to perform repairs. The inspector should communicate to the client that further evaluations from qualified service professionals may be necessary for items marked as Deficient, and that such evaluations should ideally occur before any contractual time limitations expire, such as the option period. The inspector should also note that subsequent evaluations may reveal additional deficiencies not visible during the original inspection.

The Report Limitations paragraph requires the inspector to make clear that the report is for the named client only and is based solely on observations made on the inspection date. The inspector must communicate that this is not a technically exhaustive inspection, not a code compliance inspection, and not a verification of manufacturer installation instructions. The inspector should not imply insurability or warrantability of any component. This paragraph protects both the inspector and the client by clearly defining the boundaries of the service performed.

The Notice Concerning Hazardous Conditions, Deficiencies, and Contractual Agreements paragraph addresses the reporting of conditions that may not have violated codes when the home was built but are now considered hazardous. The inspector must report these conditions as Deficient when reasonably identified, including issues such as missing GFCI or AFCI protection, ordinary glass where safety glass is now required, malfunctioning smoke or carbon monoxide alarms, improper baluster spacing, improperly installed appliances, defective safety devices, lack of electrical bonding and grounding, and lack of bonding on gas piping including CSST. The inspector should mark these items appropriately and explain each finding within the body of the report.

The final notice regarding Additional Information Provided by Inspector reminds the inspector that any contractual terms or attachments included with the form are not regulated by TREC. If the inspector includes an inspection agreement, addenda, or supplemental property information, they should advise the client to consult an attorney if any contractual term is unclear.

The body of the form covers Structural Systems, Electrical Systems, Heating, Ventilation and Air Conditioning Systems, Plumbing Systems, Appliances, and Optional Systems. For each item within these sections, the inspector must check the appropriate box (I, NI, NP, or D) and provide written explanations supporting any deficiency findings to ensure the report meets TREC's minimum requirements.

Form ERW 4-1: Notice Concerning Easements and Rights-of-Way

The Notice Concerning Easements and Rights-of-Way is a disclosure document promulgated by the Texas Real Estate Commission (TREC) for mandatory use by easement or right-of-way agents (ERW agents). The form serves as a formal notification to property owners that an ERW agent is acting on behalf of a third party seeking to acquire an easement or right-of-way for telecommunication, utility, railroad, or pipeline service. The purpose of the notice is to make sure the property owner understands the agency relationship, the implications of granting an easement, and their rights as a property owner before entering into any agreement to sell, buy, lease, or transfer an easement or right-of-way. Texas real estate licensed professionals acting as ERW agents must deliver this notice prior to negotiations or signing of any agreement.

The opening paragraph establishes the agency relationship and the purpose of the notice. It informs the property owner that the named ERW agent represents a third party (not the property owner) regarding the easement or right-of-way being negotiated. When completing this section, the licensed professional should make sure to clearly identify themselves as the agent and recognize that the disclosure must be provided before any agreement is reached. There is no blank to fill in within the body of this paragraph itself, but the licensee should review it carefully with the property owner and confirm that the property owner understands the agent does not represent their interests in the transaction. Timing of delivery matters; the licensee must present this notice early enough in the process to allow the property owner the opportunity to consider their options.

The next portion of the notice contains two bulleted disclosures that the licensee must bring to the property owner's attention. The first bullet alerts the property owner that the existence of easements or rights-of-way on the property may affect its value. The licensee should confirm that the property owner understands this potential financial impact, since an easement can permanently alter use, marketability, and resale value. The second bullet addresses eminent domain. If the third party represented by the ERW agent possesses the power of eminent domain, Section 21.0112 of the Texas Property Code requires additional notice be given to the property owner regarding their rights as a landowner. The licensee should determine whether the represented party holds eminent domain authority and, if so, deliver the supplemental Landowner's Bill of Rights notice as required by statute. This is a separate document from the TREC form, and failure to provide it when required can have legal consequences.

The following paragraph defines the nature of an easement or right-of-way agreement, describing it as a formal, legal agreement granting long-term use of the property. It also informs the property owner of their right to be represented by a real estate broker or attorney in any transaction involving an easement or right-of-way. The licensee should encourage the property owner to seek independent representation if they wish, and should never discourage the property owner from consulting legal counsel. This paragraph reinforces the boundaries of the ERW agent's representation and protects the consumer's right to obtain advice from a professional working solely on their behalf.

The final section of the form contains two blank fields that must be completed by the licensee. The first blank, "Name of Easement or Right-of-Way Agent," is where the licensed professional enters their full legal name as it appears on their TREC license. The second blank, "Name of Person Represented by Easement or Right-of-Way Agent," is where the licensee identifies the third-party client, which may be a utility company, pipeline operator, railroad, telecommunications provider, or another principal. Both names should be entered accurately and legibly, as this information establishes the formal record of the agency relationship.

In summary, this TREC form is a straightforward but important disclosure tool. The licensed professional should deliver it promptly, complete the identifying fields accurately, and confirm the property owner's understanding of the disclosures and their right to independent representation before any easement or right-of-way agreement is negotiated or signed.

Form OP-I: Texas Real Estate Consumer Notice Concerning Hazards or Deficiencies

The Texas Real Estate Consumer Notice Concerning Hazards or Deficiencies is an informational document developed and adopted by the Texas Real Estate Commission (TREC) to educate consumers - particularly buyers and sellers of residential property - about common household hazards that may cause injury, death, or property damage. Unlike many TREC documents, this notice is not a contract or a form that requires signatures, blanks to be filled in, or negotiated terms. Instead, it functions as a disclosure and educational tool that licensed real estate professionals should provide to or review with their clients to ensure consumers understand the safety considerations associated with home ownership and the inspection process. Below is a summary of each section of the notice and guidance for the Texas real estate licensed professional regarding its proper use.

The opening paragraph establishes the purpose of the notice by acknowledging that Texans suffer property damage and personal injury each year due to accidents in the home, and that many of these incidents are preventable through the identification and repair of hazardous conditions. Because this paragraph is purely informational, the licensee does not fill in any blanks. However, the licensee should make certain that the client reads and understands this introduction, as it sets the tone for why the notice exists. Agents should be prepared to explain that the notice was created to promote consumer awareness and safety, not to alarm buyers or sellers.

The next portion of the notice provides a bulleted list of examples of hazards that may exist in a home. These include malfunctioning or missing ground fault circuit interrupter (GFCI) devices, malfunctioning arc fault circuit interrupter (AFCI) devices, ordinary glass installed where safety glass is now required, malfunctioning or absent fire safety features such as smoke alarms and fire-rated doors, malfunctioning carbon monoxide alarms, excessive spacing between balusters, improperly installed appliances, defective or improperly installed safety devices, lack of electrical bonding and grounding, and the absence of bonding on gas piping, including corrugated stainless steel tubing (CSST). The licensee does not complete or modify this list. Instead, the agent should encourage clients to review each item carefully and consider these examples when deciding whether to obtain a professional inspection. Buyers, in particular, should be made aware that these conditions may not be obvious during a casual walkthrough of the property.

The following paragraph explains that TREC has adopted Standards of Practice requiring licensed inspectors to report these conditions as "Deficient" when conducting an inspection for a buyer or seller, provided the conditions can be reasonably determined. Again, no information is filled in by the licensee, but the agent should clarify to clients that licensed inspectors operate under specific guidelines established by TREC, and that any deficiencies noted in an inspection report reflect those standards.

The next paragraph clarifies that the listed conditions may not have violated the building codes or common practices that were in effect when the home was originally constructed, or that they may have been grandfathered because they predate current code requirements. The notice also explains that while TREC Standards of Practice do not require inspectors to perform a code compliance inspection, TREC has determined that the potential for injury or property loss from these hazards justifies issuing this notice. Real estate professionals should help clients understand that an older home may legally contain conditions that today would be considered deficient, and that the notice is intended to alert them to safety concerns regardless of legal compliance.

The final paragraph informs consumers that TREC contract forms include the buyer's right to have the home inspected and may include an option clause allowing the buyer to terminate the contract within a specified time. It also makes clear that neither the Standards of Practice nor TREC contract forms require a seller to repair any conditions revealed by an inspection. The decision to correct hazards or deficiencies remains with the parties to the contract. The licensee should emphasize that any repairs must be negotiated between buyer and seller as part of the transaction.

CN 1-5: Consumer Protection Notice

The Texas Real Estate Commission (TREC) Consumer Protection Notice is a disclosure document that serves as an informational resource for consumers engaging in real estate transactions in the state of Texas. Unlike contracts or agreements that require negotiation between parties, this notice is a standardized form designed to inform consumers about the regulatory body overseeing real estate professionals, the resources available for filing complaints, and the protections afforded to them under Texas law. Real estate licensed professionals are required to display or provide this notice to clients, but the form itself does not require any input or completion by the licensee. Below is a summary of each paragraph and guidance on how the licensed professional should approach the form's distribution and presentation.

The opening paragraph identifies TREC as the regulatory authority for real estate brokers, sales agents, real estate inspectors, easement and right-of-way agents, and timeshare interest providers. It directs consumers to the TREC website (www.trec.texas.gov) where they can verify the licensing status of any professional they intend to work with. Real estate licensed professionals should ensure this notice is prominently displayed in their offices and provided to clients at the appropriate time during a transaction. Since the form does not require completion, the licensee's responsibility is to make sure consumers have access to this information so they can independently verify credentials and learn about the agency that oversees the industry.

The second paragraph informs consumers of their right to file a complaint against a license holder and references the complaint form available on the TREC website. It also introduces the Real Estate Recovery Trust Account, which can be used to satisfy a civil court judgment against a broker, sales agent, or easement or right-of-way agent under certain conditions. The licensed professional does not fill in any information here, but should be prepared to answer general questions a client may have about how the complaint process works or the existence of the recovery trust account. While licensees should never discourage a client from contacting TREC, they should also be aware that this paragraph reinforces consumer rights and transparency in the profession.

The third paragraph addresses the requirement that real estate inspectors carry errors and omissions insurance to cover losses resulting from negligent or incompetent inspections. This paragraph applies specifically to inspectors rather than brokers or sales agents, but the notice is uniform across all license categories. A real estate licensed professional providing this notice should understand that this provision exists to protect consumers from financial losses tied to inspection services and may want to remind buyers to confirm an inspector's insurance status before retaining their services.

The fourth paragraph contains a "Please Note" advisory clarifying that inspectors may limit their liability through provisions contained in their contract or inspection agreement with the client. Consumers are advised to read any such contract carefully and to consult an attorney if they do not understand the terms. The licensed professional should not provide legal interpretations of inspection contracts but should encourage clients to thoroughly review any inspection agreement and seek legal counsel when necessary. This paragraph is purely informational and does not require licensee input.

The closing paragraph provides TREC's contact information for consumers who have questions or issues about license holder activities, the complaint process, or the recovery trust account. The mailing address is P.O. Box 12188, Austin, Texas 78711-2188, and the telephone number is (512) 936-3000. Real estate licensed professionals should never obscure or alter this contact information. Instead, they should make certain it is clearly visible and accessible to clients at any point during the engagement.

In conclusion, the TREC Consumer Protection Notice is a non-negotiable, informational disclosure that does not require any data entry or signature from the real estate licensed professional or the consumer. The licensee's role is to ensure that the notice is properly displayed and that clients have access to its contents, supporting transparency and consumer awareness throughout the real estate transaction process.

Chapter 7: Snapshot Review

The following review summarizes the key rules and concepts from Chapter 7.

Information About Brokerage Services (IABS 1-2)

- IABS 1-2 (effective November 3, 2025) is a required consumer disclosure provided to all prospective buyers, tenants, sellers, and landlords; it creates no contractual obligation and is not a representation agreement
- A license holder must provide IABS 1-2 before showing residential property to a buyer and before a written representation agreement is signed
- Written buyer representation agreements are now required before showing residential property or presenting an offer on behalf of a buyer; IABS 1-2 explains this requirement explicitly
- A license holder may show property to an unrepresented buyer under a limited written agreement that is non-exclusive and no longer than 14 days
- Three forms of representation are described: agent for owner, agent for buyer/tenant, and intermediary
- An intermediary must treat all parties impartially; with written consent, the intermediary may appoint separate associated license holders to each party
- The License Holder Contact Information section must be completed accurately; inaccurate information creates regulatory and civil liability
- All broker and agent fees are negotiable and not set by law

Amendment to Contract (Form 39-11)

- No term of a promulgated contract can be changed after execution except through a signed written amendment agreed to by both parties; verbal agreements are not binding
- Amendments cover changes to sales price (all three lines), additional repairs, closing date extensions, option period extensions, financing deadline changes, seller contributions to buyer expenses, and other modifications
- The 'Other Modifications' section of the amendment follows the same rules as Paragraph 11 of the main contract: only informational items may be entered; legal modifications must be drafted by a party or their attorney
- Amendments should be prepared and executed before deadlines pass; a missed deadline without an amendment may leave a party without contract protection

Non-Realty Items Addendum (Form 57-0)

- Form 57-0 is approved (not promulgated) for voluntary use when the parties agree to transfer personal property not already covered by Paragraphs 2B or 2C of the main contract
- Each item must be specifically described with model numbers, serial numbers, location, and other identifying information; vague descriptions create disputes
- Paragraph B: Seller warrants ownership of the personal property free and clear of all encumbrances
- Paragraph C: Seller does NOT warrant the condition or future performance of the personal property; the buyer accepts it as-is
- A Bill of Sale prepared by an attorney may be preferable when significant or high-value personal property is involved

HOA Addendum and Subdivision Information (Forms 36-11 and 37-5)

- Form 36-11 (HOA Addendum, effective November 7, 2022) is for properties with mandatory HOA membership; NOT for condominiums (which use Form 32-5)
- Paragraph A of Form 36-11: Subdivision Information (restrictions, bylaws, rules, resale certificate) is delivered by seller or obtained by buyer; buyer may terminate within 3 days of receipt or at any time before closing if information is not received
- Paragraph B: Seller pays all Association fees associated with the transfer except the amount negotiated in Paragraph C; regular periodic dues are prorated under Paragraph 13, not paid here
- Paragraph C: Buyer pays a specified capped dollar amount; seller pays excess; a specific dollar amount must be entered
- Paragraph D: Authorization for Association to release information; identifies who pays title company for HOA-related information requests
- Form 37-5 (Subdivision Information/Resale Certificate) is completed by the Association's board or managing agent, not the license holder or seller
- Form 37-5 covers 13 items (A-M): right of first refusal, regular assessment, special assessments, amounts owed, capital expenditure reserves, judgments, pending suits, known violations, government notices, transfer fees, managing agent, and foreclosure authority

Addendum for Sale of Other Property by Buyer (Form 10-6)

- Form 10-6 is used when the buyer cannot close on the new property unless proceeds from the sale of the buyer's existing property are received by a specified date (the Contingency)
- Paragraph A: If the Contingency is not satisfied or waived by the deadline, the contract terminates automatically and earnest money is refunded to the buyer
- Paragraph B: If the seller receives another written offer, seller notifies buyer and buyer must waive the Contingency by a specified deadline (typically 1 day) or the contract terminates
- Paragraph C: To waive the Contingency, the buyer must BOTH notify the seller in writing AND deposit additional earnest money; both steps are required
- Paragraph D: If buyer waives the Contingency but still cannot close solely because the buyer's property did not fund, and buyer notifies seller before the Closing Date, the buyer is not in default
- Time is of the essence for all provisions of Form 10-6

Addendum for Back-Up Contract (Form 11-9)

- Form 11-9 (updated July 1, 2026) allows a buyer to be in a secondary contract position on a property already under contract with another buyer
- The back-up contract is subordinate to the first contract and does not obligate the seller to sell to the back-up buyer while the first contract is active
- Earnest money and option fee timing requirements in Form 11-9 now mirror Paragraph 5 of the main contract; time is of the essence for delivery
- When the first contract terminates, the back-up contract automatically becomes the primary contract on that date; all deadlines begin running from that date
- The seller must notify the back-up buyer promptly when the first contract terminates
- If the first contract closes, the back-up contract terminates automatically

Short Sale Addendum (Form 45-2)

- Form 45-2 (effective April 1, 2021) is used when the sales price is insufficient to pay all existing liens in full and the lender(s) must agree to accept less than the full amount owed

- The entire transaction is contingent on noteholder approval of the short sale; the seller must diligently pursue all required approvals
- If approvals are not obtained or contain unacceptable conditions, either party may terminate and the earnest money is refunded to the buyer
- Short sales involve potential income tax consequences for the seller from forgiven debt and require advice from attorneys and tax professionals
- License holders should not attempt to advise buyers or sellers on the tax or legal consequences of a short sale; refer to appropriate professionals

Addendum for Reservation of Oil, Gas and Other Minerals (Form 44-3)

- Form 44-3 (effective February 1, 2023) is used whenever a seller reserves all or part of the mineral estate rather than conveying it with the surface
- Applies to any TREC-promulgated contract form, not only Farm and Ranch transactions
- Paragraph A: Identifies what mineral interests are being reserved; Paragraph B: Surface use rights; Paragraph C: Seller must provide copies of existing mineral leases
- All parties must consult a licensed attorney before proceeding with any mineral rights reservation; license holders may not advise on mineral law

Coastal Area Addenda (Forms 33-2 and 34-4)

- Form 33-2 (Addendum for Coastal Area Property) is required for any property that adjoins tidally influenced submerged lands of the state, including bays, estuaries, and Gulf shoreline properties
- Form 34-4 (Addendum for Property Located Seaward of the Gulf Intracoastal Waterway) is required for properties on barrier islands and coastal strips between the Gulf Intracoastal Waterway and the Gulf of Mexico
- Form 33-2 addresses the shifting nature of tidal boundaries and public beach access rights; Form 34-4 addresses the greater environmental and storm-related risks of properties fully exposed to the Gulf
- A property may require both addenda if it is on tidally influenced waters AND seaward of the Gulf Intracoastal Waterway; attach both in that case
- License holders working in coastal markets should be familiar with the geography of the Gulf Intracoastal Waterway and consult the title company when form selection is uncertain

Addendum Concerning Right to Terminate Due to Lender's Appraisal (Form 49-1)

- Form 49-1 modifies the Third Party Financing Addendum and is used only with conventional financing; NOT appropriate for FHA-insured or VA-guaranteed loans
- Only ONE of three boxes may be checked; selecting more than one creates ambiguity and may render the addendum unenforceable
- Full Waiver: buyer surrenders the right to terminate under Paragraph 2B of the TPF Addendum if the appraisal falls short; if the lender reduces the loan, the cash portion of the Sales Price increases by the reduction amount
- Partial Waiver: buyer waives termination rights only if the appraised value equals or exceeds a specific dollar amount written in the blank; otherwise the cash portion increases by any loan reduction
- Additional Right to Terminate: supplements existing rights under Paragraph 2B; requires entry of (1) the number of days after the Effective Date the buyer may exercise this right, and (2) the

minimum acceptable appraised value; buyer must deliver a copy of the appraisal to the seller within the stated period to terminate
- The addendum must be signed by all parties and distributed to the buyer, seller, lender, and title company

Addendum Containing Notice of Obligation to Pay Improvement District Assessment (Form 53-0)

- Used when a property lies within a public improvement district (PID) created under Subchapter A, Chapter 372, or Chapter 382 of the Texas Local Government Code
- The licensee must accurately identify the municipality or county levying the assessment and the District by its full legal name
- The licensee must indicate which enabling statute (Chapter 372 or Chapter 382) created the District; this should be confirmed with the municipality, developer, or title company, not guessed
- The all-capitalized notice paragraph is statutorily mandated and must not be altered; it informs the buyer that the assessment may be paid in full or in annual installments and that installment amounts may fluctuate
- Buyers often confuse PID assessments with property taxes or HOA dues; the licensee should clearly explain the distinction
- Failure to pay assessments may result in penalties, interest, a lien, or foreclosure; both parties must sign the addendum

Addendum for Authorizing Hydrostatic Testing (Form 48-1)

- Allows a buyer, with the seller's written permission, to engage a licensed plumber to conduct a hydrostatic plumbing test on the property at the buyer's expense
- The form includes an advisory recommending consultation with a licensed plumber about the scope and risks of testing before signing; older or compromised plumbing may be damaged by the test
- Paragraph A: Seller authorizes the test, performed by a licensed plumber at buyer's expense
- Paragraph B presents three mutually exclusive risk-allocation options; only one may be selected:
    - Option (1): Liability for damages on the seller (more favorable to buyer)
    - Option (2): Liability on the buyer (more favorable to seller; common with older properties)
    - Option (3): Liability on the buyer up to a specified dollar cap, with seller responsible above that amount
- Both buyer and seller must sign for the addendum to be enforceable

Addendum for Property in a Propane Gas System Service Area (Form 47-0)

- Promulgated under Section 141.010 of the Texas Utilities Code; used when a property lies within a designated propane gas system service area
- Notifies the buyer of potential special charges or fees associated with receiving propane service and possible waiting periods for line or facility construction
- The buyer's acknowledgment confirms receipt of the notice at or before signing the contract or at closing; timing of delivery is statutorily required
- A copy of the notice the distribution system retailer recorded in the real property records must be physically attached to the addendum; without it, the addendum is incomplete
- The seller may obtain the recorded notice from the county clerk's office or the distribution system retailer
- Both buyer and seller must sign

Addendum for Section 1031 Exchange (Form 60-0)

- Notifies the opposing party of the intent to structure the transaction as a like-kind exchange under Section 1031 of the Internal Revenue Code; the form does NOT itself create or execute the exchange
- The actual exchange must be coordinated through a qualified intermediary and structured in compliance with IRS regulations; a tax professional or attorney specializing in 1031 exchanges should be involved
- Paragraph A: Only ONE box (Seller or Buyer) is marked, identifying the exchanging party; in rare cases both parties exchange and two addenda may be appropriate
- Paragraph B: Both parties agree to reasonably cooperate with two limitations -- the non-exchanging party will not incur additional expense or liability, and the closing will not be delayed due to the exchange
- All exchange-related costs (qualified intermediary, exchange documentation, contract assignment) are borne by the exchanging party
- The licensee must not provide tax or legal advice on whether the transaction qualifies under Section 1031

Addendum Regarding Fixture Leases (Form 52-1)

- Used when the property contains fixtures the seller leases rather than owns, such as solar panels, propane tanks, water softeners, or security systems
- Paragraph A: Identifies which fixtures are leased; checkboxes are provided for solar panels, propane tanks, water softeners, and security systems, plus a blank for other leased fixtures
- Subparagraph A(1): Identifies which leases the buyer will assume; requires a dollar amount for the maximum the buyer will pay toward assumption or assignment costs, with seller responsible for the remainder
- Subparagraph A(2): Indicates whether the seller "will" or "will not" remove leased fixtures the buyer is not assuming; if removed, the seller must repair any resulting damage; remaining leased fixtures continue subject to the lessor's rights
- Paragraph B: Confirms whether the buyer has received copies of the leases (Box 1), or will receive them within 5 days with a 7-day termination right after receipt (Box 2), or discloses oral leases (Box 3)
- Paragraph C: At closing there will be no liens or security interests against the leased fixtures other than those tied to assumed leases

Addendum Regarding Residential Leases (Form 51-1)

- Used when the property is currently leased or may be subject to a lease at closing
- "Residential Lease" is defined broadly to include any lease, addendum, amendment, or move-in condition form
- After the effective date, the seller may not execute a new lease or amend an existing one without the buyer's written consent
- Paragraph A and Paragraph B are mutually exclusive; only one box may be checked
- Paragraph A: Termination of Residential Leases -- all leases must be terminated by closing and possession delivered with no tenant; the addendum itself does NOT terminate leases; seller must take separate legal steps and should consult an attorney
- Paragraph B: Assignment and Assumption of Residential Leases -- seller assigns and buyer assumes the leases at closing

- B(1): Delivery of leases (already received, to be received within 3 days with a buyer termination right, or oral leases described)
- B(2): Seller transfers security deposits to buyer at closing under §92.102 Texas Property Code; buyer delivers signed acknowledgment to each tenant
- B(3): Seller represents that each lease is in full force and effect, no tenant in default, no prepaid rent, no offsets, no claims, no side agreements
- B(4): Continuing duty to notify the buyer of any changes; seller has 7 days to cure, then buyer has 5 days to terminate with refund of earnest money

Landlord's Floodplain and Flood Notice (Form 54-1)

- TREC-approved form that must accompany a residential lease in Texas; NOT required when using a TREC Temporary Residential Lease
- Paragraph A: Landlord checks "is" or "is not" regarding location in a 100-year floodplain; if neither box is checked, the tenant should assume the property IS in a 100-year floodplain
- Tenants are directed to FEMA flood maps (free, searchable by address) and informed that most tenant insurance policies do not cover flood damage
- Paragraph B: Landlord checks "is" or "is not" aware of flooding in the dwelling within the last 5 years; failing to disclose known flooding can expose the landlord to legal consequences
- Paragraph C: Pre-printed legal definitions of "100-year floodplain," "flooding," and "dwelling"; no licensee input required, but the licensee should be prepared to explain the terms
- Both landlord and tenant sign; the notice should be attached to the lease and retained in the file

Notice of Buyer's Termination of Contract (Form 38-8)

- Allows a buyer to formally notify a seller that the buyer is exercising a right to terminate; used after the contract has been executed
- Eight enumerated termination bases:
    - (1) Unrestricted right under Paragraph 5 (option period)
    - (2) Failure to obtain Buyer Approval under TPF Addendum (lender's written denial statement must be delivered to seller)
    - (3) Failure to obtain Property Approval under TPF Addendum (lender's written statement must be delivered)
    - (4) Termination under Paragraph A of the HOA Addendum
    - (5) Termination under Paragraph 7B(2) related to the Seller's Disclosure Notice
    - (6) Termination under Paragraph (3) of the Lender's Appraisal Addendum (a copy of the appraisal must be delivered)
    - (7) Termination under Paragraph 6.D. of the standard contract or 6.C. of the Residential Condominium Contract for uncured title objections
    - (8) Other -- specify the paragraph number from the contract or addendum
- The notice does NOT constitute an election of remedies; release of earnest money is governed separately by the contract
- A separate Release of Earnest Money form is generally needed to release the funds; the form reminds the parties to consult an attorney

Notice of Seller's Termination of Contract (Form 50-0)

- Allows a seller to formally notify a buyer that the seller is terminating the contract

- Reason (1): Buyer failed to deliver earnest money within the time required under Paragraph 5; timing matters because once the buyer delivers the earnest money, even late, the right to terminate may be lost
- Reason (2): Any other contractual basis for termination, with the specific paragraph number of the contract or addendum identified clearly
- Licensees must avoid editorial commentary or legal conclusions; if the seller is uncertain about the basis, the seller must consult an attorney
- The notice does NOT constitute an election of remedies; release of earnest money is governed by the contract
- Copies should be provided to the buyer, the title company or escrow agent, and retained in the transaction file

Notice to Purchaser of Special Taxing or Assessment District (Form 59-0)

- Disclosure for properties located within a special taxing or assessment district; NOT used for Public Improvement Districts (PIDs use Form 53-0)
- Under Section 49.453 of the Texas Water Code, each district must make a notice form available; if the district provides its own notice form, that version should be used in place of Form 59-0
- Paragraph 1: Official name of the special district
- Paragraph 2: District tax rate per $100 assessed valuation, or projected rate if not yet imposed (only one box checked)
- Paragraph 3: Assessment rate or amount, or projected figures if not yet imposed (only one box checked)
- Paragraph 4: Voter-approved bonds and bonds issued, broken down by category (water/sewer/drainage, roads, parks, other)
- Paragraph 5: Standby fee amount if approved by TCEQ; unpaid standby fees become a personal obligation and a lien on the property
- Paragraph 6: District location relative to a city's ETJ or corporate boundaries
- Paragraph 7: Strategic partnership agreement with a municipality, if applicable
- Paragraph 8: Purpose of the district (water, sewer, drainage, flood control, firefighting, road, parks, other)
- All figures must be confirmed directly with the district; both seller and buyer sign

Property Inspection Report (Form REI 7-6)

- The standardized report form licensed real estate inspectors must use under TREC Standards of Practice (22 TAC 535.233)
- A visual survey only, reflecting the property's general condition on the date of inspection -- not technically exhaustive, not a code compliance inspection, not a verification of manufacturer instructions
- Items are marked Inspected (I), Not Inspected (NI), Not Present (NP), or Deficient (D); deficiencies must be explained in writing
- Inspectors are not required to identify every potential hazard, operate decommissioned equipment, move furnishings, prioritize deficiencies, or perform follow-up verification
- Deficiencies do not obligate any party to perform repairs; further evaluations by qualified service professionals may be needed before contract time limitations expire (such as the option period)
- Hazardous conditions that may not have violated codes when built but are now considered hazardous must still be reported as Deficient (missing GFCI/AFCI protection, ordinary glass where safety glass is required, malfunctioning smoke or CO alarms, improper baluster spacing, defective safety devices, lack of bonding/grounding, lack of CSST bonding)

- The body of the form covers Structural, Electrical, HVAC, Plumbing, Appliances, and Optional Systems

Notice Concerning Easements and Rights-of-Way (Form ERW 4-1)

- Disclosure required for mandatory use by easement or right-of-way (ERW) agents; notifies a property owner that the agent represents a third party (utility, pipeline, railroad, telecommunications), not the property owner
- Must be delivered before negotiations or signing of any agreement
- Two bulleted disclosures: easements may affect property value, and if the represented party has the power of eminent domain, Section 21.0112 of the Texas Property Code requires an additional Landowner's Bill of Rights notice
- The property owner has the right to be represented by a real estate broker or attorney; the licensee must not discourage independent counsel
- Two blanks must be completed: "Name of Easement or Right-of-Way Agent" (the licensee's full legal name) and "Name of Person Represented by Easement or Right-of-Way Agent" (the third-party principal)

Texas Real Estate Consumer Notice Concerning Hazards or Deficiencies (Form OP-I)

- Informational document, not a contract; no signatures, blanks, or negotiated terms required
- Educates consumers about common household hazards: missing GFCI/AFCI devices, ordinary glass where safety glass is required, missing or malfunctioning smoke alarms and fire-rated doors, malfunctioning carbon monoxide alarms, excessive baluster spacing, improperly installed appliances, defective safety devices, lack of electrical bonding and grounding, lack of CSST bonding
- Explains that TREC Standards of Practice require licensed inspectors to report these conditions as Deficient when reasonably determined
- Clarifies that the listed conditions may not have violated codes when the home was built or may have been grandfathered, but TREC has determined the safety risks justify the notice
- Reminds consumers that TREC contract forms include the right to inspection and option period termination, but no TREC form requires a seller to repair revealed conditions; repairs are negotiated between the parties

Consumer Protection Notice (Form CN 1-5)

- Standardized informational disclosure that does not require licensee or consumer input or signatures; must be displayed or provided
- Identifies TREC as the regulatory authority for brokers, sales agents, real estate inspectors, ERW agents, and timeshare interest providers; directs consumers to www.trec.texas.gov to verify licensing status
- Informs consumers of the right to file a complaint and references the Real Estate Recovery Trust Account, which can satisfy a civil court judgment against a broker, sales agent, or ERW agent under certain conditions
- Notes the requirement that real estate inspectors carry errors and omissions insurance to cover losses from negligent or incompetent inspections
- Advises consumers that inspectors may limit liability through inspection contracts; consumers should read the contract carefully and consult an attorney if needed
- Provides TREC's contact information: P.O. Box 12188, Austin, Texas 78711-2188; (512) 936-3000; this information may not be obscured or altered

Chapter 7 Quiz: Promulgated Addenda, Notices, and Other Forms

1. What type of written agreement does Texas law require a license holder to enter into before showing residential property to an unrepresented buyer?

a. A full buyer representation agreement that establishes the broker as the buyer's exclusive agent for all future transactions

b. A Non-Realty Items Addendum that identifies what personal property the buyer may examine during the showing

c. A written agreement that is non-exclusive and is limited to no more than 14 days

d. An IABS acknowledgment form signed by the buyer confirming receipt of the brokerage services disclosure

2. The IABS form describes three types of representation a Texas license holder may provide. Which of the following is one of those three types?

a. Agent for the owner, in which the broker represents the seller or landlord through a written listing or property management agreement

b. Neutral facilitator, in which the broker assists both parties without representing either party to the transaction

c. Transaction coordinator, in which the broker manages paperwork on behalf of both parties without disclosing any agency relationship

d. Designated dual agent, in which two sales agents from the same brokerage office each independently represent a different principal

3. A buyer and a seller verbally agree to extend the closing date by two weeks. What is the legal status of that verbal agreement?

a. It is binding as long as both parties confirm the extension by text or email within 24 hours of the conversation

b. It is binding because both parties have demonstrated mutual assent to the change, even without a written document

c. It is binding only if the escrow agent receives written notification of the verbal extension within three business days

d. It is not binding because only a signed written amendment agreed to by both parties can modify a promulgated contract

4. Under the Non-Realty Items Addendum (Form 57-0), what warranty does the seller make in Paragraph B?

a. The seller warrants that all personal property items listed in the addendum are in good working order as of the date the contract is signed

b. The seller warrants that the seller owns the personal property free and clear of all encumbrances, liens, and security interests

c. The seller warrants that the listed personal property will remain in working condition through the date of closing and funding

d. The seller warrants that the market value of the personal property listed equals the consideration stated in Paragraph A of the addendum

5. The Non-Realty Items Addendum (Form 57-0) is described as approved rather than promulgated by TREC. What is the practical significance of this distinction?

a. Approved means TREC has reviewed the form and finds it acceptable for use, but its use is not mandatory; a Bill of Sale prepared by an attorney may serve as an alternative

b. Approved means the form was prepared by an individual attorney rather than the Broker-Lawyer Committee and therefore may not be used in all transaction types

c. Approved means the form is required only in transactions that involve the transfer of personal property with a total value exceeding $10,000

d. Approved means the form is mandatory whenever any personal property is transferred as part of a real estate sale but may not be altered or supplemented by the parties

6. Form 37-5, the Subdivision Information Including Resale Certificate, is completed by which party?

a. The listing agent, because the listing agent has direct knowledge of the subdivision's rules and the association's current financial condition

b. The buyer's agent, to ensure the information provided in the certificate reflects an independent and unbiased perspective

c. The seller, who is required under the Texas Property Code to personally certify the accuracy of all information disclosed in the certificate

d. The association's board of directors or managing agent, not the license holder or the seller

7. Under the HOA Addendum (Form 36-11), what is the buyer's right to terminate the contract after receiving Subdivision Information from the seller?

a. The buyer may terminate at any time within 30 days after receiving the Subdivision Information, as long as written notice is delivered to the seller

b. The buyer may terminate at any time before closing, regardless of when the Subdivision Information was received from the seller

c. The buyer may terminate within three days after receiving the Subdivision Information, or before closing, whichever occurs first

d. The buyer may terminate only if the Subdivision Information reveals unpaid special assessments that are attributable to the seller

8. Under the Addendum for Sale of Other Property by Buyer (Form 10-6), if the seller receives another written offer while the contingency is in place, what must the seller do?

a. The seller must reject the new offer because the property is already under contract and the contingency period has not expired

b. The seller must notify the buyer of the accepted offer and simultaneously notify the buyer that the seller requires the buyer to waive the contingency

c. The seller must wait until the contingency deadline has passed before accepting or notifying the first buyer of any other offer received

d. The seller must immediately terminate the contract with the first buyer and proceed with the new offer

9. Under Paragraph C of the Addendum for Sale of Other Property by Buyer (Form 10-6), what two actions must the buyer take simultaneously in order to validly waive the contingency?

a. The buyer must notify the seller in writing of the waiver and must deposit a stated amount of additional earnest money with the escrow agent

b. The buyer must deliver a written lender pre-approval letter to the seller and must sign a general waiver of all contingencies in the contract

c. The buyer must notify the escrow agent in writing of the waiver and must deposit the full down payment amount directly with the title company

d. The buyer must provide written evidence that the sale of the buyer's current home is under contract and must increase the original offer price by a stated amount

10. Under the Addendum for Back-Up Contract (Form 11-9), on what date does the back-up contract automatically move into the primary contract position?

a. On the closing date specified in the first buyer's contract, if the first contract has not closed by that date

b. On the date the back-up contract's earnest money and option fee are both delivered to the escrow agent

c. On the date the seller sends written notice to the back-up buyer that the seller wishes to proceed with the back-up offer

d. On the date the first contract terminates, with all deadlines in the back-up contract running from that date forward

11. Under the Short Sale Addendum (Form 45-2), on what basis does the addendum make the entire transaction contingent?

a. On the buyer's receipt of a satisfactory home inspection and a lender appraisal at or above the contract sales price

b. On the buyer's ability to obtain full financing approval from a lender within the timeframe specified in the addendum

c. On the noteholder's approval of a sale at a price that is insufficient to pay off all existing liens in full

d. On the seller's written agreement to pay all closing costs from any proceeds that remain after the existing lien is satisfied

12. The Addendum for Reservation of Oil, Gas and Other Minerals (Form 44-3) is listed in Paragraph 22 of Form 20-19. What does this tell a license holder about the form's appropriate use?

a. It tells the license holder that Form 44-3 may be used only in transactions involving rural property or property located in a county where active mineral production occurs

b. It tells the license holder that Form 44-3 applies to any TREC-promulgated contract form, not only to the Farm and Ranch Contract

c. It tells the license holder that Form 44-3 must be attached whenever an existing mineral lease currently affects any property being sold in Texas

d. It tells the license holder that Form 44-3 is required whenever a buyer wishes to include mineral rights as part of the purchase along with the surface estate

13. Form 34-4, the Addendum for Property Located Seaward of the Gulf Intracoastal Waterway, applies to which category of Texas coastal property?

a. Any Texas property whose boundary adjoins or shares a common boundary with the tidally influenced submerged lands of the state

b. Any Texas property located within 1,000 feet of the mean high tide line along the Gulf Coast or along an inland bay

c. Any Texas property that was constructed on a barrier island at any point within the past 50 years

d. Properties located on the Gulf side of the Gulf Intracoastal Waterway, such as those on Padre Island and Galveston Island

14. Form 33-2, the Addendum for Coastal Area Property, is required when a property satisfies which geographic condition?

a. The property's boundary adjoins and shares a common boundary with the tidally influenced submerged lands of the state of Texas

b. The property is located entirely seaward of the Gulf Intracoastal Waterway on a barrier island or coastal strip

c. The property is situated within the 100-year floodplain as designated by FEMA along the Texas Gulf Coast shoreline

d. The property falls within a designated coastal management zone that is subject to the Dune Protection Act

15. When a buyer terminates a contract and provides a copy of an adverse environmental report to the seller under Form 28-2, what ongoing obligation does the seller then carry?

a. The seller must remediate any conditions identified in the report before the property may be relisted for sale

b. The seller is released from all future disclosure obligations because the report is now part of the publicly available property record

c. The seller must disclose the contents of the report to any subsequent buyer, because the seller now has actual knowledge of the condition

d. The seller must hire a qualified environmental inspector to independently verify the accuracy of the buyer's report before relisting

16. Under what geographic circumstance would a property require both Form 33-2 and Form 34-4 to be attached to the contract?

a. When a property is located in a county that has been designated both a coastal erosion zone and a hurricane evacuation zone by the state

b. When a property borders tidally influenced waters and is also located seaward of the Gulf Intracoastal Waterway

c. When a property spans the full width of a barrier island, with frontage on both the bay side and the Gulf side

d. When a property's legal description straddles the boundary line of the Gulf Intracoastal Waterway itself

17. When a license holder uses the Amendment to Contract (Form 39-11) to extend the closing date, which type of entry in the closing date blank is prohibited?

a. A phrase such as "at lender's discretion," which is imprecise and creates a legal consequence the license holder may not impose

b. Any date that falls more than 90 days beyond the original closing date that was stated in the purchase contract

c. Any date that falls on a Saturday, Sunday, or legal holiday, because real estate closings may not occur on those days under Texas law

d. Any date that extends the closing period beyond the expiration date of the buyer's current earnest money deposit agreement

---

CHAPTER 8
OTHER REAL ESTATE MATTERS

Chapter Overview

This chapter covers the legal, ethical, and regulatory framework that surrounds real estate practice beyond the mechanics of completing a contract. It begins with the purpose of the Texas Real Estate Commission and the three elements of fraud that every license holder must understand and avoid. It then examines broker compensation in the current environment, where the landscape has changed significantly following industry-wide settlement agreements and new Texas law, and the antitrust principles that govern how brokers may and may not discuss fees. The chapter then provides a thorough review of the federal Fair Housing Act, its history, its current protected classes, its prohibited practices, and the penalties that violations carry. The final sections examine the body of federal and state disclosure laws that intersect with real estate practice, including the Foreign Investment in Real Property Tax Act, the Interstate Land Sales Full Disclosure Act, Megan's Law and the sex offender registry, the Environmental Protection Agency and its statutory authority, and the national standards on occupancy that govern how housing providers must treat families with children.

Learning Objectives

Upon completing Chapter 8, the student will be able to:

1. Explain the primary purpose of the Texas Real Estate Commission and describe the three elements of fraud, using the RID acronym, with examples of each element in a real estate context.
2. Describe how broker compensation is structured and negotiated in 2026, including the role of written representation agreements, the impact of recent industry changes on how buyer agent compensation is disclosed and paid, and the antitrust prohibitions that apply to any discussion of commission rates among competing brokers.
3. Trace the history of the federal Fair Housing Act from 1866 to the present, identify all current federally protected classes, and list the categories of conduct the Act prohibits.
4. State the current civil penalty amounts for Fair Housing Act violations adjudicated before a HUD Administrative Law Judge, and describe the filing deadlines and remedies available to a person who has experienced housing discrimination.
5. Describe the disclosure and compliance obligations created by the Foreign Investment in Real Property Tax Act, the Interstate Land Sales Full Disclosure Act, and Megan's Law as they apply to Texas real estate practice.
6. Explain the role of the Environmental Protection Agency, CERCLA, and the Clean Water Act in real estate practice, and describe the occupancy standards established by the Keating Memorandum and their relationship to the Fair Housing Act's familial status protections.

Contents

- The Federal Fair Housing Act
- Fair Housing Violations and Penalties
- TREC Canons on Discriminatory Practices
- Federal Disclosure Laws Affecting Real Estate
- Environmental Laws and Real Estate
- Occupancy Standards and Fair Housing

TREC and the Purpose of Real Estate Regulation

The Texas Real Estate Commission exists for one primary purpose: to protect the public from real estate license holders who fail to follow the Texas Real Estate License Act or the rules of the Commission. That purpose shapes everything about how the Commission operates, from the forms it promulgates to the disciplinary actions it pursues against licensees who cause harm to consumers.

Using TREC's promulgated forms correctly is one of the most practical ways a license holder demonstrates competence and protects their clients. The forms are designed to require disclosure of all material information, to structure the parties' obligations clearly, and to close transactions in a way that minimizes the risk of misrepresentation. License holders who take shortcuts in completing forms, who fail to attach required addenda, or who write into contracts provisions that go beyond the scope of factual disclosure risk consequences that range from disciplinary action to civil liability to criminal prosecution when the conduct rises to the level of fraud.

The most common way a license holder puts their future in jeopardy is by failing to disclose an agency relationship or a negative property condition properly. Another frequent problem is a license holder who believes their own judgment supersedes the guidance of their designated broker. A wise license holder always asks the broker to review significant contract entries and consults the broker before any novel or unusual transaction term is used. The broker has experience, carries responsibility for the conduct of the sponsored agents, and can identify problems that an individual sales agent might miss.

Fraud: The Three Elements

Fraud in real estate is intentional misrepresentation, and it is treated with the full seriousness of a criminal offense. While most license holder mistakes are the result of carelessness or lack of knowledge rather than bad intent, deliberate deception can result in loss of license, civil damages, and imprisonment. Understanding the three elements of fraud is essential both for recognizing when fraud might be alleged and for conducting every transaction in a way that avoids even the appearance of deception.

The three elements of fraud can be remembered with the acronym RID: Reliance, Intent, and Damage. All three elements must be present for a claim of fraud to succeed. When examining any potential fraud allegation, the question is whether the person who relied on the statement had the right to do so, whether the person who made the statement intended to deceive, and whether actual harm resulted.

Reliance

Reliance asks whether the consumer had the right to rely on the representation that was made. Not every statement in a real estate context is actionable. Consider the difference between two statements. A license holder who says 'Everyone who buys through me ends up being happy with their investment' has made a general opinion statement that no reasonable person would treat as a verifiable fact. It is not actionable because no reasonable consumer would rely on a vague, positive generalization as the basis for a financial decision. Contrast that with a license holder who says 'The fence line is the property line.' That statement is specific, factual, relates directly to the transaction, and comes from a person with professional expertise in real estate. A buyer has every reason to rely on it. When a professional makes a specific, material statement in the context of their expertise, the listener has the right to rely on it, and reliance is established.

Intent

Intent is the element that distinguishes fraud from mere misrepresentation. Many real estate mistakes are made without any deceptive purpose: a license holder passes along incorrect information because they received incorrect information, or fails to discover a material defect because it was not apparent. These may still be actionable as negligence or innocent misrepresentation, but they are not fraud. Fraud requires that the person making the representation knew the statement was false or knew that the truth would harm the other party, and proceeded anyway. The only reason a person would knowingly make a false statement in a real estate transaction is to take advantage of the other party, to get a transaction to close that would not close if the truth were told, or to gain something of value through deception. All of these constitute fraud.

Damage

Damage is the third element and refers to an actual loss of something of value. In most fraud cases, damage takes the form of financial loss: a buyer who pays too much for a property because they were deceived about its condition, a seller who accepts too little because the licensee misrepresented the market, or a party who incurs costs as a result of a deception. Damage can also include non-financial harm such as mental anguish, emotional distress, and humiliation, which courts have recognized as compensable in fraud cases. Attorneys generally find damage easier to prove than the other elements because the requirement is broad. The losing party in a fraud case may face damages well beyond the amount of the actual transaction if punitive damages are awarded by a court.

Broker Compensation

How brokers are compensated for their services has undergone significant change in the past several years, and license holders practice in an environment where the old assumptions about commission structures no longer apply. Understanding the current framework is essential for every license holder.

Compensation Is Always Negotiable

Broker fees are negotiated between a broker and the broker's client. They are not set by the Texas Real Estate Commission, by the state of Texas, by any real estate association, or by any agreement among competing brokers. The IABS 1-2 form explicitly states that all broker and agent fees are not set by law and are fully negotiable. The main contract forms (Form 20-19 and all others) confirm in Paragraph 8 (Brokers' Fees) that all obligations for payment of brokers' fees are contained in separate written agreements. Effective July 1, 2026, the former Paragraph 8B was removed, and brokerage compensation is now addressed in Paragraph 12. The purchase contract itself does not set or obligate any broker's fee.

The three documents that govern broker compensation are the listing agreement (between the seller and the listing broker, establishing what the listing broker will be paid), the buyer representation agreement (between the buyer and the buyer's broker, establishing what the buyer's broker will be paid), and any cooperative compensation agreement between the listing broker and the buyer's broker if the listing broker has agreed to contribute to the buyer's broker's compensation. These are all separate from and independent of the purchase contract.

Changes in How Buyer Agent Compensation Is Structured

Historically, the dominant practice in residential real estate was for sellers to offer buyer agent compensation through the Multiple Listing Service, and for that compensation to be paid from the seller's proceeds at closing. Following a significant national settlement agreement that took effect in August 2024, this practice was substantially restructured. MLS systems may no longer require or permit offers of buyer agent compensation to be communicated in MLS listings. Sellers may still choose to offer to contribute toward a buyer's brokerage fees as a term of the transaction, but this is now handled through the purchase contract rather than through a pre-set MLS field.

Texas law (Senate Bill 1968, effective January 1, 2026) reinforced this framework by requiring that buyers have a written representation agreement with their broker before the broker performs brokerage activity for the buyer in connection with a residential property transaction. This means a buyer's broker must have a signed agreement in place before showing property or presenting an offer. The agreement must specify how the buyer's broker will be compensated and who will pay. If the seller agrees to contribute toward the buyer's broker's fee, that contribution is reflected in the purchase contract through Paragraph 12B(1) of Form 20-19, where the seller's contribution toward the buyer's broker compensation may be stated as a specific dollar amount or as a percentage of the sales price. The buyer, through their representation agreement, may have negotiated a fee structure that results in additional out-of-pocket cost if the seller's contribution is less than the agreed fee, or no additional cost if the seller's contribution is sufficient.

For the seller, the listing agreement establishes what the listing broker will be paid. It may also specify whether the listing broker intends to share any portion of the listing commission with a buyer's broker, but that sharing is a matter between the two brokers and their respective clients, not a condition imposed by the MLS. License holders should have their designated broker's guidance on how the brokerage's agreements are structured in the current environment and should ensure that all fee arrangements are in writing, clearly communicated to clients, and fully compliant with TREC rules and applicable law.

The Sherman Antitrust Act

Any discussion of broker compensation must be accompanied by a clear understanding of federal antitrust law. The Sherman Antitrust Act was enacted in 1890 to prohibit any contract, combination, or conspiracy that restrains trade or commerce. Section 1 of the Act declares illegal every contract, combination in the form of trust or otherwise, or conspiracy in restraint of trade or commerce, and provides that any person who enters into such an agreement shall be deemed guilty of a felony, subject to fine or imprisonment or both, at the discretion of the court.

The specific antitrust violation most relevant to real estate is price-fixing. Price-fixing occurs when two or more competing businesses agree with each other to charge the same price for their services or products, depriving consumers of the benefit of genuine competition. In real estate, price-fixing would occur if two or more competing brokers agreed to charge the same commission rate. Such an agreement would eliminate the incentive for any broker to compete on price, and consumers would end up paying more than they would in a genuinely competitive market.

The danger is not limited to formal written agreements. A price-fixing violation can be inferred entirely from circumstantial evidence showing parallel pricing conduct among competitors, even if no written or oral agreement is proven. The fact that similar conduct results from a meeting of competing brokers is enough to raise serious legal risk. The law does not provide a defense based on the argument that the prices agreed upon were reasonable, or that the goal of raising commissions was financially justified. If prices are fixed, the intent and reasonableness of the agreement are irrelevant.

The practical implication for every license holder is absolute. If a group of competing brokers is gathered and the conversation turns to the idea that all brokers should charge a certain commission rate, the correct response is to leave immediately. Remaining in the room during that conversation creates legal exposure even without agreeing, because a court may infer participation from presence. The correct posture is to set commissions through individual negotiation with each client, based on the services being provided and the value being delivered, without any reference to what competing brokers charge.

Antitrust law also prohibits two other anticompetitive practices that real estate license holders must be aware of. A boycott of another broker or a group of brokers (for example, a group of brokers agreeing not to cooperate with a particular brokerage) is an antitrust violation. An allocation of customers or markets (for example, an agreement between competing brokers to divide a geographic area so that each takes exclusive control of certain territory) is also a violation. Any arrangement between competing firms that restricts the freedom of clients to choose among competing services is suspect under antitrust analysis.

The Federal Fair Housing Act

History and Development

The roots of fair housing law in the United States predate the Civil Rights era by more than a century. The Civil Rights Act of 1866 was the first federal law prohibiting discrimination in the purchase or lease of real property, and it prohibited discrimination on the basis of race and color only. The law was significant in principle but had no practical enforcement mechanism: an aggrieved person had to pursue a civil lawsuit in federal court at their own expense, a financial burden that placed the law beyond the reach of most people who had actually been discriminated against.

Title VIII of the Civil Rights Act of 1968, commonly known as the Fair Housing Act, fundamentally changed this. It expanded the protected classes to include religion and national origin, and it created an enforcement mechanism through the United States Department of Housing and Urban Development. HUD has the institutional resources to investigate complaints and pursue violators without requiring the individual victim to finance the litigation. The 1968 Act was also reinforced that same year by the Supreme Court's decision in Jones v. Alfred H. Mayer Co. (1968), which held that Congress has the authority to regulate the sale of private property to prevent racial discrimination.

Subsequent amendments broadened the Act's protections. In 1974, sex was added as a protected class, covering biological male or female status (gender). In 1988, two additional protected classes were added: familial status and disability (referred to in the original legislation as handicap). Familial status protects households that include children under the age of 18, including pregnant women and persons in the process of obtaining custody of children. The disability protections cover physical and mental impairments that substantially limit one or more major life activities, including conditions such as AIDS, HIV-related illness, and mental disorders. Under these protections, a person with a disability may make reasonable modifications to a dwelling at their own expense to ensure safe access and use, provided they restore the property to its original condition when they leave.

Current Protected Classes

The Fair Housing Act currently prohibits discrimination based on the following seven protected classes: race, color, religion, sex, national origin, familial status, and disability. Texas law adds several additional protected classes through the Texas Property Code and the Texas Fair Housing Act, and many local governments in Texas have expanded protections beyond the federal floor. License holders should be aware of any local or state protections that apply in their market area.

A common point of confusion is that neither age nor income is a protected class under the federal Fair Housing Act. These characteristics may be addressed by other laws, and income limitations may be relevant in subsidized housing contexts, but they are not bases for a Fair Housing Act complaint in the sale or lease of conventional residential real property.

Prohibited Conduct

The Fair Housing Act prohibits a broad range of conduct. Refusing to sell or rent a dwelling to a person because of a protected class is the most direct form of prohibited discrimination, but the Act is much broader than this. It is also unlawful to discriminate against a person in the terms, conditions, or privileges of the sale or rental of a dwelling on a protected basis, including setting more restrictive qualification standards, applying inconsistent policies, or offering less favorable terms. Advertising a sale or rental using language or imagery that indicates a preference or restriction based on a protected class is prohibited. Making a false statement that a property is not available when it actually is available is prohibited. Blockbusting, which is using predictions of demographic change to induce property owners to sell out of fear, is prohibited. Steering, which means directing buyers or renters toward or away from certain neighborhoods based on protected characteristics, is prohibited. Coercing, threatening, or retaliating against a person for exercising or assisting others in exercising their fair housing rights is prohibited.

A professionally trained license holder would never knowingly engage in any of these behaviors, but some violations occur innocently through careless statements, unconscious assumptions, or failure to provide the same level of service to all clients regardless of their membership in a protected class. The test is not whether the license holder subjectively intended to discriminate; the test is whether the conduct had a discriminatory effect on a protected class. Disparate impact, as recognized by the Supreme Court in Texas Department of Housing and Community Affairs v. Inclusive Communities Project (2015), is a valid basis for a Fair Housing Act claim even when no discriminatory intent is present.

Fair Housing Violations and Penalties

The Fair Housing Act provides several enforcement pathways with different remedies and timelines. A person who believes they have experienced housing discrimination has one year from the discriminatory act to file a complaint with HUD. Alternatively, a person may file a civil lawsuit directly in federal court within two years of the act.

When a complaint is filed with HUD, the agency investigates and, if it finds reason to believe discrimination occurred, issues a charge of discrimination. The case then proceeds either before a federal district court (if either party elects) or before a HUD Administrative Law Judge. In the administrative process, if the ALJ finds that discrimination occurred, the ALJ may award actual damages (compensation for out-of-pocket losses and non-economic harms such as humiliation, mental anguish, and emotional distress), injunctive relief, and civil monetary penalties. The civil penalties, which are adjusted periodically for inflation, currently stand at up to $26,262 for a first violation. For a respondent who has committed a Fair Housing Act violation within the previous five years, the maximum penalty increases to approximately $65,655. For a respondent who has committed two or more violations within the previous seven years, the maximum civil penalty can reach approximately $131,308. These penalty amounts are updated by federal regulation and are subject to change with each annual inflation adjustment.

In cases brought by the Department of Justice in federal court, the civil penalties can be substantially higher. Federal court litigation can also result in punitive damages that may reach into the millions of dollars in egregious cases. In private civil lawsuits, victims of discrimination can recover actual damages, punitive damages, and attorney's fees and costs. There is no cap on punitive damages in federal court fair housing cases, making a serious violation extraordinarily expensive.

For real estate license holders, the reputational damage of a fair housing violation may be as significant as the financial consequences. TREC may also take disciplinary action against a license holder found to have violated the Fair Housing Act, potentially resulting in suspension or revocation of the license.

TREC Canons on Discriminatory Practices

The Texas Real Estate Commission's Canons of Professional Ethics and Conduct reinforce the Fair Housing Act's protections and in some respects go further. The Canons prohibit any Texas real estate license holder from inquiring about, responding to, or facilitating inquiries about, or making a disclosure that indicates or is intended to indicate any preference, limitation, or discrimination based on the following: race, color, religion, sex, national origin, ancestry, familial status, or handicap of an owner, previous or current occupant, potential purchaser, lessor, or potential lessee of real property.

The Canons specifically include as a basis for handicap protection any person who had, may have had, has, or may have AIDS, HIV-related illnesses, or HIV infection as defined by the Centers for Disease Control of the United States Public Health Service. This provision ensures that license holders may not make any disclosure about a property's history with respect to occupants who had or were suspected to have such conditions.

A license holder who is asked by a client about the racial, religious, or ethnic composition of a neighborhood must decline to answer the question directly. Referring the client to publicly available census data or demographic resources is permissible; providing information in a way that steers the client toward or away from a neighborhood based on protected characteristics is not. The professional response to such questions demonstrates both legal compliance and ethical character.

Federal Disclosure Laws Affecting Real Estate

Foreign Investment in Real Property Tax Act

The Foreign Investment in Real Property Tax Act, known as FIRPTA, requires that when a foreign person (a non-resident alien as defined by the Internal Revenue Code) sells real property in the United States, the buyer must withhold a portion of the sales proceeds and deliver that amount to the Internal Revenue Service to cover the seller's potential U.S. tax obligation. If the foreign seller were to return to their home country after closing without paying taxes on the gain from the sale, the IRS would have no practical means of collecting. FIRPTA solves this problem by making the buyer responsible for the withholding.

The standard withholding rate under FIRPTA is 15% of the amount realized on the sale. Reduced withholding rates apply in certain circumstances: when the property is acquired for use as a personal residence and the sales price is $300,000 or less, no withholding is required; when the sales price is between $300,001 and $1,000,000 and the property will be used as a personal residence, the withholding rate is 10%. The title company in a residential transaction is responsible for verifying the seller's status and ensuring that the required withholding is handled correctly. A real estate sales agent who attempts to handle a transaction involving a potentially foreign seller without the assistance of a title company and qualified tax advisor is taking on responsibility they should not accept.

Financial Crimes Enforcement Network (FinCEN) Reporting

Effective July 1, 2026, the promulgated contract forms were revised in response to federal reporting requirements administered by the U.S. Treasury's Financial Crimes Enforcement Network (FinCEN). In the One to Four Family Residential Contract (Form 20-19), a new Paragraph 20B requires the parties to provide the escrow agent with the information needed to satisfy any governmental reporting requirements and requires the buyer to pay any charges associated with gathering and reporting that information. In practice, the title or escrow agent determines what must be reported and collects the required information; the licensee should direct client questions about the reporting obligation to that agent.

Interstate Land Sales Full Disclosure Act

The Interstate Land Sales Full Disclosure Act, enacted by Congress in 1968, protects buyers from misrepresentation, fraud, and abuse in the sale or lease of land offered through interstate commerce. The Act requires developers who offer 100 or more non-exempt lots to register the subdivision with the Department of Housing and Urban Development and to provide each prospective buyer with a Property Report before the buyer signs any purchase contract or agreement. The Property Report must contain material information about the lots, the subdivision, and the developer's obligations, including any promised improvements such as roads, utilities, and recreational facilities.

The Act does not give HUD authority to force developers to complete promised facilities, but it does create private rights of action for buyers who were harmed by misrepresentations or omissions in the Property Report. A developer who misstates or omits required information, or who promises amenities in promotional materials that are not included in the Property Report, may face individual and class action lawsuits by purchasers. HUD can also pursue civil and criminal enforcement when fraudulent sales practices are involved and can suspend the developer's registration.

The Tax Reform Act of 1986

The Tax Reform Act of 1986, signed by President Reagan, was a comprehensive restructuring of the federal tax code that had significant implications for real estate investment. The Act reduced the top marginal income tax rate from 50% to 28%, broadened the overall tax base by eliminating many deductions and credits, and treated capital gains, earned income, and unearned income at the same rate for the first time.

For real estate specifically, the Act eliminated or reduced many of the tax-shelter benefits that had driven large institutional investment in multi-family rental housing during the 1970s and early 1980s. This reduction in tax incentives contributed to a contraction in the construction and rehabilitation of rental housing for a period of years after the Act. To preserve some level of investment in affordable multi-family housing, Congress created the Low-Income Housing Tax Credit program, which provides tax credits to developers who build or rehabilitate rental housing for low-income households. The Act also created specific rules for the passive activity loss deduction, including a provision allowing taxpayers with adjusted gross income under a certain threshold to deduct up to $25,000 in net rental losses annually, provided the property was not used for personal purposes for more than 14 days or 10% of rental days during the year.

Megan's Law and the Sex Offender Registry

In 1994, 7-year-old Megan Kanka was abducted, assaulted, and murdered in New Jersey by a neighbor who was a convicted sex offender. The family had no way of knowing a sex offender lived across the street because law enforcement was prohibited from disclosing that information to the public. The resulting legislation, signed by President Clinton in May 1996 and informally named Megan's Law, authorized state and local governments to make sex offender registration information available to the public. A subsequent Supreme Court decision in 2003 upheld the constitutionality of publishing sex offender information on the internet.

In Texas, Chapter 62 of the Code of Criminal Procedure establishes the Texas Sex Offender Registration Program, which requires convicted sex offenders to register with the local law enforcement authority in the city or county where they reside. The registration includes the offender's name and aliases, date of birth, physical description, photograph, fingerprints, home address, the offense of conviction, the victim's age, and the date and terms of conviction. A sex offender who fails to comply with any registration requirement may be subject to felony prosecution.

The Texas legislature has not enacted a law that either requires or prohibits a real estate license holder from disclosing to a buyer the presence of a registered sex offender near a property. This creates a genuine professional dilemma, and the answer depends entirely on the nature of the agency relationship. If the license holder is representing the buyer, the duty to disclose all material information the licensee knows applies, and the presence of a nearby registered sex offender is precisely the type of information a family with children would consider material. Withholding it from a buyer one is representing could constitute a breach of fiduciary duty. If the license holder is representing the seller and working with an unrepresented buyer, the analysis is different: the license holder has no duty to the unrepresented buyer and has a duty of loyalty to the seller client. In that situation, disclosing without the seller's consent could constitute a breach of fiduciary duty to the seller.

Every brokerage should have a written policy on this issue before the situation arises. Options include a policy of always disclosing with the seller's written permission, a policy of informing all buyers of their right to search the publicly available registry themselves, or a policy of referring all such questions to the broker and potentially an attorney. Waiting until the situation presents itself is not a policy; it is an invitation to make an uninformed decision under pressure.

Environmental Laws and Real Estate

The Environmental Protection Agency

The Environmental Protection Agency was established in 1970 by President Nixon with the mission of protecting human health and the environment. The EPA develops and enforces federal environmental regulations, conducts research, educates the public, and delegates enforcement authority to the states, including Texas, for monitoring and permitting compliance at the local level. When companies or industries fail to meet the EPA's standards, the agency can impose sanctions, fines, and corrective action orders. In Texas, the EPA's enforcement activities have produced billions of dollars in pollution controls and penalty assessments aimed at factories, industries, and other regulated entities.

The EPA's activities affect real estate both directly and indirectly. Directly, the presence of contaminated sites, brownfields, or properties with known environmental hazards affects the ability to use, develop, finance, and sell the land. Indirectly, the EPA's success in maintaining air and water quality protects the quality of life in communities throughout Texas, which in turn supports the stability of real property values. A community with unaddressed environmental contamination sees declining property values, difficulty attracting investment, and diminished quality of life for residents.

CERCLA and the Superfund

The Comprehensive Environmental Response, Compensation, and Liability Act of 1980, known as CERCLA or by its common name Superfund, created a federal fund and legal framework for cleaning up abandoned hazardous waste sites, uncontrolled releases of toxic substances, and other environmental emergencies. CERCLA gives the EPA broad authority to identify responsible parties for contamination, to compel cleanup by those responsible parties, and to conduct cleanup itself when responsible parties refuse or are unable to do so, with the right to recover costs afterward. CERCLA imposes strict, joint, and several liability, meaning that any one of the responsible parties can be held liable for the entire cost of cleanup, regardless of the relative size of their contribution to the contamination.

For real estate practitioners, CERCLA is most relevant in commercial and industrial transactions and in the purchase of properties with known or suspected contamination histories. A buyer who acquires a contaminated property without performing adequate due diligence may find themselves liable as a responsible party for cleanup costs that can reach into the millions of dollars. The Environmental Assessment, Threatened or Endangered Species, and Wetlands Addendum (Form 28-2) discussed in Chapter 4 provides a contractual mechanism for buyers to conduct environmental investigations before closing on properties where these risks may exist.

The Clean Water Act

The Federal Water Pollution Control Act Amendments of 1972, commonly known as the Clean Water Act, established the national framework for controlling water pollution. The Act made it illegal for any person or company to discharge pollutants into navigable waters of the United States without a permit from the EPA or a delegated state authority. The EPA was authorized to develop and enforce water quality standards, fund the construction of sewage treatment facilities, and regulate industrial and municipal discharges.

The Clean Water Act has direct relevance to real estate through its regulation of wetlands. Section 404 of the Act requires a permit for the discharge of dredged or fill material into waters of the United States, which has been interpreted to include certain wetland areas. A buyer who intends to fill, grade, or develop property that includes jurisdictional wetlands may be subject to federal permit requirements that significantly limit the project's scope or feasibility. This is why the Environmental Assessment Addendum flags wetland determinations as a potential basis for the buyer's termination right.

Occupancy Standards and Fair Housing

Occupancy standards set limits on how many people may live in a housing unit. These standards intersect with the Fair Housing Act because policies that limit the number of occupants can have a discriminatory effect on families with children, which is a protected class under the familial status provisions of the Act. A policy that is facially neutral (two persons per bedroom applies to everyone) may still violate the Fair Housing Act if it has the practical effect of making housing unavailable to families with children.

The Keating Memorandum

In 1998, HUD's General Counsel Frank Keating issued guidance on how housing providers should evaluate their occupancy policies for compliance with the Fair Housing Act. The Texas Commission on Human Rights adopted the standards in this guidance, which has become known as the Keating Memorandum. HUD continues to use these guidelines as its policy on occupancy standards.

The Keating Memorandum establishes that a policy of two persons per bedroom is, as a general rule, reasonable under the Fair Housing Act. However, the memorandum makes clear that this is not an automatic safe harbor. Reasonableness depends on a number of factors that must be evaluated for each specific property and situation. These factors include the size of the bedrooms and the overall unit, the configuration of the unit (whether it has additional rooms that could serve as sleeping space), the physical limitations of the housing (plumbing, egress, ventilation), applicable state or local building codes and occupancy laws, and any other relevant circumstances.

For units with unusually large bedrooms or with additional rooms such as a study, den, or large living areas, a standard two-person-per-bedroom limit may be unnecessarily restrictive and could discriminate against families with children. In those cases, the occupancy policy should allow more than two persons per bedroom to reflect the property's actual capacity. Conversely, for small studio or one-bedroom units with limited floor space and a single bathroom, a stricter standard may be justifiable based on the physical limitations of the unit.

The Keating guidelines do not specify a minimum age below which children should not be counted in the occupancy calculation, and they do not recognize a business reason defense for a policy that limits families based on the age of children. A policy that restricts children under age five, for example, has no legitimate physical basis and is very likely discriminatory.

Best Practices for License Holders Working as Landlord's Agents

A license holder acting as a landlord's agent must understand the Keating guidelines and advise the landlord accordingly. Before implementing any occupancy policy, the license holder should review the size, configuration, and condition of each unit type in the portfolio and develop a policy that reflects actual capacity without unnecessarily excluding families. The occupancy policy should be stated clearly and provided to all prospective tenants at the beginning of the leasing process, not revealed only after a family has invested time in application. All prospective tenants should be told about the occupancy policy in the same way, without targeting disclosure to families that appear to have children. Inconsistent application of the policy creates the same Fair Housing Act liability as a discriminatory policy stated on its face.

Chapter 8: Snapshot Review

The following review summarizes the key rules and concepts from Chapter 8.

TREC and Fraud

- TREC exists to protect the public from real estate license holders who do not follow TRELA or TREC rules
- The three elements of fraud are Reliance, Intent, and Damage (acronym: RID); all three must be present for a fraud claim to succeed
- Reliance: the consumer must have had the right to rely on the statement as a material, professional representation (not merely an opinion)
- Intent: the person making the statement must have known it was false or harmful; this is what distinguishes fraud from innocent misrepresentation or negligence
- Damage: an actual loss of something of value must result; damage may include financial loss, mental anguish, emotional distress, and humiliation
- Fraud is a criminal offense in Texas and can result in loss of license, civil liability, and imprisonment

Broker Compensation

- Broker fees are always negotiable between broker and client; they are not set by TREC, the state, or any organization
- The purchase contract (Form 20-19 Paragraph 8) does not create commission obligations; those are in separate written agreements
- Following the August 2024 national settlement, MLS systems may no longer communicate offers of buyer agent compensation in listing fields; buyer broker compensation is addressed in the purchase contract or in separate broker-to-broker agreements
- Texas SB 1968 (effective January 1, 2026) requires a written buyer representation agreement before showing or presenting offers on residential property
- Sellers may contribute toward buyer broker fees through Paragraph 12B(1) of Form 20-19 as a negotiated term
- All compensation disclosures must be transparent and in writing; the IABS 1-2 explicitly states fees are negotiable

The Sherman Antitrust Act

- The Sherman Antitrust Act prohibits every contract, combination, or conspiracy in restraint of trade; violations are felonies
- Price-fixing: when two or more competing brokers agree to charge the same commission rate -- this is a federal crime
- A price-fixing violation can be inferred from parallel pricing conduct even without a written or oral agreement
- It is not a defense that the fixed price was reasonable or that the goal was worthy
- Other antitrust violations: boycotting a competitor and allocating customers or markets
- If competing brokers begin discussing a standard commission rate, leave the room immediately

The Federal Fair Housing Act

- Civil Rights Act of 1866: prohibited race and color discrimination; required federal civil court action; limited enforcement

- Fair Housing Act of 1968 (Title VIII): added religion and national origin; created HUD enforcement authority
- 1974 amendment: added sex (gender)
- 1988 amendment: added familial status (households with children under 18, pregnant women, persons seeking custody) and disability (including HIV/AIDS)
- Seven current federal protected classes: race, color, religion, sex, national origin, familial status, disability
- Prohibited conduct: refusal to sell or rent; discriminatory terms or conditions; discriminatory advertising; false statements about availability; blockbusting; steering; coercion or retaliation; disparate impact (as affirmed by Supreme Court in 2015)
- Age and income are NOT protected classes under the federal Fair Housing Act

Fair Housing Penalties

- Complaint to HUD must be filed within 1 year of the discriminatory act; federal civil lawsuit may be filed within 2 years
- HUD Administrative Law Judge civil penalties (2025): up to $26,262 for a first violation; up to approximately $65,655 for a violation within the prior 5 years; up to approximately $131,308 for two or more violations within the prior 7 years (these amounts are adjusted annually for inflation)
- Federal court cases brought by the DOJ can result in even higher civil penalties
- Victims may also recover actual damages (including non-economic harms), punitive damages, and attorney's fees
- TREC may take separate disciplinary action, including license suspension or revocation, for Fair Housing Act violations

TREC Canons on Discriminatory Practices

- No Texas license holder may inquire about, facilitate inquiries about, or make disclosures that indicate any preference or discrimination based on: race, color, religion, sex, national origin, ancestry, familial status, or handicap of any owner, occupant, prospective buyer, or lessee
- Handicap expressly includes any person who has, had, or may have AIDS, HIV-related illness, or HIV infection
- When a client asks about neighborhood demographics, refer them to publicly available data rather than providing a direct answer that could constitute steering

Federal Disclosure Laws

- FIRPTA: standard withholding rate of 15% of proceeds when a foreign person sells U.S. real property; reduced rates for personal residences at lower price points; title company handles verification and withholding
- Interstate Land Sales Full Disclosure Act (1968): requires developers of 100 or more non-exempt lots to register with HUD and provide a Property Report to each buyer before the contract is signed
- Tax Reform Act of 1986: eliminated many real estate tax shelter benefits, reduced top marginal rate from 50% to 28%, created the Low-Income Housing Tax Credit
- Megan's Law: authorized public disclosure of sex offender registry information; Texas Sex Offender Registration Program requires registration with local law enforcement
- Texas has not specifically required or prohibited license holder disclosure of nearby sex offenders; the answer depends on agency relationship; brokers must have a written office policy before the situation arises

Environmental Laws

- EPA (established 1970): protects human health and environment; develops and enforces federal environmental regulations; delegates enforcement to states
- CERCLA / Superfund (1980): provides federal authority and funding to clean up abandoned hazardous waste sites; strict, joint, and several liability applies to responsible parties; buyers who acquire contaminated property without due diligence may inherit cleanup liability
- Clean Water Act (1972): made it illegal to discharge pollutants into U.S. waters without a permit; regulates wetlands through Section 404; wetland designations can significantly restrict property development
- Form 28-2 (Environmental Assessment Addendum) gives buyers a contractual right to investigate environmental conditions before closing

Occupancy Standards and Fair Housing

- Occupancy policies that are too restrictive can discriminate against families with children and violate the Fair Housing Act's familial status protection
- The Keating Memorandum (HUD guidance): two persons per bedroom is generally reasonable but is not an automatic safe harbor
- Reasonableness depends on: bedroom and unit size, configuration of the unit, physical limitations of the housing, local building codes, and other factors
- Large bedrooms or units with extra rooms (den, study) may require a more generous policy; small units may justify a stricter one
- There is no basis for excluding children under any specific age from the occupancy count
- All prospective tenants must be told the occupancy policy consistently and early; inconsistent application creates Fair Housing liability

Chapter 8 Quiz: Other Real Estate Matters

1. The three elements of fraud are represented by the acronym RID. Which element distinguishes fraud from innocent misrepresentation or negligence?

a. Reliance, because the consumer's right to rely on a statement is what triggers legal liability for any misstatement

b. Damage, because no fraud claim can succeed without documented proof of an actual financial loss

c. Reliance, because any statement that is relied upon by a consumer is inherently fraudulent regardless of the speaker's state of mind

d. Intent, because fraud requires that the person making the statement knew it was false or knew that the truth would harm the other party

2. Under the reliance element of fraud, which of the following statements made by a license holder is most likely to be actionable?

a. "Everyone who buys through me ends up being happy with their investment."

b. "The fence line is the property line."

c. "This neighborhood has great appreciation potential in a rising market."

d. "You will love living here; it is a wonderful community with great neighbors."

3. Under Texas Senate Bill 1968 (effective January 1, 2026), what must a buyer's broker have in place before showing residential property or presenting an offer on behalf of a buyer?

a. A signed written buyer representation agreement that specifies how the buyer's broker will be compensated and who will pay that compensation

b. A copy of the Third Party Financing Addendum confirming that the buyer has obtained a written lender pre-approval

c. A completed IABS 1-2 acknowledgment form signed by the buyer confirming receipt of the brokerage services disclosure

d. A written authorization from the seller confirming the seller agrees to contribute toward the buyer's broker compensation

4. Price-fixing in real estate occurs when which of the following situations takes place?

a. A broker sets a commission rate that is higher than the prevailing rate charged by other brokers who operate in the same market area

b. A broker offers to reduce the commission rate in exchange for the seller agreeing to a lower listing price for the property

c. Two or more competing brokers agree with each other to charge the same commission rate, thereby eliminating price competition

d. A buyer's broker and a listing broker negotiate a cooperative compensation split that departs from the most common practice in the local area

5. Which of the following characteristics is NOT a protected class under the federal Fair Housing Act?

a. Familial status
b. National origin
c. Disability
d. Age

6. The federal Fair Housing Act was amended in 1974 to add which protected class?

a. Sex
b. Disability
c. Familial status
d. National origin

7. A person who believes that he or she has experienced housing discrimination has how long to file a complaint with the U.S. Department of Housing and Urban Development?

a. 6 months from the date of the discriminatory act
b. 1 year from the date of the discriminatory act
c. 2 years from the date of the discriminatory act
d. 3 years from the date of the discriminatory act

8. Under FIRPTA, what is the standard withholding rate that applies when a foreign person sells U.S. real property?

a. 5% of the amount realized on the sale
b. 8% of the amount realized on the sale
c. 10% of the amount realized on the sale
d. 15% of the amount realized on the sale

9. Megan's Law, signed by President Clinton in May 1996, authorized what action by state and local governments?

a. The creation of a national database that requires all sex offenders to register with the FBI before moving to a new state
b. The mandatory disclosure by real estate license holders of any registered sex offender located within one mile of any listed property
c. The public disclosure of sex offender registration information to alert communities to the presence of convicted sex offenders
d. The mandatory posting of warning signs in neighborhoods where convicted sex offenders currently are registered to live

10. The Keating Memorandum establishes what general rule as a starting point for evaluating a reasonable occupancy policy under the Fair Housing Act?

a. One person per bedroom is the only occupancy standard that fully protects familial status under all circumstances

b. Two persons per bedroom is, as a general rule, a reasonable occupancy policy, though it is not an automatic safe harbor in every situation

c. Three persons per bedroom is required in properties with unusually large bedrooms in order to avoid liability for familial status discrimination

d. Occupancy policies are always presumed reasonable if they are applied consistently to all applicants, regardless of how many persons per bedroom are allowed

---

CHAPTER 9
FORM APPLICATION WORKSHOP

Chapter Overview

This chapter is a hands-on workshop. Rather than introducing new law, it asks you to apply what the preceding chapters have covered by completing TREC promulgated forms from realistic transaction facts. Three case studies are presented. For each one you are given the facts of a transaction and a completion worksheet that lists, paragraph by paragraph, the entries a license holder would make on the form. Fill in each blank using only the information a license holder may properly supply, and leave a blank or write not applicable where the facts do not call for an entry. When you have finished a case, compare your work against the matching answer in the Form Application Workshop: Completed Forms section at the back of the book. The completed versions include brief notes that explain why each entry is made and point out the entries that most often cause errors. Throughout, remember that a license holder completes only the factual and business-detail blanks on a promulgated form and never adds to, deletes from, or modifies the pre-printed language; anything that would create or change a legal right belongs with an attorney.

Learning Objectives

After completing this workshop you will be able to:

- Complete the One to Four Family Residential Contract (Form 20-19) from a set of transaction facts, including the parties, property, sales price, financing, earnest money and termination option, title and survey elections, and property condition elections.
- Complete the Third Party Financing Addendum (Form 40-11) and coordinate it with the main contract.
- Record a seller's contribution toward the buyer's broker compensation in the correct provision of Paragraph 12, and identify which addenda must be checked in Paragraph 22 and attached.
- Complete the New Home Contract (Completed Construction) (Form 24-20) and recognize how it differs from the resale contract.
- Recognize entries that a license holder may not make and that require referral to an attorney.

How to Use This Workshop

Work the cases in order; they build in complexity. Read the facts carefully and complete the worksheet before turning to the completed version. Where an entry depends on a negotiated term that the facts supply, such as the option fee or the number of option days, use the figure given; where the facts are silent, the correct response is often to leave the blank empty or to mark the provision not applicable, and the completed versions note where that is so. All form references are to the versions in effect July 1, 2026.

Case A: A Conventional-Financed Resale

Transaction Facts

Howard and Lillian Pruitt are selling their home at 1428 Brookhaven Lane, Round Rock, Williamson County, Texas, legally described as Lot 14, Block 3, Brookhaven Estates, Section Two. The buyers are Maria Ortega and Daniel Ortega. The agreed sales price is $385,000. The Ortegas will pay $77,000 of the price in cash and finance the remaining $308,000 with a conventional loan, due in full in 30 years, with interest not to exceed 7.5 percent per year; they will apply promptly and must obtain credit approval within 21 days after the effective date. The Ortegas deposit $5,000 in earnest money with Heritage Title Company, 200 East Main Street, Round Rock, and pay a $300 option fee for the unrestricted right to terminate within 10 days after the effective date. The sellers will pay for the owner's title policy, which will be issued by Heritage Title Company. The sellers have an existing survey from when they bought the home; the parties agree the buyers will use that survey if it is acceptable to the title company and the lender, and that the buyers will pay for a new survey if one is required. The Ortegas accept the property in its present condition and are not asking the sellers to make repairs. Neither party and no family member of either party is a real estate license holder. There are no special provisions. The effective date is September 8, 2026, closing is set for October 9, 2026, and possession transfers to the buyers at closing and funding.

Completion Worksheet

Complete the following entries on Form 20-19 and the Third Party Financing Addendum (Form 40-11).

Paragraph 1 - Parties

Seller(s): ______________________________

Buyer(s): ______________________________

Paragraph 2 - Property

Lot / Block / Addition / Section: ______________________________

City / County: ______________________________

Street address: ______________________________

Paragraph 3 - Sales Price

3A. Cash portion payable by Buyer: $ ______________________________

3B. Sum of all financing: $ ______________________________

3C. Sales Price (3A + 3B): $ ______________________________

Paragraph 4 - Leases

Applicable leases (residential, fixture, or natural resource), if any:

____

Paragraph 5 - Earnest Money and Termination Option

Earnest money: $ ______________________________

Escrow agent (name and address): ______________________________

Option fee: $ ______________________________

Option period (days after effective date): ______________________________

Paragraph 6 - Title Policy and Survey

Owner's title policy paid by (Seller / Buyer): ______________________________

Title company: ______________________________

Survey: which option and who pays: ______________________________

Paragraph 7 - Property Condition

Acceptance (present condition, or with listed repairs): ______________________________

Repairs requested by Buyer, if any: ______________________________

Paragraph 8 - Broker and Sales Agent Disclosure

Disclosure required (yes/no); if yes, state it: ______________________________

Paragraph 9 - Closing

Closing Date: ______________________________

Paragraph 10 - Possession

Possession (upon closing and funding, or per temporary lease):

____

Paragraph 11 - Special Provisions

Entries (factual and business details only), if any: ______________________________

Final Page

Effective Date: ______________________________

Third Party Financing Addendum (Form 40-11)

Type of financing (Conventional / FHA / VA / USDA / Other):

____

Principal loan amount: $ ______________________________

Term: ______________________________ years

Interest not to exceed: ______________________________ percent

Credit approval to be obtained within (days after effective date):

____

Case B: A Resale With HOA Membership, a Seller Contribution to the Buyer's Broker, and a Temporary Lease

Transaction Facts

Robert Feldman is selling the home at 92 Camden Court, Frisco, Collin County, Texas, legally described as Lot 7, Block B, Camden Park, Phase 1, to the buyer, Priya Nair. The sales price is $612,000, with $122,400 in cash and $489,600 financed through a conventional loan, due in full in 30 years, with interest not to exceed 7.25 percent per year; the buyer must obtain credit approval within 25 days after the effective date. Camden Park has mandatory membership in a property owners association, so the parties attach the Addendum for Property Subject to Mandatory Membership in a Property Owners Association (Form 36-11). Mr. Feldman delivered the Seller's Disclosure Notice (Form 55-1) to Ms. Nair before she made her offer. Ms. Nair is represented by Carla Dominguez of Northstar Realty under a written buyer representation agreement that calls for the buyer's broker to be paid 3 percent of the sales price; Mr. Feldman has agreed to contribute 2.5 percent of the sales price toward the buyer's broker's compensation, and Ms. Nair will pay any remaining difference directly to her own broker. Mr. Feldman has also agreed to contribute up to $4,000 toward the buyer's other closing costs. Earnest money is $10,000 held by Collin County Title Company, 1500 Preston Road, Frisco; the option fee is $500 for a 12-day option period. Because Ms. Nair must relocate before the sale can close, the parties agree that she will take possession five days before closing under a Buyer's Temporary Residential Lease (Form 16-7). The effective date is September 15, 2026; the temporary lease begins October 15, 2026; and closing is set for October 20, 2026.

Completion Worksheet

Complete the following on Form 20-19, together with the addenda and lease the facts require. Items already practiced in Case A are abbreviated here so you can focus on the provisions that distinguish this transaction.

Paragraph 1 - Parties

Seller(s): ______________________________

Buyer(s): ______________________________

Paragraph 2 - Property

Legal description, city, county, and street address: ______________________________

Paragraph 3 - Sales Price

3A. Cash: $ ______________________________

3B. Financing: $ ______________________________

3C. Sales Price: $ ______________________________

Paragraph 5 - Earnest Money and Termination Option

Earnest money: $ ______________________________

Escrow agent: ______________________________

Option fee: $ ______________________________

Option period (days): ______________________________

Paragraph 6E - Required Notices

Mandatory HOA membership (is / is not), and addendum attached:

____

Paragraph 7B - Seller's Disclosure Notice

Notice received by Buyer (yes/no): ______________________________

Paragraph 12 - Settlement and Other Expenses

12A(1)(b). Seller's contribution to Buyer's expenses other than broker compensation (dollar amount): $ ____________________________

12B(1). Seller's contribution to Buyer's broker's compensation ($ or %):

____

12B(2). Buyer's contribution to Seller's broker's compensation ($ or %):

____

Paragraph 9 - Closing

Closing Date: ____________________________

Paragraph 10 - Possession

Possession (upon closing and funding, or per temporary lease):

____

Paragraph 22 - Agreement of Parties

Addenda to check and attach: ____________________________

Final Page

Effective Date: ____________________________

Buyer's Temporary Residential Lease (Form 16-7)

Commencement date and term (days): ____________________________

Daily rental and deposit: ____________________________

Case C: A New Home, Completed Construction

Transaction Facts

Evergreen Builders, LLC is selling a newly completed home at 305 Mesquite Trail, Georgetown, Williamson County, Texas, legally described as Lot 22, Block 5, Sundance Ridge, Section 4, to the buyer, Aaron Whitfield. Evergreen Builders constructed the home, and it has never been occupied. The sales price is $448,000, with $44,800 in cash and $403,200 financed through a conventional loan, due in full in 30 years, with interest not to exceed 7.5 percent per year; the buyer must obtain credit approval within 21 days after the effective date. Because the seller is a builder selling a new home for the first time, the Texas Property Code does not require a Seller's Disclosure Notice, and none is provided. The builder provides its standard limited warranty as a separate written document, and any manufacturers' warranties pass to the buyer at closing. The home's insulation, as disclosed by the builder, is R-38 blown fiberglass in the ceiling and R-15 batt fiberglass in the exterior walls. Earnest money is $6,000 held by Sundance Title Company; the option fee is $400 for a 7-day option period. The effective date is September 22, 2026, closing is set for October 23, 2026, and possession transfers at closing and funding.

Completion Worksheet

Complete the following on the New Home Contract (Completed Construction) (Form 24-20). Note the provisions that differ from the resale contract.

Paragraph 1 - Parties

Seller (builder): ______________________________

Buyer: ______________________________

Paragraph 2 - Property

Legal description, city, county, and street address: ______________________________

Paragraph 3 - Sales Price

3A. Cash: $ ______________________________

3B. Financing: $ ______________________________

3C. Sales Price: $ ______________________________

Paragraph 5 - Earnest Money and Termination Option

Earnest money: $ ______________________________

Escrow agent: ______________________________

Option fee: $ ______________________________

Option period (days): ______________________________

Paragraph 7 - Property Condition (new construction)

Seller's Disclosure Notice provided (yes/no/exempt): ______________________________

Builder warranty (how provided): ______________________________

Manufacturers' warranties (treatment): ______________________________

Insulation disclosure - ceiling (type and R-value): ______________________________

Insulation disclosure - exterior walls (type and R-value): ______________________________

Paragraph 9 - Closing

Closing Date: ______________________________

Paragraph 10 - Possession

Possession: ______________________________

Final Page

Effective Date: ______________________________

Third Party Financing Addendum (Form 40-11)

Type, principal, term, interest cap, and approval days: ______________________________

ANSWER KEY TO CHAPTER QUIZZES

Answer Key - Chapter 1

1. b 1949

2. d 13

3. a A written document

4. c Void

5. b A contract for the sale of real estate

6. a Good consideration

7. d A material breach occurs that may allow the non-breaching party to terminate the contract

8. c The Parol Evidence Rule

9. b Both parties are released from any further obligation under that contract

10. d Unilateral, because only the seller makes a promise to pay if the broker produces a qualified buyer

11. a 18

12. c A specific calendar date

Answer Key - Chapter 2

1. b Real estate commissions are negotiable

2. d Giving a client an opinion about the legal effect of a contract term

3. a Rescission

4. c The governor of Texas

5. b The original offer is terminated and cannot be revived by either party

6. d The licensee is acting as a principal in the transaction, buying or selling property for himself or herself

7. a Price fixing

8. c When all parties have signed and acceptance has been communicated to the other side

9. b Raise the concern directly with the other licensee rather than overlooking the errors

10. d Mutual mistake

Answer Key - Chapter 3

1. d The number of times the form has been revised since it was first issued

2. a Ask the seller to remove the chandelier before any buyer views the property

3. c 3A = $24,000; 3B = $216,000; 3C = $240,000

4. b Paragraph 4B, with the Addendum Regarding Fixture Leases (Form 52-1) attached

5. d It is retained by the seller and is not refundable to the buyer under any circumstances

6. a 3 days

7. c 20 days

8. b The seller

9. d 15 days

10. a Form 36-11, Addendum for Property Subject to Mandatory Membership in a Property Owners Association

11. c 7B(1), because the buyer already received the notice before making the offer

12. b 5%

13. a A buyer who is purchasing the property entirely in cash with no financing of any kind

14. d 5% of the installment amount

15. c Complete both Paragraphs A and B, because each paragraph addresses a separate and distinct purpose

Answer Key - Chapter 4

1. c It demonstrates the buyer's good faith, and it serves as liquidated damages that are agreed upon in advance in the event of a default

2. a A title that can be transferred to a buyer even though certain encumbrances, such as utility easements, exist on the property

3. d The Owner's Policy, because it is issued to the buyer and insures against defects not disclosed on the title commitment

4. b Schedule C

5. a A cash purchase or an owner-financed transaction where no lender is independently requiring a title search

6. d The seller, because the form requires disclosure of the seller's actual knowledge of the property's condition

7. c By lot number, block number, and the name of the recorded subdivision plat filed in the county records

8. b 1978

9. a The earnest money is refunded to the buyer, and the seller retains the Option Fee as compensation for taking the property off the market

10. d The Environmental Assessment, Threatened or Endangered Species, and Wetlands Addendum (Form 28-2)

11. b Whenever a license holder receives any form of compensation from a residential service company in connection with a transaction

12. c No coverage, because the Mortgagee's Policy is issued to and protects the lender only, not the buyer

Answer Key - Chapter 5

1. b Both spouses must sign the deed, even if only one spouse's name appears on the deed or title

2. d License holders often write language in this paragraph that creates, modifies, or removes legal rights, which constitutes unauthorized practice of law

3. a Appropriate, because it is a factual disclosure that the buyer is required to make in order to avoid a DTPA violation

4. c A tenancy at sufferance, which provides minimal legal protection for either party and creates uncertainty about insurance

5. d The buyer, because the buyer holds title to the property after closing and funding have occurred

6. b At the time of closing and funding, as part of the closing and settlement process

7. c 90 days

8. a At the time the buyer takes possession when the lease commences, with any adjustments for actual versus anticipated term settled at closing

9. d The buyer is responsible for all equipment and appliances in addition to the yard, trees, and shrubs

10. b This is an executory contract that requires referral to an attorney and cannot be handled using Form 16-7 or any other promulgated TREC form

11. c Paragraph 12B(1), which may be stated as a dollar amount or a percentage of the sales price; the former Paragraph 8B was removed in the 2026 revision

12. d Require the seller to reduce the sales price by the full replacement cost of the damage; Paragraph 14 gives the buyer only the three options described in the other choices

13. b Sent to a party or that party's agent by a permitted method; the 2026 revision clarified the acceptable delivery methods and added contact lines for each party's agent

14. b It has been combined into Paragraph 5, Earnest Money and Termination Option; Consult an Attorney Before Signing is now Paragraph 23, the contract's final numbered paragraph

Answer Key - Chapter 6

1. c Form 20-19, because the seller owns the land, making this a fee simple sale rather than a condominium transaction

2. a The interior airspace of the unit from wall paint to wall paint and floor to ceiling, plus an undivided interest in the common elements of the project

3. d The Effective Date is amended to the date the buyer receives the Association's written certification that the right of first refusal has been complied with or waived by all eligible parties

4. b The condominium association's board of directors or managing agent, not the license holder or the seller

5. c The seller retains the right to harvest all growing crops until delivery of possession, unless the parties specifically agree otherwise in writing

6. a 33 and one-third inches

7. d Not sign this section if a separate written agreement for payment of brokers' fees already exists between the parties

8. b The buyer's right to object if any portion of the property is located in a FEMA special flood hazard area

9. c Whenever the seller intends to retain all or any portion of the mineral estate rather than conveying it to the buyer

10. d The Federal Trade Commission's R-value rule, which requires new home sellers to disclose the thermal performance characteristics of the insulation installed in the structure

11. a When a buyer contracts to purchase a spec house that a builder is currently constructing before construction is complete

Answer Key - Chapter 7

1. c A written agreement that is non-exclusive and is limited to no more than 14 days

2. a Agent for the owner, in which the broker represents the seller or landlord through a written listing or property management agreement

3. d It is not binding because only a signed written amendment agreed to by both parties can modify a promulgated contract

4. b The seller warrants that the seller owns the personal property free and clear of all encumbrances, liens, and security interests

5. a Approved means TREC has reviewed the form and finds it acceptable for use, but its use is not mandatory; a Bill of Sale prepared by an attorney may serve as an alternative

6. d The association's board of directors or managing agent, not the license holder or the seller

7. c The buyer may terminate within three days after receiving the Subdivision Information, or before closing, whichever occurs first

8. b The seller must notify the buyer of the accepted offer and simultaneously notify the buyer that the seller requires the buyer to waive the contingency

9. a The buyer must notify the seller in writing of the waiver and must deposit a stated amount of additional earnest money with the escrow agent

10. d On the date the first contract terminates, with all deadlines in the back-up contract running from that date forward

11. c On the noteholder's approval of a sale at a price that is insufficient to pay off all existing liens in full

12. b It tells the license holder that Form 44-3 applies to any TREC-promulgated contract form, not only to the Farm and Ranch Contract

13. d Properties located on the Gulf side of the Gulf Intracoastal Waterway, such as those on Padre Island and Galveston Island

14. a The property's boundary adjoins and shares a common boundary with the tidally influenced submerged lands of the state of Texas

15. c The seller must disclose the contents of the report to any subsequent buyer, because the seller now has actual knowledge of the condition

16. b When a property borders tidally influenced waters and is also located seaward of the Gulf Intracoastal Waterway

17. a A phrase such as "at lender's discretion," which is imprecise and creates a legal consequence the license holder may not impose

Answer Key - Chapter 8

1. d Intent, because fraud requires that the person making the statement knew it was false or knew that the truth would harm the other party

2. b "The fence line is the property line."

3. a A signed written buyer representation agreement that specifies how the buyer's broker will be compensated and who will pay that compensation

4. c Two or more competing brokers agree with each other to charge the same commission rate, thereby eliminating price competition

5. d Age

6. a Sex

7. b 1 year from the date of the discriminatory act

8. d 15% of the amount realized on the sale

9. c The public disclosure of sex offender registration information to alert communities to the presence of convicted sex offenders

10. b Two persons per bedroom is, as a general rule, a reasonable occupancy policy, though it is not an automatic safe harbor in every situation

FORM APPLICATION WORKSHOP
COMPLETED FORMS

The completed worksheets below correspond to the three case studies in Chapter 9. Compare your entries against them. Where the facts did not call for an entry, the correct response is a blank or not applicable, and that is shown. The notes explain the entries that most often cause errors.

Case A: Completed Form

Paragraph 1 - Parties

Seller(s): Howard Pruitt and Lillian Pruitt
Buyer(s): Maria Ortega and Daniel Ortega

Paragraph 2 - Property

Lot / Block / Addition / Section: Lot 14, Block 3, Brookhaven Estates, Section Two
City / County: Round Rock, Williamson County
Street address: 1428 Brookhaven Lane

Paragraph 3 - Sales Price

3A. Cash portion: $ 77,000
3B. Sum of all financing: $ 308,000
3C. Sales Price: $ 385,000

Note: The cash portion (3A) plus the financing (3B) must equal the sales price (3C). A mismatch among these three figures is one of the most common completion errors.

Paragraph 4 - Leases

Applicable leases: None

Paragraph 5 - Earnest Money and Termination Option

Earnest money: $ 5,000
Escrow agent: Heritage Title Company, 200 East Main Street, Round Rock
Option fee: $ 300
Option period: 10 days after the effective date

Paragraph 6 - Title Policy and Survey

Owner's title policy paid by: Seller
Title company: Heritage Title Company
Survey: Buyer will use the Seller's existing survey if acceptable to the title company and the lender; if a new survey is required, Buyer pays for it

Paragraph 7 - Property Condition

Acceptance: Buyer accepts the Property in its present condition
Repairs requested: None

Paragraph 8 - Broker and Sales Agent Disclosure

Disclosure required: No; leave blank

Note: Paragraph 8 is a disclosure that applies only when a party or a family member of a party is a license holder. It is not a place to state commission terms; brokerage compensation is addressed in Paragraph 12 and in the parties' separate written agreements.

Paragraph 9 - Closing
Closing Date: October 9, 2026

Paragraph 10 - Possession
Possession: Upon closing and funding

Paragraph 11 - Special Provisions
Entries: None

Final Page
Effective Date: September 8, 2026

Third Party Financing Addendum (Form 40-11)
Type of financing: Conventional
Principal loan amount: $ 308,000
Term: 30 years
Interest not to exceed: 7.5 percent
Credit approval within: 21 days after the effective date
Note: The financing addendum must be checked and attached in Paragraph 22, and its principal amount must match Paragraph 3B. The 40-11 in effect July 1, 2026 uses a credit-approval framework: the buyer applies promptly and must obtain credit approval within the stated number of days.

Case B: Completed Form

Paragraph 1 - Parties
Seller(s): Robert Feldman
Buyer(s): Priya Nair

Paragraph 2 - Property
Legal description / city / county / address: Lot 7, Block B, Camden Park, Phase 1; Frisco, Collin County; 92 Camden Court

Paragraph 3 - Sales Price
3A. Cash: $ 122,400
3B. Financing: $ 489,600
3C. Sales Price: $ 612,000

Paragraph 5 - Earnest Money and Termination Option
Earnest money: $ 10,000
Escrow agent: Collin County Title Company, 1500 Preston Road, Frisco
Option fee: $ 500
Option period: 12 days

Paragraph 6E - Required Notices
Mandatory HOA membership: Check the is box; attach Form 36-11 and reference it in Paragraph 22

Paragraph 7B - Seller's Disclosure Notice
Notice received by Buyer: Yes; delivered before the offer (Form 55-1)

Paragraph 12 - Settlement and Other Expenses
12A(1)(b). Seller's contribution to Buyer's other expenses: $ 4,000

12B(1). Seller's contribution to Buyer's broker's compensation: 2.5 percent of the sales price
12B(2). Buyer's contribution to Seller's broker's compensation: None; leave blank

Note: This is the entry most likely to be done incorrectly. The seller's 2.5 percent contribution toward the buyer's broker goes in Paragraph 12B(1), not in 12A(1)(b). The separate $4,000 the seller agreed to put toward the buyer's other closing costs goes in 12A(1)(b) and must be a dollar amount. Paragraph 12B(2) is left blank because the buyer is not contributing toward the seller's broker. The half-percent difference the buyer owes her own broker is governed by her buyer representation agreement, not by the contract.

Paragraph 9 - Closing

Closing Date: October 20, 2026

Paragraph 10 - Possession

Possession: Per the Buyer's Temporary Residential Lease (Form 16-7), beginning October 15, 2026

Paragraph 22 - Agreement of Parties

Addenda checked and attached: Third Party Financing Addendum (40-11); Addendum for Property Subject to Mandatory Membership in a Property Owners Association (36-11); Buyer's Temporary Residential Lease (16-7)

Note: Each addendum that applies must be both attached and checked in Paragraph 22. Because possession passes before closing, Paragraph 10 points to the temporary lease, and Form 16-7 is attached.

Final Page

Effective Date: September 15, 2026

Buyer's Temporary Residential Lease (Form 16-7)

Commencement and term: October 15, 2026; 5 days, through closing on October 20, 2026
Daily rental and deposit: Negotiated business terms entered from the parties' agreement; the facts do not fix a figure, so these blanks are completed from what the parties agree

Case C: Completed Form

Paragraph 1 - Parties

Seller (builder): Evergreen Builders, LLC
Buyer: Aaron Whitfield

Paragraph 2 - Property

Legal description / city / county / address: Lot 22, Block 5, Sundance Ridge, Section 4; Georgetown, Williamson County; 305 Mesquite Trail

Paragraph 3 - Sales Price

3A. Cash: $ 44,800
3B. Financing: $ 403,200
3C. Sales Price: $ 448,000

Paragraph 5 - Earnest Money and Termination Option

Earnest money: $ 6,000
Escrow agent: Sundance Title Company
Option fee: $ 400
Option period: 7 days

Paragraph 7 - Property Condition (new construction)

Seller's Disclosure Notice: Not provided; a builder selling a new home for the first time is exempt under the Texas Property Code (do not attach Form 55-1)

Builder warranty: Provided as a separate written document

Manufacturers' warranties: Pass to the Buyer at closing

Insulation - ceiling: R-38 blown fiberglass

Insulation - exterior walls: R-15 batt fiberglass

Note: The defining difference from the resale contract is the absence of a Seller's Disclosure Notice. The insulation disclosure is required by federal law (the FTC R-value rule) and is completed from the figures the builder supplies; the license holder records, but does not generate, those figures.

Paragraph 9 - Closing

Closing Date: October 23, 2026

Paragraph 10 - Possession

Possession: Upon closing and funding

Final Page

Effective Date: September 22, 2026

Third Party Financing Addendum (Form 40-11)

Type / principal / term / interest cap / approval: Conventional; $403,200; 30 years; not to exceed 7.5 percent; credit approval within 21 days

APPENDIX
TREC FORMS

The following pages reproduce the current Texas Real Estate Commission (TREC) forms referenced throughout this text, provided so that you can study and practice on the same documents you will use in practice. They are grouped by function, and within each group the forms appear in the order TREC publishes them. Each form is identified by its form number and effective date. Forms are revised periodically, so always confirm you are using the current version at trec.texas.gov before relying on any form in a live transaction.

How This Appendix Is Organized

The forms are divided into six groups. Each group begins on its own divider page and is followed by the forms in that group:

Promulgated Contracts (6 forms): the TREC sale contracts.

Amendment (1 form): the Amendment to Contract.

Promulgated Addenda (23 forms): addenda attached to a promulgated contract.

Resale Certificates (2 forms): owners association and condominium resale certificates.

Promulgated Notices and Disclosures (9 forms): notices and disclosures used with a promulgated contract.

Required Disclosures (1 form): the Information About Brokerage Services notice.

In all, 42 forms are reproduced. Each group divider lists its forms with form numbers and effective dates.

PROMULGATED CONTRACTS
The Six TREC Promulgated Sale Contracts

Farm and Ranch Contract (Form 25-17, effective 07/01/2026)
New Home Contract (Completed Construction) (Form 24-20, effective 07/01/2026)
New Home Contract (Incomplete Construction) (Form 23-20, effective 07/01/2026)
One to Four Family Residential Contract (Resale) (Form 20-19, effective 07/01/2026)
Residential Condominium Contract (Resale) (Form 30-18, effective 07/01/2026)
Unimproved Property Contract (Form 9-18, effective 07/01/2026)

PROMULGATED BY THE TEXAS REAL ESTATE COMMISSION (TREC) 05-04-2026

FARM AND RANCH CONTRACT

NOTICE: Designed For Use In Sales Of Existing Farms Or Ranches Of Any Size. Not For Use In Complex Transactions.

1. PARTIES: The parties to this contract are ______________________________ (Seller) and ______________________________ (Buyer). Seller agrees to sell and convey to Buyer and Buyer agrees to buy from Seller the Property defined below.

2. PROPERTY: The land, improvements, accessories and crops except for the exclusions and reservations, are collectively referred to as the Property (Property).

A. LAND: The land situated in the County (or Counties) of ______________________________ ______________________________, Texas, described as follows: ______________________________ ______________________________ ______________________________ or as described on attached exhibit, also known as ______________________________ (address/zip code), together with all rights, privileges, and appurtenances pertaining thereto.

B. IMPROVEMENTS:

(1) FARM and RANCH IMPROVEMENTS: The following **permanently installed and built-in items**, if any: windmills, tanks, barns, pens, fences, gates, sheds, outbuildings, and corrals.

(2) RESIDENTIAL IMPROVEMENTS: Any houses, garages, and all other fixtures and improvements attached to the above-described real property, including without limitation, the following **permanently installed and built-in items,** if any: all equipment and appliances, valances, screens, shutters, awnings, wall-to-wall carpeting, mirrors, ceiling fans, attic fans, mail boxes, television antennas, mounts and brackets for televisions and speakers, heating and air-conditioning units, security and fire detection equipment, wiring, plumbing and lighting fixtures, chandeliers, water softener system, kitchen equipment, garage door openers, cleaning equipment, shrubbery, landscaping, outdoor cooking equipment, generators, and all other property attached to the above described real property.

C. ACCESSORIES:

(1) FARM AND RANCH ACCESSORIES: The following described related accessories: (check boxes of conveyed accessories) ❑ portable buildings ❑ hunting blinds ❑ game feeders ❑ livestock feeders and troughs ❑ irrigation equipment ❑ fuel tanks ❑ submersible pumps ❑ pressure tanks ❑ corrals ❑ gates ❑ chutes ❑ other: ______________________________ ______________________________.

(2) RESIDENTIAL ACCESSORIES: The following described related accessories, if any: window air conditioning units, stove, fireplace screens, curtains and rods, blinds, window shades, draperies and rods, door keys, mailbox keys, above ground pool, swimming pool equipment and maintenance accessories, artificial fireplace logs, security systems that are not fixtures, and controls for: (i) garage doors, (ii) entry gates, and (iii) other improvements and accessories. "Controls" includes Seller's transferable rights to the (i) software and applications used to access and control improvements or accessories, and (ii) hardware used solely to control improvements or accessories.

D. CROPS: Unless otherwise agreed in writing, Seller has the right to harvest all growing crops until delivery of possession of the Property.

E. EXCLUSIONS: The following improvements, accessories, and crops will be retained by Seller and must be removed prior to delivery of possession: ______________________________ ______________________________.

F. RESERVATIONS: Any reservation for oil, gas, or other minerals, water, timber, or other interests is made in accordance with an attached addendum.

3. SALES PRICE:

A. Cash portion of Sales Price payable by Buyer at closing .... $____________
The term "Cash portion of the Sales Price" does not include proceeds from borrowing of any kind or selling other real property except as disclosed in this contract.

B. Sum of all financing described in the attached: ❑ Third Party Financing Addendum, ❑ Loan Assumption Addendum, ❑ Seller Financing Addendum .. $____________

C. Sales Price (Sum of A and B) .... $____________

D. The Sales Price ❑ will ❑ will not be adjusted based on the survey required by Paragraph 6C. If the Sales Price is adjusted, the Sales Price will be adjusted based on the difference between _______ acres and the acreage set forth in the survey required by Paragraph 6C. The difference in acreage (either increased or decreased) shall be multiplied by the sum of $________ per acre and either added to or subtracted from the Sales Price stated in Paragraph 3C. If the Sales Price is adjusted by more than 10%, either party may terminate this contract by providing written notice to the other party within ____ days after the terminating party receives the survey. If neither party terminates this contract or if the variance is 10% or less, the adjustment will be made to the amount in ❑ 3A ❑ 3B ❑ proportionately to 3A and 3B.

4. LEASES: Except as disclosed in this contract, Seller is not aware of any leases affecting the Property. After the Effective Date, Seller may not, without Buyer's written consent, create a new lease, amend any existing lease, or convey any interest in the Property. (Check all applicable boxes)

❑ A. RESIDENTIAL LEASES: The Property is subject to one or more residential leases and the Addendum Regarding Residential Leases is attached to this contract.

❑ B. FIXTURE LEASES: Fixtures on the Property are subject to one or more fixture leases (for example, solar panels, propane tanks, water softener, security system) and the Addendum Regarding Fixture Leases is attached to this contract.

Initialed for identification by Buyer______ ______ and Seller _______ ______ TREC NO. 25-17

❑ C. NATURAL RESOURCE LEASES: "Natural Resource Lease" means an existing oil and gas, mineral, geothermal, water, or other natural resource lease affecting the Property to which Seller is a party.

❑ (1) Seller has delivered to Buyer a copy of all the Natural Resource Leases.

❑ (2) Seller has not delivered to Buyer a copy of all the Natural Resource Leases. Seller shall provide to Buyer a copy of all the Natural Resource Leases within 3 days after the Effective Date. Buyer may terminate the contract within _____ days after the date the Buyer receives all the Natural Resource Leases and the earnest money shall be refunded to Buyer.

❑ D. SURFACE LEASES: "Surface Lease" means an existing lease for the surface only of the Property (for example, grazing leases, hunting leases, agricultural leases, recreational leases, wind leases, solar leases, timber or forestry leases). (Check all applicable boxes)

❑ (1) Seller has delivered to Buyer a copy of all written Surface Leases.

❑ (2) Seller provides Buyer with notice of the following oral Surface Lease(s), identifying the type of lease, name of the tenant(s), rental amount, and term:__________________________________
____.

❑ (3) Seller has not delivered to Buyer all Surface Leases (whether written or oral). Seller shall provide to Buyer a copy of all the written Surface Leases and notice of all oral Surface Leases, identifying the type of lease, the name of the tenant(s), rental amount, and term, within 3 days after the Effective Date. Buyer may terminate the contract within _____ days after the date the Buyer receives all the Surface Leases and the earnest money shall be refunded to Buyer.

5. EARNEST MONEY AND TERMINATION OPTION:

A. DELIVERY OF EARNEST MONEY AND OPTION FEE: Within 3 days after the Effective Date, Buyer must deliver to ___________________________________ (Escrow Agent) at ___________ ____(address): $__________________ as earnest money and $_________________ as the option fee. The earnest money and option fee shall be made payable to escrow agent and may be paid separately or combined in a single payment.

(1) Buyer shall deliver additional earnest money of $_____________ to Escrow Agent within _____ days after the Effective Date of this contract.

(2) If the last day to deliver the earnest money, option fee, or the additional earnest money falls on a Saturday, Sunday, or Legal Holiday, the time to deliver the earnest money, option fee, or the additional earnest money, as applicable, is extended until the end of the next day that is not a Saturday, Sunday, or Legal Holiday. "Legal Holiday" means a legal holiday described in Sections 662.003(a) and 662.003(b)(4) and (6), Texas Government Code.

(3) The amount(s) Escrow Agent receives under this paragraph shall be applied first to the option fee, then to the earnest money, and then to the additional earnest money.

(4) Buyer authorizes Escrow Agent to release and deliver the option fee to Seller at any time without further notice to or consent from Buyer, and releases Escrow Agent from liability for delivery of the option fee to Seller. The option fee will be credited to the Sales Price at closing.

B. TERMINATION OPTION: For nominal consideration, the receipt of which Seller acknowledges, and Buyer's agreement to pay the option fee within the time required, Seller grants Buyer the unrestricted right to terminate this contract by giving notice of termination to Seller within _______ days after the Effective Date of this contract (Option Period). Notices under this paragraph must be given by 5:00 p.m. (local time where the Property is located) by the date specified. If Buyer gives notice of termination within the time prescribed: (i) the option fee will not be refunded and Escrow Agent shall release any option fee remaining with Escrow Agent to Seller; and (ii) any earnest money will be refunded to Buyer.

C. FAILURE TO TIMELY DELIVER EARNEST MONEY: If Buyer fails to deliver the earnest money within the time required, Seller may terminate this contract or exercise Seller's remedies under Paragraph 15, or both, by providing notice to Buyer before Buyer delivers the earnest money.

D. FAILURE TO TIMELY DELIVER OPTION FEE: If no dollar amount is stated as the option fee or if Buyer fails to deliver the option fee within the time required, Buyer shall not have the unrestricted right to terminate this contract under this Paragraph 5.

E. TIME: **Time is of the essence for this paragraph and strict compliance with the time for performance is required.**

6. TITLE POLICY AND SURVEY:

A. TITLE POLICY: Seller shall furnish to Buyer at ❑ Seller's ❑ Buyer's expense an owner policy of title insurance (Title Policy) issued by: ___________________________________ (Title Company) in the amount of the Sales Price, dated at or after closing, insuring Buyer against loss under the provisions of the Title Policy, subject to the promulgated exclusions (including existing building and zoning ordinances) and the following exceptions:

(1) The standard printed exception for standby fees, taxes and assessments.
(2) Liens created as part of the financing described in Paragraph 3.
(3) Reservations or exceptions otherwise permitted by this contract or as may be approved by Buyer in writing.
(4) The standard printed exception as to marital rights.
(5) The standard printed exception as to waters, tidelands, beaches, streams, and related matters.
(6) The standard printed exception as to discrepancies, conflicts, shortages in area or boundary lines, encroachments or protrusions, or overlapping improvements:

❑ (i) will not be amended or deleted from the title policy; or
❑ (ii) will be amended to read, "shortages in area" at the expense of ❑ Buyer ❑ Seller.

(7) The exception or exclusion regarding minerals approved by the Texas Department of Insurance.

B. COMMITMENT: Within 20 days after the Title Company receives a copy of this contract, Seller shall furnish to Buyer a commitment for title insurance (Commitment) and, at Buyer's expense, legible copies of restrictive covenants and documents evidencing exceptions in the Commitment (Exception Documents) other than the standard printed exceptions. Seller authorizes the Title Company to deliver the Commitment and Exception Documents to Buyer at Buyer's address shown in Paragraph 21. If the Commitment and Exception Documents are not delivered to Buyer within the specified time, the time for delivery will be automatically extended up to 15 days or 3 days before the Closing Date, whichever is earlier. If the Commitment and Exception Documents are not delivered within the time required, Buyer may terminate this contract and the earnest money will be refunded to Buyer.

C. SURVEY: The survey must be made by a registered professional land surveyor acceptable to the Title Company and Buyer's lender(s). (Check one box only):

❑ (1) Within ______ days after the Effective Date of this contract, Seller shall furnish to Buyer and Title Company Seller's existing survey of the Property and a Residential Real Property Affidavit or Declaration promulgated by the Texas Department of Insurance (T-47 Affidavit or T-47.1 Declaration). Buyer shall obtain a new survey at Seller's expense no later than 3 days prior to Closing Date if Seller fails to furnish within the time prescribed both the: (i) existing survey; and (ii) affidavit or declaration. If the Title Company or Buyer's lender does not accept the existing survey, or the affidavit or declaration, Buyer shall obtain a new survey at ❑ Seller's ❑ Buyer's expense no later than 3 days prior to Closing Date.

❑ (2) Within ______ days after the Effective Date of this contract, Buyer may obtain a new survey at Buyer's expense. Buyer is deemed to receive the survey on the date of actual receipt or the date specified in this paragraph, whichever is earlier. If Buyer fails to obtain the survey, Buyer may not terminate the contract under Paragraph 2B of the Third Party Financing Addendum because the survey was not obtained.

❑ (3) Within ______ days after the Effective Date of this contract, Seller, at Seller's expense shall furnish a new survey to Buyer.

❑ (4) No survey is required.

D. OBJECTIONS: Buyer may object in writing to (i) defects, exceptions, or encumbrances to title disclosed on the survey other than items 6A(1) through (5) above; or disclosed in the Commitment other than items 6A(1) through (7) above; (ii) any portion of the Property lying in a special flood hazard area (Zone V or A) as shown on the current Federal Emergency Management Agency map; or (iii) any exceptions which prohibit the following use or activity:______________________
____
____.
Buyer must object the earlier of (i) the Closing Date or (ii) ______ days after Buyer receives the Commitment, Exception Documents, and the survey. Buyer's failure to object within the time allowed will constitute a waiver of Buyer's right to object; except that the requirements in Schedule C of the Commitment are not waived by Buyer. Provided Seller is not obligated to incur any expense, Seller shall cure any timely objections of Buyer or any third party lender within 15 days after Seller receives the objections (Cure Period) and the Closing Date will be extended as necessary. If objections are not cured within the Cure Period, Buyer may, by delivering notice to Seller within 5 days after the end of the Cure Period: (i) terminate this contract and the earnest money will be refunded to Buyer; or (ii) waive the objections. If Buyer does not terminate within the time required, Buyer shall be deemed to have waived the objections. If the Commitment or survey is revised or any new Exception Document(s) is delivered, Buyer may object to any new matter revealed in the revised Commitment or survey or new Exception Document(s) within the same time stated in this paragraph to make objections beginning when the revised Commitment, survey, or Exception Document(s) is delivered to Buyer.

E. EXCEPTION DOCUMENTS: Prior to the execution of the contract, Seller has provided Buyer with copies of the Exception Documents listed below or on the attached exhibit. Matters reflected in the Exception Documents listed below or on the attached exhibit will be permitted exceptions in the Title Policy and will not be a basis for objection to title:

Document	Date	Recording Reference
____________	____________	____________
____________	____________	____________
____________	____________	____________

F. SURFACE LEASES: The following Surface Leases will be permitted exceptions in the Title Policy and will not be a basis for objection to title:______________________________________
____.

G. TITLE NOTICES:

(1) ABSTRACT OR TITLE POLICY: Broker advises Buyer to have an abstract of title covering the Property examined by an attorney of Buyer's selection, or Buyer should be furnished with or obtain a Title Policy. If a Title Policy is furnished, the Commitment should be promptly reviewed by an attorney of Buyer's choice due to the time limitations on Buyer's right to object.

(2) STATUTORY TAX DISTRICTS: If the Property is situated in a utility or other statutorily created district providing water, sewer, drainage, or flood control facilities and services, Chapter 49,

Texas Water Code, requires Seller to deliver and Buyer to sign the statutory notice relating to the tax rate, bonded indebtedness, or standby fee of the district prior to final execution of this contract.

(3) TIDE WATERS: If the Property abuts the tidally influenced waters of the state, §33.135, Texas Natural Resources Code, requires a notice regarding coastal area property to be included in the contract.

(4) ANNEXATION: If the Property is located outside the limits of a municipality, Seller notifies Buyer under §5.011, Texas Property Code, that the Property may now or later be included in the extraterritorial jurisdiction of a municipality and may now or later be subject to annexation by the municipality. Each municipality maintains a map that depicts its boundaries and extraterritorial jurisdiction. To determine if the Property is located within a municipality's extraterritorial jurisdiction or is likely to be located within a municipality's extraterritorial jurisdiction, contact all municipalities located in the general proximity of the Property for further information.

(5) PROPERTY LOCATED IN A CERTIFICATED SERVICE AREA OF A UTILITY SERVICE PROVIDER: Notice required by §13.257, Water Code: The real property, described in Paragraph 2, that you are about to purchase may be located in a certificated water or sewer service area, which is authorized by law to provide water or sewer service to the properties in the certificated area. If your property is located in a certificated area there may be special costs or charges that you will be required to pay before you can receive water or sewer service. There may be a period required to construct lines or other facilities necessary to provide water or sewer service to your property. You are advised to determine if the property is in a certificated area and contact the utility service provider to determine the cost that you will be required to pay and the period, if any, that is required to provide water or sewer service to your property. The undersigned Buyer hereby acknowledges receipt of the foregoing notice at or before the execution of a binding contract for the purchase of the real property described in Paragraph 2 or at closing of purchase of the real property.

(6) PUBLIC IMPROVEMENT DISTRICTS: If the Property is in a public improvement district, Seller must give Buyer written notice as required by §5.014, Property Code.

(7) TEXAS AGRICULTURAL DEVELOPMENT DISTRICT: The Property ☐ is ☐ is not located in a Texas Agricultural Development District. For additional information contact the Texas Department of Agriculture

(8) TRANSFER FEES: If the Property is subject to a private transfer fee obligation, §5.205, Property Code, requires Seller to notify Buyer as follows: The private transfer fee obligation may be governed by Chapter 5, Subchapter G of the Texas Property Code.

(9) PROPANE GAS SYSTEM SERVICE AREA: If the Property is located in a propane gas system service area owned by a distribution system retailer, Seller must give Buyer written notice as required by §141.010, Texas Utilities Code.

(10) NOTICE OF WATER LEVEL FLUCTUATIONS: If the Property adjoins an impoundment of water, including a reservoir or lake, constructed and maintained under Chapter 11, Water Code, that has a storage capacity of at least 5,000 acre-feet at the impoundment's normal operating level, Seller hereby notifies Buyer: "The water level of the impoundment of water adjoining the Property fluctuates for various reasons, including as a result of: (1) an entity lawfully exercising its right to use the water stored in the impoundment; or (2) drought or flood conditions."

(11) CERTIFICATE OF MOLD REMEDIATION: If the Property has been remediated for mold, Seller must provide to Buyer each certificate of mold damage remediation issued under §1958.154, Occupations Code, during the 5 years preceding the sale of the Property.

7. PROPERTY CONDITION:

A. ACCESS, INSPECTIONS AND UTILITIES: Seller shall permit Buyer and Buyer's agents access to the Property at reasonable times. Buyer may have the Property inspected by inspectors selected by Buyer and licensed by TREC or otherwise permitted by law to make inspections. Any hydrostatic testing must be separately authorized by Seller in writing. Seller at Seller's expense shall immediately cause existing utilities to be turned on and shall keep the utilities on during the time this contract is in effect .

NOTICE: Buyer should determine the availability of utilities to the Property suitable to satisfy Buyer's needs.

B. SELLER'S DISCLOSURE NOTICE PURSUANT TO §5.008, TEXAS PROPERTY CODE (Seller's Disclosure Notice):
(Check one box only)

☐ (1) Buyer has received the Seller's Disclosure Notice

☐ (2) Buyer has not received the Seller's Disclosure Notice. Within _______ days after the Effective Date of this contract, Seller shall deliver the Seller's Disclosure Notice to Buyer. If Buyer does not receive the Seller's Disclosure Notice, Buyer may terminate this contract at any time prior to the closing and the earnest money will be refunded to Buyer. If Seller delivers the Seller's Disclosure Notice, Buyer may terminate this contract for any reason within 7 days after Buyer receives the Seller's Disclosure Notice or prior to the closing, whichever first occurs, and the earnest money will be refunded to Buyer.

☐ (3) The Texas Property Code does not require this Seller to furnish the Seller's Disclosure Notice.

C. SELLER'S DISCLOSURE OF LEAD-BASED PAINT AND LEAD-BASED PAINT HAZARDS is required by Federal law for a residential dwelling constructed prior to 1978.

D. ACCEPTANCE OF PROPERTY CONDITION: "As Is" means the present condition of the Property with any and all defects and without warranty except for the warranties of title and the warranties in this contract. Buyer's agreement to accept the Property As Is under Paragraph 7D(1) or (2) does not preclude Buyer from inspecting the Property under Paragraph 7A, from negotiating repairs or treatments in a subsequent amendment, or from terminating this contract during the Option Period, if any.

(Check one box only)

❑ (1) Buyer accepts the Property As Is.

❑ (2) Buyer accepts the Property As Is provided Seller, at Seller's expense, shall complete the following specific repairs and treatments: ____

____.

(Do not insert general phrases, such as "subject to inspections," that do not identify specific repairs and treatments.)

E. COMPLETION OF REPAIRS AND TREATMENTS: Unless otherwise agreed in writing, Seller shall complete all agreed repairs and treatments prior to the Closing Date and obtain any required permits. The repairs and treatments must be performed by persons who are licensed to provide such repairs or treatments or, if no license is required by law, are commercially engaged in the trade of providing such repairs or treatments. Seller shall: (i) provide Buyer with copies of documentation from the repair person(s) showing the scope of work and payment for the work completed; and (ii) at Seller's expense, arrange for the transfer of any transferable warranties with respect to the repairs to Buyer at closing. If Seller fails to complete any agreed repairs prior to the Closing Date, Buyer may exercise remedies under Paragraph 15 or extend the Closing Date up to 5 days if necessary for Seller to complete repairs.

F. LENDER REQUIRED REPAIRS AND TREATMENTS: Unless otherwise agreed in writing, neither party is obligated to pay for lender required repairs, which includes treatment for wood destroying insects. If the parties do not agree to pay for the lender required repairs or treatments, this contract will terminate and the earnest money will be refunded to Buyer. If the cost of lender required repairs and treatments exceeds 5% of the Sales Price, Buyer may terminate this contract and the earnest money will be refunded to Buyer.

G. ENVIRONMENTAL MATTERS: Buyer is advised that the presence of wetlands, toxic substances, including asbestos and wastes or other environmental hazards, or the presence of a threatened or endangered species or its habitat may affect Buyer's intended use of the Property. If Buyer is concerned about these matters, an addendum promulgated by TREC or required by the parties should be used.

H. SELLER'S DISCLOSURE:

(1) Seller ❑ is ❑ is not aware of any flooding of the Property which has had a material adverse effect on the use of the Property.

(2) Seller ❑ is ❑ is not aware of any pending or threatened litigation, condemnation, or special assessment affecting the Property.

(3) Seller ❑ is ❑ is not aware of any environmental hazards that materially and adversely affect the Property.

(4) Seller ❑ is ❑ is not aware of any dumpsite, landfill, or underground tanks or containers now or previously located on the Property.

(5) Seller ❑ is ❑ is not aware of any wetlands, as defined by federal or state law or regulation, affecting the Property.

(6) Seller ❑ is ❑ is not aware of any threatened or endangered species or their habitat affecting the Property.

(7) Seller ❑ is ❑ is not aware that the Property is located ❑ wholly ❑ partly in a floodplain.

(8) Seller ❑ is ❑ is not aware that a tree or trees located on the Property has oak wilt.

If Seller is aware of any of the items above, explain (attach additional sheets if necessary): ____.

I. RESIDENTIAL SERVICE CONTRACTS: Buyer may purchase a residential service contract from a provider or administrator licensed by the Texas Department of Licensing and Regulation. If Buyer purchases a residential service contract, Seller shall reimburse Buyer at closing for the cost of the residential service contract in an amount not exceeding $_______________. Buyer should review any residential service contract for the scope of coverage, exclusions and limitations. **The purchase of a residential service contract is optional. Similar coverage may be purchased from various companies authorized to do business in Texas.**

J. GOVERNMENT PROGRAMS: The Property is subject to the government programs listed below or on the attached exhibit: ____

____.

Seller shall provide Buyer with copies of all governmental program agreements. Any allocation or proration of payment under governmental programs is made by separate agreement between the parties which will survive closing.

K. SELLER'S DISCLOSURE ABOUT GROUNDWATER AND SURFACE WATER RIGHTS (Seller's Water Disclosure): Access to surface water or groundwater on the Property may be regulated, restricted, or prohibited, including but not limited to the right to drill or operate water wells and the right to withdraw water from surface water sources on or adjoining the Property. The parties shall use the Seller's Water Disclosure published by TREC to identify information related to groundwater and surface water rights. (Check one box only)

❑ (1) Buyer has received the Seller's Water Disclosure.

❑ (2) Buyer has not received the Seller's Water Disclosure. Within ____days after the Effective Date of this contract, Seller shall deliver the Seller's Water Disclosure to Buyer. If Buyer does not receive the Seller's Water Disclosure, Buyer may terminate this contract at any time prior to the closing and the earnest money will be refunded to Buyer. If Seller delivers the Seller's Water Disclosure, Buyer may terminate this contract for any reason within 7 days after Buyer receives the Seller's Water Disclosure or prior to the closing, whichever first occurs, and the earnest money will be refunded to Buyer.

❑ (3) Seller is not required to deliver the Seller's Water Disclosure to Buyer because all of the following are true:

(a) Seller is not aware of a water well on the Property (in use or not in use);
(b) Seller is not aware of a pond, lake, or water tank on the Property;
(c) Seller is not aware of any certificate of adjudication, certified filing, or permit for surface water rights associated with the Property administered by the Texas Commission on Environmental Quality;
(d) Seller is not aware that any groundwater rights to the Property have been severed, sold, or leased in whole or in part; and
(e) the Property receives water only from the following municipality (City), municipal utility district (MUD) or other special district, water supply corporation (WSC), or private water supply company (PWC):____
____.

8. BROKER OR SALES AGENT DISCLOSURE:
Texas law requires a real estate broker or sales agent who is a party to a transaction or acting on behalf of a spouse, parent, child, business entity in which the broker or sales agent owns more than 10%, or a trust for which the broker or sales agent acts as a trustee or of which the broker or sales agent or the broker or sales agent's spouse, parent or child is a beneficiary, to notify the other party in writing before entering into a contract of sale. Disclose if applicable:__________________
____.

9. CLOSING:
A. The closing of the sale will be on or before ____________________, 20_____, or within 7 days after objections made under Paragraph 6D have been cured or waived, whichever date is later (Closing Date). If either party fails to close the sale by the Closing Date, the non-defaulting party may exercise the remedies contained in Paragraph 15.

B. At closing:
(1) Seller shall execute and deliver a general warranty deed conveying title to the Property to Buyer and showing no additional exceptions to those permitted in Paragraph 6, an assignment of Leases, and furnish tax statements or certificates showing no delinquent taxes on the Property.
(2) Buyer shall pay the Sales Price in good funds acceptable to the Escrow Agent.
(3) Seller and Buyer shall execute and deliver any notices, statements, certificates, affidavits, releases, loan documents, transfer of any warranties, and other documents reasonably required for the closing of the sale and the issuance of the Title Policy.
(4) There will be no liens, assessments, or security interests against the Property which will not be satisfied out of the sales proceeds unless securing the payment of any loans assumed by Buyer and assumed loans will not be in default.
(5) Private transfer fees (as defined by Chapter 5, Subchapter G of the Texas Property Code) will be the obligation of Seller unless provided otherwise in this contract. Transfer fees assessed by a property owners' association are governed by the Addendum for Property Subject to Mandatory Membership in a Property Owners Association.

10. POSSESSION:
A. BUYER'S POSSESSION: Seller shall deliver to Buyer possession of the Property in its present or required condition, ordinary wear and tear excepted: ❑ upon closing and funding ❑ according to a temporary residential lease form promulgated by TREC or other written lease required by the parties. Any possession by Buyer prior to closing or by Seller after closing which is not authorized by a written lease will establish a tenancy at sufferance relationship between the parties. **Consult your insurance agent prior to change of ownership and possession because insurance coverage may be limited or terminated. The absence of a written lease or appropriate insurance coverage may expose the parties to economic loss.**

B. SMART DEVICES: "Smart Device" means a device that connects to the internet to enable remote use, monitoring, and management of: (i) the Property; (ii) items identified in any Non-Realty Items Addendum; or (iii) items in a Fixture Lease assigned to Buyer. At the time Seller delivers possession of the Property to Buyer, Seller shall:
(1) deliver to Buyer written information containing all access codes, usernames, passwords, and applications Buyer will need to access, operate, manage, and control the Smart Devices; and
(2) terminate and remove all access and connections to the improvements and accessories from any of Seller's personal devices including but not limited to phones and computers.

11. SPECIAL PROVISIONS: (This paragraph is intended to be used only for additional informational items. An informational item is a statement that completes a blank in a contract form, discloses factual information, or provides instructions. Real estate brokers and sales agents are prohibited from practicing law and shall not add to, delete, or modify any provision of this contract unless drafted by a party to this contract or a party's attorney.)______________________________________
____.

12. SETTLEMENT AND OTHER EXPENSES:
A. EXPENSES: The following expenses must be paid at or prior to closing:
(1) Seller shall pay the following expenses (Seller's Expenses):
(a) releases of existing liens, including prepayment penalties and recording fees; release of Seller's loan liability; tax statements or certificates; preparation of deed; one-half of escrow fee; and other expenses payable by Seller under this contract;
(b) an amount not to exceed $_______________ to be applied to Buyer's Expenses other than brokerage compensation or contributions under Paragraph 12B below.

(2) Buyer shall pay the following expenses (Buyer's Expenses) Appraisal fees; loan application fees; origination charges; credit reports; preparation of loan documents; interest on the notes from date of disbursement to one month prior to dates of first monthly payments; recording fees; copies of easements and restrictions; loan title policy with endorsements required by lender; loan-related inspection fees; photos; amortization schedules; one-half of escrow fee; all prepaid items, including required premiums for flood and hazard insurance, reserve deposits for insurance, ad valorem taxes and special governmental assessments; final compliance inspection; courier fee; repair inspection; underwriting fee; wire transfer fee; expenses incident to any loan; Private Mortgage Insurance Premium (PMI), VA Loan Funding Fee, or FHA Mortgage Insurance Premium (MIP) as required by the lender; and other expenses payable by Buyer under this contract.

B. BROKERAGE COMPENSATION: Brokerage compensation is not set by law and is fully negotiable. Each party shall pay their respective brokers pursuant to the terms of the parties' obligations to compensate their brokers contained in separate written agreements. **The contributions under 12B(1) and 12B(2) below shall be applied to and shall not change the parties' obligations to pay compensation pursuant to those agreements.** The following contributions must be paid at closing:

❑ (1) Seller will pay (check one box only): ❑ $__________ or ❑______% of the Sales Price to be applied toward the brokerage compensation owed by Buyer to Buyer's broker.

❑ (2) Buyer will pay (check one box only): ❑ $__________ or ❑______% of the Sales Price to be applied toward the brokerage compensation owed by Seller to Seller's broker.

C. EXPENSE LIMITATION: If a governmental loan program regulation prohibits Buyer from paying charges or fees, then the amount of any concession in 12A(1)(b) shall be first applied to pay such prohibited expenses and then to other Buyer's Expenses but not brokerage compensation or contribution.

13. PRORATIONS AND ROLLBACK TAXES:

A. PRORATIONS: Taxes for the current year, interest, rents, and regular periodic maintenance fees, assessments, and dues (including prepaid items) will be prorated through the Closing Date. The tax proration may be calculated taking into consideration any change in exemptions that will affect the current year's taxes. If taxes for the current year vary from the amount prorated at closing, the parties shall adjust the prorations when tax statements for the current year are available. If taxes are not paid at or prior to closing, Buyer shall pay taxes for the current year. Rentals which are unknown at time of closing will be prorated between Buyer and Seller when they become known.

B. ROLLBACK TAXES: If this sale or Buyer's use of the Property after closing results in the assessment of additional taxes, penalties or interest (Assessments) for periods prior to closing, the Assessments will be the obligation of Buyer. If Assessments are imposed because of Seller's use or change in use of the Property prior to closing, the Assessments will be the obligation of Seller. Obligations imposed by this paragraph will survive closing.

14. CASUALTY LOSS: If any part of the Property is damaged or destroyed by fire or other casualty after the Effective Date of this contract, Seller shall restore the Property to its previous condition as soon as reasonably possible, but in any event by the Closing Date. If Seller fails to do so due to factors beyond Seller's control, Buyer may (a) terminate this contract and the earnest money will be refunded to Buyer, (b) extend the time for performance up to 15 days and the Closing Date will be extended as necessary or (c) accept the Property in its damaged condition with an assignment of insurance proceeds, if permitted by Seller's insurance carrier, and receive credit from Seller at closing in the amount of the deductible under the insurance policy. Seller's obligations under this paragraph are independent of any other obligations of Seller under this contract.

15. DEFAULT: If Buyer fails to comply with this contract, Buyer will be in default, and Seller may (a) enforce specific performance, seek such other relief as may be provided by law, or both, or (b) terminate this contract and receive the earnest money as liquidated damages, thereby releasing both parties from this contract. If Seller fails to comply with this contract for any other reason, Seller will be in default and Buyer may (a) enforce specific performance, seek such other relief as may be provided by law, or both, or (b) terminate this contract and receive the earnest money, thereby releasing both parties from this contract.

16. MEDIATION: It is the policy of the State of Texas to encourage resolution of disputes through alternative dispute resolution procedures such as mediation. Any dispute between Seller and Buyer related to this contract which is not resolved through informal discussion will be submitted to a mutually acceptable mediation service or provider. The parties to the mediation shall bear the mediation costs equally. This paragraph does not preclude a party from seeking equitable relief from a court of competent jurisdiction.

17. ATTORNEY'S FEES: A Buyer, Seller, Seller's broker, Buyer's broker, or Escrow Agent who prevails in any legal proceeding related to this contract is entitled to recover reasonable attorney's fees and all costs of such proceeding.

18. ESCROW:

A. ESCROW: The Escrow Agent is not (i) a party to this contract and does not have liability for the performance or nonperformance of any party to this contract, (ii) liable for interest on the earnest money and (iii) liable for the loss of any earnest money caused by the failure of any financial institution in which the earnest money has been deposited unless the financial institution is acting as Escrow Agent. Escrow Agent may require any disbursement made in connection with this contract to be conditioned on Escrow Agent's collection of good funds acceptable to Escrow Agent.

B. EXPENSES: At closing, the earnest money must be applied first to any cash down payment, then to Buyer's Expenses and any excess refunded to Buyer. If no closing occurs, Escrow Agent may: (i) require a written release of liability of the Escrow Agent from all parties before releasing any earnest money; and (ii) require payment of unpaid expenses incurred on behalf of a party. Escrow Agent may deduct authorized expenses from the earnest money payable to a party. "Authorized expenses" means expenses incurred by Escrow Agent on behalf of the party entitled to the earnest money that were authorized by this contract or that party.

C. DEMAND: Upon termination of this contract, either party or the Escrow Agent may send a release of earnest money to each party and the parties shall execute counterparts of the release and deliver same to the Escrow Agent. If either party fails to execute the release, either party may make a written demand to the Escrow Agent for the earnest money. If only one party makes written demand for the earnest money, Escrow Agent shall promptly provide a copy of the demand to the other party. If Escrow Agent does not receive written objection to the demand from the other party within 15 days, Escrow Agent may disburse the earnest money to the party making demand reduced by the amount of unpaid expenses incurred on behalf of the party receiving the earnest money and Escrow Agent may pay the same to the creditors. If Escrow Agent complies with the provisions of this paragraph, each party hereby releases Escrow Agent from all adverse claims related to the disbursal of the earnest money.

D. DAMAGES: Any party who wrongfully fails or refuses to sign a release acceptable to the Escrow Agent within 7 days of receipt of the request will be liable to the other party for (i) damages; (ii) the earnest money; (iii) reasonable attorney's fees; and (iv) all costs of suit.

E. NOTICES: Escrow Agent's notices will be effective when sent in compliance with Paragraph 21. Notice of objection to the demand will be deemed effective upon receipt by Escrow Agent.

19. REPRESENTATIONS: All covenants, representations and warranties in this contract survive closing. If any representation of Seller in this contract is untrue on the Closing Date, Seller will be in default. Unless expressly prohibited by written agreement, Seller may continue to show the Property and receive, negotiate and accept back up offers.

20. GOVERNMENTAL REQUIREMENTS:

A. If Seller is a "foreign person," as defined by Internal Revenue Code and its regulations, or if Seller fails to deliver an affidavit or a certificate of non-foreign status to Buyer that Seller is not a "foreign person," then Buyer shall withhold from the sales proceeds an amount sufficient to comply with applicable tax law and deliver the same to the Internal Revenue Service together with appropriate tax forms. Internal Revenue Service regulations require filing written reports if currency in excess of specified amounts is received in the transaction.

B. Seller and Buyer shall promptly execute and deliver any statements, documents, and information requested by Escrow Agent required by governmental reporting requirements (for example, reporting to the U.S. Treasury or its bureaus).

C. The Agriculture Foreign Investment Disclosure Act (AFIDA) of 1978 requires that a foreign person who acquires, disposes of, or holds an interest in United States agricultural land must disclose such transactions and holdings to the Secretary of Agriculture. Foreign persons must file an FSA-153 in the Farm Service Agency (FSA) Service Center where the land is physically located within 90 days of the date of the transaction. Failure to report is subject to civil penalty up to 25 percent of the fair market value of the land on the date the penalty is assessed. Consult an attorney or tax professional.

21. NOTICES: All notices from one party or their agent to the other must be in writing. Notices are effective when mailed to, hand-delivered at, sent by overnight courier to, or transmitted by electronic transmission to the other party or their agent.

To Buyer(s) at:	**To Seller(s) at:**
Address:______________________	Address:______________________
______________________	______________________
Phone(s):______________________	Phone(s):______________________
______________________	______________________
Email(s):______________________	Email(s):______________________
______________________	______________________
To Buyer's agent at:	**To Seller's agent at:**
Address:______________________	Address:______________________
______________________	______________________
Phone:______________________	Phone:______________________
Email:______________________	Email:______________________

22. AGREEMENT OF PARTIES: This contract contains the entire agreement of the parties and cannot be changed except by their written agreement. Addenda and notices which are a part of this contract are (check all applicable boxes):

Financial

- ☐ Third Party Financing Addendum
- ☐ Addendum for Sale of Other Property by Buyer
- ☐ Addendum Concerning Right to Terminate Due to Lender's Appraisal
- ☐ Seller Financing Addendum
- ☐ Addendum for Section 1031 Exchange
- ☐ Short Sale Addendum
- ☐ Loan Assumption Addendum
- ☐ Addendum for Release of Liability on Assumed Loan and/or Restoration of Seller's VA Entitlement

Leases

- ☐ Addendum Regarding Residential Leases
- ☐ Addendum Regarding Fixture Leases
- ☐ Buyer's Temporary Residential Lease
- ☐ Seller's Temporary Residential Lease

Additional Tests and Reports

- ☐ Addendum for Authorizing Hydrostatic Testing
- ☐ Environmental Assessment, Threatened or Endangered Species, and Wetlands Addendum

Statutory Disclosures and Notices

- ☐ Addendum for Seller's Disclosure of Information on Lead-Based Paint and Lead-Based Paint Hazards as Required by Federal Law
- ☐ Addendum for Property in a Propane Gas System Service Area
- ☐ Addendum for Property Located Seaward of the Gulf Intercoastal Waterway
- ☐ Addendum for Coastal Area Property
- ☐ The following utility, water, drainage, public improvement, and other district notices (list all that have been given or are attached):______________________________
____

NOTICE: Seller's failure to provide applicable Statutory Disclosures and Notices may provide Buyer with remedies or rights to terminate this contract.

Other

- ☐ Addendum for Property Subject to Mandatory Membership in a Property Owners Association
- ☐ Non-Realty Items Addendum
- ☐ Addendum for "Back-Up" Contract
- ☐ Addendum for Reservation of Oil, Gas, and Other Minerals
- ☐ Other:______________________________
____

23. CONSULT AN ATTORNEY BEFORE SIGNING: TREC rules prohibit real estate brokers and sales agents from giving legal advice. READ THIS CONTRACT CAREFULLY.

Buyer's		Seller's	
Buyer's Attorney is:	______________	Seller's Attorney is:	______________
Phone:	( ) ______________	Phone:	( ) ______________
Fax:	( ) ______________	Fax:	( ) ______________
E-mail:	______________	E-mail:	______________

EXECUTED the _______day of __________________________, 20_____ (Effective Date).
(BROKER: FILL IN THE DATE OF FINAL ACCEPTANCE.)

______________________________	______________________________
Buyer	Seller
______________________________	______________________________
Buyer	Seller

RATIFICATION OF FEE

Seller's broker has agreed to pay Buyer's broker ______________________________ of the total Sales Price when Seller's broker's fee is received. Escrow Agent is authorized and directed to pay Buyer's broker from Seller's broker's fee at closing.

Buyer's broker: Seller's broker:

By: ______________________________ By: ______________________________

BROKER CONTACT INFORMATION AND AGREEMENT FOR PAYMENT OF BROKERS' FEES

The brokers to this sale are:

______________________________ (Broker Firm) **represents Seller only as Seller's agent**.

Address:______________________________
Broker Firm License No.:______________________________
Associate's Name:______________________________
Team Name:______________________________
Associate's Email:______________________________
Associate's Phone No.:____________________Associate's License No.:____________________
Licensed Supervisor of Associate:______________________________
Phone No. of Licensed Supervisor:____________________License No.:____________________

______________________________ (Broker Firm) **represents Buyer only as Buyer's agent**.

Address:______________________________
Broker Firm License No.:______________________________
Associate's Name:______________________________
Team Name:______________________________
Associate's Email:______________________________
Associate's Phone No.:____________________Associate's License No.:____________________
Licensed Supervisor of Associate:______________________________
Phone No. of Licensed Supervisor:____________________License No.:____________________

Intermediary

______________________________ (Broker Firm) **represents Seller and Buyer as an intermediary**.

Address:______________________________
Broker Firm License No.:______________________________
Associate's Name (for Seller):______________________________
Team Name:______________________________
Associate's Email:______________________________
Associate's Phone No.:____________________Associate's License No.:____________________
Licensed Supervisor of Associate:______________________________
Phone No. of Licensed Supervisor:____________________License No.:____________________
Associate's Name (for Buyer):______________________________
Team Name:______________________________
Associate's Email:______________________________
Associate's Phone No.:____________________Associate's License No.:____________________
Licensed Supervisor of Associate:______________________________
Phone No. of Licensed Supervisor:____________________License No.:____________________

Upon closing of the sale by Seller to Buyer of the Property described in the contract to which this fee agreement is attached: (a) ❑Seller ❑ Buyer will pay Seller's broker ❑a cash fee of $______________ or ❑ ______% of the total Sales Price; and (b) ❑Seller ❑ Buyer will pay Buyer's broker ❑a cash fee of $______________ or ❑ ______% of the total Sales Price. Seller/Buyer authorizes and directs Escrow Agent to pay the brokers from the proceeds at closing.

DO NOT SIGN IF THERE IS A SEPARATE AGREEMENT FOR PAYMENT OF BROKERS' FEES OR IF CONTRIBUTIONS ARE TO BE PAID UNDER PARAGRAPH 12B(1) OR (2). Brokers' fees are negotiable. Brokers' fees or the sharing of fees between brokers are not fixed, controlled, recommended, suggested or maintained by the Texas Real Estate Commission.

______________________________ ______________________________
Seller Buyer

______________________________ ______________________________
Seller Buyer

OPTION FEE RECEIPT

Receipt of $_______________ option fee in the form of ______________________________
is acknowledged.

______________________________ ______________________________
Escrow Agent Date

EARNEST MONEY RECEIPT

Receipt of $_______________ earnest money in the form of ______________________________
is acknowledged.

______________________________ ______________________________
Escrow Agent Received by Email Address Date/Time

______________________________ ______________________________
Address Phone

______________________________ ______________________________
City State Zip Fax

CONTRACT RECEIPT

Receipt of the contract is acknowledged.

______________________________ ______________________________
Escrow Agent Received by Email Address Date

______________________________ ______________________________
Address Phone

______________________________ ______________________________
City State Zip Fax

ADDITIONAL EARNEST MONEY RECEIPT

Receipt of $_______________ additional earnest money in the form of ______________________________
is acknowledged.

______________________________ ______________________________
Escrow Agent Received by Email Address Date/Time

______________________________ ______________________________
Address Phone

______________________________ ______________________________
City State Zip Fax

PROMULGATED BY THE TEXAS REAL ESTATE COMMISSION (TREC) 05-04-2026

NEW HOME CONTRACT

(Completed Construction)

NOTICE: Not For Use For Condominium Transactions or Closings Prior to Completion of Construction

1. PARTIES: The parties to this contract are ______________________________________ (Seller) and ____(Buyer). Seller agrees to sell and convey to Buyer and Buyer agrees to buy from Seller the Property defined below.

2. PROPERTY: Lot ______________________,Block____________________________________, ____Addition, City of_____________________________,County of_______________________________, Texas, known as ____ (address/zip code), or as described on attached exhibit, together with: (i) improvements, fixtures and all other property located thereon; and (ii) all rights, privileges and appurtenances thereto. All property sold by this contract is called the Property (Property).

RESERVATIONS: Any reservation for oil, gas, or other minerals, water, timber, or other interests is made in accordance with an attached addendum.

3. SALES PRICE:

A. Cash portion of Sales Price payable by Buyer at closing .... $________________
The term "Cash portion of the Sales Price" does not include proceeds from borrowing of any kind or selling other real property except as disclosed in this contract.

B. Sum of all financing described in the attached: ❑ Third Party Financing Addendum, ❑ Loan Assumption Addendum, ❑ Seller Financing Addendum ...... $________________

C. Sales Price (Sum of A and B) .... $________________

4. LEASES: Except as disclosed in this contract, Seller is not aware of any leases affecting the Property. After the Effective Date, Seller may not, without Buyer's written consent, create a new lease, amend any existing lease, or convey any interest in the Property. (Check all applicable boxes)

❑ A. RESIDENTIAL LEASES: The Property is subject to one or more residential leases and the Addendum Regarding Residential Leases is attached to this contract.

❑ B. FIXTURE LEASES: Fixtures on the Property are subject to one or more fixture leases (for example, solar panels, propane tanks, water softener, security system) and the Addendum Regarding Fixture Leases is attached to this contract.

❑ C. NATURAL RESOURCE LEASES: "Natural Resource Lease" means an existing oil and gas, mineral, geothermal, water, wind, or other natural resource lease affecting the Property to which Seller is a party.

❑ (1) Seller has delivered to Buyer a copy of all the Natural Resource Leases.

❑ (2) Seller has not delivered to Buyer a copy of all the Natural Resource Leases. Seller shall provide to Buyer a copy of all the Natural Resource Leases within 3 days after the Effective Date. Buyer may terminate the contract within ______ days after the date the Buyer receives all the Natural Resource Leases and the earnest money shall be refunded to Buyer.

5. EARNEST MONEY AND TERMINATION OPTION:

A. DELIVERY OF EARNEST MONEY AND OPTION FEE: Within 3 days after the Effective Date, Buyer must deliver to ________________________________ (Escrow Agent) at __________ ________________________________(address): $______________ as earnest money and $_____________ as the option fee. The earnest money and option fee shall be made payable to Escrow Agent and may be paid separately or combined in a single payment.

(1) Buyer shall deliver additional earnest money of $_______________ to Escrow Agent within ______ days after the Effective Date of this contract.

(2) If the last day to deliver the earnest money, option fee, or the additional earnest money falls on a Saturday, Sunday, or Legal Holiday, the time to deliver the earnest money, option fee, or the additional earnest money, as applicable, is extended until the end of the next day that is not a Saturday, Sunday, or Legal Holiday. "Legal Holiday" means a legal holiday described in Sections 662.003(a) and 662.003(b)(4) and (6), Texas Government Code.

(3) The amount(s) Escrow Agent receives under this paragraph shall be applied first to the option fee, then to the earnest money, and then to the additional earnest money.

(4) Buyer authorizes Escrow Agent to release and deliver the option fee to Seller at any time without further notice to or consent from Buyer, and releases Escrow Agent from liability for delivery of the option fee to Seller. The option fee will be credited to the Sales Price at closing.

B. TERMINATION OPTION: For nominal consideration, the receipt of which Seller acknowledges, and Buyer's agreement to pay the option fee within the time required, Seller grants Buyer the unrestricted right to terminate this contract by giving notice of termination to Seller within _______ days after the Effective Date of this contract (Option Period). Notices under this paragraph must be given by 5:00 p.m. (local time where the Property is located) by the date specified. If Buyer gives notice of termination within the time prescribed: (i) the option fee will not be refunded and Escrow Agent shall release any option fee remaining with Escrow Agent to Seller; and (ii) any earnest money will be refunded to Buyer.

C. FAILURE TO TIMELY DELIVER EARNEST MONEY: If Buyer fails to deliver the earnest money within the time required, Seller may terminate this contract or exercise Seller's remedies under Paragraph 15, or both, by providing notice to Buyer before Buyer delivers the earnest money.

D. FAILURE TO TIMELY DELIVER OPTION FEE: If no dollar amount is stated as the option fee or if Buyer fails to deliver the option fee within the time required, Buyer shall not have the unrestricted right to terminate this contract under this Paragraph 5.

E. TIME: **Time is of the essence for this paragraph and strict compliance with the time for performance is required.**

6. TITLE POLICY AND SURVEY:

A. TITLE POLICY: Seller shall furnish to Buyer at ❑Seller's ❑Buyer's expense an owner policy of title insurance (Title Policy) issued by ______________________________ (Title Company) in the amount of the Sales Price, dated at or after closing, insuring Buyer against loss under the provisions of the Title Policy, subject to the promulgated exclusions (including existing building and zoning ordinances) and the following exceptions:

(1) Restrictive covenants common to the platted subdivision in which the Property is located.
(2) The standard printed exception for standby fees, taxes and assessments.
(3) Liens created as part of the financing described in Paragraph 3.
(4) Utility easements created by the dedication deed or plat of the subdivision in which the Property is located.
(5) Reservations or exceptions otherwise permitted by this contract or as may be approved by Buyer in writing.
(6) The standard printed exception as to marital rights.
(7) The standard printed exception as to waters, tidelands, beaches, streams, and related matters.
(8) The standard printed exception as to discrepancies, conflicts, shortages in area or boundary lines, encroachments or protrusions, or overlapping improvement:

❑ (i) will not be amended or deleted from the title policy; or

❑ (ii) will be amended to read, "shortages in area" at the expense of ❑Buyer ❑Seller.

(9) The exception or exclusion regarding minerals approved by the Texas Department of Insurance.

B. COMMITMENT: Within 20 days after the Title Company receives a copy of this contract, Seller shall furnish to Buyer a commitment for title insurance (Commitment) and, at Buyer's expense, legible copies of restrictive covenants and documents evidencing exceptions in the Commitment (Exception Documents) other than the standard printed exceptions. Seller authorizes the Title Company to deliver the Commitment and Exception Documents to Buyer at Buyer's address shown in Paragraph 21. If the Commitment and Exception Documents are not delivered to Buyer within the specified time, the time for delivery will be automatically extended up to 15 days or 3 days before the Closing Date, whichever is earlier. If the Commitment and Exception Documents are not delivered within the time required, Buyer may terminate this contract and the earnest money will be refunded to Buyer.

C. SURVEY: The survey must be made by a registered professional land surveyor acceptable to the Title Company and Buyer's lender(s). (Check one box only)

❑ (1) Within ______ days after the Effective Date of this contract, Seller shall furnish to Buyer and Title Company Seller's existing survey of the Property and a Residential Real Property Affidavit or Declaration promulgated by the Texas Department of Insurance (T-47 Affidavit or T-47.1 Declaration). Buyer shall obtain a new survey at Seller's expense no later than 3 days prior to Closing Date if Seller fails to furnish within the time prescribed both the: (i) existing survey; and (ii) affidavit or declaration. If the Title Company or Buyer's lender does not accept the existing survey, or the affidavit or declaration, Buyer shall obtain a new survey at ❑ Seller's ❑ Buyer's expense no later than 3 days prior to Closing Date.

❑ (2) Within ______ days after the Effective Date of this contract, Buyer may obtain a new survey at Buyer's expense. Buyer is deemed to receive the survey on the date of actual receipt or the date specified in this paragraph, whichever is earlier. If Buyer fails to obtain the survey, Buyer may not terminate the contract under Paragraph 2B of the Third Party Financing Addendum because the survey was not obtained.

❑ (3) Within ______ days after the Effective Date of this contract, Seller, at Seller's expense shall furnish a new survey to Buyer.

D. OBJECTIONS: Buyer may object in writing to defects, exceptions, or encumbrances to title: disclosed on the survey other than items 6A(1) through (7) above; disclosed in the Commitment other than items 6A(1) through (9) above; or which prohibit the following use or activity: ____
____.

Buyer must object the earlier of (i) the Closing Date or (ii) ______ days after Buyer receives the Commitment, Exception Documents, and the survey. Buyer's failure to object within the time allowed will constitute a waiver of Buyer's right to object; except that the requirements in Schedule C of the Commitment are not waived by Buyer. Provided Seller is not obligated to incur any expense, Seller shall cure any timely objections of Buyer or any third party lender within 15 days after Seller receives the objections (Cure Period) and the Closing Date will be extended as necessary. If objections are not cured within the Cure Period, Buyer may, by delivering notice to Seller within 5 days after the end of the Cure Period: (i) terminate this contract and the earnest money will be refunded to Buyer; or (ii) waive the objections. If

Buyer does not terminate within the time required, Buyer shall be deemed to have waived the objections. If the Commitment or survey is revised or any new Exception Document(s) is delivered, Buyer may object to any new matter revealed in the revised Commitment or survey or new Exception Document(s) within the same time stated in this paragraph to make objections beginning when the revised Commitment, survey, or Exception Document(s) is delivered to Buyer.

E. TITLE NOTICES:

(1) ABSTRACT OR TITLE POLICY: Broker advises Buyer to have an abstract of title covering the Property examined by an attorney of Buyer's selection, or Buyer should be furnished with or obtain a Title Policy. If a Title Policy is furnished, the Commitment should be promptly reviewed by an attorney of Buyer's choice due to the time limitations on Buyer's right to object.

(2) MEMBERSHIP IN PROPERTY OWNERS ASSOCIATION(S): The Property ☐ is ☐ is not subject to mandatory membership in a property owners association(s). If the Property is subject to mandatory membership in a property owners association(s), Seller notifies Buyer under §5.012, Texas Property Code, that, as a purchaser of property in the residential community identified in Paragraph 2A in which the Property is located, you are obligated to be a member of the property owners association(s). Restrictive covenants governing the use and occupancy of the Property and all dedicatory instruments governing the establishment, maintenance, and operation of this residential community have been or will be recorded in the Real Property Records of the county in which the Property is located. Copies of the restrictive covenants and dedicatory instruments may be obtained from the county clerk. **You are obligated to pay assessments to the property owners association(s). The amount of the assessments is subject to change. Your failure to pay the assessments could result in enforcement of the association's lien on and the foreclosure of the Property.**

Section 207.003, Property Code, entitles an owner to receive copies of any document that governs the establishment, maintenance, or operation of a subdivision, including, but not limited to, restrictions, bylaws, rules and regulations, and a resale certificate from a property owners' association. A resale certificate contains information including, but not limited to, statements specifying the amount and frequency of regular assessments and the style and cause number of lawsuits to which the property owners' association is a party, other than lawsuits relating to unpaid ad valorem taxes of an individual member of the association. These documents must be made available to you by the property owners' association or the association's agent on your request.

If Buyer is concerned about these matters, the TREC promulgated Addendum for Property Subject to Mandatory Membership in a Property Owners Association should be used.

(3) STATUTORY TAX DISTRICTS: If the Property is situated in a utility or other statutorily created district providing water, sewer, drainage, or flood control facilities and services, Chapter 49, Texas Water Code, requires Seller to deliver and Buyer to sign the statutory notice relating to the tax rate, bonded indebtedness, or standby fee of the district prior to final execution of this contract.

(4) TIDE WATERS: If the Property abuts the tidally influenced waters of the state, §33.135, Texas Natural Resources Code, requires a notice regarding coastal area property to be included in the contract.

(5) ANNEXATION: If the Property is located outside the limits of a municipality, Seller notifies Buyer under §5.011, Texas Property Code, that the Property may now or later be included in the extraterritorial jurisdiction of a municipality and may now or later be subject to annexation by the municipality. Each municipality maintains a map that depicts its boundaries and extraterritorial jurisdiction. To determine if the Property is located within a municipality's extraterritorial jurisdiction or is likely to be located within a municipality's extraterritorial jurisdiction, contact all municipalities located in the general proximity of the Property for further information.

(6) PROPERTY LOCATED IN A CERTIFICATED SERVICE AREA OF A UTILITY SERVICE PROVIDER: Notice required by §13.257, Water Code: The real property, described in Paragraph 2, that you are about to purchase may be located in a certificated water or sewer service area, which is authorized by law to provide water or sewer service to the properties in the certificated area. If your property is located in a certificated area there may be special costs or charges that you will be required to pay before you can receive water or sewer service. There may be a period required to construct lines or other facilities necessary to provide water or sewer service to your property. You are advised to determine if the property is in a certificated area and contact the utility service provider to determine the cost that you will be required to pay and the period, if any, that is required to provide water or sewer service to your property. The undersigned Buyer hereby acknowledges receipt of the foregoing notice at or before the execution of a binding contract for the purchase of the real property described in Paragraph 2 or at closing of purchase of the real property.

(7) PUBLIC IMPROVEMENT DISTRICTS: If the Property is in a public improvement district, Seller must give Buyer written notice as required by §5.014, Property Code.

(8) TRANSFER FEES: If the Property is subject to a private transfer fee obligation, §5.205, Property Code, requires Seller to notify Buyer as follows: The private transfer fee obligation may be governed by Chapter 5, Subchapter G of the Texas Property Code.

(9) PROPANE GAS SYSTEM SERVICE AREA: If the Property is located in a propane gas system service area owned by a distribution system retailer, Seller must give Buyer written notice as required by §141.010, Texas Utilities Code.

(10) NOTICE OF WATER LEVEL FLUCTUATIONS: If the Property adjoins an impoundment of water, including a reservoir or lake, constructed and maintained under Chapter 11, Water Code, that has a storage capacity of at least 5,000 acre-feet at the impoundment's normal operating level, Seller hereby notifies Buyer: "The water level of the impoundment of water adjoining the Property fluctuates for various reasons, including as a result of: (1) an entity lawfully exercising its right to use the water stored in the impoundment; or (2) drought or flood conditions."

(11) CERTIFICATE OF MOLD REMEDIATION: If the Property has been remediated for mold, Seller must provide to Buyer each certificate of mold damage remediation issued under §1958.154, Occupations Code, during the 5 years preceding the sale of the Property.

7. PROPERTY CONDITION:

A. ACCESS, INSPECTIONS AND UTILITIES: Seller shall permit Buyer and Buyer's agents access to the Property at reasonable times. Buyer may have the Property inspected by inspectors selected by Buyer and licensed by TREC or otherwise permitted by law to make inspections. Seller at Seller's expense shall immediately cause existing utilities to be turned on and shall keep the utilities on during the time this contract is in effect.

B. ACCEPTANCE OF PROPERTY CONDITION: "As Is" means the present condition of the Property with any and all defects and without warranty except for the warranties of title and the warranties in this contract. Buyer's agreement to accept the Property As Is under Paragraph 7B (1) or (2) does not preclude Buyer from inspecting the Property under Paragraph 7A, from negotiating repairs or treatments in a subsequent amendment, or from terminating this contract during the Option Period, if any.

(Check one box only)

☐ (1) Buyer accepts the Property As Is.

☐ (2) Buyer accepts the Property As Is provided Seller, at Seller's expense, shall complete the following specific repairs and treatments: ____________________________________

(Do not insert general phrases, such as "subject to inspections," that do not identify specific repairs and treatments.)

C. WARRANTIES: Except as expressly set forth in this contract, a separate writing, or provided by law, Seller makes no other express warranties. Seller shall assign to Buyer at closing all assignable manufacturer warranties.

D. INSULATION: As required by Federal Trade Commission Regulations, the information relating to the insulation installed or to be installed in the Improvements at the Property is: (check only one box below)

☐ (1) as shown in the attached specifications.

☐ (2) as follows:

(a) Exterior walls of improved living areas: insulated with ______________________ insulation to a thickness of ________ inches which yields an R-Value of ____________ ______________________________.

(b) Walls in other areas of the home: insulated with ______________________________ insulation to a thickness of ________ inches which yields an R-Value of ____________ ______________________________.

(c) Ceilings in improved living areas: insulated with ______________________________ insulation to a thickness of ________ inches which yields an R-Value of ____________ ______________________________.

(d) Floors of improved living areas not applied to a slab foundation: insulated with _______ ______________________________ insulation to a thickness of _______ inches which yields an R-Value of ______________________________.

(e) Other insulated areas: insulated with ____________________________insulation to a thickness of _________ inches which yields an R-Value of ______________________.

All stated R-Values are based on information provided by the manufacturer of the insulation.

E. LENDER REQUIRED REPAIRS AND TREATMENTS: Unless otherwise agreed in writing, neither party is obligated to pay for lender required repairs, which includes treatment for wood destroying insects. If the parties do not agree to pay for the lender required repairs or treatments, this contract will terminate and the earnest money will be refunded to Buyer. If the cost of lender required repairs and treatments exceeds 5% of the Sales Price, Buyer may terminate this contract and the earnest money will be refunded to Buyer.

F. COMPLETION OF REPAIRS, TREATMENTS, AND IMPROVEMENTS: Unless otherwise agreed in writing, Seller shall complete all agreed repairs, treatments, and improvements (Work) prior to the Closing Date and obtain any required permits. The Work must be performed by persons who are licensed to provide such Work or, if no license is required by law, are commercially engaged in the trade of providing such Work. Seller shall: (i) provide Buyer with copies of documentation from the repair person(s) showing the scope of work and payment for the work completed; and (ii) at Seller's expense, arrange for the transfer of any transferable warranties with respect to the Work to Buyer at closing. If Seller fails to complete any agreed Work prior to the Closing Date, Buyer may exercise remedies under Paragraph 15 or extend the Closing Date up to 5 days if necessary for Seller to complete Work.

G. ENVIRONMENTAL MATTERS: Buyer is advised that the presence of wetlands, toxic substances, including asbestos and wastes or other environmental hazards or the presence of a threatened or endangered species or its habitat may affect Buyer's intended use of the Property. If Buyer is concerned about these matters, an addendum promulgated by TREC or required by the parties should be used.

H. SELLER'S DISCLOSURE:

(1) Seller ☐ is ☐ is not aware of any flooding of the Property which has had a material adverse effect on the use of the Property.
(2) Seller ☐ is ☐ is not aware of any pending or threatened litigation, condemnation, or special assessment affecting the Property.
(3) Seller ☐ is ☐ is not aware of any environmental hazards that materially and adversely affect the Property.
(4) Seller ☐ is ☐ is not aware of any dumpsite, landfill, or underground tanks or containers now or previously located on the Property.
(5) Seller ☐ is ☐ is not aware of any wetlands, as defined by federal or state law or regulation, affecting the Property.
(6) Seller ☐ is ☐ is not aware of any threatened or endangered species or their habitat affecting the Property.
(7) Seller ☐ is ☐ is not aware that the Property is located ☐ wholly ☐ partly in a floodplain.
(8) Seller ☐ is ☐ is not aware that a tree or trees located on the Property has oak wilt.

If Seller is aware of any of the items above, explain (attach additional sheets if necessary): ____.

I. RESIDENTIAL SERVICE CONTRACTS: Buyer may purchase a residential service contract from a provider or administrator licensed by the Texas Department of Licensing and Regulation. If Buyer purchases a residential service contract, Seller shall reimburse Buyer at closing for the cost of the residential service contract in an amount not exceeding $____________. Buyer should review any residential service contract for the scope of coverage, exclusions and limitations. **The purchase of a residential service contract is optional. Similar coverage may be purchased from various companies authorized to do business in Texas.**

J. SELLER'S DISCLOSURE ABOUT GROUNDWATER AND SURFACE WATER RIGHTS (Seller's Water Disclosure): Access to surface water or groundwater on the Property may be regulated, restricted, or prohibited, including but not limited to the right to drill or operate water wells and the right to withdraw water from surface water sources on or adjoining the Property. The parties shall use the Seller's Water Disclosure published by TREC to identify information related to groundwater and surface water rights. (Check one box only)

☐ (1) Buyer has received the Seller's Water Disclosure.

☐ (2) Buyer has not received the Seller's Water Disclosure. Within _____ days after the Effective Date of this contract, Seller shall deliver the Seller's Water Disclosure to Buyer. If Buyer does not receive the Seller's Water Disclosure, Buyer may terminate this contract at any time prior to the closing and the earnest money will be refunded to Buyer. If Seller delivers the Seller's Water Disclosure, Buyer may terminate this contract for any reason within 7 days after Buyer receives the Seller's Water Disclosure or prior to the closing, whichever first occurs, and the earnest money will be refunded to Buyer.

☐ (3) Seller is not required to deliver the Seller's Water Disclosure to Buyer because all of the following are true:

(a) Seller is not aware of a water well on the Property (in use or not in use);
(b) Seller is not aware of a pond, lake, or water tank on the Property;
(c) Seller is not aware of any certificate of adjudication, certified filing, or permit for surface water rights associated with the Property administered by the Texas Commission on Environmental Quality;
(d) Seller is not aware that any groundwater rights to the Property have been severed, sold, or leased in whole or in part; and
(e) the Property receives water only from the following municipality (City), municipal utility district (MUD) or other special district, water supply corporation (WSC), or private water supply company (PWC):______________________________________
____.

8. BROKER OR SALES AGENT DISCLOSURE:

Texas law requires a real estate broker or sales agent who is a party to a transaction or acting on behalf of a spouse, parent, child, business entity in which the broker or sales agent owns more than 10%, or a trust for which the broker or sales agent acts as a trustee or of which the broker or sales agent or the broker or sales agent's spouse, parent or child is a beneficiary, to notify the other party in writing before entering into a contract of sale. Disclose if applicable:__
____.

9. CLOSING:

A. The closing of the sale will be on or before ____________________, 20_____, or within 7 days after objections made under Paragraph 6D have been cured or waived, whichever date is later (Closing Date). If either party fails to close the sale by the Closing Date, the non-defaulting party may exercise the remedies contained in Paragraph 15.

B. At closing:

(1) Seller shall execute and deliver a general warranty deed conveying title to the Property to Buyer and showing no additional exceptions to those permitted in Paragraph 6 and furnish tax statements or certificates showing no delinquent taxes on the Property.

(2) Buyer shall pay the Sales Price in good funds acceptable to the Escrow Agent.
(3) Seller and Buyer shall execute and deliver any notices, statements, certificates, affidavits, releases, loan documents, transfer of any warranties, and other documents reasonably required for the closing of the sale and the issuance of the Title Policy.
(4) There will be no liens, assessments, or security interests against the Property which will not be satisfied out of the sales proceeds unless securing the payment of any loans assumed by Buyer and assumed loans will not be in default.
(5) Private transfer fees (as defined by Chapter 5, Subchapter G of the Texas Property Code) will be the obligation of Seller unless provided otherwise in this contract. Transfer fees assessed by a property owners' association are governed by the Addendum for Property Subject to Mandatory Membership in a Property Owners Association.

10. POSSESSION:

A. BUYER'S POSSESSION: Seller shall deliver to Buyer possession of the Property in its present or required condition, ordinary wear and tear excepted: ❑ upon closing and funding ❑ according to a temporary residential lease form promulgated by TREC or other written lease required by the parties. Any possession by Buyer prior to closing or by Seller after closing which is not authorized by a written lease will establish a tenancy at sufferance relationship between the parties. **Consult your insurance agent prior to change of ownership and possession because insurance coverage may be limited or terminated. The absence of a written lease or appropriate insurance coverage may expose the parties to economic loss.**

B. SMART DEVICES: "Smart Device" means a device that connects to the internet to enable remote use, monitoring, and management of: (i) the Property; (ii) items identified in any Non-Realty Items Addendum; or (iii) items in a Fixture Lease assigned to Buyer. At the time Seller delivers possession of the Property to Buyer, Seller shall:
(1) deliver to Buyer written information containing all access codes, usernames, passwords, and applications Buyer will need to access, operate, manage, and control the Smart Devices; and
(2) terminate and remove all access and connections to the improvements and accessories from any of Seller's personal devices including but not limited to phones and computers.

11. SPECIAL PROVISIONS: (This paragraph is intended to be used only for additional informational items. An informational item is a statement that completes a blank in a contract form, discloses factual information, or provides instructions. Real estate brokers and sales agents are prohibited from practicing law and shall not add to, delete, or modify any provision of this contract unless drafted by a party to this contract or a party's attorney.)________________
____.

12. SETTLEMENT AND OTHER EXPENSES:

A. EXPENSES: The following expenses must be paid at or prior to closing:
(1) Seller shall pay the following expenses (Seller's Expenses):
(a) releases of existing liens, including prepayment penalties and recording fees; release of Seller's loan liability; tax statements or certificates; preparation of deed; one-half of escrow fee; and other expenses payable by Seller under this contract;
(b) an amount not to exceed $ __________ to be applied to Buyer's Expenses other than brokerage compensation or contributions under Paragraph 12B below.
(2) Buyer shall pay the following expenses (Buyer's Expenses): Appraisal fees; loan application fees; origination charges; credit reports; preparation of loan documents; interest on the notes from date of disbursement to one month prior to dates of first monthly payments; recording fees; copies of easements and restrictions; loan title policy with endorsements required by lender; loan-related inspection fees; photos; amortization schedules; one-half of escrow fee; all prepaid items, including required premiums for flood and hazard insurance, reserve deposits for insurance, ad valorem taxes and special governmental assessments; final compliance inspection; courier fee; repair inspection; underwriting fee; wire transfer fee; expenses incident to any loan; Private Mortgage Insurance Premium (PMI), VA Loan Funding Fee, or FHA Mortgage Insurance Premium (MIP) as required by the lender; and other expenses payable by Buyer under this contract.

B. BROKERAGE COMPENSATION: Brokerage compensation is not set by law and is fully negotiable. Each party shall pay their respective brokers pursuant to the terms of the parties' obligations to compensate their brokers contained in separate written agreements. **The contributions under 12B(1) and 12B(2) below shall be applied to and shall not change the parties' obligations to pay compensation pursuant to those agreements.** The following contributions must be paid at closing:
❑ (1) Seller will pay (check one box only): ❑ $__________ or ❑ ______% of the Sales Price to be applied toward the brokerage compensation owed by Buyer to Buyer's broker.
❑ (2) Buyer will pay (check one box only): ❑ $__________ or ❑ ______% of the Sales Price to be applied toward the brokerage compensation owed by Seller to Seller's broker.

C. EXPENSE LIMITATION: If a governmental loan program regulation prohibits Buyer from paying charges or fees, then the amount of any concession in 12A(1)(b) shall be first applied to pay such prohibited expenses and then to other Buyer's Expenses but not brokerage compensation or contribution.

13. PRORATIONS AND ROLLBACK TAXES:

A. PRORATIONS: Taxes for the current year, interest, rents, and regular periodic maintenance fees, assessments, and dues (including prepaid items) will be prorated through the Closing Date. The tax proration may be calculated taking into consideration any change in exemptions that will affect the current year's taxes. If taxes for the current year vary from the amount prorated at closing, the parties shall adjust the prorations when tax statements for the current year are available. If taxes are not paid at or prior to closing, Buyer will be obligated to pay taxes for the current year.

B. ROLLBACK TAXES: If additional taxes, penalties, or interest (Assessments) are imposed because of Seller's use or change in use of the Property prior to closing, the Assessments will be the obligation of Seller. Obligations imposed by this paragraph will survive closing.

14. CASUALTY LOSS: If any part of the Property is damaged or destroyed by fire or other casualty after the Effective Date of this contract, Seller shall restore the Property to its previous condition as soon as reasonably possible, but in any event by the Closing Date. If Seller fails to do so due to factors beyond Seller's control, Buyer may (a) terminate this contract and the earnest money will be refunded to Buyer (b) extend the time for performance up to 15 days and the Closing Date will be extended as necessary or (c) accept the Property in its damaged condition with an assignment of insurance proceeds, if permitted by Seller's insurance carrier, and receive credit from Seller at closing in the amount of the deductible under the insurance policy. Seller's obligations under this paragraph are independent of any other obligations of Seller under this contract.

15. DEFAULT: If Buyer fails to comply with this contract, Buyer will be in default, and Seller may (a) enforce specific performance, seek such other relief as may be provided by law, or both, or (b) terminate this contract and receive the earnest money as liquidated damages, thereby releasing both parties from this contract. If Seller fails to comply with this contract Seller will be in default and Buyer may (a) enforce specific performance, seek such other relief as may be provided by law, or both, or (b) terminate this contract and receive the earnest money, thereby releasing both parties from this contract.

16. MEDIATION: It is the policy of the State of Texas to encourage resolution of disputes through alternative dispute resolution procedures such as mediation. Subject to applicable law, any dispute between Seller and Buyer related to this contract which is not resolved through informal discussion will be submitted to a mutually acceptable mediation service or provider. The parties to the mediation shall bear the mediation costs equally. This paragraph does not preclude a party from seeking equitable relief from a court of competent jurisdiction.

17. ATTORNEY'S FEES: A Buyer, Seller, Seller's broker, Buyer's broker, or Escrow Agent who prevails in any legal proceeding related to this contract is entitled to recover reasonable attorney's fees and all costs of such proceeding.

18. ESCROW:

A. ESCROW: The Escrow Agent is not (i) a party to this contract and does not have liability for the performance or nonperformance of any party to this contract, (ii) liable for interest on the earnest money and (iii) liable for the loss of any earnest money caused by the failure of any financial institution in which the earnest money has been deposited unless the financial institution is acting as Escrow Agent. Escrow Agent may require any disbursement made in connection with this contract to be conditioned on Escrow Agent's collection of good funds acceptable to Escrow Agent.

B. EXPENSES: At closing, the earnest money must be applied first to any cash down payment, then to Buyer's Expenses and any excess refunded to Buyer. If no closing occurs, Escrow Agent may: (i) require a written release of liability of the Escrow Agent from all parties before releasing any earnest money; and (ii) require payment of unpaid expenses incurred on behalf of a party. Escrow Agent may deduct authorized expenses from the earnest money payable to a party. "Authorized expenses" means expenses incurred by Escrow Agent on behalf of the party entitled to the earnest money that were authorized by this contract or that party.

C. DEMAND: Upon termination of this contract, either party or the Escrow Agent may send a release of earnest money to each party and the parties shall execute counterparts of the release and deliver same to the Escrow Agent. If either party fails to execute the release, either party may make a written demand to the Escrow Agent for the earnest money. If only one party makes written demand for the earnest money, Escrow Agent shall promptly provide a copy of the demand to the other party. If Escrow Agent does not receive written objection to the demand from the other party within 15 days, Escrow Agent may disburse the earnest money to the party making demand reduced by the amount of unpaid expenses incurred on behalf of the party receiving the earnest money and Escrow Agent may pay the same to the creditors. If Escrow Agent complies with the provisions of this paragraph, each party hereby releases Escrow Agent from all adverse claims related to the disbursal of the earnest money.

D. DAMAGES: Any party who wrongfully fails or refuses to sign a release acceptable to the Escrow Agent within 7 days of receipt of the request will be liable to the other party for (i) damages; (ii) the earnest money; (iii) reasonable attorney's fees; and (iv) all costs of suit.

E. NOTICES: Escrow Agent's notices will be effective when sent in compliance with Paragraph 21. Notice of objection to the demand will be deemed effective upon receipt by Escrow Agent.

19. REPRESENTATIONS: All covenants, representations and warranties in this contract survive closing. If any representation of Seller in this contract is untrue on the Closing Date, Seller will be in default. Unless expressly prohibited by written agreement, Seller may continue to show the Property and receive, negotiate and accept back up offers.

20. GOVERNMENTAL REQUIREMENTS:

A. If Seller is a "foreign person," as defined by Internal Revenue Code and its regulations, or if Seller fails to deliver an affidavit or a certificate of non-foreign status to Buyer that Seller is not a "foreign person," then Buyer shall withhold from the sales proceeds an amount sufficient to comply with applicable tax law and deliver the same to the Internal Revenue Service together with appropriate tax forms. Internal Revenue Service regulations require filing written reports if currency in excess of specified amounts is received in the transaction.

B. Seller and Buyer shall promptly execute and deliver any statements, documents, and information requested by Escrow Agent required by governmental reporting requirements (for example, reporting to the U.S. Treasury or its bureaus).

21. NOTICES: All notices from one party or their agent to the other must be in writing. Notices are effective when mailed to, hand-delivered at, sent by overnight courier to, or transmitted by electronic transmission to the other party or their agent.

To Buyer(s) at:
Address:______________________________
____
Phone(s):______________________________
____
Email(s):______________________________
____

To Seller(s) at:
Address:______________________________
____
Phone(s):______________________________
____
Email(s):______________________________
____

To Buyer's agent at:
Address:______________________________
____
Phone:______________________________
Email:______________________________

To Seller's agent at:
Address:______________________________
____
Phone:______________________________
Email:______________________________

22. AGREEMENT OF PARTIES: This contract contains the entire agreement of the parties and cannot be changed except by their written agreement. Addenda and notices which are a part of this contract are (check all applicable boxes):

Financial
- ❑ Third Party Financing Addendum
- ❑ Addendum for Sale of Other Property by Buyer
- ❑ Addendum Concerning Right to Terminate Due to Lender's Appraisal
- ❑ Seller Financing Addendum
- ❑ Addendum for Section 1031 Exchange
- ❑ Short Sale Addendum
- ❑ Loan Assumption Addendum

Leases
- ❑ Addendum Regarding Residential Leases
- ❑ Addendum Regarding Fixture Leases
- ❑ Buyer's Temporary Residential Lease
- ❑ Seller's Temporary Residential Lease

Additional Tests and Reports
- ❑ Addendum for Authorizing Hydrostatic Testing
- ❑ Environmental Assessment, Threatened or Endangered Species, and Wetlands Addendum

Statutory Disclosures and Notices
- ❑ Addendum for Property in a Propane Gas System Service Area
- ❑ Addendum for Property Located Seaward of the Gulf Intercoastal Waterway
- ❑ Addendum for Coastal Area Property
- ❑ The following utility, water, drainage, public improvement, and other district notices (list all that have been given or are attached):______________________________
____

NOTICE: Seller's failure to provide applicable Statutory Disclosures and Notices may provide Buyer with remedies or rights to terminate this contract.

Other
- ❑ Addendum for Property Subject to Mandatory Membership in a Property Owners Association
- ❑ Non-Realty Items Addendum
- ❑ Addendum for "Back-Up" Contract
- ❑ Addendum for Reservation of Oil, Gas, and Other Minerals
- ❑ Other:______________________________
____

23. CONSULT AN ATTORNEY BEFORE SIGNING: TREC rules prohibit real estate license brokers and sales agents from giving legal advice. READ THIS CONTRACT CAREFULLY.

Buyer's Attorney is: ______________________	Seller's Attorney is: ______________________
______________________	______________________
Phone: ( ) ______________	Phone: ( ) ______________
Fax: ( ) ______________	Fax: ( ) ______________
E-mail: ______________	E-mail: ______________

EXECUTED the ______day of ________________________, 20____ (Effective Date).
(BROKER: FILL IN THE DATE OF FINAL ACCEPTANCE.)

This contract is subject to Chapter 27 of the Texas Property Code. The provisions of that chapter may affect your right to recover damages arising from a construction defect. If you have a complaint concerning a construction defect and that defect has not been corrected as may be required by law or by contract, you must provide the notice required by Chapter 27 of the Texas Property Code to the contractor by certified mail, return receipt requested, not later than the 60th day before the date you file suit to recover damages in a court of law or initiate arbitration. The notice must refer to Chapter 27 of the Texas Property Code and must describe the construction defect. If requested by the contractor, you must provide the contractor an opportunity to inspect and cure the defect as provided by Section 27.004 of the Texas Property Code.

____
Buyer

____
Buyer

____
Seller

____
Seller

BROKER CONTACT INFORMATION
(Print name(s) only. Do not sign)

The brokers to this sale are:

_______________________________ (Broker Firm) **represents Seller only as Seller's agent.**
Address: _______________________________
Broker Firm License No.: _______________________________
Associate's Name: _______________________________
Team Name: _______________________________
Associate's Email: _______________________________
Associate's Phone No.: ______________ Associate's License No.: ______________
Licensed Supervisor of Associate: _______________________________
Phone No. of Licensed Supervisor: ______________ License No.: ______________

_______________________________ (Broker Firm) **represents Buyer only as Buyer's agent.**
Address: _______________________________
Broker Firm License No.: _______________________________
Associate's Name: _______________________________
Team Name: _______________________________
Associate's Email: _______________________________
Associate's Phone No.: ______________ Associate's License No.: ______________
Licensed Supervisor of Associate: _______________________________
Phone No. of Licensed Supervisor: ______________ License No.: ______________

Intermediary

_______________________________ (Broker Firm) **represents Seller and Buyer as an intermediary.**
Address: _______________________________
Broker Firm License No.: _______________________________
Associate's Name (for Seller): _______________________________
Team Name: _______________________________
Associate's Email: _______________________________
Associate's Phone No.: ______________ Associate's License No.: ______________
Licensed Supervisor of Associate: _______________________________
Phone No. of Licensed Supervisor: ______________ License No.: ______________
Associate's Name (for Buyer): _______________________________
Team Name: _______________________________
Associate's Email: _______________________________
Associate's Phone No.: ______________ Associate's License No.: ______________
Licensed Supervisor of Associate: _______________________________
Phone No. of Licensed Supervisor: ______________ License No.: ______________

OPTION FEE RECEIPT

Receipt of $________________ option fee in the form of ___________________________
is acknowledged.

_______________________________________ _______________________________________
Escrow Agent Date

EARNEST MONEY RECEIPT

Receipt of $________________ earnest money in the form of ___________________________
is acknowledged.

_______________________________________ _______________________________________
Escrow Agent Received by Email Address Date/Time

_______________________________________ _______________________________________
Address Phone

_______________________________________ _______________________________________
City State Zip Fax

CONTRACT RECEIPT

Receipt of the contract is acknowledged.

_______________________________________ _______________________________________
Escrow Agent Received by Email Address Date

_______________________________________ _______________________________________
Address Phone

_______________________________________ _______________________________________
City State Zip Fax

ADDITIONAL EARNEST MONEY RECEIPT

Receipt of $________________ additional earnest money in the form of ___________________________
is acknowledged.

_______________________________________ _______________________________________
Escrow Agent Received by Email Address Date/Time

_______________________________________ _______________________________________
Address Phone

_______________________________________ _______________________________________
City State Zip Fax

PROMULGATED BY THE TEXAS REAL ESTATE COMMISSION (TREC) 05-04-2026

NEW HOME CONTRACT

(Incomplete Construction)

NOTICE: Not For Use For Condominium Transactions or Closings Prior to Completion of Construction

1.PARTIES: The parties to this contract are ______________________________________ (Seller) and ______________________________________(Buyer). Seller agrees to sell and convey to Buyer and Buyer agrees to buy from Seller the Property defined below.

2.PROPERTY: Lot ____________,Block__________, ______________________________ Addition, City of____________________________,County of ________________Texas, known as ____(address/zip code), or as described on attached exhibit, together with: (i) improvements, fixtures and all other property described in the Construction Documents; and (ii) all rights, privileges and appurtenances thereto All property sold by this contract is called the Property (Property).
RESERVATIONS: Any reservation for oil, gas, or other minerals, water, timber, or other interests is made in accordance with an attached addendum.

3.SALES PRICE:

A. Cash portion of Sales Price payable by Buyer at closing .... $________________
The term "Cash portion of the Sales Price" does not include proceeds from borrowing of any kind or selling other real property except as disclosed in this contract.

B. Sum of all financing described in the attached: ☐ Third Party Financing Addendum, ☐ Loan Assumption Addendum, ☐ Seller Financing Addendum .... $________________

C. Sales Price (Sum of A and B)... $________________

4.LEASES:

A. Except as disclosed in this contract, Seller is not aware of any leases affecting the Property. After the Effective Date, Seller may not, without Buyer's written consent, create a new lease, amend any existing lease, or convey any interest in the Property.

B. NATURAL RESOURCE LEASES: "Natural Resource Lease" means an existing oil and gas, mineral, geothermal, water, wind, or other natural resource lease affecting the Property to which Seller is a party. Seller ☐ is ☐ is not a party to a Natural Resource Lease. If Seller is a party to a Natural Resource Lease, check one of the following:

☐ (1) Seller has delivered to Buyer a copy of all the Natural Resource Leases.

☐ (2) Seller has not delivered to Buyer a copy of all the Natural Resource Leases. Seller shall provide to Buyer a copy of all the Natural Resource Leases within 3 days after the Effective Date. Buyer may terminate the contract within ______ days after the date the Buyer receives all the Natural Resource Leases and the earnest money shall be refunded to Buyer.

5.EARNEST MONEY AND TERMINATION OPTION:

A. DELIVERY OF EARNEST MONEY AND OPTION FEE: Within 3 days after the Effective Date, Buyer must deliver to ________________________________(Escrow Agent) at ______________ ____(address): $________________ as earnest money and $________________ as the option fee. The earnest money and option fee shall be made payable to Escrow Agent and may be paid separately or combined in a single payment.

(1) Buyer shall deliver additional earnest money of $________________ to Escrow Agent within ______ days after the Effective Date of this contract.

(2) If the last day to deliver the earnest money, option fee, or the additional earnest money falls on a Saturday, Sunday, or Legal Holiday, the time to deliver the earnest money, option fee, or the additional earnest money, as applicable, is extended until the end of the next day that is not a Saturday, Sunday, or Legal Holiday. "Legal Holiday" means a legal holiday described in Sections 662.003(a) and 662.003(b)(4) and (6), Texas Government Code.

(3) The amount(s) Escrow Agent receives under this paragraph shall be applied first to the option fee, then to the earnest money, and then to the additional earnest money.

(4) Buyer authorizes Escrow Agent to release and deliver the option fee to Seller at any time without further notice to or consent from Buyer, and releases Escrow Agent from liability for delivery of the option fee to Seller. The option fee will be credited to the Sales Price at closing.

B. TERMINATION OPTION: For nominal consideration, the receipt of which Seller acknowledges, and Buyer's agreement to pay the option fee within the time required, Seller grants Buyer the unrestricted right to terminate this contract by giving notice of termination to Seller within _______ days after the Effective Date of this contract (Option Period). Notices under this paragraph must be given by 5:00 p.m. (local time where the Property is located) by the date specified. If Buyer gives notice of termination within the time prescribed: (i) the option fee will not be refunded and Escrow Agent shall release any option fee remaining with Escrow Agent to Seller; and (ii) any earnest money will be refunded to Buyer.

C. FAILURE TO TIMELY DELIVER EARNEST MONEY: If Buyer fails to deliver the earnest money within the time required, Seller may terminate this contract or exercise Seller's remedies under Paragraph 15, or both, by providing notice to Buyer before Buyer delivers the earnest money.

D. FAILURE TO TIMELY DELIVER OPTION FEE: If no dollar amount is stated as the option fee or if Buyer fails to deliver the option fee within the time required, Buyer shall not have the unrestricted right to terminate this contract under this Paragraph 5.

E. TIME: **Time is of the essence for this paragraph and strict compliance with the time for performance is required.**

Initialed for identification by Buyer_____ _____ and Seller ______ _____ TREC NO. 23-20

6.TITLE POLICY AND SURVEY:

A. TITLE POLICY: Seller shall furnish to Buyer at ❑Seller's ❑Buyer's expense an owner policy of title insurance (Title Policy) issued by ______________________________(Title Company) in the amount of the Sales Price, dated at or after closing, insuring Buyer against loss under the provisions of the Title Policy, subject to the promulgated exclusions (including existing building and zoning ordinances) and the following exceptions:

(1) Restrictive covenants common to the platted subdivision in which the Property is located.
(2) The standard printed exception for standby fees, taxes and assessments.
(3) Liens created as part of the financing described in Paragraph 3.
(4) Utility easements created by the dedication deed or plat of the subdivision in which the Property is located.
(5) Reservations or exceptions otherwise permitted by this contract or as may be approved by Buyer in writing.
(6)The standard printed exception as to marital rights.
(7) The standard printed exception as to waters, tidelands, beaches, streams, and related matters.
(8) The standard printed exception as to discrepancies, conflicts, shortages in area or boundary lines, encroachments or protrusions, or overlapping improvements:
❑ (i) will not be amended or deleted from the title policy; or
❑ (ii) will be amended to read, "shortages in area" at the expense of ❑Buyer ❑Seller.
(9) The exception or exclusion regarding minerals approved by the Texas Department of Insurance.

B. COMMITMENT: Within 20 days after the Title Company receives a copy of this contract, Seller shall furnish to Buyer a commitment for title insurance (Commitment) and, at Buyer's expense, legible copies of restrictive covenants and documents evidencing exceptions in the Commitment (Exception Documents) other than the standard printed exceptions. Seller authorizes the Title Company to deliver the Commitment and Exception Documents to Buyer at Buyer's address shown in Paragraph 21. If the Commitment and Exception Documents are not delivered to Buyer within the specified time, the time for delivery will be automatically extended up to 15 days or 3 days before the Closing Date, whichever is earlier. If the Commitment and Exception Documents are not delivered within the time required, Buyer may terminate this contract and the earnest money will be refunded to Buyer.

C. SURVEY: The survey must be made after the Substantial Completion Date by a registered professional land surveyor acceptable to the Title Company and Buyer's lender(s). (Check one box only)
❑ (1) At least _______ days prior to the Closing Date, Seller, at Seller's expense, shall provide a new survey to Buyer.
❑ (2) At least ______ days prior to the Closing Date, Buyer, at Buyer's expense, may obtain a new survey. Buyer is deemed to receive the survey on the date of actual receipt or the date specified in this paragraph, whichever is earlier. If Buyer fails to obtain the survey, Buyer may not terminate the contract under Paragraph 2B of the Third Party Financing Addendum because the survey was not obtained.

D. OBJECTIONS: Buyer may object in writing to defects, exceptions, or encumbrances to title: disclosed on the survey other than items 6A(1) through (7) above; disclosed in the Commitment other than items 6A(1) through (9) above; or which prohibit the following use or activity: _____
____.
Buyer must object the earlier of (i) the Closing Date or (ii) ______ days after Buyer receives the Commitment, Exception Documents, and the survey. Buyer's failure to object within the time allowed will constitute a waiver of Buyer's right to object; except that the requirements in Schedule C of the Commitment are not waived by Buyer. Provided Seller is not obligated to incur any expense, Seller shall cure any timely objections of Buyer or any third party lender within 15 days after Seller receives the objections (Cure Period) and the Closing Date will be extended as necessary. If objections are not cured within the Cure Period, Buyer may, by delivering notice to Seller within 5 days after the end of the Cure Period: (i) terminate this contract and the earnest money will be refunded to Buyer; or (ii) waive the objections. If Buyer does not terminate within the time required, Buyer shall be deemed to have waived the objections. If the Commitment or survey is revised or any new Exception Document(s) is delivered, Buyer may object to any new matter revealed in the revised Commitment or survey or new Exception Document(s) within the same time stated in this paragraph to make objections beginning when the revised Commitment, survey, or Exception Document(s) is delivered to Buyer.

E. TITLE NOTICES:
(1) ABSTRACT OR TITLE POLICY: Broker advises Buyer to have an abstract of title covering the Property examined by an attorney of Buyer's selection, or Buyer should be furnished with or obtain a Title Policy. If a Title Policy is furnished, the Commitment should be promptly reviewed by an attorney of Buyer's choice due to the time limitations on Buyer's right to object.
(2) MEMBERSHIP IN PROPERTY OWNERS ASSOCIATION(S): The Property ❑is ❑is not subject to mandatory membership in a property owners association(s). If the Property is subject to mandatory membership in a property owners association(s), Seller notifies Buyer under §5.012, Texas Property Code, that, as a purchaser of property in the residential community identified in Paragraph 2A in which the Property is located, you are obligated to be a member

of the property owners association(s). Restrictive covenants governing the use and occupancy of the Property and all dedicatory instruments governing the establishment, maintenance, and operation of this residential community have been or will be recorded in the Real Property Records of the county in which the Property is located. Copies of the restrictive covenants and dedicatory instruments may be obtained from the county clerk. **You are obligated to pay assessments to the property owners association(s). The amount of the assessments is subject to change. Your failure to pay the assessments could result in enforcement of the association's lien on and the foreclosure of the Property.**
Section 207.003, Property Code, entitles an owner to receive copies of any document that governs the establishment, maintenance, or operation of a subdivision, including, but not limited to, restrictions, bylaws, rules and regulations, and a resale certificate from a property owners' association. A resale certificate contains information including, but not limited to, statements specifying the amount and frequency of regular assessments and the style and cause number of lawsuits to which the property owners' association is a party, other than lawsuits relating to unpaid ad valorem taxes of an individual member of the association. These documents must be made available to you by the property owners' association or the association's agent on your request.
If Buyer is concerned about these matters, the TREC promulgated Addendum for Property Subject to Mandatory Membership in a Property Owners Association should be used.

(3) STATUTORY TAX DISTRICTS: If the Property is situated in a utility or other statutorily created district providing water, sewer, drainage, or flood control facilities and services, Chapter 49, Texas Water Code, requires Seller to deliver and Buyer to sign the statutory notice relating to the tax rate, bonded indebtedness, or standby fee of the district prior to final execution of this contract.

(4) TIDE WATERS: If the Property abuts the tidally influenced waters of the state, §33.135, Texas Natural Resources Code, requires a notice regarding coastal area property to be included in the contract.

(5) ANNEXATION: If the Property is located outside the limits of a municipality, Seller notifies Buyer under §5.011, Texas Property Code, that the Property may now or later be included in the extraterritorial jurisdiction of a municipality and may now or later be subject to annexation by the municipality. Each municipality maintains a map that depicts its boundaries and extraterritorial jurisdiction. To determine if the Property is located within a municipality's extraterritorial jurisdiction or is likely to be located within a municipality's extraterritorial jurisdiction, contact all municipalities located in the general proximity of the Property for further information.

(6) PROPERTY LOCATED IN A CERTIFICATED SERVICE AREA OF A UTILITY SERVICE PROVIDER: Notice required by §13.257, Water Code: The real property, described in Paragraph 2, that you are about to purchase may be located in a certificated water or sewer service area, which is authorized by law to provide water or sewer service to the properties in the certificated area. If your property is located in a certificated area there may be special costs or charges that you will be required to pay before you can receive water or sewer service. There may be a period required to construct lines or other facilities necessary to provide water or sewer service to your property. You are advised to determine if the property is in a certificated area and contact the utility service provider to determine the cost that you will be required to pay and the period, if any, that is required to provide water or sewer service to your property. The undersigned Buyer hereby acknowledges receipt of the foregoing notice at or before the execution of a binding contract for the purchase of the real property described in Paragraph 2 or at closing of purchase of the real property.

(7) PUBLIC IMPROVEMENT DISTRICTS: If the Property is in a public improvement district, Seller must give Buyer written notice as required by §5.014, Property Code.

(8) TRANSFER FEES: If the Property is subject to a private transfer fee obligation, §5.205, Property Code, requires Seller to notify Buyer as follows: The private transfer fee obligation may be governed by Chapter 5, Subchapter G of the Texas Property Code.

(9) PROPANE GAS SYSTEM SERVICE AREA: If the Property is located in a propane gas system service area owned by a distribution system retailer, Seller must give Buyer written notice as required by §141.010, Texas Utilities Code.

(10) NOTICE OF WATER LEVEL FLUCTUATIONS: If the Property adjoins an impoundment of water, including a reservoir or lake, constructed and maintained under Chapter 11, Water Code, that has a storage capacity of at least 5,000 acre-feet at the impoundment's normal operating level, Seller hereby notifies Buyer: "The water level of the impoundment of water adjoining the Property fluctuates for various reasons, including as a result of: (1) an entity lawfully exercising its right to use the water stored in the impoundment; or (2) drought or flood conditions."

(11) CERTIFICATE OF MOLD REMEDIATION: If the Property has been remediated for mold, Seller must provide to Buyer each certificate of mold damage remediation issued under §1958.154, Occupations Code, during the 5 years preceding the sale of the Property.

7. PROPERTY CONDITION:

A. ACCESS AND INSPECTIONS: Seller shall permit Buyer and Buyer's agents access to the Property at reasonable times. Buyer may have the Property inspected by inspectors selected by Buyer and licensed by TREC or otherwise permitted by law to make inspections.

B. CONSTRUCTION DOCUMENTS: Seller shall complete all improvements to the Property with due diligence in accordance with the Construction Documents. "Construction Documents" means the plans and specifications, the finish out schedules, any change orders, and any allowances related to the plans and specifications, finish out schedules, and change orders. The Construction Documents have been signed by the parties and are incorporated into this contract by reference.

C. COST ADJUSTMENTS: All change orders must be in writing. Increase in costs resulting from change orders or items selected by Buyer which exceed the allowances specified in the Construction Documents will be paid by Buyer as follows:______________________________
____.
A decrease in costs resulting from change orders and unused allowances will reduce the Sales Price, with proportionate adjustments to the amounts in Paragraphs 3A and 3B as required by lender.

D. BUYER'S SELECTIONS: If the Construction Documents permit selections by Buyer, Buyer's selections will conform to Seller's normal standards as set out in the Construction Documents or will not, in Seller's judgment, adversely affect the marketability of the Property. Buyer will make required selections within ______ days after notice from Seller.

E. COMPLETION: Seller must commence construction no later than _______ days after the Effective Date of this contract. The improvements will be substantially completed in accordance with the Construction Documents and ready for occupancy not later than _____________________, 20___ . The improvements will be deemed to be substantially completed in accordance with the Construction Documents upon the final inspection and approval by all applicable governmental authorities and any lender (Substantial Completion Date). Construction delays caused by acts of God, fire or other casualty, strikes, boycotts or nonavailability of materials for which no substitute of comparable quality and price is available will be added to the time allowed for substantial completion of the construction. However, in no event may the time for substantial completion extend beyond the Closing Date. Seller may substitute materials, equipment and appliances of comparable quality for those specified in the Construction Documents.

F. WARRANTIES: Except as expressly set forth in this contract, a separate writing, or provided by law, Seller makes no other express warranties. Seller shall assign to Buyer at closing all assignable manufacturer warranties.

G. INSULATION: As required by Federal Trade Commission Regulations, the information relating to the insulation installed or to be installed in the Improvements at the Property is: (check only one box below)

❑ (1) as shown in the attached specifications.
❑ (2) as follows:

(a) Exterior walls of improved living areas: insulated with ______________________ insulation to a thickness of ________ inches which yields an R-Value of ____________ ____.

(b) Walls in other areas of the home: insulated with______________________ insulation to a thickness of ________ inches which yields an R-Value of ____________ ____.

(c) Ceilings in improved living areas: insulated with______________________ insulation to a thickness of ________ inches which yields an R-Value of ____________ ____.

(d) Floors of improved living areas not applied to a slab foundation: insulated with_______ ______________________________insulation to a thickness of __________ inches which yields an R-Value of ____.

(e) Other insulated areas: insulated with ______________________________ insulation to a thickness of ________ inches which yields an R-Value of _______________________.

All stated R-Values are based on information provided by the manufacturer of the insulation.

H. ENVIRONMENTAL MATTERS: Buyer is advised that the presence of wetlands, toxic substances, including asbestos and wastes or other environmental hazards, or the presence of a threatened or endangered species or its habitat may affect Buyer's intended use of the Property. If Buyer is concerned about these matters, an addendum promulgated by TREC or required by the parties should be used.

I. SELLER'S DISCLOSURE:

(1) Seller ❑ is ❑ is not aware of any flooding of the Property which has had a material adverse effect on the use of the Property.
(2) Seller ❑ is ❑ is not aware of any pending or threatened litigation, condemnation, or special assessment affecting the Property.
(3) Seller ❑ is ❑ is not aware of any environmental hazards that materially and adversely affect the Property.
(4) Seller ❑ is ❑ is not aware of any dumpsite, landfill, or underground tanks or containers now or previously located on the Property.
(5) Seller ❑ is ❑ is not aware of any wetlands, as defined by federal or state law or regulation, affecting the Property.
(6) Seller ❑ is ❑ is not aware of any threatened or endangered species or their habitat affecting the Property.
(7) Seller ❑ is ❑ is not aware that the Property is located ❑ wholly ❑ partly in a floodplain.
(8) Seller ❑ is ❑ is not aware that a tree or trees located on the Property has oak wilt.

If Seller is aware of any of the items above, explain (attach additional sheets if necessary):____
____.

J. RESIDENTIAL SERVICE CONTRACTS: Buyer may purchase a residential service contract from a provider or administrator licensed by the Texas Department of Licensing and Regulation. If Buyer purchases a residential service contract, Seller shall reimburse Buyer at closing for the cost of the residential service contract in an amount not exceeding $_______________. Buyer should review any residential service contract for the scope of coverage, exclusions and limitations. **The purchase of a residential service contract is optional. Similar coverage may be purchased from various companies authorized to do business in Texas.**

K. SELLER'S DISCLOSURE ABOUT GROUNDWATER AND SURFACE WATER RIGHTS (Seller's Water Disclosure): Access to surface water or groundwater on the Property may be regulated, restricted, or prohibited, including but not limited to the right to drill or operate water wells and the right to withdraw water from surface water sources on or adjoining the Property. The parties shall use the Seller's Water Disclosure published by TREC to identify information related to groundwater and surface water rights. (Check one box only)

❑ (1) Buyer has received the Seller's Water Disclosure.

❑ (2) Buyer has not received the Seller's Water Disclosure. Within _____ days after the Effective Date of this contract, Seller shall deliver the Seller's Water Disclosure to Buyer. If Buyer does not receive the Water Notice, Buyer may terminate this contract at any time prior to the closing and the earnest money will be refunded to Buyer. If Seller delivers the Seller's Water Disclosure, Buyer may terminate this contract for any reason within 7 days after Buyer receives the Water Notice or prior to the closing, whichever first occurs, and the earnest money will be refunded to Buyer.

❑ (3) Seller is not required to deliver the Seller's Water Disclosure to Buyer because all of the following are true:
- (a) Seller is not aware of a water well on the Property (in use or not in use);
- (b) Seller is not aware of a pond, lake, or water tank on the Property;
- (c) Seller is not aware of any certificate of adjudication, certified filing, or permit for surface water rights associated with the Property administered by the Texas Commission on Environmental Quality;
- (d) Seller is not aware that any groundwater rights to the Property have been severed, sold, or leased in whole or in part; and
- (e) the Property receives water only from the following municipality (City), municipal utility district (MUD) or other special district, water supply corporation (WSC), or private water supply company (PWC):____
____.

8.BROKER OR SALES AGENT DISCLOSURE:
Texas law requires a real estate broker or sales agent who is a party to a transaction or acting on behalf of a spouse, parent, child, business entity in which the broker or sales agent owns more than 10%, or a trust for which the broker or sales agent acts as a trustee or of which the broker or sales agent or the broker or sales agent's spouse, parent or child is a beneficiary, to notify the other party in writing before entering into a contract of sale. Disclose if applicable:____________
____.

9.CLOSING:

A. The closing of the sale will be on or before ____________________, 20_____, or within 7 days after objections made under Paragraph 6D have been cured or waived, whichever date is later (Closing Date). If either party fails to close the sale by the Closing Date, the non-defaulting party may exercise the remedies contained in Paragraph 15.

B. At closing:
- (1) Seller shall execute and deliver a general warranty deed conveying title to the Property to Buyer and showing no additional exceptions to those permitted in Paragraph 6 and furnish tax statements or certificates showing no delinquent taxes on the Property.
- (2) Buyer shall pay the Sales Price in good funds acceptable to the Escrow Agent.
- (3) Seller and Buyer shall execute and deliver any notices, statements, certificates, affidavits, releases, loan documents, transfer of any warranties, and other documents reasonably required for the closing of the sale and the issuance of the Title Policy.
- (4) There will be no liens, assessments, or security interests against the Property which will not be satisfied out of the sales proceeds unless securing payment of any loans assumed by Buyer and assumed loans will not be in default.
- (5) Private transfer fees (as defined by Chapter 5, Subchapter G of the Texas Property Code) will be the obligation of Seller unless provided otherwise in this contract. Transfer fees assessed by a property owners' association are governed by the Addendum for Property Subject to Mandatory Membership in a Property Owners Association.

10.POSSESSION:

A. BUYER'S POSSESSION: Seller shall deliver to Buyer possession of the Property: ❑ upon closing and funding ❑ according to a temporary residential lease form promulgated by TREC or other written lease required by the parties. Any possession by Buyer prior to closing or by Seller after closing which is not authorized by a written lease will establish a tenancy at sufferance relationship between the parties. **Consult your insurance agent prior to change of ownership and possession because insurance coverage may be limited or terminated. The absence of a written lease or appropriate insurance coverage may expose the parties to economic loss.**

B. SMART DEVICES: "Smart Device" means a device that connects to the internet to enable remote use, monitoring, and management of: (i) the Property; (ii) items identified in any Non-Realty Items Addendum; or (iii) items in a fixture lease assigned to Buyer. At the time Seller delivers possession of the Property to Buyer, Seller shall:
- (1) deliver to Buyer written information containing all access codes, usernames, passwords, and applications Buyer will need to access, operate, manage, and control the Smart Devices; and
- (2) terminate and remove all access and connections to the improvements and accessories from any of Seller's personal devices including but not limited to phones and computers.

11.SPECIAL PROVISIONS: (This paragraph is intended to be used only for additional informational items. An informational item is a statement that completes a blank in a contract form, discloses factual information, or provides instructions. Real estate brokers and sales agents are prohibited

from practicing law and shall not add to, delete, or modify any provision of this contract unless drafted by a party to this contract or a party's attorney.) ______________________________
____.

12. SETTLEMENT AND OTHER EXPENSES:

A. EXPENSES: The following expenses must be paid at or prior to closing:

(1) Seller shall pay the following expenses (Seller's Expenses):

(a) releases of existing liens, including prepayment penalties and recording fees; release of Seller's loan liability; tax statements or certificates; preparation of deed; one-half of escrow fee; and other expenses payable by Seller under this contract;

(b) an amount not to exceed $ ___________ to be applied to Buyer's Expenses other than brokerage compensation or contributions under Paragraph 12B below.

(2) Buyer shall pay the following expenses (Buyer's Expenses): Appraisal fees; loan application fees; origination charges; credit reports; preparation of loan documents; interest on the notes from date of disbursement to one month prior to dates of first monthly payments; recording fees; copies of easements and restrictions; loan title policy with endorsements required by lender; loan-related inspection fees; photos; amortization schedules; one-half of escrow fee; all prepaid items, including required premiums for flood and hazard insurance, reserve deposits for insurance, ad valorem taxes and special governmental assessments; final compliance inspection; courier fee; repair inspection; underwriting fee; wire transfer fee; expenses incident to any loan; Private Mortgage Insurance Premium (PMI), VA Loan Funding Fee, or FHA Mortgage Insurance Premium (MIP) as required by the lender; and other expenses payable by Buyer under this contract.

B. BROKERAGE COMPENSATION: Brokerage compensation is not set by law and is fully negotiable. Each party shall pay their respective brokers pursuant to the terms of the parties' obligations to compensate their brokers contained in separate written agreements. **The contributions under 12B(1) and 12B(2) below shall be applied to and shall not change the parties' obligations to pay compensation pursuant to those agreements.** The following contributions must be paid at closing:

❑ (1) Seller will pay (check one box only): ❑ $__________ or ❑ _______% of the Sales Price to be applied toward the brokerage compensation owed by Buyer to Buyer's broker.

❑ (2) Buyer will pay (check one box only): ❑ $__________ or ❑ _______% of the Sales Price to be applied toward the brokerage compensation owed by Seller to Seller's broker.

C. EXPENSE LIMITATION: If a governmental loan program regulation prohibits Buyer from paying charges or fees, then the amount of any concession in 12A(1)(b) shall be first applied to pay such prohibited expenses and then to other Buyer's Expenses but not brokerage compensation or contribution.

13. PRORATIONS AND ROLLBACK TAXES:

A. PRORATIONS: Taxes for the current year, interest, rents, and regular periodic maintenance fees, assessments, and dues (including prepaid items) will be prorated through the Closing Date. The tax proration may be calculated taking into consideration any change in exemptions that will affect the current year's taxes. If taxes for the current year vary from the amount prorated at closing, the parties shall adjust the prorations when tax statements for the current year are available. If taxes are not paid at or prior to closing, Buyer will be obligated to pay taxes for the current year.

B. ROLLBACK TAXES: If additional taxes, penalties, or interest (Assessments) are imposed because of Seller's use or change in use of the Property prior to closing, the Assessments will be the obligation of Seller. Obligations imposed by this paragraph will survive closing.

14. CASUALTY LOSS: If any part of the Property is damaged or destroyed by fire or other casualty after the Effective Date of this contract, Seller shall restore the Property to its previous condition as soon as reasonably possible, but in any event by the Closing Date. If Seller fails to do so due to factors beyond Seller's control, Buyer may (a) terminate this contract and the earnest money will be refunded to Buyer (b) extend the time for performance up to 45 days and the Closing Date will be extended as necessary or (c) accept the Property in its damaged condition with an assignment of insurance proceeds, if permitted by Seller's insurance carrier, and receive credit from Seller at closing in the amount of the deductible under the insurance policy. Seller's obligations under this paragraph are independent of any other obligations of Seller under this contract.

15. DEFAULT: If Buyer fails to comply with this contract, Buyer will be in default, and Seller may (a) enforce specific performance, seek such other relief as may be provided by law, or both, or (b) terminate this contract and receive the earnest money as liquidated damages, thereby releasing both parties from this contract. If Seller fails to comply with this contract Seller will be in default and Buyer may (a) enforce specific performance, seek such other relief as may be provided by law, or both, or (b) terminate this contract and receive the earnest money, thereby releasing both parties from this contract.

16. MEDIATION: It is the policy of the State of Texas to encourage resolution of disputes through alternative dispute resolution procedures such as mediation. Subject to applicable law, any dispute between Seller and Buyer related to this contract which is not resolved through informal discussion will be submitted to a mutually acceptable mediation service or provider. The parties to the mediation shall bear the mediation costs equally. This paragraph does not preclude a party from seeking equitable relief from a court of competent jurisdiction.

17. ATTORNEY'S FEES: A Buyer, Seller, Seller's broker, Buyer's broker, or Escrow Agent who prevails in any legal proceeding related to this contract is entitled to recover reasonable attorney's fees and all costs of such proceeding.

18. ESCROW:

A. ESCROW: The Escrow Agent is not (i) a party to this contract and does not have liability for the performance or nonperformance of any party to this contract, (ii) liable for interest on the earnest money and (iii) liable for the loss of any earnest money caused by the failure of any financial institution in which the earnest money has been deposited unless the financial institution is acting as Escrow Agent. Escrow Agent may require any disbursement made in connection with this contract to be conditioned on Escrow Agent's collection of good funds acceptable to Escrow Agent.

B. EXPENSES: At closing, the earnest money must be applied first to any cash down payment, then to Buyer's Expenses and any excess refunded to Buyer. If no closing occurs, Escrow Agent may: (i) require a written release of liability of the Escrow Agent from all parties before releasing any earnest money; and (ii) require payment of unpaid expenses incurred on behalf of a party. Escrow Agent may deduct authorized expenses from the earnest money payable to a party. "Authorized expenses" means expenses incurred by Escrow Agent on behalf of the party entitled to the earnest money that were authorized by this contract or that party.

C. DEMAND: Upon termination of this contract, either party or the Escrow Agent may send a release of earnest money to each party and the parties shall execute counterparts of the release and deliver same to the Escrow Agent. If either party fails to execute the release, either party may make a written demand to the Escrow Agent for the earnest money. If only oneparty makes written demand for the earnest money, Escrow Agent shall promptly provide a copy of the demand to the other party. If Escrow Agent does not receive written objection to the demand from the other party within 15 days, Escrow Agent may disburse the earnest money to the party making demand reduced by the amount of unpaid expenses incurred on behalf of the party receiving the earnest money and Escrow Agent may pay the same to the creditors. If Escrow Agent complies with the provisions of this paragraph, each party hereby releases Escrow Agent from all adverse claims related to the disbursal of the earnest money.

D. DAMAGES: Any party who wrongfully fails or refuses to sign a release acceptable to the Escrow Agent within 7 days of receipt of the request will be liable to the other party for (i) damages (ii) the earnest money; (iii) reasonable attorney's fees; and (iv) all costs of suit.

E. NOTICES: Escrow Agent's notices will be effective when sent in compliance with Paragraph 21. Notice of objection to the demand will be deemed effective upon receipt by Escrow Agent.

19. REPRESENTATIONS: All covenants, representations and warranties in this contract survive closing. If any representation of Seller in this contract is untrue on the Closing Date, Seller will be in default. Unless expressly prohibited by written agreement, Seller may continue to show the Property and receive, negotiate and accept back up offers.

20. GOVERNMENTAL REQUIREMENTS:

A. If Seller is a "foreign person," as defined by Internal Revenue Code and its regulations, or if Seller fails to deliver an affidavit or a certificate of non-foreign status to Buyer that Seller is nota "foreign person," then Buyer shall withhold from the sales proceeds an amount sufficient to comply with applicable tax law and deliver the same to the Internal Revenue Service together with appropriate tax forms. Internal Revenue Service regulations require filing written reports if currency in excess of specified amounts is received in the transaction.

B. Seller and Buyer shall promptly execute and deliver any statements, documents, and information requested by Escrow Agent required by governmental reporting requirements (for example, reporting to the U.S. Treasury or its bureaus).

21. NOTICES: All notices from one party or their agent to the other must be in writing. Notices are effective when mailed to, hand-delivered at, sent by overnight courier to, or transmitted by electronic transmission to the other party or their agent.

To Buyer(s) at:	**To Seller(s) at:**
Address: ______________________	Address: ______________________
______________________	______________________
Phone(s): ______________________	Phone(s): ______________________
______________________	______________________
Email(s): ______________________	Email(s): ______________________
______________________	______________________
To Buyer's agent at:	**To Seller's agent at:**
Address: ______________________	Address: ______________________
______________________	______________________
Phone: ______________________	Phone: ______________________
Email: ______________________	Email: ______________________

22. AGREEMENT OF PARTIES: This contract contains the entire agreement of the parties and cannot be changed except by their written agreement. Addenda and notices which are a part of this contract are (check all applicable boxes):

Financial
- ❑ Third Party Financing Addendum
- ❑ Addendum for Sale of Other Property by Buyer
- ❑ Addendum Concerning Right to Terminate Due to Lender's Appraisal
- ❑ Seller Financing Addendum
- ❑ Addendum for Section 1031 Exchange
- ❑ Short Sale Addendum
- ❑ Loan Assumption Addendum

Leases
- ❑ Addendum Regarding Residential Leases
- ❑ Addendum Regarding Fixture Leases
- ❑ Buyer's Temporary Residential Lease
- ❑ Seller's Temporary Residential Lease

Additional Tests and Reports
- ❑ Addendum for Authorizing Hydrostatic Testing
- ❑ Environmental Assessment, Threatened or Endangered Species, and Wetlands Addendum

Statutory Disclosures and Notices
- ❑ Addendum for Property in a Propane Gas System Service Area
- ❑ Addendum for Property Located Seaward of the Gulf Intercoastal Waterway
- ❑ Addendum for Coastal Area Property
- ❑ The following utility, water, drainage, public improvement, and other district notices (list all that have been given or are attached):____
____

NOTICE: Seller's failure to provide applicable Statutory Disclosures and Notices may provide Buyer with remedies or rights to terminate this contract.

Other
- ❑ Addendum for Property Subject to Mandatory Membership in a Property Owners Association
- ❑ Non-Realty Items Addendum
- ❑ Addendum for "Back-Up" Contract
- ❑ Addendum for Reservation of Oil, Gas, and Other Minerals
- ❑ Other:____
____

23. CONSULT AN ATTORNEY BEFORE SIGNING: TREC rules prohibit real estate brokers and sales agents from giving legal advice. READ THIS CONTRACT CAREFULLY.

Buyer's Attorney is: ______________________	Seller's Attorney is: ______________________
______________________	______________________
Phone: ( ) ______________	Phone: ( ) ______________
Fax: ( ) ______________	Fax: ( ) ______________
E-mail: ______________	E-mail: ______________

EXECUTED the _______day of ___________________________, 20_____ (Effective Date).
(BROKER: FILL IN THE DATE OF FINAL ACCEPTANCE.)

This contract is subject to Chapter 27 of the Texas Property Code. The provisions of that chapter may affect your right to recover damages arising from a construction defect. If you have a complaint concerning a construction defect and that defect has not been corrected as may be required by law or by contract, you must provide the notice required by Chapter 27 of the Texas Property Code to the contractor by certified mail, return receipt requested, not later than the 60th day before the date you file suit to recover damages in a court of law or initiate arbitration. The notice must refer to Chapter 27 of the Texas Property Code and must describe the construction defect. If requested by the contractor, you must provide the contractor an opportunity to inspect and cure the defect as provided by Section 27.004 of the Texas Property Code.

____
Buyer

____
Buyer

____
Seller

____
Seller

BROKER CONTACT INFORMATION
(Print name(s) only. Do not sign)

The brokers to this sale are:

______________________ (Broker Firm) **represents Seller only as Seller's agent.**

Address: ______________________
Broker Firm License No.: ______________________
Associate's Name: ______________________
Team Name: ______________________
Associate's Email: ______________________
Associate's Phone No.: ______________ Associate's License No.: ______________
Licensed Supervisor of Associate: ______________________
Phone No. of Licensed Supervisor: ______________ License No.: ______________

______________________ (Broker Firm) **represents Buyer only as Buyer's agent.**

Address: ______________________
Broker Firm License No.: ______________________
Associate's Name: ______________________
Team Name: ______________________
Associate's Email: ______________________
Associate's Phone No.: ______________ Associate's License No.: ______________
Licensed Supervisor of Associate: ______________________
Phone No. of Licensed Supervisor: ______________ License No.: ______________

Intermediary

______________________ (Broker Firm) **represents Seller and Buyer as an intermediary.**

Address: ______________________
Broker Firm License No.: ______________________
Associate's Name (for Seller): ______________________
Team Name: ______________________
Associate's Email: ______________________
Associate's Phone No.: ______________ Associate's License No.: ______________
Licensed Supervisor of Associate: ______________________
Phone No. of Licensed Supervisor: ______________ License No.: ______________
Associate's Name (for Buyer): ______________________
Team Name: ______________________
Associate's Email: ______________________
Associate's Phone No.: ______________ Associate's License No.: ______________
Licensed Supervisor of Associate: ______________________
Phone No. of Licensed Supervisor: ______________ License No.: ______________

OPTION FEE RECEIPT

Receipt of $________________________ option fee in the form of ________________________ is acknowledged.

Escrow Agent ______________________ Date ______________________

EARNEST MONEY RECEIPT

Receipt of $________________________ earnest money in the form of ________________________
is acknowledged.

Escrow Agent ______ Received by ______ Email Address ______ Date/Time ______

Address ______ Phone ______

City ______ State ______ Zip ______ Fax ______

CONTRACT RECEIPT

Receipt of the contract is acknowledged.

Escrow Agent ______ Received by ______ Email Address ______ Date ______

Address ______ Phone ______

City ______ State ______ Zip ______ Fax ______

ADDITIONAL EARNEST MONEY RECEIPT

Receipt of $____________________ additional earnest money in the form of ________________________
is acknowledged.

Escrow Agent ______ Received by ______ Email Address ______ Date/Time ______

Address ______ Phone ______

City ______ State ______ Zip ______ Fax ______

05-04-2026

PROMULGATED BY THE TEXAS REAL ESTATE COMMISSION (TREC)

ONE TO FOUR FAMILY RESIDENTIAL CONTRACT (RESALE)

NOTICE: Not For Use For Condominium Transactions

1. PARTIES: The parties to this contract are _______________________________ (Seller) and _______________________________ (Buyer). Seller agrees to sell and convey to Buyer and Buyer agrees to buy from Seller the Property defined below.

2. PROPERTY: The land, improvements and accessories are collectively referred to as the Property (Property).

A. LAND: Lot __________ Block _____________, _______________________________ Addition, City of ____________________________, County of ____________________________, Texas, known as _______________________________ (address/zip code), or as described on attached exhibit.

B. IMPROVEMENTS: The house, garage and all other fixtures and improvements attached to the above-described real property, including without limitation, the following **permanently installed and built-in items,** if any: all equipment and appliances, valances, screens, shutters, awnings, wall-to-wall carpeting, mirrors, ceiling fans, attic fans, mail boxes, television antennas, mounts and brackets for televisions and speakers, heating and air-conditioning units, security and fire detection equipment, wiring, plumbing and lighting fixtures, chandeliers, water softener system, kitchen equipment, garage door openers, cleaning equipment, shrubbery, landscaping, outdoor cooking equipment, generators, and all other property attached to the above described real property.

C. ACCESSORIES: The following described related accessories, if any: window air conditioning units, stove, fireplace screens, curtains and rods, blinds, window shades, draperies and rods, door keys, mailbox keys, above ground pool, swimming pool equipment and maintenance accessories, artificial fireplace logs, security systems that are not fixtures, and controls for: (i) garage doors, (ii) entry gates, and (iii) other improvements and accessories. "Controls" includes Seller's transferable rights to the (i) software and applications used to access and control improvements or accessories, and (ii) hardware used solely to control improvements or accessories.

D. EXCLUSIONS: The following improvements and accessories will be retained by Seller and must be removed prior to delivery of possession: _______________________________ _______________________________.

E. RESERVATIONS: Any reservation for oil, gas, or other minerals, water, timber, or other interests is made in accordance with an attached addendum.

3. SALES PRICE:

A. Cash portion of Sales Price payable by Buyer at closing .... $_______________
The term "Cash portion of the Sales Price" does not include proceeds from borrowing of any kind or selling other real property except as disclosed in this contract.

B. Sum of all financing described in the attached: ☐ Third Party Financing Addendum, ☐ Loan Assumption Addendum, ☐ Seller Financing Addendum .... $_______________

C. Sales Price (Sum of A and B) .... $_______________

4. LEASES: Except as disclosed in this contract, Seller is not aware of any leases affecting the Property. After the Effective Date, Seller may not, without Buyer's written consent, create a new lease, amend any existing lease, or convey any interest in the Property. (Check all applicable boxes)

☐ A. RESIDENTIAL LEASES: The Property is subject to one or more residential leases and the Addendum Regarding Residential Leases is attached to this contract.

☐ B. FIXTURE LEASES: Fixtures on the Property are subject to one or more fixture leases (for example, solar panels, propane tanks, water softener, security system) and the Addendum Regarding Fixture Leases is attached to this contract.

☐ C. NATURAL RESOURCE LEASES: "Natural Resource Lease" means an existing oil and gas, mineral, geothermal, water, wind, or other natural resource lease affecting the Property to which Seller is a party.

☐ (1) Seller has delivered to Buyer a copy of all the Natural Resource Leases.

☐ (2) Seller has not delivered to Buyer a copy of all the Natural Resource Leases. Seller shall provide to Buyer a copy of all the Natural Resource Leases within 3 days after the Effective Date. Buyer may terminate the contract within _____ days after the date the Buyer receives all the Natural Resource Leases and the earnest money shall be refunded to Buyer.

5. EARNEST MONEY AND TERMINATION OPTION:

A. DELIVERY OF EARNEST MONEY AND OPTION FEE: Within 3 days after the Effective Date, Buyer must deliver to________________________ (Escrow Agent) at ____________________________ ________________________(address): $__________ as earnest money and $___________ as the option fee. The earnest money and option fee shall be made payable to Escrow Agent and may be paid separately or combined in a single payment.

(1) Buyer shall deliver additional earnest money of $________________ to Escrow Agent within ______ days after the Effective Date of this contract.

(2) If the last day to deliver the earnest money, option fee, or the additional earnest money falls on a Saturday, Sunday, or Legal Holiday, the time to deliver the earnest money, option fee, or the additional earnest money, as applicable, is extended until the end of the next day that is not a Saturday, Sunday, or Legal Holiday. "Legal Holiday" means a legal holiday described in Sections 662.003(a) and 662.003(b)(4) and (6), Texas Government Code.

(3) The amount(s) Escrow Agent receives under this paragraph shall be applied first to the option fee, then to the earnest money, and then to the additional earnest money.

(4) Buyer authorizes Escrow Agent to release and deliver the option fee to Seller at any time without further notice to or consent from Buyer, and releases Escrow Agent from liability for delivery of the option fee to Seller. The option fee will be credited to the Sales Price at closing.

B. TERMINATION OPTION: For nominal consideration, the receipt of which Seller acknowledges, and Buyer's agreement to pay the option fee within the time required, Seller grants Buyer the unrestricted right to terminate this contract by giving notice of termination to Seller within _____ days after the Effective Date of this contract (Option Period). Notices under this paragraph must be given by 5:00 p.m. (local time where the Property is located) by the date specified. If Buyer gives notice of termination within the time prescribed: (i) the option fee will not be refunded and Escrow Agent shall release any option fee remaining with Escrow Agent to Seller; and (ii) any earnest money will be refunded to Buyer.

C. FAILURE TO TIMELY DELIVER EARNEST MONEY: If Buyer fails to deliver the earnest money within the time required, Seller may terminate this contract or exercise Seller's remedies under Paragraph 15, or both, by providing notice to Buyer before Buyer delivers the earnest money.

D. FAILURE TO TIMELY DELIVER OPTION FEE: If no dollar amount is stated as the option fee or if Buyer fails to deliver the option fee within the time required, Buyer shall not have the unrestricted right to terminate this contract under this paragraph 5.

E. TIME: **Time is of the essence for this paragraph and strict compliance with the time for performance is required.**

6. TITLE POLICY AND SURVEY:

A. TITLE POLICY: Seller shall furnish to Buyer at ❑ Seller's ❑ Buyer's expense an owner policy of title insurance (Title Policy) issued by ______________________________(Title Company) in the amount of the Sales Price, dated at or after closing, insuring Buyer against loss under the provisions of the Title Policy, subject to the promulgated exclusions (including existing building and zoning ordinances) and the following exceptions:

(1) Restrictive covenants common to the platted subdivision in which the Property is located.

(2) The standard printed exception for standby fees, taxes and assessments.

(3) Liens created as part of the financing described in Paragraph 3.

(4) Utility easements created by the dedication deed or plat of the subdivision in which the Property is located.

(5) Reservations or exceptions otherwise permitted by this contract or as may be approved by Buyer in writing.

(6) The standard printed exception as to marital rights.

(7) The standard printed exception as to waters, tidelands, beaches, streams, and related matters.

(8) The standard printed exception as to discrepancies, conflicts, shortages in area or boundary lines, encroachments or protrusions, or overlapping improvements:

❑ (i) will not be amended or deleted from the title policy; or

❑ (ii) will be amended to read, "shortages in area" at the expense of ❑ Buyer ❑ Seller.

(9) The exception or exclusion regarding minerals approved by the Texas Department of Insurance.

B. COMMITMENT: Within 20 days after the Title Company receives a copy of this contract, Seller shall furnish to Buyer a commitment for title insurance (Commitment) and, at Buyer's expense, legible copies of restrictive covenants and documents evidencing exceptions in the Commitment (Exception Documents) other than the standard printed exceptions. Seller authorizes the Title Company to deliver the Commitment and Exception Documents to Buyer at Buyer's address shown in Paragraph 21. If the Commitment and Exception Documents are not delivered to Buyer within the specified time, the time for delivery will be automatically extended up to 15 days or 3 days before the Closing Date, whichever is earlier. If the Commitment and Exception Documents are not delivered within the time required, Buyer may terminate this contract and the earnest money will be refunded to Buyer.

C. SURVEY: The survey must be made by a registered professional land surveyor acceptable to the Title Company and Buyer's lender(s). (Check one box only)

❑ (1) Within _____ days after the Effective Date of this contract, Seller shall furnish to Buyer and Title Company Seller's existing survey of the Property and a Residential Real Property Affidavit or Declaration promulgated by the Texas Department of Insurance (T-47 Affidavit or T-47.1 Declaration). Buyer shall obtain a new survey at Seller's expense no later than 3 days prior to Closing Date if Seller fails to furnish within the time prescribed both the: (i) existing survey; and (ii) affidavit or declaration. If the Title Company or Buyer's lender does not accept the existing survey, or the affidavit or declaration, Buyer shall obtain a new survey at ❑ Seller's ❑ Buyer's expense no later than 3 days prior to Closing Date.

❑ (2) Within ______ days after the Effective Date of this contract, Buyer may obtain a new survey at Buyer's expense. Buyer is deemed to receive the survey on the date of actual receipt or the date specified in this paragraph, whichever is earlier. If Buyer fails to obtain the survey, Buyer may not terminate the contract under Paragraph 2B of the Third Party Financing Addendum because the survey was not obtained.

❑(3) Within ______ days after the Effective Date of this contract, Seller, at Seller's expense shall furnish a new survey to Buyer.

D. OBJECTIONS: Buyer may object in writing to defects, exceptions, or encumbrances to title: disclosed on the survey other than items 6A(1) through (7) above; disclosed in the Commitment other than items 6A(1) through (9) above; or which prohibit the following use or activity: ____.
Buyer must object the earlier of (i) the Closing Date or (ii) ______ days after Buyer receives the Commitment, Exception Documents, and the survey. Buyer's failure to object within the time allowed will constitute a waiver of Buyer's right to object; except that the requirements in Schedule C of the Commitment are not waived by Buyer. Provided Seller is not obligated to incur any expense, Seller shall cure any timely objections of Buyer or any third party lender within 15 days after Seller receives the objections (Cure Period) and the Closing Date will be extended as necessary. If objections are not cured within the Cure Period, Buyer may, by delivering notice to Seller within 5 days after the end of the Cure Period: (i) terminate this contract and the earnest money will be refunded to Buyer; or (ii) waive the objections. If Buyer does not terminate within the time required, Buyer shall be deemed to have waived the objections. If the Commitment or survey is revised or any new Exception Document(s) is delivered, Buyer may object to any new matter revealed in the revised Commitment or survey or new Exception Document(s) within the same time stated in this paragraph to make objections beginning when the revised Commitment, survey, or Exception Document(s) is delivered to Buyer.

E. TITLE NOTICES:

(1) ABSTRACT OR TITLE POLICY: Broker advises Buyer to have an abstract of title covering the Property examined by an attorney of Buyer's selection, or Buyer should be furnished with or obtain a Title Policy. If a Title Policy is furnished, the Commitment should be promptly reviewed by an attorney of Buyer's choice due to the time limitations on Buyer's right to object.

(2) MEMBERSHIP IN PROPERTY OWNERS ASSOCIATION(S): The Property ❑is ❑is not subject to mandatory membership in a property owners association(s). If the Property is subject to mandatory membership in a property owners association(s), Seller notifies Buyer under §5.012, Texas Property Code, that, as a purchaser of property in the residential community identified in Paragraph 2A in which the Property is located, you are obligated to be a member of the property owners association(s). Restrictive covenants governing the use and occupancy of the Property and all dedicatory instruments governing the establishment, maintenance, or operation of this residential community have been or will be recorded in the Real Property Records of the county in which the Property is located. Copies of the restrictive covenants and dedicatory instruments may be obtained from the county clerk. **You are obligated to pay assessments to the property owners association(s). The amount of the assessments is subject to change. Your failure to pay the assessments could result in enforcement of the association's lien on and the foreclosure of the Property.**
Section 207.003, Property Code, entitles an owner to receive copies of any document that governs the establishment, maintenance, or operation of a subdivision, including, but not limited to, restrictions, bylaws, rules and regulations, and a resale certificate from a property owners' association. A resale certificate contains information including, but not limited to, statements specifying the amount and frequency of regular assessments and the style and cause number of lawsuits to which the property owners' association is a party, other than lawsuits relating to unpaid ad valorem taxes of an individual member of the association. These documents must be made available to you by the property owners' association or the association's agent on your request. **If Buyer is concerned about these matters, the TREC promulgated Addendum for Property Subject to Mandatory Membership in a Property Owners Association(s) should be used.**

(3) STATUTORY TAX DISTRICTS: If the Property is situated in a utility or other statutorily created district providing water, sewer, drainage, or flood control facilities and services, Chapter 49, Texas Water Code, requires Seller to deliver and Buyer to sign the statutory notice relating to the tax rate, bonded indebtedness, or standby fee of the district prior to final execution of this contract.

(4) TIDE WATERS: If the Property abuts the tidally influenced waters of the state, §33.135, Texas Natural Resources Code, requires a notice regarding coastal area property to be included in the contract.

(5) ANNEXATION: If the Property is located outside the limits of a municipality, Seller notifies Buyer under §5.011, Texas Property Code, that the Property may now or later be included in the extraterritorial jurisdiction of a municipality and may now or later be subject to annexation by the municipality. Each municipality maintains a map that depicts its boundaries and extraterritorial jurisdiction. To determine if the Property is located within a municipality's extraterritorial jurisdiction or is likely to be located within a municipality's extraterritorial jurisdiction, contact all municipalities located in the general proximity of the Property for further information.

(6) PROPERTY LOCATED IN A CERTIFICATED SERVICE AREA OF A UTILITY SERVICE PROVIDER: Notice required by §13.257, Water Code: The real property, described in Paragraph 2, that you are about to purchase may be located in a certificated water or sewer service area, which is authorized by law to provide water or sewer service to the properties in the certificated area. If your property is located in a certificated area there may be special costs or charges that you will be required to pay before you can receive water or sewer service. There may be a period required to construct lines or other facilities necessary to provide water or sewer service to your property. You are advised to determine if the property is in a certificated area and contact the utility service provider to determine the cost that you will be required to pay and the period, if any, that is required to provide water or sewer service to your property. The undersigned Buyer hereby acknowledges receipt of the foregoing notice at or before the execution of a binding contract for the purchase of the real property described in Paragraph 2 or at closing of purchase of the real property.

(7) PUBLIC IMPROVEMENT DISTRICTS: If the Property is in a public improvement district, Seller must give Buyer written notice as required by §5.014, Property Code.

(8) TRANSFER FEES: If the Property is subject to a private transfer fee obligation, §5.205, Property Code, requires Seller to notify Buyer as follows: The private transfer fee obligation may be governed by Chapter 5, Subchapter G of the Texas Property Code.

(9) PROPANE GAS SYSTEM SERVICE AREA: If the Property is located in a propane gas system service area owned by a distribution system retailer, Seller must give Buyer written notice as required by §141.010, Texas Utilities Code.

(10) NOTICE OF WATER LEVEL FLUCTUATIONS: If the Property adjoins an impoundment of water, including a reservoir or lake, constructed and maintained under Chapter 11, Water Code, that has a storage capacity of at least 5,000 acre-feet at the impoundment's normal operating level, Seller hereby notifies Buyer: "The water level of the impoundment of water adjoining the Property fluctuates for various reasons, including as a result of: (1) an entity lawfully exercising its right to use the water stored in the impoundment; or (2) drought or flood conditions."

(11) CERTIFICATE OF MOLD REMEDIATION: If the Property has been remediated for mold, Seller must provide to Buyer each certificate of mold damage remediation issued under §1958.154, Occupations Code, during the 5 years preceding the sale of the Property.

7. PROPERTY CONDITION:

A. ACCESS, INSPECTIONS AND UTILITIES: Seller shall permit Buyer and Buyer's agents access to the Property at reasonable times. Buyer may have the Property inspected by inspectors selected by Buyer and licensed by TREC or otherwise permitted by law to make inspections. Any hydrostatic testing must be separately authorized by Seller in writing. Seller at Seller's expense shall immediately cause existing utilities to be turned on and shall keep the utilities on during the time this contract is in effect.

B. SELLER'S DISCLOSURE NOTICE PURSUANT TO §5.008, TEXAS PROPERTY CODE (Seller's Disclosure Notice):
(Check one box only)

❑ (1) Buyer has received the Seller's Disclosure Notice.

❑ (2) Buyer has not received the Seller's Disclosure Notice. Within _________ days after the Effective Date of this contract, Seller shall deliver the Seller's Disclosure Notice to Buyer. If Buyer does not receive the Seller's Disclosure Notice, Buyer may terminate this contract at any time prior to the closing and the earnest money will be refunded to Buyer. If Seller delivers the Seller's Disclosure Notice, Buyer may terminate this contract for any reason within 7 days after Buyer receives the Seller's Disclosure Notice or prior to the closing, whichever first occurs, and the earnest money will be refunded to Buyer.

❑ (3) The Seller is not required to furnish the Seller's Disclosure Notice under the Texas Property Code.

C. SELLER'S DISCLOSURE OF LEAD-BASED PAINT AND LEAD-BASED PAINT HAZARDS is required by Federal law for a residential dwelling constructed prior to 1978.

D. ACCEPTANCE OF PROPERTY CONDITION: "As Is" means the present condition of the Property with any and all defects and without warranty except for the warranties of title and the warranties in this contract. Buyer's agreement to accept the Property As Is under Paragraph 7D (1) or (2) does not preclude Buyer from inspecting the Property under Paragraph 7A, from negotiating repairs or treatments in a subsequent amendment, or from terminating this contract during the Option Period, if any.

(Check one box only)

❑ (1) Buyer accepts the Property As Is.

❑ (2) Buyer accepts the Property As Is provided Seller, at Seller's expense, shall complete the following specific repairs and treatments: ____

____

(Do not insert general phrases, such as "subject to inspections" that do not identify specific repairs and treatments.)

E. LENDER REQUIRED REPAIRS AND TREATMENTS: Unless otherwise agreed in writing, neither party is obligated to pay for lender required repairs, which includes treatment for wood destroying insects. If the parties do not agree to pay for the lender required repairs or treatments, this contract will terminate and the earnest money will be refunded to Buyer. If the cost of lender required repairs and treatments exceeds 5% of the Sales Price, Buyer may terminate this contract and the earnest money will be refunded to Buyer.

F. COMPLETION OF REPAIRS AND TREATMENTS: Unless otherwise agreed in writing, Seller shall complete all agreed repairs and treatments prior to the Closing Date and obtain any required permits. The repairs and treatments must be performed by persons who are licensed to provide such repairs or treatments or, if no license is required by law, are commercially engaged in the trade of providing such repairs or treatments. Seller shall: (i) provide Buyer with copies of documentation from the repair person(s) showing the scope of work and payment for the work completed; and (ii) at Seller's expense, arrange for the transfer of any transferable warranties with respect to the repairs and treatments to Buyer at closing. If Seller fails to complete any agreed repairs and treatments prior to the Closing Date, Buyer may exercise remedies under Paragraph 15 or extend the Closing Date up to 5 days if necessary for Seller to complete the repairs and treatments.

G. ENVIRONMENTAL MATTERS: Buyer is advised that the presence of wetlands, toxic substances, including asbestos and wastes or other environmental hazards, or the presence of a threatened or endangered species or its habitat may affect Buyer's intended use of the Property. If Buyer is concerned about these matters, an addendum promulgated by TREC or required by the parties should be used.

H. RESIDENTIAL SERVICE CONTRACTS: Buyer may purchase a residential service contract from a provider or administrator licensed by the Texas Department of Licensing and Regulation. If Buyer purchases a residential service contract, Seller shall reimburse Buyer at closing for the cost of the residential service contract in an amount not exceeding $______________. Buyer should review any residential service contract for the scope of coverage, exclusions and limitations. **The purchase of a residential service contract is optional. Similar coverage may be purchased from various companies authorized to do business in Texas.**

I. SELLER'S DISCLOSURE ABOUT GROUNDWATER AND SURFACE WATER RIGHTS (Seller's Water Disclosure): Access to surface water or groundwater on the Property may be regulated, restricted, or prohibited, including but not limited to the right to drill or operate water wells and the right to withdraw water from surface water sources on or adjoining the Property. The parties shall use the Seller's Water Disclosure published by TREC to identify information related to groundwater and surface water rights. (Check one box only)

❑ (1) Buyer has received the Seller's Water Disclosure.

❑ (2) Buyer has not received the Seller's Water Disclosure. Within ______ days after the Effective Date of this contract, Seller shall deliver the Seller's Water Disclosure to Buyer. If Buyer does not receive the Seller's Water Disclosure, Buyer may terminate this contract at any time prior to the closing and the earnest money will be refunded to Buyer. If Seller delivers the Seller's Water Disclosure, Buyer may terminate this contract for any reason within 7 days after Buyer receives the Seller's Water Disclosure or prior to the closing, whichever first occurs, and the earnest money will be refunded to Buyer.

❑ (3) Seller is not required to deliver the Seller's Water Disclosure to Buyer because all of the following are true:

(a) Seller is not aware of a water well on the Property (in use or not in use);
(b) Seller is not aware of a pond, lake, or water tank on the Property;
(c) Seller is not aware of any certificate of adjudication, certified filing, or permit for surface water rights associated with the Property administered by the Texas Commission on Environmental Quality;
(d) Seller is not aware that any groundwater rights to the Property have been severed, sold, or leased in whole or in part; and
(e) the Property receives water only from the following municipality (City), municipal utility district (MUD) or other special district, water supply corporation (WSC), or private water supply company (PWC): ____

____

8. BROKER OR SALES AGENT DISCLOSURE:

Texas law requires a real estate broker or sales agent who is a party to a transaction or acting on behalf of a spouse, parent, child, business entity in which the broker or sales agent owns more than 10%, or a trust for which the broker or sales agent acts as a trustee or of which the broker

or sales agent or the broker or sales agent's spouse, parent or child is a beneficiary, to notify the other party in writing before entering into a contract of sale. Disclose if applicable: ____________
____
____.

9. CLOSING:

A. The closing of the sale will be on or before ____________________, 20____, or within 7 days after objections made under Paragraph 6D have been cured or waived, whichever date is later (Closing Date). If either party fails to close the sale by the Closing Date, the non-defaulting party may exercise the remedies contained in Paragraph 15.

B. At closing:

(1) Seller shall execute and deliver a general warranty deed conveying title to the Property to Buyer and showing no additional exceptions to those permitted in Paragraph 6 and furnish tax statements or certificates showing no delinquent taxes on the Property.

(2) Buyer shall pay the Sales Price in good funds acceptable to the Escrow Agent.

(3) Seller and Buyer shall execute and deliver any notices, statements, certificates, affidavits, releases, loan documents, transfer of any warranties, and other documents reasonably required for the closing of the sale and the issuance of the Title Policy.

(4) There will be no liens, assessments, or security interests against the Property which will not be satisfied out of the sales proceeds unless securing the payment of any loans assumed by Buyer and assumed loans will not be in default.

(5) Private transfer fees (as defined by Chapter 5, Subchapter G of the Texas Property Code) will be the obligation of Seller unless provided otherwise in this contract. Transfer fees assessed by a property owners' association are governed by the Addendum for Property Subject to Mandatory Membership in a Property Owners Association.

10. POSSESSION:

A. BUYER'S POSSESSION: Seller shall deliver to Buyer possession of the Property in its present or required condition, ordinary wear and tear excepted: ❑ upon closing and funding ❑ according to a temporary residential lease form promulgated by TREC or other written lease required by the parties. Any possession by Buyer prior to closing or by Seller after closing which is not authorized by a written lease will establish a tenancy at sufferance relationship between the parties. **Consult your insurance agent prior to change of ownership and possession because insurance coverage may be limited or terminated. The absence of a written lease or appropriate insurance coverage may expose the parties to economic loss.**

B. SMART DEVICES: "Smart Device" means a device that connects to the internet to enable remote use, monitoring, and management of: (i) the Property; (ii) items identified in any Non-Realty Items Addendum; or (iii) items in a Fixture Lease assigned to Buyer. At the time Seller delivers possession of the Property to Buyer, Seller shall:

(1) deliver to Buyer written information containing all access codes, usernames, passwords, and applications Buyer will need to access, operate, manage, and control the Smart Devices; and

(2) terminate and remove all access and connections to the improvements and accessories from any of Seller's personal devices including but not limited to phones and computers.

11. SPECIAL PROVISIONS: (This paragraph is intended to be used only for additional informational items. An informational item is a statement that completes a blank in a contract form, discloses factual information, or provides instructions. Real estate brokers and sales agents are prohibited from practicing law and shall not add to, delete, or modify any provision of this contract unless drafted by a party to this contract or a party's attorney.) ________________________________
____
____.

12. SETTLEMENT AND OTHER EXPENSES:

A. EXPENSES: The following expenses must be paid at or prior to closing:

(1) Seller shall pay the following expenses (Seller's Expenses):

(a) releases of existing liens, including prepayment penalties and recording fees; release of Seller's loan liability; tax statements or certificates; preparation of deed; one-half of escrow fee; and other expenses payable by Seller under this contract; and

(b) an amount not to exceed $_____________ to be applied to Buyer's Expenses other than brokerage compensation or contributions under Paragraph 12B below.

(2) Buyer shall pay the following expenses (Buyer's Expenses): Appraisal fees; loan application fees; origination charges; credit reports; preparation of loan documents; interest on the notes from date of disbursement to one month prior to dates of first monthly payments; recording fees; copies of easements and restrictions; loan title policy with endorsements required by lender; loan-related inspection fees; photos; amortization schedules; one-half of escrow fee; all prepaid items, including required premiums for flood and hazard insurance, reserve deposits for insurance, ad valorem taxes and special governmental assessments; final compliance inspection; courier fee; repair inspection; underwriting fee; wire transfer fee; expenses incident to any loan; Private Mortgage Insurance Premium

(PMI), VA Loan Funding Fee, or FHA Mortgage Insurance Premium (MIP) as required by the lender; and other expenses payable by Buyer under this contract.

B. BROKERAGE COMPENSATION: Brokerage compensation is not set by law and is fully negotiable. Each party shall pay their respective brokers pursuant to the terms of the parties' obligations to compensate their brokers contained in separate written agreements. **The contributions under 12B(1) and 12B(2) below shall be applied to and shall not change the parties' obligations to pay compensation pursuant to those agreements.** The following contributions must be paid at closing:

❑ (1) Seller will pay (check one box only): ❑ $_________ or ❑ ______% of the Sales Price to be applied toward the brokerage compensation owed by Buyer to Buyer's broker.

❑ (2) Buyer will pay (check one box only): ❑ $_________ or ❑ ______% of the Sales Price to be applied toward the brokerage compensation owed by Seller to Seller's broker.

C. EXPENSE LIMITATION: If a governmental loan program regulation prohibits Buyer from paying charges or fees, then the amount of any concession in 12A(1)(b) shall be first applied to pay such prohibited expenses and then to other Buyer's Expenses but not brokerage compensation or contribution.

13. **PRORATIONS:** Taxes for the current year, interest, rents, and regular periodic maintenance fees, assessments, and dues (including prepaid items) will be prorated through the Closing Date. The tax proration may be calculated taking into consideration any change in exemptions that will affect the current year's taxes. If taxes for the current year vary from the amount prorated at closing, the parties shall adjust the prorations when tax statements for the current year are available. If taxes are not paid at or prior to closing, Buyer shall pay taxes for the current year.

14. **CASUALTY LOSS:** If any part of the Property is damaged or destroyed by fire or other casualty after the Effective Date of this contract, Seller shall restore the Property to its previous condition as soon as reasonably possible, but in any event by the Closing Date. If Seller fails to do so due to factors beyond Seller's control, Buyer may (a) terminate this contract and the earnest money will be refunded to Buyer (b) extend the time for performance up to 15 days and the Closing Date will be extended as necessary or (c) accept the Property in its damaged condition with an assignment of insurance proceeds, if permitted by Seller's insurance carrier, and receive credit from Seller at closing in the amount of the deductible under the insurance policy. Seller's obligations under this paragraph are independent of any other obligations of Seller under this contract.

15. **DEFAULT:** If Buyer fails to comply with this contract, Buyer will be in default, and Seller may (a) enforce specific performance, seek such other relief as may be provided by law, or both, or (b) terminate this contract and receive the earnest money as liquidated damages, thereby releasing both parties from this contract. If Seller fails to comply with this contract, Seller will be in default and Buyer may (a) enforce specific performance, seek such other relief as may be provided by law, or both, or (b) terminate this contract and receive the earnest money, thereby releasing both parties from this contract.

16. **MEDIATION:** It is the policy of the State of Texas to encourage resolution of disputes through alternative dispute resolution procedures such as mediation. Any dispute between Seller and Buyer related to this contract which is not resolved through informal discussion will be submitted to a mutually acceptable mediation service or provider. The parties to the mediation shall bear the mediation costs equally. This paragraph does not preclude a party from seeking equitable relief from a court of competent jurisdiction.

17. **ATTORNEY'S FEES:** A Buyer, Seller, Seller's broker, Buyer's broker, or Escrow Agent who prevails in any legal proceeding related to this contract is entitled to recover reasonable attorney's fees and all costs of such proceeding.

18. **ESCROW:**

A. ESCROW: The Escrow Agent is not (i) a party to this contract and does not have liability for the performance or nonperformance of any party to this contract, (ii) liable for interest on the earnest money and (iii) liable for the loss of any earnest money caused by the failure of any financial institution in which the earnest money has been deposited unless the financial institution is acting as Escrow Agent. Escrow Agent may require any disbursement made in connection with this contract to be conditioned on Escrow Agent's collection of good funds acceptable to Escrow Agent.

B. EXPENSES: At closing, the earnest money must be applied first to any cash down payment, then to Buyer's Expenses and any excess refunded to Buyer. If no closing occurs, Escrow Agent may: (i) require a written release of liability of the Escrow Agent from all parties before releasing any earnest money; and (ii) require payment of unpaid expenses incurred on behalf of a party. Escrow Agent may deduct authorized expenses from the earnest money payable to a party. "Authorized expenses" means expenses incurred by Escrow Agent on behalf of the party entitled to the earnest money that were authorized by this contract or that party.

C. DEMAND: Upon termination of this contract, either party or the Escrow Agent may send a release of earnest money to each party and the parties shall execute counterparts of the release and deliver same to the Escrow Agent. If either party fails to execute the release, either party may make a written demand to the Escrow Agent for the earnest money. If only one party makes written demand for the earnest money, Escrow Agent shall promptly provide a copy of the demand to the other party. If Escrow Agent does not receive written objection to the demand from the other party within 15 days, Escrow Agent may disburse the earnest money to the party making demand reduced by the amount of unpaid expenses incurred on behalf of the party receiving the earnest money and Escrow Agent may pay the same to the creditors. If Escrow Agent complies with the provisions of this paragraph, each party hereby releases Escrow Agent from all adverse claims related to the disbursal of the earnest money.

D. DAMAGES: Any party who wrongfully fails or refuses to sign a release acceptable to the Escrow Agent within 7 days of receipt of the request will be liable to the other party for (i) damages; (ii) the earnest money; (iii) reasonable attorney's fees; and (iv) all costs of suit.

E. NOTICES: Escrow Agent's notices will be effective when sent in compliance with Paragraph 21. Notice of objection to the demand will be deemed effective upon receipt by Escrow Agent.

19. REPRESENTATIONS: All covenants, representations and warranties in this contract survive closing. If any representation of Seller in this contract is untrue on the Closing Date, Seller will be in default. Unless expressly prohibited by written agreement, Seller may continue to show the Property and receive, negotiate and accept back up offers.

20. GOVERNMENTAL REQUIREMENTS:

A. If Seller is a "foreign person," as defined by Internal Revenue Code and its regulations, or if Seller fails to deliver an affidavit or a certificate of non-foreign status to Buyer that Seller is not a "foreign person," then Buyer shall withhold from the sales proceeds an amount sufficient to comply with applicable tax law and deliver the same to the Internal Revenue Service together with appropriate tax forms. Internal Revenue Service regulations require filing written reports if currency in excess of specified amounts is received in the transaction.

B. Seller and Buyer shall promptly execute and deliver any statements, documents, and information requested by Escrow Agent required by governmental reporting requirements (for example, reporting to the U.S. Treasury or its bureaus).

21. NOTICES: All notices from one party or their agent to the other must be in writing. Notices are effective when mailed to, hand-delivered at, sent by overnight courier to, or transmitted by electronic transmission to the other party or their agent.

To Buyer(s) at:

Address: ______________________________

____

Phone(s): ______________________________

____

Email(s): ______________________________

____

To Seller(s) at:

Address: ______________________________

____

Phone(s): ______________________________

____

Email(s): ______________________________

____

To Buyer's agent at:

Address: ______________________________

____

Phone: ______________________________

Email: ______________________________

To Seller's agent at:

Address: ______________________________

____

Phone: ______________________________

Email: ______________________________

22. AGREEMENT OF PARTIES: This contract contains the entire agreement of the parties and cannot be changed except by their written agreement. Addenda and notices which are a part of this contract are (check all applicable boxes):

Financial

- ❑ Third Party Financing Addendum
- ❑ Addendum for Sale of Other Property by Buyer
- ❑ Addendum Concerning Right to Terminate Due to Lender's Appraisal
- ❑ Seller Financing Addendum
- ❑ Addendum for Section 1031 Exchange
- ❑ Short Sale Addendum
- ❑ Loan Assumption Addendum
- ❑ Addendum for Release of Liability on Assumed Loan and/or Restoration of Seller's VA Entitlement

Leases

- ❑ Addendum Regarding Residential Leases
- ❑ Addendum Regarding Fixture Leases
- ❑ Buyer's Temporary Residential Lease
- ❑ Seller's Temporary Residential Lease

Additional Tests and Reports

- ❑ Addendum for Authorizing Hydrostatic Testing
- ❑ Environmental Assessment, Threatened or Endangered Species, and Wetlands Addendum

Statutory Disclosures and Notices

- ❑ Addendum for Seller's Disclosure of Information on Lead-Based Paint and Lead-Based Paint Hazards as Required by Federal Law
- ❑ Addendum for Property in a Propane Gas System Service Area
- ❑ Addendum for Property Located Seaward of the Gulf Intercoastal Waterway
- ❑ Addendum for Coastal Area Property
- ❑ The following utility, water, drainage, public improvement, and other district notices (list all that have been given or are attached):____
____

NOTICE: Seller's failure to provide applicable Statutory Disclosures and Notices may provide Buyer with remedies or rights to terminate this contract.

Other

- ❑ Addendum for Property Subject to Mandatory Membership in a Property Owners Association
- ❑ Non-Realty Items Addendum
- ❑ Addendum for "Back-Up" Contract
- ❑ Addendum for Reservation of Oil, Gas, and Other Minerals
- ❑ Other:____
____

23. CONSULT AN ATTORNEY BEFORE SIGNING: TREC rules prohibit real estate brokers and sales agents from giving legal advice. READ THIS CONTRACT CAREFULLY.

Buyer's Attorney is: ______________________	Seller's Attorney is: ______________________
______________________	______________________
Phone: ( ) ______________________	Phone: ( ) ______________________
Fax: ( ) ______________________	Fax: ( ) ______________________
E-mail: ______________________	E-mail: ______________________

EXECUTED the ______day of ______________________, 20____ (Effective Date).
(BROKER: FILL IN THE DATE OF FINAL ACCEPTANCE.)

______________________	______________________
Buyer	Seller
______________________	______________________
Buyer	Seller

BROKER CONTACT INFORMATION
(Print name(s) only. Do not sign)

The brokers to this sale are:

______________________ (Broker Firm) **represents Seller only as Seller's agent**.
Address:______________________
Broker Firm License No.:______________________
Associate's Name:______________________
Team Name:______________________
Associate's Email:______________________
Associate's Phone No.:______________ Associate's License No.:______________
Licensed Supervisor of Associate:______________________
Phone No. of Licensed Supervisor:______________ License No.:______________

______________________ (Broker Firm) **represents Buyer only as Buyer's agent**.
Address:______________________
Broker Firm License No.:______________________
Associate's Name:______________________
Team Name:______________________
Associate's Email:______________________
Associate's Phone No.:______________ Associate's License No.:______________
Licensed Supervisor of Associate:______________________
Phone No. of Licensed Supervisor:______________ License No.:______________

Intermediary

______________________ (Broker Firm) **represents Seller and Buyer as an intermediary**.
Address:______________________
Broker Firm License No.:______________________
Associate's Name (for Seller):______________________
Team Name:______________________
Associate's Email:______________________
Associate's Phone No.:______________ Associate's License No.:______________
Licensed Supervisor of Associate:______________________
Phone No. of Licensed Supervisor:______________ License No.:______________
Associate's Name (for Buyer):______________________
Team Name:______________________
Associate's Email:______________________
Associate's Phone No.:______________ Associate's License No.:______________
Licensed Supervisor of Associate:______________________
Phone No. of Licensed Supervisor:______________ License No.:______________

OPTION FEE RECEIPT

Receipt of $_______________ option fee in the form of _______________________
is acknowledged.

_______________________ _______________________
Escrow Agent Date

EARNEST MONEY RECEIPT

Receipt of $_______________ earnest money in the form of _______________________
is acknowledged.

_______________________ _______________________
Escrow Agent Received by Email Address Date/Time

_______________________ _______________________
Address Phone

_______________________ _______________________
City State Zip Fax

CONTRACT RECEIPT

Receipt of the contract is acknowledged.

_______________________ _______________________
Escrow Agent Received by Email Address Date

_______________________ _______________________
Address Phone

_______________________ _______________________
City State Zip Fax

ADDITIONAL EARNEST MONEY RECEIPT

Receipt of $_______________ additional earnest money in the form of _______________________
is acknowledged.

_______________________ _______________________
Escrow Agent Received by Email Address Date/Time

_______________________ _______________________
Address Phone

_______________________ _______________________
City State Zip Fax

RESIDENTIAL CONDOMINIUM CONTRACT (RESALE)

NOTICE: Not For Use Where Seller Owns Fee Simple Title To Land Beneath Unit

1. PARTIES: The parties to this contract are ______________________________(Seller) and ______________________________(Buyer). Seller agrees to sell and convey to Buyer and Buyer agrees to buy from Seller the Property defined below.

2. PROPERTY AND CONDOMINIUM DOCUMENTS:

A. The Condominium Unit, improvements and accessories described below are collectively referred to as the Property (Property).

(1) CONDOMINIUM UNIT: Unit ___________, in Building ______________________, of ____, a condominium project, located at ____

(address/zip code), City of _________________________,County of _______________, ____,

Texas, described in the Condominium Declaration and Plat and any amendments thereto of record in said County; together with such Unit's undivided interest in the Common Elements designated by the Declaration, including those areas reserved as Limited Common Elements appurtenant to the Unit and such other rights to use the Common Elements which have been specifically assigned to the Unit in any other manner. Parking areas assigned to the Unit are:____.

(2) IMPROVEMENTS: All fixtures and improvements attached to the above described real property including without limitation, the following **permanently installed and built-in items**, if any: all equipment and appliances, valances, screens, shutters, awnings, wall-to-wall carpeting, mirrors, ceiling fans, attic fans, mail boxes, television antennas, mounts and brackets for televisions and speakers, heating and air conditioning units, security and fire detection equipment, wiring, plumbing and lighting fixtures, chandeliers, shrubbery, landscaping, outdoor cooking equipment, generators, and all other property attached to the above described Condominium Unit.

(3) ACCESSORIES: The following described related accessories, if any: window air conditioning units, stove, fireplace screens, curtains and rods, blinds, window shades, draperies and rods, door keys, mailbox keys, above ground pool, swimming pool equipment and maintenance accessories, artificial fireplace logs, security systems that are not fixtures, and controls for: (i) garage doors, (ii) entry gates, and (iii) other improvements and accessories. "Controls" includes Seller's transferable rights to the (i) software and applications used to access and control improvements or accessories, and (ii) hardware used solely to control improvements or accessories.

(4) EXCLUSIONS: The following improvements and accessories will be retained by Seller and must be removed prior to delivery of possession:______________________________.

B. The Declaration, Bylaws and any Rules of the Association are called "Documents". (Check one box only):

❑ (1) Buyer has received a copy of the Documents. Buyer is advised to read the Documents before signing the contract.

❑ (2) Buyer has not received a copy of the Documents. Seller, at Seller's expense, shall deliver the Documents to Buyer within _______ days after the Effective Date of the contract. Buyer may terminate the contract within 7 days after Buyer receives the Documents by giving written notice of termination to Seller. If Buyer terminates the contract pursuant to this paragraph, the earnest money will be refunded to Buyer. Buyer retains rights to terminate under Section 82.156, Texas Property Code.

C. The Resale Certificate from the condominium owners association (the Association) is called the "Certificate". The Certificate must be in a form promulgated by TREC or required by the parties. The Certificate must have been prepared, at Seller's expense, no more than 3 months before the date it is delivered to Buyer and must contain at a minimum the information required by Section 82.157, Texas Property Code.

(Check one box only):

❑ (1) Buyer has received the Certificate.

❑ (2) Buyer has not received the Certificate. Seller shall deliver the Certificate to Buyer within _______ days after the Effective Date of the contract. Buyer may terminate the contract within 7 days after the date Buyer receives the Certificate by giving written notice of termination to Seller. If Buyer terminates the contract pursuant to this paragraph, the earnest money will be refunded to Buyer. Buyer retains rights to terminate under Section 82.156, Texas Property Code.

❑ (3) Buyer has received Seller's affidavit that Seller requested information from the Association concerning its financial condition as required by the Texas Property Code, and that the Association did not provide a Certificate or information required in the Certificate. Buyer and Seller agree to waive the requirement to furnish the Certificate.

D. If the Documents reveal that the Property is subject to a right of refusal under which the Association or a member of the Association may purchase the Property, the Effective Date shall be amended to the date that Buyer receives a copy of the Association's certification that: (i) Seller has complied with the requirements under the right of refusal; and (ii) all persons who may exercise the right of refusal have not exercised or have waived the right to buy the Property. If Buyer does not receive the Association's certification within _______days after the Effective Date or if the right of refusal is exercised, this contract shall terminate and the earnest money shall be refunded to Buyer.

3. SALES PRICE:

A. Cash portion of Sales Price payable by Buyer at closing ....$____________________
The term "Cash portion of the Sales Price" does not include proceeds from borrowing of any kind or selling other real property except as disclosed in this contract.

B. Sum of all financing described in the attached: ❑ Third Party Financing Addendum, ❑ Loan Assumption Addendum, ❑ Seller Financing Addendum ....$____________________

C. Sales Price (Sum of A and B) ....$____________________

4. LEASES: Except as disclosed in this contract, Seller is not aware of any leases affecting the Property. After the Effective Date, Seller may not, without Buyer's written consent, create a new lease, amend any existing lease, or convey any interest in the Property. (Check all applicable boxes)

❑ A. RESIDENTIAL LEASES: The Property is subject to one or more residential leases and the Addendum Regarding Residential Leases is attached to this contract.

❑ B. FIXTURE LEASES: Fixtures on the Property are subject to one or more fixture leases (for example, solar panels, propane tanks, water softener, security system) and the Addendum Regarding Fixture Leases is attached to this contract.

5. EARNEST MONEY AND TERMINATION OPTION.

A. DELIVERY OF EARNEST MONEY AND OPTION FEE: Within 3 days after the Effective Date, Buyer must deliver to ________________________________ (Escrow Agent) at __________ ____(address): $________________ as earnest money and $______________ as the option fee. The earnest money and option fee shall be made payable to Escrow Agent and may be paid separately or combined in a single payment.

(1) Buyer shall deliver additional earnest money of $________________ to Escrow Agent within _______ days after the Effective Date of this contract.

(2) If the last day to deliver the earnest money, option fee, or the additional earnest money falls on a Saturday, Sunday, or Legal Holiday, the time to deliver the earnest money, option fee, or the additional earnest money, as applicable, is extended until the end of the next day that is not a Saturday, Sunday, or Legal Holiday. "Legal Holiday" means a legal holiday described in Sections 662.003(a) and 662.003(b)(4) and (6), Texas Government Code.

(3) The amount(s) Escrow Agent receives under this paragraph shall be applied first to the option fee, then to the earnest money, and then to the additional earnest money.

(4) Buyer authorizes Escrow Agent to release and deliver the option fee to Seller at any time without further notice to or consent from Buyer, and releases Escrow Agent from liability for delivery of the option fee to Seller. The option fee will be credited to the Sales Price at closing.

B. TERMINATION OPTION: For nominal consideration, the receipt of which Seller acknowledges, and Buyer's agreement to pay the option fee within the time required, Seller grants Buyer the unrestricted right to terminate this contract by giving notice of termination to Seller within _______ days after the Effective Date of this contract (Option Period). Notices under this paragraph must be given by 5:00 p.m. (local time where the Property is located) by the date specified. If Buyer gives notice of termination within the time prescribed: (i) the option fee will not be refunded and Escrow Agent shall release any option fee remaining with Escrow Agent to Seller; and (ii) any earnest money will be refunded to Buyer.

C. FAILURE TO TIMELY DELIVER EARNEST MONEY: If Buyer fails to deliver the earnest money within the time required, Seller may terminate this contract or exercise Seller's remedies under Paragraph 15, or both, by providing notice to Buyer before Buyer delivers the earnest money.

D. FAILURE TO TIMELY DELIVER OPTION FEE: If no dollar amount is stated as the option fee or if Buyer fails to deliver the option fee within the time required, Buyer shall not have the unrestricted right to terminate this contract under this Paragraph 5.

E. TIME: **Time is of the essence for this paragraph and strict compliance with the time for performance is required.**

6. TITLE POLICY:

A. TITLE POLICY: Seller shall furnish to Buyer at ❑Seller's ❑Buyer's expense an owner policy of title insurance (Title Policy) issued by ________________________________ (Title Company) in the amount of the Sales Price, dated at or after closing, insuring Buyer against loss under the provisions of the Title Policy, subject to the promulgated exclusions (including existing building and zoning ordinances) and the following exceptions:

(1) Restrictive covenants common to the platted subdivision in which the Property is located.
(2) The standard printed exception for standby fees, taxes and assessments.
(3) Liens created as part of the financing described in Paragraph 3.
(4) Terms and provisions of the Documents including the assessments and platted easements.
(5) Reservations or exceptions otherwise permitted by this contract or as may be approved by Buyer in writing.
(6) The standard printed exception as to marital rights.
(7) The standard printed exception as to waters, tidelands, beaches, streams, and related matters.
(8) The standard printed exception as to discrepancies, conflicts, shortages in area or boundary lines, encroachments or protrusions, or overlapping improvements.
(9) The exception or exclusion regarding minerals approved by the Texas Department of Insurance.

B. COMMITMENT: Within 20 days after the Title Company receives a copy of this contract, Seller shall furnish to Buyer a commitment for title insurance (Commitment) and, at Buyer's expense, legible copies of restrictive covenants and documents evidencing exceptions in the Commitment (Exception Documents) other than the standard printed exceptions. Seller authorizes the Title Company to deliver the Commitment and Exception Documents to Buyer at Buyer's address shown in Paragraph 21. If the Commitment and Exception Documents are not delivered to Buyer within the specified time, the time for delivery will be automatically extended up to 15 days or 3 days before the Closing Date, whichever is earlier. If the Commitment and Exception Documents are not delivered within the time required, Buyer may terminate this contract and the earnest money will be refunded to Buyer.

C. OBJECTIONS: Buyer may object in writing to defects, exceptions, or encumbrances to title: disclosed in the Commitment other than items 6A(1) through (9) above; or which prohibit the following use or activity: ____

____.

Buyer must object the earlier of (i) the Closing Date or (ii) ______ days after Buyer receives the Commitment and Exception Documents. Buyer's failure to object within the time allowed will constitute a waiver of Buyer's right to object; except that the requirements in Schedule C of the Commitment are not waived by Buyer. Provided Seller is not obligated to incur any expense, Seller shall cure any timely objections of Buyer or any third party lender within 15 days after Seller receives the objections (Cure Period) and the Closing Date will be extended as necessary. If objections are not cured within the Cure Period, Buyer may, by delivering notice to Seller within 5 days after the end of the Cure Period: (i) terminate this contract and the earnest money will be refunded to Buyer; or (ii) waive the objections. If Buyer does not terminate within the time required, Buyer shall be deemed to have waived the objections. If the Commitment is revised or any new Exception Document(s) is delivered, Buyer may object to any new matter revealed in the revised Commitment or new Exception Document(s) within the same time stated in this paragraph to make objections beginning when the revised Commitment or Exception Document(s) is delivered to Buyer.

D. TITLE NOTICES:

(1) ABSTRACT OR TITLE POLICY: Broker advises Buyer to have an abstract of title covering the Property examined by an attorney of Buyer's selection, or Buyer should be furnished with or obtain a Title Policy. If a Title Policy is furnished, the Commitment should be promptly reviewed by an attorney of Buyer's choice due to the time limitations on Buyer's right to object.

(2) STATUTORY TAX DISTRICTS: If the Property is situated in a utility or other statutorily created district providing water, sewer, drainage, or flood control facilities and services, Chapter 49, Texas Water Code, requires Seller to deliver and Buyer to sign the statutory notice relating to the tax rate, bonded indebtedness, or standby fee of the district prior to final execution of this contract.

(3) TIDE WATERS: If the Property abuts the tidally influenced waters of the state, §33.135, Texas Natural Resources Code, requires a notice regarding coastal area property to be included in the contract.

(4) ANNEXATION: If the Property is located outside the limits of a municipality, Seller notifies Buyer under §5.011, Texas Property Code, that the Property may now or later be included in the extraterritorial jurisdiction of a municipality and may now or later be subject to annexation by the municipality. Each municipality maintains a map that depicts its boundaries and extraterritorial jurisdiction. To determine if the Property is located within a municipality's extraterritorial jurisdiction or is likely to be located within a municipality's extraterritorial jurisdiction, contact all municipalities located in the general proximity of the Property for further information.

(5) PROPERTY LOCATED IN A CERTIFICATED SERVICE AREA OF A UTILITY SERVICE PROVIDER: Notice required by §13.257, Water Code: The real property, described in Paragraph 2, that you are about to purchase may be located in a certificated water or sewer service area, which is authorized by law to provide water or sewer service to the properties in the certificated area. If your property is located in a certificated area there may be special costs or charges that you will be required to pay before you can receive water or sewer service. There may be a period required to construct lines or other facilities necessary to provide water or sewer service to your property. You are advised to determine if the property is in a certificated area and contact the utility service provider to determine the cost that you will be required to pay and the period, if any, that is required to provide water or sewer service to your property. The undersigned Buyer hereby acknowledges receipt of the foregoing notice at or before the execution of a binding contract for the purchase of the real property described in Paragraph 2 or at closing of purchase of the real property.

(6) PUBLIC IMPROVEMENT DISTRICTS: If the Property is in a public improvement district, Seller must give Buyer written notice as required by §5.014, Property Code.

(7) TRANSFER FEES: If the Property is subject to a private transfer fee obligation, §5.205, Property Code, requires Seller to notify Buyer as follows: The private transfer fee obligation may be governed by Chapter 5, Subchapter G of the Texas Property Code.

(8) PROPANE GAS SYSTEM SERVICE AREA: If the Property is located in a propane gas system service area owned by a distribution system retailer, Seller must give Buyer written notice as required by §141.010, Texas Utilities Code.

(9) NOTICE OF WATER LEVEL FLUCTUATIONS: If the Property adjoins an impoundment of water, including a reservoir or lake, constructed and maintained under Chapter 11, Water Code, that has a storage capacity of at least 5,000 acre-feet at the impoundment's normal

operating level, Seller hereby notifies Buyer: "The water level of the impoundment of water adjoining the Property fluctuates for various reasons, including as a result of:
(1) an entity lawfully exercising its right to use the water stored in the impoundment; or
(2) drought or flood conditions."

(10) CERTIFICATE OF MOLD REMEDIATION: If the Property has been remediated for mold, Seller must provide to Buyer each certificate of mold damage remediation issued under §1958.154, Occupations Code, during the 5 years preceding the sale of the Property.

7. PROPERTY CONDITION:

A. ACCESS, INSPECTIONS AND UTILITIES: Seller shall permit Buyer and Buyer's agents access to the Property at reasonable times. Buyer may have the Property inspected by inspectors selected by Buyer and licensed by TREC or otherwise permitted by law to make inspections. Any hydrostatic testing must be separately authorized by Seller in writing. Seller at Seller's expense shall immediately cause existing utilities to be turned on and shall keep the utilities on during the time this contract is in effect .

B. SELLER'S DISCLOSURE NOTICE PURSUANT TO §5.008, TEXAS PROPERTY CODE (Seller's Disclosure Notice):
(Check one box only)

☐ (1) Buyer has received the Seller's Disclosure Notice.

☐ (2) Buyer has not received the Seller's Disclosure Notice. Within ______ days after the Effective Date of this contract, Seller shall deliver the Seller's Disclosure Notice to Buyer. If Buyer does not receive the Seller's Disclosure Notice, Buyer may terminate this contract at any time prior to the closing and the earnest money will be refunded to Buyer. If Seller delivers the Seller's Disclosure Notice, Buyer may terminate this contract for any reason within 7 days after Buyer receives the Seller's Disclosure Notice or prior to the closing, whichever first occurs, and the earnest money will be refunded to Buyer.

☐ (3) The Texas Property Code does not require this Seller to furnish the Seller's Disclosure Notice.

C. SELLER'S DISCLOSURE OF LEAD-BASED PAINT AND LEAD-BASED PAINT HAZARDS is required by Federal law for a residential dwelling constructed prior to 1978.

D. ACCEPTANCE OF PROPERTY CONDITION: "As Is" means the present condition of the Property with any and all defects and without warranty except for the warranties of title and the warranties in this contract. Buyer's agreement to accept the Property As Is under Paragraph 7D (1) or (2) does not preclude Buyer from inspecting the Property under Paragraph 7A, from negotiating repairs or treatments in a subsequent amendment, or from terminating this contract during the Option Period, if any.
(Check one box only)

☐ (1) Buyer accepts the Property As Is.

☐ (2) Buyer accepts the Property As Is provided Seller, at Seller's expense, shall complete the following specific repairs and treatments:____
____.
(Do not insert general phrases, such as "subject to inspections," that do not identify specific repairs and treatments.)

E. LENDER REQUIRED REPAIRS AND TREATMENTS: Unless otherwise agreed in writing, neither party is obligated to pay for lender required repairs, which includes treatment for wood destroying insects. If the parties do not agree to pay for the lender required repairs or treatments, this contract will terminate and the earnest money will be refunded to Buyer. If the cost of lender required repairs and treatments exceeds 5% of the Sales Price, Buyer may terminate this contract and the earnest money will be refunded to Buyer.

F. COMPLETION OF REPAIRS AND TREATMENTS: Unless otherwise agreed in writing, Seller shall complete all agreed repairs and treatments prior to the Closing Date and obtain any required permits. The repairs and treatments must be performed by persons who are licensed to provide such repairs or treatments or, if no license is required by law, are commercially engaged in the trade of providing such repairs or treatments. Seller shall: (i) provide Buyer with copies of documentation from the repair person(s) showing the scope of work and payment for the work completed; and (ii) at Seller's expense, arrange for the transfer of any transferable warranties received with respect to the repairs and treatments to Buyer at closing. If Seller fails to complete any agreed repairs and treatments prior to the Closing Date, Buyer may exercise remedies under Paragraph 15 or extend the Closing Date up to 5 days if necessary for Seller to complete repairs and treatments.

G. ENVIRONMENTAL MATTERS: Buyer is advised that the presence of wetlands, toxic substances, including asbestos and wastes or other environmental hazards or the presence of a threatened or endangered species or its habitat may affect Buyer's intended use of the Property. If Buyer is concerned about these matters, an addendum promulgated by TREC or required by the parties should be used.

H. RESIDENTIAL SERVICE CONTRACTS: Buyer may purchase a residential service contract from a provider or administrator licensed by the Texas Department of Licensing and Regulation. If Buyer purchases a residential service contract, Seller shall reimburse Buyer at closing for the cost of the residential service contract in an amount not exceeding $_______________. Buyer should review any residential service contract for the scope of coverage, exclusions and limitations. **The purchase of a residential service contract is optional. Similar coverage may be purchased from various companies authorized to do business in Texas.**

8. BROKER OR SALES AGENT DISCLOSURE:

Texas law requires a real estate broker or sales agent who is a party to a transaction or acting on behalf of a spouse, parent, child, business entity in which the broker or sales agent owns more than 10%, or a trust for which the broker or sales agent acts as a trustee or of which the broker or sales agent or the broker or sales agent's spouse, parent or child is a beneficiary, to notify the other party in writing before entering into a contract of sale. Disclose if applicable:____.

9. CLOSING:

A. The closing of the sale will be on or before ______________________, 20____, or within 7 days after objections to matters disclosed in the Commitment have been cured, whichever date is later (Closing Date). If either party fails to close the sale by the Closing Date, the non-defaulting party may exercise the remedies contained in Paragraph 15.

B. At closing:

(1) Seller shall execute and deliver a general warranty deed conveying title to the Property to Buyer and showing no additional exceptions to those permitted in Paragraph 6 and furnish tax statements or certificates showing no delinquent taxes on the Property.

(2) Buyer shall pay the Sales Price in good funds acceptable to the Escrow Agent.

(3) Seller and Buyer shall execute and deliver any notices, statements, certificates, affidavits, releases, loan documents, transfer of any warranties, and other documents reasonably required for the closing of the sale and the issuance of the Title Policy.

(4) There will be no liens, assessments, or security interests against the Property which will not be satisfied out of the sales proceeds unless securing the payment of any loans assumed by Buyer and assumed loans will not be in default.

(5) Private transfer fees (as defined by Chapter 5, Subchapter G of the Texas Property Code) will be the obligation of Seller unless provided otherwise in this contract. This paragraph does not apply to fees assessed by the Association.

10. POSSESSION:

A. BUYER'S POSSESSION: Seller shall deliver to Buyer possession of the Property in its present or required condition, ordinary wear and tear excepted: ❑ upon closing and funding ❑ according to a temporary residential lease form promulgated by TREC or other written lease required by the parties. Any possession by Buyer prior to closing or by Seller after closing which is not authorized by a written lease will establish a tenancy at sufferance relationship between the parties. **Consult your insurance agent prior to change of ownership and possession because insurance coverage may be limited or terminated. The absence of a written lease or appropriate insurance coverage may expose the parties to economic loss.**

B. SMART DEVICES: "Smart Device" means a device that connects to the internet to enable remote use, monitoring, and management of: (i) the Property; (ii) items identified in any Non-Realty Items Addendum; or (iii) items in a Fixture Lease assigned to Buyer. At the time Seller delivers possession of the Property to Buyer, Seller shall:

(1) deliver to Buyer written information containing all access codes, usernames, passwords, and applications Buyer will need to access, operate, manage, and control the Smart Devices; and

(2) terminate and remove all access and connections to the improvements and accessories from any of Seller's personal devices including but not limited to phones and computers.

11. SPECIAL PROVISIONS: (This paragraph is intended to be used only for additional informational items. An informational item is a statement that completes a blank in a contract form, discloses factual information, or provides instructions. Real estate brokers and sales agents are prohibited from practicing law and shall not add to, delete, or modify any provision of this contract unless drafted by a party to this contract or a party's attorney.)______________________________
____
____.

12. SETTLEMENT AND OTHER EXPENSES:

A. EXPENSES: The following expenses must be paid at or prior to closing:

(1) Seller shall pay the following expenses (Seller's Expenses):

(a) releases of existing liens, including prepayment penalties and recording fees; lender, FHA, or VA completion requirements; tax statements or certificates; preparation of deed; one-half of escrow fee; and other expenses payable by Seller under this contract;

(b) an amount not to exceed $ _____________ to be applied to Buyer's Expenses other than brokerage compensation or contributions under Paragraph 12B below.

(2) Buyer shall pay the following expenses (Buyer's Expenses): Appraisal fees; loan application fees; origination charges; credit reports; preparation of loan documents; interest on the notes from date of disbursement to one month prior to dates of first monthly payments; recording fees; copies of easements and restrictions; loan title policy with endorsements required by lender; loan-related inspection fees; photos; amortization schedules; one-half of escrow fee; all prepaid items, including required premiums for flood and hazard insurance, reserve deposits for insurance, ad valorem taxes and special governmental assessments; final compliance inspection; courier fee; repair inspection; underwriting fee; wire transfer fee; expenses incident to any loan; Private Mortgage Insurance Premium (PMI), VA Loan Funding Fee, or FHA Mortgage Insurance Premium (MIP) as required by the lender; and other expenses payable by Buyer under this contract.

(3) Buyer shall pay any and all Association fees, deposits, reserves and other charges resulting from the transfer of the Property not to exceed $_______________ and Seller shall pay any excess. This paragraph does not apply to: (i) regular periodic maintenance fees, assessments, or dues (including prepaid items) that are prorated by Paragraph 13, and (ii) costs and fees provided by Paragraph 2.

B. BROKERAGE COMPENSATION: Brokerage compensation is not set by law and is fully negotiable. Each party shall pay their respective brokers pursuant to the terms of the parties' obligations to compensate their brokers contained in separate written agreements. **The contributions under 12B(1) and 12B(2) below shall be applied to and shall not change the parties' obligations to pay compensation pursuant to those agreements.** The following contributions must be paid at closing:

❑ (1) Seller will pay (check one box only): ❑ $_________ or ❑ ______% of the Sales Price to be applied toward the brokerage compensation owed by Buyer to Buyer's broker.

❑ (2) Buyer will pay (check one box only): ❑ $_________ or ❑ ______% of the Sales Price to be applied toward the brokerage compensation owed by Seller to Seller's broker.

C. EXPENSE LIMITATION: If a governmental loan program regulation prohibits Buyer from paying charges or fees, then the amount of any concession in 12A(1)(b) shall be first applied to pay such prohibited expenses and then to other Buyer's Expenses but not brokerage compensation or contribution.

13. PRORATIONS: Taxes for the current year, interest, rents, and regular periodic maintenance fees, assessments, and dues (including prepaid items) will be prorated through the Closing Date. The tax proration may be calculated taking into consideration any change in exemptions that will affect the current year's taxes. If taxes for the current year vary from the amount prorated at closing, the parties shall adjust the prorations when tax statements for the current year are available. If taxes are not paid at or prior to closing, Buyer shall pay taxes for the current year. Cash reserves from regular condominium assessments for deferred maintenance or capital improvements established by the Association will not be credited to Seller. Any special condominium assessment due and unpaid at closing will be the obligation of Seller.

14. CASUALTY LOSS: If any part of the Unit which Seller is solely obligated to maintain and repair under the terms of the Declaration is damaged or destroyed by fire or other casualty, Seller shall restore the same to its previous condition as soon as reasonably possible, but in any event by the Closing Date. If Seller fails to do so due to factors beyond Seller's control, Buyer may (a) terminate this contract and the earnest money will be refunded to Buyer, (b) extend the time for performance up to 15 days and the Closing Date will be extended as necessary or (c) accept the Property in its damaged condition with an assignment of insurance proceeds, if permitted by Seller's insurance carrier, and receive credit from Seller at closing in the amount of the deductible under the insurance policy. If any part of the Common Elements or Limited Common Elements appurtenant to the Unit is damaged or destroyed by fire or other casualty loss, Buyer will have 7 days from receipt of notice of such casualty loss within which to notify Seller in writing that the contract will be terminated unless Buyer receives written confirmation from the Association that the damaged condition will be restored to its previous condition within a reasonable time at no cost to Buyer. Unless Buyer gives such notice within such time, Buyer will be deemed to have accepted the Property without confirmation of such restoration. Seller will have 7 days from the date of receipt of Buyer's notice within which to cause to be delivered to Buyer such confirmation. If written confirmation is not delivered to Buyer as required above, Buyer may terminate this contract and the earnest money will be refunded to Buyer. Seller's obligations under this paragraph are independent of any other obligations of Seller under this contract.

15. DEFAULT: If Buyer fails to comply with this contract, Buyer will be in default, and Seller may (a) enforce specific performance, seek such other relief as may be provided by law, or both, or (b) terminate this contract and receive the earnest money as liquidated damages, thereby releasing both parties from this contract. If Seller fails to comply with this contract for any other reason, Seller will be in default and Buyer may (a) enforce specific performance, seek such other relief as may be provided by law, or both, or (b) terminate this contract and receive the earnest money, thereby releasing both parties from this contract.

16. MEDIATION: It is the policy of the State of Texas to encourage resolution of disputes through alternative dispute resolution procedures such as mediation. Any dispute between Seller and Buyer related to this contract which is not resolved through informal discussion will be submitted to a mutually acceptable mediation service or provider. The parties to the mediation shall bear the mediation costs equally. This paragraph does not preclude a party from seeking equitable relief from a court of competent jurisdiction.

17. ATTORNEY'S FEES: A Buyer, Seller, Seller's broker, Buyer's broker, or Escrow Agent who prevails in any legal proceeding related to this contract is entitled to recover reasonable attorney's fees and all costs of such proceeding.

18. ESCROW:

A. ESCROW: The Escrow Agent is not (i) a party to this contract and does not have liability for the performance or nonperformance of any party to this contract, (ii) liable for interest on the earnest money and (iii) liable for the loss of any earnest money caused by the failure of any financial institution in which the earnest money has been deposited unless the financial institution is acting as Escrow Agent. Escrow Agent may require any disbursement made in connection with this contract to be conditioned on Escrow Agent's collection of good funds acceptable to Escrow Agent.

B. EXPENSES: At closing, the earnest money must be applied first to any cash down payment, then to Buyer's Expenses and any excess refunded to Buyer. If no closing occurs, Escrow Agent may: (i) require a written release of liability of the Escrow Agent from all parties before releasing any earnest money; and (ii) require payment of unpaid expenses incurred on behalf of a party. Escrow Agent may deduct authorized expenses from the earnest money payable to a party. "Authorized expenses" means expenses incurred by Escrow Agent on behalf of the party entitled to the earnest money that were authorized by this contract or that party.

C. DEMAND: Upon termination of this contract, either party or the Escrow Agent may send a release of earnest money to each party and the parties shall execute counterparts of the release and deliver same to the Escrow Agent. If either party fails to execute the release, either party may make a written demand to the Escrow Agent for the earnest money. If only one party makes written demand for the earnest money, Escrow Agent shall promptly provide a copy of the demand to the other party. If Escrow Agent does not receive written objection to the demand from the other party within 15 days, Escrow Agent may disburse the earnest money to the party making demand reduced by the amount of unpaid expenses incurred on behalf of the party receiving the earnest money and Escrow Agent may pay the same to the creditors. If Escrow Agent complies with the provisions of this paragraph, each party hereby releases Escrow Agent from all adverse claims related to the disbursal of the earnest money.

D. DAMAGES: Any party who wrongfully fails or refuses to sign a release acceptable to the Escrow Agent within 7 days of receipt of the request will be liable to the other party for (i) damages; (ii) the earnest money; (iii) reasonable attorney's fees; and (iv) all costs of suit.

E. NOTICES: Escrow Agent's notices will be effective when sent in compliance with Paragraph 21. Notice of objection to the demand will be deemed effective upon receipt by Escrow Agent.

19. REPRESENTATIONS: All covenants, representations and warranties in this contract survive closing. If any representation of Seller in this contract is untrue on the Closing Date, Seller will be in default. Unless expressly prohibited by written agreement, Seller may continue to show the Property and receive, negotiate and accept back up offers.

20. GOVERNMENTAL REQUIREMENTS:

A. If Seller is a "foreign person," as defined by Internal Revenue Code and its regulations, or if Seller fails to deliver an affidavit or a certificate of non-foreign status to Buyer that Seller is not a "foreign person," then Buyer shall withhold from the sales proceeds an amount sufficient to comply with applicable tax law and deliver the same to the Internal Revenue Service together with appropriate tax forms. Internal Revenue Service regulations require filing written reports if currency in excess of specified amounts is received in the transaction.

B. Seller and Buyer shall promptly execute and deliver any statements, documents, and information requested by Escrow Agent required by governmental reporting requirements (for example, reporting to the U.S. Treasury or its bureaus).

21. NOTICES: All notices from one party or their agent to the other must be in writing. Notices are effective when mailed to, hand-delivered at, sent by overnight courier to, or transmitted by electronic transmission to the other party or their agent.

To Buyer(s) at:
Address:______________________________
____
Phone(s):______________________________
____
Email(s): ______________________________
____

To Seller(s) at:
Address:______________________________
____
Phone(s):______________________________
____
Email(s):______________________________
____

To Buyer's agent at:
Address:______________________________
____
Phone:______________________________
Email: ______________________________

To Seller's agent at:
Address:______________________________
____
Phone:______________________________
Email: ______________________________

22. AGREEMENT OF PARTIES: This contract contains the entire agreement of the parties and cannot be changed except by their written agreement. Addenda and notices which are a part of this contract are (check all applicable boxes):

Financial

- ❑ Third Party Financing Addendum
- ❑ Addendum for Sale of Other Property by Buyer
- ❑ Addendum Concerning Right to Terminate Due to Lender's Appraisal
- ❑ Seller Financing Addendum
- ❑ Addendum for Section 1031 Exchange
- ❑ Short Sale Addendum
- ❑ Loan Assumption Addendum
- ❑ Addendum for Release of Liability on Assumed Loan and/or Restoration of Seller's VA Entitlement

Leases

- ❑ Addendum Regarding Residential Leases
- ❑ Addendum Regarding Fixture Leases
- ❑ Buyer's Temporary Residential Lease
- ❑ Seller's Temporary Residential Lease

Additional Tests and Reports

- ❑ Addendum for Authorizing Hydrostatic Testing
- ❑ Environmental Assessment, Threatened or Endangered Species, and Wetlands Addendum

Statutory Disclosures and Notices

- ❑ Addendum for Seller's Disclosure of Information on Lead-Based Paint and Lead-Based Paint Hazards as Required by Federal Law
- ❑ Addendum for Property in a Propane Gas System Service Area
- ❑ Addendum for Property Located Seaward of the Gulf Intercoastal Waterway
- ❑ Addendum for Coastal Area Property
- ❑ The following utility, water, drainage, public improvement, and other district notices (list all that have been given or are attached):______________________________
____

NOTICE: Seller's failure to provide applicable Statutory Disclosures and Notices may provide Buyer with remedies or rights to terminate this contract.

Other

- ❑ Non-Realty Items Addendum
- ❑ Addendum for "Back-Up" Contract
- ❑ Other:______________________________
____

23. CONSULT AN ATTORNEY BEFORE SIGNING: TREC rules prohibit real estate brokers and sales agents from giving legal advice. READ THIS CONTRACT CAREFULLY.

Buyer's Attorney is:	______________________	Seller's Attorney is:	______________________
	______________________		______________________
Phone:	( )	Phone:	( )
Fax:	( )	Fax:	( )
E-mail:	______________________	E-mail:	______________________

EXECUTED the ______day of ______________________________, 20_____ (Effective Date).
(BROKER: FILL IN THE DATE OF FINAL ACCEPTANCE.)

______________________________ ______________________________
Buyer Seller

______________________________ ______________________________
Buyer Seller

BROKER CONTACT INFORMATION
(Print name(s) only. Do not sign)

The brokers to this sale are:

______________________________ (Broker Firm) **represents Seller only as Seller's agent.**

Address:______________________________
Broker Firm License No.:______________________________
Associate's Name:______________________________
Team Name:______________________________
Associate's Email:______________________________
Associate's Phone No.:______________Associate's License No.:______________
Licensed Supervisor of Associate:______________________________
Phone No. of Licensed Supervisor:______________License No.:______________

______________________________ (Broker Firm) **represents Buyer only as Buyer's agent.**

Address:______________________________
Broker Firm License No.:______________________________
Associate's Name:______________________________
Team Name:______________________________
Associate's Email:______________________________
Associate's Phone No.:______________Associate's License No.:______________
Licensed Supervisor of Associate:______________________________
Phone No. of Licensed Supervisor:______________License No.:______________

Intermediary

______________________________ (Broker Firm) **represents Seller and Buyer as an intermediary.**

Address:______________________________
Broker Firm License No.:______________________________
Associate's Name (for Seller):______________________________
Team Name:______________________________
Associate's Email:______________________________
Associate's Phone No.:______________Associate's License No.:______________
Licensed Supervisor of Associate:______________________________
Phone No. of Licensed Supervisor:______________License No.:______________
Associate's Name (for Buyer):______________________________
Team Name:______________________________
Associate's Email:______________________________
Associate's Phone No.:______________Associate's License No.:______________
Licensed Supervisor of Associate:______________________________
Phone No. of Licensed Supervisor:______________License No.:______________

OPTION FEE RECEIPT

Receipt of $ ____________________ option fee in the form of ______________________________________
is acknowledged.

_______________________________________ _______________________________________
Escrow Agent Date

EARNEST MONEY RECEIPT

Receipt of $ ____________________ earnest money in the form of ________________________________
is acknowledged.

_______________________________________ _______________________________________
Escrow Agent Received by Email Address Date/Time

_______________________________________ _______________________________________
Address Phone

_______________________________________ _______________________________________
City State Zip Fax

CONTRACT RECEIPT

Receipt of the contract is acknowledged.

_______________________________________ _______________________________________
Escrow Agent Received by Email Address Date

_______________________________________ _______________________________________
Address Phone

_______________________________________ _______________________________________
City State Zip Fax

ADDITIONAL EARNEST MONEY RECEIPT

Receipt of $ ____________________ additional earnest money in the form of __________________________
is acknowledged.

_______________________________________ _______________________________________
Escrow Agent Received by Email Address Date/Time

_______________________________________ _______________________________________
Address Phone

_______________________________________ _______________________________________
City State Zip Fax

PROMULGATED BY THE TEXAS REAL ESTATE COMMISSION (TREC) 05-04-2026

TREC
TEXAS REAL ESTATE COMMISSION

UNIMPROVED PROPERTY CONTRACT

NOTICE: Not For Use For Condominium Transactions

EQUAL HOUSING OPPORTUNITY

1. PARTIES: The parties to this contract are ________________________________(Seller) and ____(Buyer). Seller agrees to sell and convey to Buyer and Buyer agrees to buy from Seller the Property defined below.

2. PROPERTY: Lot ____________________, Block ______________________________, ____Addition, City of ___________________________, County of___________________________, Texas, known as____ (address/zip code), or as described on attached exhibit together with all rights, privileges and appurtenances pertaining thereto (Property).

RESERVATIONS: Any reservation for oil, gas, or other minerals, water, timber, or other interests is made in accordance with an attached addendum.

3. SALES PRICE:

A. Cash portion of Sales Price payable by Buyer at closing .... $______________
The term "Cash portion of the Sales Price" does not include proceeds from borrowing of any kind or selling other real property except as disclosed in this contract.

B. Sum of all financing described in the attached: ❑ Third Party Financing Addendum, ❑ Loan Assumption Addendum, ❑ Seller Financing Addendum .... $______________

C. Sales Price (Sum of A and B) .... $______________

D. The Sales Price ❑ will ❑ will not be adjusted based on the survey required by Paragraph 6C. If the Sales Price is adjusted, the Sales Price will be adjusted based on the difference between _______ acres and the acreage set forth in the survey required by Paragraph 6C. The difference in acreage (either increased or decreased) shall be multiplied by the sum of $________ per acre and either added to or subtracted from the Sales Price stated in Paragraph 3C. If the Sales Price is adjusted by more than 10%, either party may terminate this contract by providing written notice to the other party within ____ days after the terminating party receives the survey. If neither party terminates this contract or if the variance is 10% or less, the adjustment will be made to the amount in ❑ 3A ❑ 3B ❑ proportionately to 3A and 3B.

4. LEASES:

A. Except as disclosed in this contract, Seller is not aware of any leases affecting the Property. After the Effective Date, Seller may not, without Buyer's written consent, create a new lease, amend any existing lease, or convey any interest in the Property.

B. NATURAL RESOURCE LEASES: "Natural Resource Lease" means an existing oil and gas, mineral, geothermal, water, wind, or other natural resource lease affecting the Property to which Seller is a party. Seller ❑ is ❑ is not a party to a Natural Resource Lease. If Seller is a party to a Natural Resource Lease, check one of the following:

❑ (1) Seller has delivered to Buyer a copy of all the Natural Resource Leases.

❑ (2) Seller has not delivered to Buyer a copy of all the Natural Resource Leases. Seller shall provide to Buyer a copy of all the Natural Resource Leases within 3 days after the Effective Date. Buyer may terminate the contract within ______ days after the date the Buyer receives all the Natural Resource Leases and the earnest money shall be refunded to Buyer.

5. EARNEST MONEY AND TERMINATION OPTION:

A. DELIVERY OF EARNEST MONEY AND OPTION FEE: Within 3 days after the Effective Date, Buyer must deliver to ____________________________________ (Escrow Agent) at _________ ____(address): $__________________ as earnest money and $_______________ as the option fee. The earnest money and option fee shall be made payable to Escrow Agent and may be paid separately or combined in a single payment.

(1) Buyer shall deliver additional earnest money of $________________ to Escrow Agent within ______ days after the Effective Date of this contract.

(2) If the last day to deliver the earnest money, option fee, or the additional earnest money falls on a Saturday, Sunday, or Legal Holiday, the time to deliver the earnest money, option fee, or the additional earnest money, as applicable, is extended until the end of the next day that is not a Saturday, Sunday, or Legal Holiday. "Legal Holiday" means a legal holiday described in Sections 662.003(a) and 662.003(b)(4) and (6), Texas Government Code.

(3) The amount(s) Escrow Agent receives under this paragraph shall be applied first to the option fee, then to the earnest money, and then to the additional earnest money.

(4) Buyer authorizes Escrow Agent to release and deliver the option fee to Seller at any time without further notice to or consent from Buyer, and releases Escrow Agent from liability for delivery of the option fee to Seller. The option fee will be credited to the Sales Price at closing.

B. TERMINATION OPTION: For nominal consideration, the receipt of which Seller acknowledges, and Buyer's agreement to pay the option fee within the time required, Seller grants Buyer the unrestricted right to terminate this contract by giving notice of termination to Seller within ______ days after the Effective Date of this contract (Option Period). Notices under this paragraph must be given by 5:00 p.m. (local time where the Property is located) by the date specified. If Buyer gives notice of termination within the time prescribed: (i) the option fee will not be refunded and Escrow Agent shall release any option fee remaining with Escrow Agent to Seller; and (ii) any earnest money will be refunded to Buyer.

C. FAILURE TO TIMELY DELIVER EARNEST MONEY: If Buyer fails to deliver the earnest money within the time required, Seller may terminate this contract or exercise Seller's remedies under Paragraph 15, or both, by providing notice to Buyer before Buyer delivers the earnest money.

D. FAILURE TO TIMELY DELIVER OPTION FEE: If no dollar amount is stated as the option fee or if Buyer fails to deliver the option fee within the time required, Buyer shall not have the unrestricted right to terminate this contract under this Paragraph 5.

E. TIME: **Time is of the essence for this paragraph and strict compliance with the time for performance is required.**

6. TITLE POLICY AND SURVEY:

A. TITLE POLICY: Seller shall furnish to Buyer at ❑Seller's ❑Buyer's expense an owner's policy of title insurance (Title Policy) issued by____ (Title Company) in the amount of the Sales Price, dated at or after closing, insuring Buyer against loss under the provisions of the Title Policy, subject to the promulgated exclusions (including existing building and zoning ordinances) and the following exceptions:

(1) Restrictive covenants common to the platted subdivision in which the Property is located.
(2) The standard printed exception for standby fees, taxes and assessments.
(3) Liens created as part of the financing described in Paragraph 3.
(4) Utility easements created by the dedication deed or plat of the subdivision in which the Property is located.
(5) Reservations or exceptions otherwise permitted by this contract or as may be approved by Buyer in writing.
(6) The standard printed exception as to marital rights.
(7) The standard printed exception as to waters, tidelands, beaches, streams, and related matters.
(8) The standard printed exception as to discrepancies, conflicts, shortages in area or boundary lines, encroachments or protrusions, or overlapping improvements:
❑ (i) will not be amended or deleted from the title policy; or
❑ (ii) will be amended to read, "shortages in area" at the expense of ❑ Buyer ❑ Seller.
(9) The exception or exclusion regarding minerals approved by the Texas Department of Insurance.

B. COMMITMENT: Within 20 days after the Title Company receives a copy of this contract, Seller shall furnish to Buyer a commitment for title insurance (Commitment) and, at Buyer's expense, legible copies of restrictive covenants and documents evidencing exceptions in the Commitment (Exception Documents) other than the standard printed exceptions. Seller authorizes the Title Company to deliver the Commitment and Exception Documents to Buyer at Buyer's address shown in Paragraph 21. If the Commitment and Exception Documents are not delivered to Buyer within the specified time, the time for delivery will be automatically extended up to 15 days or 3 days before the Closing Date, whichever is earlier. If the Commitment and Exception Documents are not delivered within the time required, Buyer may terminate this contract and the earnest money will be refunded to Buyer.

C. SURVEY: The survey must be made by a registered professional land surveyor acceptable to the Title Company and Buyer's lender(s). (Check one box only)

❑ (1) Within _____ days after the Effective Date of this contract, Seller shall furnish to Buyer and Title Company Seller's existing survey of the Property and a Residential Real Property Affidavit or Declaration promulgated by the Texas Department of Insurance (T-47 Affidavit or T-47.1 Declaration). Buyer shall obtain a new survey at Seller's expense no later than 3 days prior to Closing Date if Seller fails to furnish within the time prescribed both the: (i) existing survey; and (ii) affidavit or declaration. If the Title Company or Buyer's lender does not accept the existing survey, or the affidavit or declaration, Buyer shall obtain a new survey at ❑ Seller's ❑ Buyer's expense no later than 3 days prior to Closing Date.

❑ (2) Within ______ days after the Effective Date of this contract, Buyer may obtain a new survey at Buyer's expense. Buyer is deemed to receive the survey on the date of actual receipt or the date specified in this paragraph, whichever is earlier. If Buyer fails to obtain the survey, Buyer may not terminate the contract under Paragraph 2B of the Third Party Financing Addendum because the survey was not obtained.

❑ (3) Within ______ days after the Effective Date of this contract, Seller, at Seller's expense shall furnish a new survey to Buyer.

D. OBJECTIONS: Buyer may object in writing to (i) defects, exceptions, or encumbrances to title: disclosed on the survey other than items 6A(1) through (7) above; or disclosed in the Commitment other than items 6A(1) through (9) above; (ii) any portion of the Property lying in a special flood hazard area (Zone V or A) as shown on the current Federal Emergency Management Agency map; or (iii) any exceptions which prohibit the following use or activity: ____.

Buyer must object the earlier of (i) the Closing Date or (ii) ______ days after Buyer receives the Commitment, Exception Documents, and the survey. Buyer's failure to object within the time allowed will constitute a waiver of Buyer's right to object; except that the requirements in Schedule C of the Commitment are not waived. Provided Seller is not obligated to incur any expense, Seller shall cure any timely objections of Buyer or any third party lender within 15 days after Seller receives the objections (Cure Period) and the Closing Date will be extended as necessary. If objections are not cured within the Cure Period, Buyer may, by delivering notice to Seller within 5 days after the end of the Cure Period: (i) terminate this contract and the earnest money will be refunded to Buyer; or (ii) waive the objections. If Buyer does not terminate within the time required, Buyer shall be deemed to have waived the objections. If the Commitment or survey is revised or any new Exception Document(s) is delivered, Buyer may object to any new matter revealed in the revised Commitment or survey or new Exception Document(s) within the same time stated in this paragraph to make objections beginning when the revised Commitment, survey, or Exception Document(s) is delivered to Buyer.

E. TITLE NOTICES:

(1) ABSTRACT OR TITLE POLICY: Broker advises Buyer to have an abstract of title covering the Property examined by an attorney of Buyer's selection, or Buyer should be furnished with or obtain a Title Policy. If a Title Policy is furnished, the Commitment should be promptly reviewed by an attorney of Buyer's choice due to the time limitations on Buyer's right to object.

(2) MEMBERSHIP IN PROPERTY OWNERS ASSOCIATION(S): The Property ❑is ❑is not subject to mandatory membership in a property owners association(s). If the Property is subject to mandatory membership in a property owners association(s), Seller notifies Buyer under §5.012, Texas Property Code, that, as a purchaser of property in the residential community identified in Paragraph 2 in which the Property is located, you are obligated to be a member of the property owners association(s). Restrictive covenants governing the use and occupancy of the Property and all dedicatory instruments governing the establishment, maintenance, and operation of this residential community have been or will be recorded in the Real Property Records of the county in which the Property is located. Copies of the restrictive covenants and dedicatory instruments may be obtained from the county clerk. **You are obligated to pay assessments to the property owners association(s). The amount of the assessments is subject to change. Your failure to pay the assessments could result in enforcement of the association's lien on and the foreclosure of the Property.**

Section 207.003, Property Code, entitles an owner to receive copies of any document that governs the establishment, maintenance, or operation of a subdivision, including, but not limited to, restrictions, bylaws, rules and regulations, and a resale certificate from a property owners' association. A resale certificate contains information including, but not limited to, statements specifying the amount and frequency of regular assessments and the style and cause number of lawsuits to which the property owners' association is a party, other than lawsuits relating to unpaid ad valorem taxes of an individual member of the association. These documents must be made available to you by the property owners' association or the association's agent on your request.

If Buyer is concerned about these matters, the TREC promulgated Addendum for Property Subject to Mandatory Membership in a Property Owners Association should be used.

(3) STATUTORY TAX DISTRICTS: If the Property is situated in a utility or other statutorily created district providing water, sewer, drainage, or flood control facilities and services, Chapter 49, Texas Water Code, requires Seller to deliver and Buyer to sign the statutory notice relating to the tax rate, bonded indebtedness, or standby fee of the district prior to final execution of this contract.

(4) TIDE WATERS: If the Property abuts the tidally influenced waters of the state, §33.135, Texas Natural Resources Code, requires a notice regarding coastal area property to be included in the contract.

(5) ANNEXATION: If the Property is located outside the limits of a municipality, Seller notifies Buyer under §5.011, Texas Property Code, that the Property may now or later be included in the extraterritorial jurisdiction of a municipality and may now or later be subject to annexation by the municipality. Each municipality maintains a map that depicts its boundaries and extraterritorial jurisdiction. To determine if the Property is located within a municipality's extraterritorial jurisdiction or is likely to be located within a municipality's extraterritorial jurisdiction, contact all municipalities located in the general proximity of the Property for further information.

(6) PROPERTY LOCATED IN A CERTIFICATED SERVICE AREA OF A UTILITY SERVICE PROVIDER: Notice required by §13.257, Water Code: The real property, described in Paragraph 2, that you are about to purchase may be located in a certificated water or sewer service area, which is authorized by law to provide water or sewer service to the properties in the certificated area. If your property is located in a certificated area there may be special costs or charges that you will be required to pay before you can receive water or sewer service. There may be a period required to construct lines or other facilities necessary to provide water or sewer service to your property. You are advised to determine if the property is in a certificated area and contact the utility service provider to determine the cost that you will be required to pay and the period, if any, that is required to provide water or sewer service to your property. The undersigned Buyer hereby acknowledges receipt of the foregoing notice at or before the execution of a binding contract for the purchase of the real property described in Paragraph 2 or at closing of purchase of the real property.

(7) PUBLIC IMPROVEMENT DISTRICTS: If the Property is in a public improvement district, Seller must give Buyer written notice as required by §5.014, Property Code.

(8) TEXAS AGRICULTURAL DEVELOPMENT DISTRICT: The Property ❑ is ❑ is not located in a Texas Agricultural Development District. For additional information, contact the Texas Department of Agriculture.

(9) TRANSFER FEES: If the Property is subject to a private transfer fee obligation, §5.205, Property Code requires Seller to notify Buyer as follows: The private transfer fee obligation may be governed by Chapter 5, Subchapter G of the Texas Property Code.

(10) PROPANE GAS SYSTEM SERVICE AREA: If the Property is located in a propane gas system service area owned by a distribution system retailer, Seller must give Buyer written notice as required by §141.010, Texas Utilities Code.

(11) NOTICE OF WATER LEVEL FLUCTUATIONS: If the Property adjoins an impoundment of water, including a reservoir or lake, constructed and maintained under Chapter 11, Water Code, that has a storage capacity of at least 5,000 acre-feet at the impoundment's normal operating level, Seller hereby notifies Buyer: "The water level of the impoundment of water adjoining the Property fluctuates for various reasons, including as a result of: (1) an entity lawfully exercising its right to use the water stored in the impoundment; or (2) drought or flood conditions."

7. PROPERTY CONDITION:

A. ACCESS, INSPECTIONS AND UTILITIES: Seller shall permit Buyer and Buyer's agents access to the Property at reasonable times. Buyer may have the Property inspected by inspectors selected by Buyer and licensed by TREC or otherwise permitted by law to make inspections. Seller at Seller's expense shall immediately cause existing utilities to be turned on and shall keep the utilities on during the time this contract is in effect.
NOTICE: Buyer should determine the availability of utilities to the Property suitable to satisfy Buyer's needs.

B. ACCEPTANCE OF PROPERTY CONDITION: "As Is" means the present condition of the Property with any and all defects and without warranty except for the warranties of title and the warranties in this contract. Buyer's agreement to accept the Property As Is under Paragraph 7B (1) or (2) does not preclude Buyer from inspecting the Property under Paragraph 7A, from negotiating repairs or treatments in a subsequent amendment, or from terminating this contract during the Option Period, if any.
(Check one box only)
❑ (1) Buyer accepts the Property As Is.
❑ (2) Buyer accepts the Property As Is provided Seller, at Seller's expense, shall complete the following specific repairs and treatments: ______________________________________
____.
(Do not insert general phrases, such as "subject to inspections" that do not identify specific repairs and treatments.)

C. COMPLETION OF REPAIRS AND TREATMENTS: Unless otherwise agreed in writing, Seller shall complete all agreed repairs and treatments prior to the Closing Date and obtain any required permits. The repairs and treatments must be performed by persons who are licensed to provide such repairs or treatments or, if no license is required by law, are commercially engaged in the trade of providing such repairs or treatments. Seller shall: (i) provide Buyer with copies of documentation from the repair person(s) showing the scope of work and payment for the work completed; and (ii) at Seller's expense, arrange for the transfer of any transferable warranties with respect to the repairs and treatments to Buyer at closing. If Seller fails to complete any agreed repairs and treatments prior to the Closing Date, Buyer may exercise remedies under Paragraph 15 or extend the Closing Date up to 5 days, if necessary, for Seller to complete repairs and treatments.

D. ENVIRONMENTAL MATTERS: Buyer is advised that the presence of wetlands, toxic substances, including asbestos and wastes or other environmental hazards, or the presence of a threatened or endangered species or its habitat may affect Buyer's intended use of the Property. If Buyer is concerned about these matters, an addendum promulgated by TREC or required by the parties should be used.

E. SELLER'S DISCLOSURE:
(1) Seller ❑ is ❑ is not aware of any flooding of the Property which has had a material adverse effect on the use of the Property.
(2) Seller ❑ is ❑ is not aware of any pending or threatened litigation, condemnation, or special assessment affecting the Property.
(3) Seller ❑ is ❑ is not aware of any environmental hazards that materially and adversely affect the Property.
(4) Seller ❑ is ❑ is not aware of any dumpsite, landfill, or underground tanks or containers now or previously located on the Property.
(5) Seller ❑ is ❑ is not aware of any wetlands, as defined by federal or state law or regulation, affecting the Property.
(6) Seller ❑ is ❑ is not aware of any threatened or endangered species or their habitat affecting the Property.
(7) Seller ❑ is ❑ is not aware that the Property is located ❑ wholly ❑ partly in a floodplain.
(8) Seller ❑ is ❑ is not aware that a tree or trees located on the Property has oak wilt.
If Seller is aware of any of the items above, explain (attach additional sheets if necessary): __
____.

F. SELLER'S DISCLOSURE ABOUT GROUNDWATER AND SURFACE WATER RIGHTS (Seller's Water Disclosure): Access to surface water or groundwater on the Property may be regulated, restricted, or prohibited, including but not limited to the right to drill or operate water wells and the right to withdraw water from surface water sources on or adjoining the Property. The parties shall use the Seller's Water Disclosure published by TREC to identify information related to groundwater and surface water rights. (Check one box only)

❑ (1) Buyer has received the Seller's Water Disclosure.

❑ (2) Buyer has not received the Seller's Water Disclosure. Within _____ days after the Effective Date of this contract, Seller shall deliver the Seller's Water Disclosure to Buyer. If Buyer does not receive the Seller's Water Disclosure, Buyer may terminate this contract at any time prior to the closing and the earnest money will be refunded to Buyer. If Seller delivers the Seller's Water Disclosure, Buyer may terminate this contract for any reason within 7 days after Buyer receives the Seller's Water Disclosure or prior to the closing, whichever first occurs, and the earnest money will be refunded to Buyer.

❑ (3) Seller is not required to deliver the Seller's Water Disclosure to Buyer because all of the following are true:
(a) Seller is not aware of a water well on the Property (in use or not in use);
(b) Seller is not aware of a pond, lake, or water tank on the Property;
(c) Seller is not aware of any certificate of adjudication, certified filing, or permit for surface water rights associated with the Property administered by the Texas Commission on Environmental Quality;
(d) Seller is not aware that any groundwater rights to the Property have been severed, sold, or leased in whole or in part; and
(e) the Property receives water only from the following municipality (City), municipal utility district (MUD) or other special district, water supply corporation (WSC), or private water supply company (PWC):______________________________________
____.

8. BROKER OR SALES AGENT DISCLOSURE:
Texas law requires a real estate broker or sales agent who is a party to a transaction or acting on behalf of a spouse, parent, child, business entity in which the broker or sales agent owns more than 10%, or a trust for which the broker or sales agent acts as a trustee or of which the broker or sales agent or the broker or sales agent's spouse, parent or child is a beneficiary, to notify the other party in writing before entering into a contract of sale. Disclose if applicable:___________
____.

9. CLOSING:
A. The closing of the sale will be on or before __________________, 20_____, or within 7 days after objections made under Paragraph 6D have been cured or waived, whichever date is later (Closing Date). If either party fails to close the sale by the Closing Date, the non-defaulting party may exercise the remedies contained in Paragraph 15.
B. At closing:
(1) Seller shall execute and deliver a general warranty deed conveying title to the Property to Buyer and showing no additional exceptions to those permitted in Paragraph 6 and furnish tax statements or certificates showing no delinquent taxes on the Property.
(2) Buyer shall pay the Sales Price in good funds acceptable to the Escrow Agent.
(3) Seller and Buyer shall execute and deliver any notices, statements, certificates, affidavits, releases, loan documents, transfer of any warranties, and other documents reasonably required for the closing of the sale and the issuance of the Title Policy.
(4) There will be no liens, assessments, or security interests against the Property which will not be satisfied out of the sales proceeds unless securing the payment of any loans assumed by Buyer and assumed loans will not be in default.
(5) Private transfer fees (as defined by Chapter 5, Subchapter G of the Texas Property Code) will be the obligation of Seller unless provided otherwise in this contract. Transfer fees assessed by a property owners' association are governed by the Addendum for Property Subject to Mandatory Membership in a Property Owners Association.

10. POSSESSION: Seller shall deliver to Buyer possession of the Property in its present or required condition upon closing and funding.

11. SPECIAL PROVISIONS: (This paragraph is intended to be used only for additional informational items. An informational item is a statement that completes a blank in a contract form, discloses factual information, or provides instructions. Real estate brokers and sales agents are prohibited from practicing law and shall not add to, delete, or modify any provision of this contract unless drafted by a party to this contract or a party's attorney.)______________________________
____.

12. SETTLEMENT AND OTHER EXPENSES:
A. EXPENSES: The following expenses must be paid at or prior to closing:
(1) Seller shall pay the following expenses (Seller's Expenses):
(a) releases of existing liens, including prepayment penalties and recording fees; release of Seller's loan liability; tax statements or certificates; preparation of deed; one-half of escrow fee; and other expenses payable by Seller under this contract; and
(b) an amount not to exceed $ __________ to be applied to Buyer's Expenses other than brokerage compensation or contributions under Paragraph 12B below.
(2) Buyer shall pay the following expenses (Buyer's Expenses): Appraisal fees; loan application fees; origination charges; credit reports; preparation of loan documents; interest on the notes from date of disbursement to one month prior to dates of first monthly payments; recording fees; copies of easements and restrictions; loan title policy with endorsements required by lender; loan-related inspection fees; photos; amortization schedules; one-half of escrow fee; all prepaid items, including required premiums for flood and hazard

insurance, reserve deposits for insurance, ad valorem taxes and special governmental assessments; final compliance inspection; courier fee; repair inspection; underwriting fee; wire transfer fee; expenses incident to any loan; Private Mortgage Insurance Premium (PMI), VA Loan Funding Fee, or FHA Mortgage Insurance Premium (MIP) as required by the lender; and other expenses payable by Buyer under this contract.

B. BROKERAGE COMPENSATION: Brokerage compensation is not set by law and is fully negotiable. Each party shall pay their respective brokers pursuant to the terms of the parties' obligations to compensate their brokers contained in separate written agreements. **The contributions under 12B(1) and 12B(2) below shall be applied to and shall not change the parties' obligations to pay compensation pursuant to those agreements.** The following contributions must be paid at closing:

❑ (1) Seller will pay (check one box only): ❑ $_________ or ❑_______% of the Sales Price to be applied toward the brokerage compensation owed by Buyer to Buyer's broker.

❑ (2) Buyer will pay (check one box only): ❑ $_________ or ❑_______% of the Sales Price to be applied toward the brokerage compensation owed by Seller to Seller's broker.

C. EXPENSE LIMITATION: If a governmental loan program regulation prohibits Buyer from paying charges or fees, then the amount of any concession in 12A(1)(b) shall be first applied to pay such prohibited expenses and then to other Buyer's Expenses but not brokerage compensation or contribution.

13. PRORATIONS AND ROLLBACK TAXES:

A. PRORATIONS: Taxes for the current year, interest, rents, and regular periodic maintenance fees, assessments, and dues (including prepaid items) will be prorated through the Closing Date. The tax proration may be calculated taking into consideration any change in exemptions that will affect the current year's taxes. If taxes for the current year vary from the amount prorated at closing, the parties shall adjust the prorations when tax statements for the current year are available. If taxes are not paid at or prior to closing, Buyer shall pay taxes for the current year.

B. ROLLBACK TAXES: If this sale or Buyer's use of the Property after closing results in the assessment of additional taxes, penalties or interest (Assessments) for periods prior to closing, the Assessments will be the obligation of Buyer. If Assessments are imposed because of Seller's use or change in use of the Property prior to closing, the Assessments will be the obligation of Seller. Obligations imposed by this paragraph will survive closing.

14. CASUALTY LOSS: If any part of the Property is damaged or destroyed by fire or other casualty after the Effective Date of this contract, Seller shall restore the Property to its previous condition as soon as reasonably possible, but in any event by the Closing Date. If Seller fails to do so due to factors beyond Seller's control, Buyer may (a) terminate this contract and the earnest money will be refunded to Buyer (b) extend the time for performance up to 15 days and the Closing Date will be extended as necessary or (c) accept the Property in its damaged condition with an assignment of insurance proceeds, if permitted by Seller's insurance carrier, and receive credit from Seller at closing in the amount of the deductible under the insurance policy. Seller's obligations under this paragraph are independent of any other obligations of Seller under this contract.

15. DEFAULT: If Buyer fails to comply with this contract, Buyer will be in default, and Seller may (a) enforce specific performance, seek such other relief as may be provided by law, or both, or (b) terminate this contract and receive the earnest money as liquidated damages, thereby releasing both parties from this contract. If Seller fails to comply with this contract, Seller will be in default and Buyer may (a) enforce specific performance, seek such other relief as may be provided by law, or both, or (b) terminate this contract and receive the earnest money, thereby releasing both parties from this contract.

16. MEDIATION: It is the policy of the State of Texas to encourage resolution of disputes through alternative dispute resolution procedures such as mediation. Any dispute between Seller and Buyer related to this contract which is not resolved through informal discussion will be submitted to a mutually acceptable mediation service or provider. The parties to the mediation shall bear the mediation costs equally. This paragraph does not preclude a party from seeking equitable relief from a court of competent jurisdiction.

17. ATTORNEY'S FEES: A Buyer, Seller, Seller's broker, Buyer's broker, or Escrow Agent who prevails in any legal proceeding related to this contract is entitled to recover reasonable attorney's fees and all costs of such proceeding.

18. ESCROW:

A. ESCROW: The Escrow Agent is not (i) a party to this contract and does not have liability for the performance or nonperformance of any party to this contract, (ii) liable for interest on the earnest money and (iii) liable for the loss of any earnest money caused by the failure of any financial institution in which the earnest money has been deposited unless the financial institution is acting as Escrow Agent. Escrow Agent may require any disbursement made in connection with this contract to be conditioned on Escrow Agent's collection of good funds acceptable to Escrow Agent.

B. EXPENSES: At closing, the earnest money must be applied first to any cash down payment, then to Buyer's Expenses and any excess refunded to Buyer. If no closing occurs, Escrow Agent may: (i) require a written release of liability of the Escrow Agent from all parties before releasing any earnest money; and (ii) require payment of unpaid expenses incurred on behalf of a party. Escrow Agent may deduct authorized expenses from the earnest money payable to a party. "Authorized expenses" means expenses incurred by Escrow Agent on behalf of the party entitled to the earnest money that were authorized by this contract or that party.

C. DEMAND: Upon termination of this contract, either party or the Escrow Agent may send a release of earnest money to each party and the parties shall execute counterparts of the release and deliver same to the Escrow Agent. If either party fails to execute the release, either party may make a written demand to the Escrow Agent for the earnest money. If only one party makes written demand for the earnest money, Escrow Agent shall promptly provide a copy of the demand to the other party. If Escrow Agent does not receive written objection to the demand from the other party within 15 days, Escrow Agent may disburse the earnest money to the party making demand reduced by the amount of unpaid expenses incurred on behalf of the party receiving the earnest money and Escrow Agent may pay the same to the creditors. If Escrow Agent complies with the provisions of this paragraph, each party hereby releases Escrow Agent from all adverse claims related to the disbursal of the earnest money.

D. DAMAGES: Any party who wrongfully fails or refuses to sign a release acceptable to the Escrow Agent within 7 days of receipt of the request will be liable to the other party for (i) damages; (ii) the earnest money; (iii) reasonable attorney's fees; and (iv) all costs of suit.

E. NOTICES: Escrow Agent's notices will be effective when sent in compliance with Paragraph 21. Notice of objection to the demand will be deemed effective upon receipt by Escrow Agent.

19. REPRESENTATIONS: All covenants, representations and warranties in this contract survive closing. If any representation of Seller in this contract is untrue on the Closing Date, Seller will be in default. Unless expressly prohibited by written agreement, Seller may continue to show the Property and receive, negotiate and accept back up offers.

20. GOVERNMENTAL REQUIREMENTS:

A. If Seller is a "foreign person," as defined by Internal Revenue Code and its regulations, or if Seller fails to deliver an affidavit or a certificate of non-foreign status to Buyer that Seller is not a "foreign person," then Buyer shall withhold from the sales proceeds an amount sufficient to comply with applicable tax law and deliver the same to the Internal Revenue Service together with appropriate tax forms. Internal Revenue Service regulations require filing written reports if currency in excess of specified amounts is received in the transaction.

B. Seller and Buyer shall promptly execute and deliver any statements, documents, and information requested by Escrow Agent required by governmental reporting requirements (for example, reporting to the U.S. Treasury or its bureaus).

21. NOTICES: All notices from one party or their agent to the other must be in writing. Notices are effective when mailed, hand-delivered, sent by overnight courier to, or transmitted by electronic transmission to the other party or their agent.

To Buyer(s) at:	**To Seller(s) at:**
Address: ______________________	Address: ______________________
______________________	______________________
Phone(s): ______________________	Phone(s): ______________________
______________________	______________________
Email(s): ______________________	Email(s): ______________________
______________________	______________________
To Buyer's agent at:	**To Seller's agent at:**
Address: ______________________	Address: ______________________
______________________	______________________
Phone: ______________________	Phone: ______________________
Email: ______________________	Email: ______________________

22. AGREEMENT OF PARTIES: This contract contains the entire agreement of the parties and cannot be changed except by their written agreement. Addenda and notices which are a part of this contract are (check all applicable boxes):

Financial

- ❑ Third Party Financing Addendum
- ❑ Addendum for Sale of Other Property by Buyer
- ❑ Addendum Concerning Right to Terminate Due to Lender's Appraisal
- ❑ Seller Financing Addendum
- ❑ Addendum for Section 1031 Exchange
- ❑ Short Sale Addendum
- ❑ Loan Assumption Addendum
- ❑ Addendum for Release of Liability on Assumed Loan and/or Restoration of Seller's VA Entitlement

Leases

- ❑ Addendum Regarding Residential Leases
- ❑ Addendum Regarding Fixture Leases
- ❑ Buyer's Temporary Residential Lease
- ❑ Seller's Temporary Residential Lease

Additional Tests and Reports

- ❑ Addendum for Authorizing Hydrostatic Testing
- ❑ Environmental Assessment, Threatened or Endangered Species, and Wetlands Addendum

Statutory Disclosures and Notices

- ❑ Addendum for Property in a Propane Gas System Service Area
- ❑ Addendum for Property Located Seaward of the Gulf Intercoastal Waterway
- ❑ Addendum for Coastal Area Property
- ❑ The following utility, water, drainage, public improvement, and other district notices (list all that have been given or are attached):____
  ____

NOTICE: Seller's failure to provide applicable Statutory Disclosures and Notices may provide Buyer with remedies or rights to terminate this contract.

Other

- ❑ Addendum for Property Subject to Mandatory Membership in a Property Owners Association
- ❑ Non-Realty Items Addendum
- ❑ Addendum for "Back-Up" Contract
- ❑ Addendum for Reservation of Oil, Gas, and Other Minerals
- ❑ Other:____
  ____

23. CONSULT AN ATTORNEY BEFORE SIGNING: TREC rules prohibit real estate brokers and sales agents from giving legal advice. READ THIS CONTRACT CAREFULLY.

Buyer's	Seller's
Attorney is: ______________________	Attorney is: ______________________
______________________	______________________
Phone: ( ) ______________________	Phone: ( ) ______________________
Fax: ( ) ______________________	Fax: ( ) ______________________
E-mail: ______________________	E-mail: ______________________

EXECUTED the ______day of _______________________________, 20_____ (Effective Date).
(BROKER: FILL IN THE DATE OF FINAL ACCEPTANCE.)

________________________________	________________________________
Buyer	Seller
________________________________	________________________________
Buyer	Seller

BROKER CONTACT INFORMATION
(Print name(s) only. Do not sign)

The brokers to this sale are:

______________________ (Broker Firm) **represents Seller only as Seller's agent**.
Address: ______________________
Broker Firm License No.: ______________________
Associate's Name: ______________________
Team Name: ______________________
Associate's Email: ______________________
Associate's Phone No.: ______________ Associate's License No.: ______________
Licensed Supervisor of Associate: ______________________
Phone No. of Licensed Supervisor: ______________ License No.: ______________

______________________ (Broker Firm) **represents Buyer only as Buyer's agent**.
Address: ______________________
Broker Firm License No.: ______________________
Associate's Name: ______________________
Team Name: ______________________
Associate's Email: ______________________
Associate's Phone No.: ______________ Associate's License No.: ______________
Licensed Supervisor of Associate: ______________________
Phone No. of Licensed Supervisor: ______________ License No.: ______________

Intermediary

______________________ (Broker Firm) **represents Seller and Buyer as an intermediary**.
Address: ______________________
Broker Firm License No.: ______________________
Associate's Name (for Seller): ______________________
Team Name: ______________________
Associate's Email: ______________________
Associate's Phone No.: ______________ Associate's License No.: ______________
Licensed Supervisor of Associate: ______________________
Phone No. of Licensed Supervisor: ______________ License No.: ______________
Associate's Name (for Buyer): ______________________
Team Name: ______________________
Associate's Email: ______________________
Associate's Phone No.: ______________ Associate's License No.: ______________
Licensed Supervisor of Associate: ______________________
Phone No. of Licensed Supervisor: ______________ License No.: ______________

OPTION FEE RECEIPT

Receipt of $______________ option fee in the form of ______________________ is acknowledged.

______________________________ ______________________________
Escrow Agent Date

EARNEST MONEY RECEIPT

Receipt of $______________ earnest money in the form of __________________ is acknowledged.

______________________________ ______________________________
Escrow Agent Received by Email Address Date/Time

______________________________ ______________________________
Address Phone

______________________________ ______________________________
City State Zip Fax

CONTRACT RECEIPT

Receipt of the contract is acknowledged.

______________________________ ______________________________
Escrow Agent Received by Email Address Date

______________________________ ______________________________
Address Phone

______________________________ ______________________________
City State Zip Fax

ADDITIONAL EARNEST MONEY RECEIPT

Receipt of $______________ additional earnest money in the form of ______________________
is acknowledged.

______________________________ ______________________________
Escrow Agent Received by Email Address Date/Time

______________________________ ______________________________
Address Phone

______________________________ ______________________________
City State Zip Fax

AMENDMENT
Amendment to a Promulgated Contract

Amendment to Contract (Form 39-11, effective 07/01/2026)

PROMULGATED BY THE TEXAS REAL ESTATE COMMISSION (TREC) 05-04-2026

TREC
TEXAS REAL ESTATE COMMISSION

AMENDMENT

TO CONTRACT CONCERNING THE PROPERTY AT

EQUAL HOUSING OPPORTUNITY

____

(Street Address and City)

Seller and Buyer amend the contract as follows: (check each applicable box)

❑(1) The Sales Price in Paragraph 3 of the contract is:
A. Cash portion of Sales Price payable by Buyer at closing .... $______________
B. Sum of financing described in the contract .... $______________
C. Sales Price (Sum of A and B) .... $______________

❑(2) In addition to any repairs and treatments otherwise required by the contract, Seller, at Seller's expense, shall complete the following repairs and treatments: (Notice: Paragraph 7 of the contract governs the completion, delivery of documentation, and transfer of warranties of repairs and treatments.)____
____
____
____.

❑(3) The date in Paragraph 9 of the contract is changed to ________________________, 20______.

❑(4) The amount in Paragraph 12A(1)(b) of the contract is changed to $________________.

❑(5) The amounts in Paragraph 12B of the contract are changed as follows (check applicable boxes):
❑ (1) Seller will pay (check one box only): ❑ $_________ or ❑ _____% of the Sales Price.
❑ (2) Buyer will pay (check one box only): ❑ $_________ or ❑ _____% of the Sales Price.

❑(6) The cost of lender required repairs and treatment, as itemized on the attached list, will be paid as follows: $ ______________________ by Seller; $ ______________________ by Buyer.

❑(7) Buyer has paid Seller an additional option fee of $ _________________ for an extension of the unrestricted right to terminate the contract on or before 5:00 p.m. on ______________________, 20______. This additional option fee ❑ will ❑ will not be credited to the Sales Price.

❑(8) Buyer waives the unrestricted right to terminate the contract for which the option fee was paid.

❑(9) The date for Buyer to give written notice to Seller that Buyer cannot obtain Buyer Approval as set forth in the Third Party Financing Addendum is changed to ________________, 20______.

❑(10) **Other Modifications**: (Real estate brokers and sales agents are prohibited from practicing law.)_____
____
____
____.

CONSULT AN ATTORNEY BEFORE SIGNING: TREC rules prohibit real estate brokers and sales agents from giving legal advice. READ THIS FORM CAREFULLY.

EXECUTED the ______day of ____________________________, 20_____ . (BROKER: FILL IN THE DATE OF FINAL ACCEPTANCE.)

______________________ Buyer	______________________ Seller
______________________ Buyer	______________________ Seller

TREC
TEXAS REAL ESTATE COMMISSION

This form has been approved by the Texas Real Estate Commission for use with similarly approved or promulgated contract forms. Such approval relates to this form only. TREC forms are intended for use only by trained real estate license holders. No representation is made as to the legal validity or adequacy of any provision in any specific transactions. It is not intended for complex transactions. Texas Real Estate Commission, P.O. Box 12188, Austin, TX 78711-2188, 512-936-3000 (http://www.trec.texas.gov) TREC No. 39-11. This form replaces TREC No. 39-10.

PROMULGATED ADDENDA

Addenda Attached to a Promulgated Contract

Addendum Concerning Right to Terminate Due to Lender's Appraisal (Form 49-1, effective 03/01/2019)

Addendum Containing Notice of Obligation to Pay Improvement District Assessment (Form 53-0, effective 09/01/2021)

Addendum for "Back-Up" Contract (Form 11-9, effective 07/01/2026)

Addendum for Authorizing Hydrostatic Testing (Form 48-1, effective 03/01/2020)

Addendum for Coastal Area Property (Form 33-2, effective 12/05/2011)

Addendum for Property in a Propane Gas System Service Area (Form 47-0, effective 02/01/2014)

Addendum for Property Located Seaward of the Gulf Intercoastal Waterway (Form 34-4, effective 12/05/2011)

Addendum for Property Subject to Mandatory Membership in a Property Owners Association (Form 36-11, effective 07/01/2026)

Addendum for Release of Liability on Assumed Loan and/or Restoration of Seller's VA Entitlement (Form 12-3, effective 12/05/2011)

Addendum for Reservation of Oil, Gas, and Other Minerals (Form 44-3, effective 02/01/2023)

Addendum for Sale of Other Property by Buyer (Form 10-6, effective 12/05/2011)

Addendum for Section 1031 Exchange (Form 60-0, effective 01/03/2025)

Addendum for Seller's Disclosure of Information on Lead-Based Paint and Lead-Based Paint Hazards as Required by Federal Law (Form 56-0, effective 05/28/2026)

Addendum Regarding Fixture Leases (Form 52-1, effective 02/01/2023)

Addendum Regarding Residential Leases (Form 51-1, effective 02/01/2023)

Buyer's Temporary Residential Lease (Form 16-7, effective 01/05/2026)

Environmental Assessment, Threatened or Endangered Species, and Wetlands Addendum (Form 28-2, effective 12/05/2011)

Loan Assumption Addendum (Form 41-3, effective 02/01/2023)

Non-Realty Items Addendum (Form 57-0, effective 09/03/2025)

Seller Financing Addendum (Form 26-8, effective 02/01/2023)

Seller's Temporary Residential Lease (Form 15-7, effective 01/05/2026)

Short Sale Addendum (Form 45-2, effective 04/01/2021)

Third Party Financing Addendum (Form 40-11, effective 01/03/2025)

PROMULGATED BY THE TEXAS REAL ESTATE COMMISSION (TREC) 11-15-18

ADDENDUM CONCERNING RIGHT TO TERMINATE DUE TO LENDER'S APPRAISAL

Use only if the Third Party Financing Addendum is attached to the contract and the transaction does not involve FHA insured or VA guaranteed financing

CONCERNING THE PROPERTY AT:____
(Street Address and City)

The financing described in the Third Party Financing Addendum attached to the contract for the sale of the above-referenced Property does not involve FHA or VA financing. *(Check one box only)*

☐ (1) **WAIVER.** Buyer waives Buyer's right to terminate the contract under Paragraph 2B of the Third Party Financing Addendum if Property Approval is not obtained because the opinion of value in the appraisal does not satisfy lender's underwriting requirements.

If the lender reduces the amount of the loan due to the opinion of value, the cash portion of Sales Price is increased by the amount the loan is reduced due to the appraisal.

☐ (2) **PARTIAL WAIVER.** Buyer waives Buyer's right to terminate the contract under Paragraph 2B of the Third Party Financing Addendum if:

(i) Property Approval is not obtained because the opinion of value in the appraisal does not satisfy lender's underwriting requirements; and

(ii) the opinion of value is $________________ or more.

If the lender reduces the amount of the loan due to the opinion of value, the cash portion of Sales Price is increased by the amount the loan is reduced due to the appraisal.

☐ (3) **ADDITIONAL RIGHT TO TERMINATE.** In addition to Buyer's right to terminate under Paragraph 2B of the Third Party Financing Addendum, Buyer may terminate the contract within _______ days after the Effective Date if:

(i) the appraised value, according to the appraisal obtained by Buyer's lender, is less than $________________; and

(ii) Buyer delivers a copy of the appraisal to the Seller.

If Buyer terminates under this paragraph, the earnest money will be refunded to Buyer.

______________________________ ______________________________
Buyer Seller

______________________________ ______________________________
Buyer Seller

TREC NO. 49-1

PROMULGATED BY THE TEXAS REAL ESTATE COMMISSION (TREC) 11-08-2021

ADDENDUM CONTAINING NOTICE OF OBLIGATION TO PAY IMPROVEMENT DISTRICT ASSESSMENT TO ______________________ ,TEXAS CONCERNING THE FOLLOWING PROPERTY

(insert name of municipality or county levying assessment)

____
(insert property address)

As the purchaser of the real property described above, you are obligated to pay assessments to ______________________ (insert name of municipality or county, as applicable), Texas, for the costs of a portion of a public improvement or services project (the "Authorized Improvements") undertaken for the benefit of the property within ______________________ (insert name of public improvement district) (the "District") created under ______________________ (insert Subchapter A, Chapter 372, Local Government Code, or Chapter 382, Local Government Code, as applicable).

AN ASSESSMENT HAS BEEN LEVIED AGAINST YOUR PROPERTY FOR THE AUTHORIZED IMPROVEMENTS, WHICH MAY BE PAID IN FULL AT ANY TIME. IF THE ASSESSMENT IS NOT PAID IN FULL, IT WILL BE DUE AND PAYABLE IN ANNUAL INSTALLMENTS THAT WILL VARY FROM YEAR TO YEAR DEPENDING ON THE AMOUNT OF INTEREST PAID, COLLECTION COSTS, ADMINISTRATIVE COSTS, AND DELINQUENCY COSTS.

The exact amount of the assessment may be obtained from ______________________ (insert name of municipality or county, as applicable). The exact amount of each annual installment will be approved each year by ______________________ (insert name of city council or county commissioners court, as applicable) in the annual service plan update for the district. More information about the assessments, including the amounts and due dates, may be obtained from ______________________ (insert name of municipality or county, as applicable).

Your failure to pay any assessment or any annual installment may result in penalties and interest being added to what you owe or in a lien on and the foreclosure of your property.

Signature of Seller	Date	Signature of Seller	Date

The undersigned purchaser acknowledges receipt of this notice before the effective date of a binding contract for the purchase of the real property at the address described above.

Signature of Buyer	Date	Signature of Buyer	Date

TREC
TEXAS REAL ESTATE COMMISSION

This form has been approved by the Texas Real Estate Commission for use with similarly approved or promulgated contract forms. Such approval relates to this form only. TREC forms are intended for use only by trained real estate license holders. No representation is made as to the legal validity or adequacy of any provision in any specific transactions. It is not suitable for complex transactions. Texas Real Estate Commission, P.O. Box 12188, Austin, TX 78711-2188, (512) 936-3000 (http://www.trec.texas.gov) TREC No. 53-0.

PROMULGATED BY THE TEXAS REAL ESTATE COMMISSION (TREC) 05-04-2026

ADDENDUM FOR "BACK-UP" CONTRACT

TO CONTRACT CONCERNING THE PROPERTY AT

____
(Address of Property)

A. The contract to which this Addendum is attached (the Back-Up Contract) is binding upon execution by the parties, and the earnest money and any option fee must be paid as follows:

(1) Buyer shall deliver the earnest money and option fee as provided in Paragraph 5 of the Back-Up Contract; and

(2) Buyer shall deliver additional earnest money of $_________ and an additional option fee of $_________ to Escrow Agent within ______ days after the Amended Effective Date of the Back-Up Contract defined below.

B. If the last day to deliver the additional earnest money or the additional option fee falls on a Saturday, Sunday, or Legal Holiday, the time to deliver the additional earnest money or additional option fee, as applicable, is extended until the end of the next day that is not a Saturday, Sunday, or Legal Holiday.

C. The amount(s) Escrow Agent receives under Paragraph A(2) of this Addendum shall be applied first to the additional option fee and then to the additional earnest money.

D. Buyer authorizes Escrow Agent to release and deliver the additional option fee to Seller at any time without further notice to or consent from Buyer, and releases Escrow Agent from liability for delivery of the additional option fee to Seller. The additional option fee will be credited to the Sales Price at closing.

E. FAILURE TO TIMELY DELIVER ADDITIONAL EARNEST MONEY: If Buyer fails to deliver the additional earnest money within the time required, Seller may terminate this contract or exercise Seller's remedies under Paragraph 15, or both, by providing notice to Buyer before Buyer delivers the additional earnest money.

F. FAILURE TO TIMELY DELIVER ADDITIONAL OPTION FEE: If Buyer fails to deliver any required additional option fee within the time required, Buyer shall not have the unrestricted right to terminate this contract as provided in Paragraph 5(B) of the contract.

G. The Back-Up Contract is contingent upon the termination of a previous contract (the First Contract) dated ____________________________, 20______, for the sale of Property. Except as provided by this Addendum, neither party is required to perform under the Back-Up Contract while it is contingent upon the termination of the First Contract.

H. If the First Contract does not terminate on or before __________________________, 20______, the Back-Up Contract terminates and the earnest money will be refunded to Buyer. Seller must notify Buyer immediately of the termination of the First Contract. For purposes of performance, the Effective Date of the Back-Up Contract changes to the date Seller delivers notice of termination of the First Contract to Buyer (Amended Effective Date).

I. An amendment or modification of the First Contract will not terminate the First Contract.

J. If Buyer has the unrestricted right to terminate the Back-Up Contract, the time for giving notice of termination begins on the Effective Date of the Back-Up Contract, continues after the Amended Effective Date and ends upon the expiration of Buyer's unrestricted right to terminate the Back-Up Contract.

Initialed for identification by Buyer__________ and Seller__________ TREC No. 11-9

K. For purposes of this Addendum, time is of the essence. Strict compliance with the times for performance stated herein is required.

______________________________ Buyer	______________________________ Seller
______________________________ Buyer	______________________________ Seller

TREC
TEXAS REAL ESTATE COMMISSION

TREC

TEXAS REAL ESTATE COMMISSION

PROMULGATED BY THE TEXAS REAL ESTATE COMMISSION (TREC)

11-19-19

ADDENDUM FOR AUTHORIZING HYDROSTATIC TESTING

EQUAL HOUSING OPPORTUNITY

CONCERNING THE PROPERTY AT:____
(Street Address and City)

Consult a licensed plumber about the scope of hydrostatic testing and risks associated with the testing before signing this form.

A. **AUTHORIZATION:** Seller authorizes Buyer, at Buyer's expense, to engage a licensed plumber to perform a hydrostatic plumbing test on the Property.

B. **ALLOCATION OF RISK**:

- ☐ (1) Seller shall be liable for damages caused by the hydrostatic plumbing test.
- ☐ (2) Buyer shall be liable for damages caused by the hydrostatic plumbing test.
- ☐ (3) Buyer shall be liable for damages caused by the hydrostatic plumbing test in an amount not to exceed $______________________.

______________________________	______________________________
Buyer	Seller
______________________________	______________________________
Buyer	Seller

TREC

TEXAS REAL ESTATE COMMISSION

The form of this addendum has been approved by the Texas Real Estate Commission for use only with similarly approved or promulgated forms of contracts. Such approval relates to this contract form only. TREC forms are intended for use only by trained real estate license holders. No representation is made as to the legal validity or adequacy of any provision in any specific transactions. It is not intended for complex transactions. Texas Real Estate Commission, P.O. Box 12188, Austin, TX 78711-2188, (512) 936-3000 (www.trec.texas.gov) TREC No. 48-1.

PROMULGATED BY THE TEXAS REAL ESTATE COMMISSION (TREC)

12-05-11

ADDENDUM FOR COASTAL AREA PROPERTY

(SECTION 33.135, TEXAS NATURAL RESOURCES CODE)

TO CONTRACT CONCERNING THE PROPERTY AT

____

(Address of Property)

NOTICE REGARDING COASTAL AREA PROPERTY

1. The real property described in and subject to this contract adjoins and shares a common boundary with the tidally influenced submerged lands of the state. The boundary is subject to change and can be determined accurately only by a survey on the ground made by a licensed state land surveyor in accordance with the original grant from the sovereign. The owner of the property described in this contract may gain or lose portions of the tract because of changes in the boundary.

2. The seller, transferor, or grantor has no knowledge of any prior fill as it relates to the property described in and subject to this contract except:______________________________________
____
____.

3. State law prohibits the use, encumbrance, construction, or placing of any structure in, on, or over state-owned submerged lands below the applicable tide line, without proper permission.

4. The purchaser or grantee is hereby advised to seek the advice of an attorney or other qualified person as to the legal nature and effect of the facts set forth in this notice on the property described in and subject to this contract. Information regarding the location of the applicable tide line as to the property described in and subject to this contract may be obtained from the surveying division of the General Land Office in Austin.

______________________ Buyer	______________________ Seller
______________________ Buyer	______________________ Seller

PROMULGATED BY THE TEXAS REAL ESTATE COMMISSION (TREC) 2-10-2014

TREC
TEXAS REAL ESTATE COMMISSION

EQUAL HOUSING OPPORTUNITY

ADDENDUM FOR PROPERTY IN A PROPANE GAS SYSTEM SERVICE AREA

(Section 141.010, Utilities Code)

CONCERNING THE PROPERTY AT ______________________________
(Street Address and City)

NOTICE

The above referenced real property that you are about to purchase may be located in a propane gas system service area, which is authorized by law to provide propane gas service to the properties in the area pursuant to Chapter 141, Utilities Code. If your property is located in a propane gas system service area, there may be special costs or charges that you will be required to pay before you can receive propane gas service. There may be a period required to construct lines or other facilities necessary to provide propane gas service to your property. You are advised to determine if the property is in a propane gas system service area and contact the distribution system retailer to determine the cost that you will be required to pay and the period, if any, that is required to provide propane gas service to your property.

Buyer hereby acknowledges receipt of this notice at or before execution of a binding contract for the purchase of the above referenced real property or at the closing of the real property.

Section 141.010(a), Utilities Code, requires this notice to include a copy of the notice the distribution system retailer is required to record in the real property records. A copy of the recorded notice is attached.

NOTE: Seller can obtain a copy of the required recorded notice from the county clerk's office where the property is located or from the distribution system retailer.

Buyer	Date	Seller	Date
Buyer	Date	Seller	Date

TREC
TEXAS REAL ESTATE COMMISSION

PROMULGATED BY THE TEXAS REAL ESTATE COMMISSION (TREC) 12-05-11

TREC
TEXAS REAL ESTATE COMMISSION

EQUAL HOUSING OPPORTUNITY

ADDENDUM FOR PROPERTY LOCATED SEAWARD OF THE GULF INTRACOASTAL WATERWAY

(SECTION 61.025, TEXAS NATURAL RESOURCES CODE)

TO CONTRACT CONCERNING THE PROPERTY AT

____

(Address of Property)

DISCLOSURE NOTICE CONCERNING LEGAL AND ECONOMIC RISKS OF PURCHASING COASTAL REAL PROPERTY NEAR A BEACH

WARNING: THE FOLLOWING NOTICE OF POTENTIAL RISKS OF ECONOMIC LOSS TO YOU AS THE PURCHASER OF COASTAL REAL PROPERTY IS REQUIRED BY STATE LAW.

- READ THIS NOTICE CAREFULLY. DO NOT SIGN THIS CONTRACT UNTIL YOU FULLY UNDERSTAND THE RISKS YOU ARE ASSUMING.
- BY PURCHASING THIS PROPERTY, YOU MAY BE ASSUMING ECONOMIC RISKS OVER AND ABOVE THE RISKS INVOLVED IN PURCHASING INLAND REAL PROPERTY.
- IF YOU OWN A STRUCTURE LOCATED ON COASTAL REAL PROPERTY NEAR A GULF COAST BEACH, IT MAY COME TO BE LOCATED ON THE PUBLIC BEACH BECAUSE OF COASTAL EROSION AND STORM EVENTS.
- AS THE OWNER OF A STRUCTURE LOCATED ON THE PUBLIC BEACH, YOU COULD BE SUED BY THE STATE OF TEXAS AND ORDERED TO REMOVE THE STRUCTURE.
- THE COSTS OF REMOVING A STRUCTURE FROM THE PUBLIC BEACH AND ANY OTHER ECONOMIC LOSS INCURRED BECAUSE OF A REMOVAL ORDER WOULD BE SOLELY YOUR RESPONSIBILITY.

The real property described in this contract is located seaward of the Gulf Intracoastal Waterway to its southernmost point and then seaward of the longitudinal line also known as 97 degrees, 12', 19" which runs southerly to the international boundary from the intersection of the centerline of the Gulf Intracoastal Waterway and the Brownsville Ship Channel. If the property is in close proximity to a beach fronting the Gulf of Mexico, the purchaser is hereby advised that the public has acquired a right of use or easement to or over the area of any public beach by prescription, dedication, or presumption, or has retained a right by virtue of continuous right in the public since time immemorial, as recognized in law and custom.

The extreme seaward boundary of natural vegetation that spreads continuously inland customarily marks the landward boundary of the public easement. If there is no clearly marked natural vegetation line, the landward boundary of the easement is as provided by Sections 61.016 and 61.017, Natural Resources Code.

Much of the Gulf of Mexico coastline is eroding at rates of more than five feet per year. Erosion rates for all Texas Gulf property subject to the open beaches act are available from the Texas General Land Office.

State law prohibits any obstruction, barrier, restraint, or interference with the use of the public easement, including the placement of structures seaward of the landward boundary of the easement. OWNERS OF STRUCTURES ERECTED SEAWARD OF THE VEGETATION LINE (OR OTHER APPLICABLE EASEMENT BOUNDARY) OR THAT BECOME SEAWARD OF THE VEGETATION LINE AS A RESULT OF PROCESSES SUCH AS SHORELINE EROSION ARE SUBJECT TO A LAWSUIT BY THE STATE OF TEXAS TO REMOVE THE STRUCTURES.

The purchaser is hereby notified that the purchaser should: (1) determine the rate of shoreline erosion in the vicinity of the real property; and (2) seek the advice of an attorney or other qualified person before executing this contract or instrument of conveyance as to the relevance of these statutes and facts to the value of the property the purchaser is hereby purchasing or contracting to purchase.

Buyer	Seller
Buyer	Seller

TREC
TEXAS REAL ESTATE COMMISSION

PROMULGATED BY THE TEXAS REAL ESTATE COMMISSION (TREC)

05-04-2026

ADDENDUM FOR PROPERTY SUBJECT TO MANDATORY MEMBERSHIP IN A PROPERTY OWNERS ASSOCIATION

(NOT FOR USE WITH CONDOMINIUMS)

ADDENDUM TO CONTRACT CONCERNING THE PROPERTY AT

____

(Street Address and City)

____

(Name of Property Owners Association, (Association) and Phone Number)

A. SUBDIVISION INFORMATION: "Subdivision Information" means: (i) a current copy of the restrictions applying to the subdivision and bylaws and rules of the Association, and (ii) a resale certificate, all of which are described by Section 207.003 of the Texas Property Code.

(Check only one box):

❑ 1. Within ____________ days after the effective date of the contract, Seller shall obtain, pay for, and deliver the Subdivision Information to the Buyer. If Seller delivers the Subdivision Information, Buyer may terminate the contract within 3 days after Buyer receives the Subdivision Information or prior to closing, whichever occurs first, and the earnest money will be refunded to Buyer. If Buyer does not receive the Subdivision Information, Buyer, as Buyer's sole remedy, may terminate the contract at any time prior to closing and the earnest money will be refunded to Buyer.

❑ 2. Within ____________ days after the Effective Date of the contract, Buyer shall obtain the Subdivision Information at Buyer's expense. Buyer is deemed to receive the Subdivision Information on the date of actual receipt or date specified in this paragraph, whichever is earlier. Buyer may terminate the contract within 3 days after Buyer receives the Subdivision Information or prior to closing, whichever occurs first, and the earnest money will be refunded to Buyer.

❑ 3. Buyer has received and approved the Subdivision Information before signing the contract. Buyer ❑ does ❑ does not require an updated resale certificate. If Buyer requires an updated resale certificate, Seller, at Buyer's expense, shall deliver it to Buyer within 10 days after receiving payment for the updated resale certificate from Buyer. Buyer may terminate this contract and the earnest money will be refunded to Buyer if Seller fails to deliver the updated resale certificate within the time required.

❑ 4. Buyer does not require delivery of the Subdivision Information.

The title company or its agent is authorized to act on behalf of the parties to obtain the Subdivision Information ONLY upon receipt of the required fee for the Subdivision Information from the party obligated to pay.

B. MATERIAL CHANGES. If Seller becomes aware of any material changes in the Subdivision Information, Seller shall promptly give notice to Buyer. Buyer may terminate the contract prior to closing by giving written notice to Seller if: (i) any of the Subdivision Information provided was not true; or (ii) any material adverse change in the Subdivision Information occurs prior to closing, and the earnest money will be refunded to Buyer.

C. FEES AND DEPOSITS FOR RESERVES: Buyer shall pay any and all Association fees, deposits, reserves, and other charges associated with the transfer of the Property not to exceed $______________ and Seller shall pay any excess. This paragraph does not apply to: (i) regular periodic maintenance fees, assessments, or dues (including prepaid items) that are prorated by Paragraph 13, and (ii) costs and fees provided by Paragraphs A and D. If this paragraph conflicts with any allocation of charges in the Subdivision Information, this paragraph will control.

D. AUTHORIZATION: Seller authorizes the Association to release and provide the Subdivision Information and any updated resale certificate if requested by the Buyer, the Title Company, or any broker to this sale. If Buyer does not require the Subdivision Information or an updated resale certificate, and the Title Company requires information from the Association (such as the status of dues, special assessments, violations of covenants and restrictions, and a waiver of any right of first refusal), ❑ Buyer ❑ Seller shall pay the Title Company the cost of obtaining the information prior to the Title Company ordering the information.

NOTICE TO BUYER REGARDING REPAIRS BY THE ASSOCIATION: The Association may have the sole responsibility to make certain repairs to the Property. If you are concerned about the condition of any part of the Property which the Association is required to repair, you should not sign the contract unless you are satisfied that the Association will make the desired repairs.

______________________ Buyer	______________________ Seller
______________________ Buyer	______________________ Seller

PROMULGATED BY THE TEXAS REAL ESTATE COMMISSION (TREC) 12-05-11

EQUAL HOUSING OPPORTUNITY

ADDENDUM FOR RELEASE OF LIABILITY ON ASSUMED LOAN AND/OR RESTORATION OF SELLER'S VA ENTITLEMENT

TO CONTRACT CONCERNING THE PROPERTY AT

____

(Address of Property)

☐ **A. RELEASE OF SELLER'S LIABILITY ON LOAN TO BE ASSUMED:**

Within ____________ days after the effective date of this contract Seller and Buyer shall apply for release of Seller's liability from (a) any conventional lender, (b) VA and any lender whose loan has been guaranteed by VA, or (c) FHA and any lender whose loan has been insured by FHA. Seller and Buyer shall furnish all required information and documents. If any release of liability has not been approved by the Closing Date: (check one box only)

☐ (1) This contract will terminate and the earnest money will be refunded to Buyer.

☐ (2) Failure to obtain release approval will not delay closing.

☐ **B. RESTORATION OF SELLER'S ENTITLEMENT FOR VA LOAN:**

Within ___________ days after the effective date of this contract Seller and Buyer shall apply for restoration of Seller's VA entitlement and shall furnish all information and documents required by VA. If restoration has not been approved by the Closing Date: (check one box only)

☐ (1) This contract will terminate and the earnest money will be refunded to Buyer.

☐ (2) Failure to obtain restoration approval will not delay closing.

NOTICE: VA will not restore Seller's VA entitlement unless Buyer: (a) is a veteran, (b) has sufficient unused VA entitlement and (c) is otherwise qualified. If Seller desires restoration of VA entitlement, paragraphs A and B should be used.

Seller shall pay the cost of securing the release and restoration.

Seller's deed will contain any loan assumption clause required by FHA, VA or any lender.

______________________	______________________
Buyer	Seller
______________________	______________________
Buyer	Seller

This form has been approved by the Texas Real Estate Commission for use with similarly approved or promulgated contract forms. Such approval relates to this form only. TREC forms are intended for use only by trained real estate licensees. No representation is made as to the legal validity or adequacy of any provision in any specific transactions. It is not suitable for complex transactions. Texas Real Estate Commission, P.O. Box 12188, Austin, TX 78711-2188, 512-936-3000 (http://www.trec.texas.gov) TREC No. 12-3. This form replaces TREC No. 12-2.

PROMULGATED BY THE TEXAS REAL ESTATE COMMISSION (TREC) 11-07-2022

TREC
TEXAS REAL ESTATE COMMISSION

ADDENDUM FOR RESERVATION OF OIL, GAS, AND OTHER MINERALS

EQUAL HOUSING OPPORTUNITY

ADDENDUM TO CONTRACT CONCERNING THE PROPERTY AT

____

(Street Address and City)

NOTICE: For use ONLY if Seller reserves all or a portion of the Mineral Estate.

A. "Mineral Estate" means all oil, gas, and other minerals in and under and that may be produced from the Property, any royalty under any existing or future mineral lease covering any part of the Property, executive rights (including the right to sign a mineral lease covering any part of the Property), implied rights of ingress and egress, exploration and development rights, production and drilling rights, mineral lease payments, and all related rights and benefits. The Mineral Estate does NOT include water, sand, gravel, limestone, building stone, caliche, surface shale, near-surface lignite, and iron, but DOES include the reasonable use of these surface materials for mining, drilling, exploring, operating, developing, or removing the oil, gas, and other minerals from the Property.

B. *Subject to Section C below,* the Mineral Estate owned by Seller, if any, will be conveyed unless reserved as follows (check one box only):

❑ (1) Seller reserves all of the Mineral Estate owned by Seller.

❑ (2) Seller reserves an undivided ________interest in the Mineral Estate owned by Seller. *NOTE: If Seller does not own all of the Mineral Estate, Seller reserves only this percentage or fraction of Seller's interest.*

C. Seller ❑ does ❑ does *not* waive rights of ingress and egress and of reasonable use of the Property (including surface materials) that are part of the Mineral Estate for mining, drilling, exploring, operating, developing, or removing the oil, gas, and other minerals. *NOTE: Surface rights that may be held by other owners of the Mineral Estate who are not parties to this transaction (including existing mineral lessees) will NOT be affected by Seller's election. Seller's failure to complete Section C will be deemed an election to convey all surface rights described herein.*

D. If Seller does not reserve all of Seller's interest in the Mineral Estate, Seller shall, within 7 days after the Effective Date, provide Buyer with the current contact information of any existing mineral lessee known to Seller.

<u>IMPORTANT NOTICE</u>: The Mineral Estate affects important rights, the full extent of which may be unknown to Seller. A full examination of the title to the Property completed by an attorney with expertise in this area is the only proper means for determining title to the Mineral Estate with certainty. In addition, attempts to convey or reserve certain interest out of the Mineral Estate separately from other rights and benefits owned by Seller may have unintended consequences. Precise contract language is essential to preventing disagreements between present and future owners of the Mineral Estate.

If Seller or Buyer has any questions about their respective rights and interests in the Mineral Estate and how such rights and interests may be affected by this contract, they are strongly encouraged to consult an attorney with expertise in this area.

CONSULT AN ATTORNEY BEFORE SIGNING: TREC rules prohibit real estate brokers and sales agents from giving legal advice. READ THIS FORM CAREFULLY.

________________________	________________________
Buyer	Seller
________________________	________________________
Buyer	Seller

TREC
TEXAS REAL ESTATE COMMISSION

PROMULGATED BY THE TEXAS REAL ESTATE COMMISSION (TREC)

12-05-11

EQUAL HOUSING OPPORTUNITY

ADDENDUM FOR SALE OF OTHER PROPERTY BY BUYER

TO CONTRACT CONCERNING THE PROPERTY AT

____

(Address of Property)

A. The contract is contingent upon Buyer's receipt of the proceeds from the sale of Buyer's property at____ (Address) on or before ____________________, 20______ (the Contingency). If the Contingency is not satisfied or waived by Buyer by the above date, the contract will terminate automatically and the earnest money will be refunded to Buyer.

NOTICE: The date inserted in this Paragraph should be no later than the Closing Date specified in Paragraph 9 of the contract.

B. If Seller accepts a written offer to sell the Property, Seller shall notify Buyer (1) of such acceptance AND (2) that Seller requires Buyer to waive the Contingency. Buyer must waive the Contingency on or before the ______________ day after Seller's notice to Buyer; otherwise the contract will terminate automatically and the earnest money will be refunded to Buyer.

C. Buyer may waive the Contingency only by notifying Seller of the waiver and depositing $__________ with escrow agent as additional earnest money. All notices and waivers must be in writing and are effective when delivered in accordance with the contract.

D. If Buyer waives the Contingency and fails to close and fund solely due to Buyer's non-receipt of proceeds from Buyer's property described in Paragraph A above, Buyer will be in default. If such default occurs, Seller may exercise the remedies specified in Paragraph 15 of the contract.

E. For purposes of this Addendum time is of the essence; strict compliance with the times for performance stated herein is required.

______________________ Buyer	______________________ Seller
______________________ Buyer	______________________ Seller

PROMULGATED BY THE TEXAS REAL ESTATE COMMISSION (TREC) 11-04-2024

TREC
TEXAS REAL ESTATE COMMISSION

EQUAL HOUSING OPPORTUNITY

ADDENDUM FOR SECTION 1031 EXCHANGE

CONCERNING THE PROPERTY AT:____
(Street Address and City)

A. ☐ Seller ☐ Buyer intends to use this Property to accomplish an exchange of like-kind properties under Section 1031 of the Internal Revenue Code, as amended.

B. The parties will reasonably cooperate to accomplish the exchange provided: (i) the non-exchanging party will not incur any additional expense or liability; and (ii) closing will not be delayed as a result of the exchange.

______________________________	______________________________
Buyer	Seller
______________________________	______________________________
Buyer	Seller

TREC
TEXAS REAL ESTATE COMMISSION

APPROVED BY THE TEXAS REAL ESTATE COMMISSION 05-04-2026

ADDENDUM FOR SELLER'S DISCLOSURE OF INFORMATION ON LEAD-BASED PAINT AND LEAD-BASED PAINT HAZARDS AS REQUIRED BY FEDERAL LAW

CONCERNING THE PROPERTY AT ____
(Street Address and City)

A. LEAD WARNING STATEMENT: "Every purchaser of any interest in residential real property on which a residential dwelling was built prior to 1978 is notified that such property may present exposure to lead from lead-based paint that may place young children at risk of developing lead poisoning. Lead poisoning in young children may produce permanent neurological damage, including learning disabilities, reduced intelligence quotient, behavioral problems, and impaired memory. Lead poisoning also poses a particular risk to pregnant women. The seller of any interest in residential real property is required to provide the buyer with any information on lead-based paint hazards from risk assessments or inspections in the seller's possession and notify the buyer of any known lead-based paint hazards. A risk assessment or inspection for possible lead-paint hazards is recommended prior to purchase."

NOTICE: Inspector must be properly certified as required by federal law.

B. SELLER'S DISCLOSURE:

1. PRESENCE OF LEAD-BASED PAINT AND/OR LEAD-BASED PAINT HAZARDS (check one box only):
   - ☐ (a) Known lead-based paint and/or lead-based paint hazards are present in the Property (explain): __________
   ____.
   - ☐ (b) Seller has no actual knowledge of lead-based paint and/or lead-based paint hazards in the Property.
2. RECORDS AND REPORTS AVAILABLE TO SELLER (check one box only):
   - ☐ (a) Seller has provided the purchaser with all available records and reports pertaining to lead-based paint and/or lead-based paint hazards in the Property (list documents): ______________________
   ____.
   - ☐ (b) Seller has no reports or records pertaining to lead-based paint and/or lead-based paint hazards in the Property.

C. BUYER'S RIGHTS (check one box only)**:**

- ☐ 1. Buyer waives the opportunity to conduct a risk assessment or inspection of the Property for the presence of lead-based paint or lead-based paint hazards.
- ☐ 2. Within ten days after the effective date of this contract, Buyer may have the Property inspected by inspectors selected by Buyer. If lead-based paint or lead-based paint hazards are present, Buyer may terminate this contract by giving Seller written notice within 14 days after the effective date of this contract, and the earnest money will be refunded to Buyer.

D. BUYER'S ACKNOWLEDGMENT (check applicable boxes)**:**

- ☐ 1. Buyer has received copies of all information listed above.
- ☐ 2. Buyer has received the pamphlet *Protect Your Family from Lead in Your Home*.

E. BROKERS' ACKNOWLEDGMENT: Brokers have informed Seller of Seller's obligations under 42 U.S.C. 4852d to: (a) provide Buyer with the federally approved pamphlet on lead poisoning prevention; (b) complete this addendum; (c) disclose any known lead-based paint and/or lead-based paint hazards in the Property; (d) deliver all records and reports to Buyer pertaining to lead-based paint and/or lead-based paint hazards in the Property; (e) provide Buyer a period of up to 10 days to have the Property inspected; and (f) retain a completed copy of this addendum for at least 3 years following the sale. Brokers are aware of their responsibility to ensure compliance.

F. CERTIFICATION OF ACCURACY: The following persons have reviewed the information above and certify, to the best of their knowledge, that the information they have provided is true and accurate.

Buyer	Date	Seller	Date
Buyer	Date	Seller	Date
Buyer's Broker	Date	Seller's Broker	Date

The form of this addendum has been approved by the Texas Real Estate Commission for use only with similarly approved or promulgated forms of contracts. Such approval relates to this contract form only. TREC forms are intended for use only by trained real estate license holders. No representation is made as to the legal validity or adequacy of any provision in any specific transactions. It is not suitable for complex transactions. Texas Real Estate Commission, P.O. Box 12188, Austin, TX 78711-2188, 512-936-3000 (http://www.trec.texas.gov)

TREC NO. 56-0

PROMULGATED BY THE TEXAS REAL ESTATE COMMISSION (TREC)

ADDENDUM REGARDING FIXTURE LEASES

EQUAL HOUSING OPPORTUNITY

CONCERNING THE PROPERTY AT: ____
(Street Address and City)

A. Leased Fixtures are those fixtures in or on the Property that Seller leases and does not own, specifically the: ❑ solar panels, ❑ propane tanks, ❑ water softener, ❑ security system, ❑ ______________ (collectively, the Leased Fixtures). All rights to the Leased Fixtures are governed by Fixture Leases.

(1) At closing, Buyer shall assume and Seller shall assign to Buyer the following Fixture Leases: ❑ solar panel lease, ❑ propane tank lease, ❑ water softener lease, ❑ security system lease, ❑ ________________________________. Buyer shall pay the first $______________ of any cost necessary to assume or receive an assignment of the Fixture Leases and Seller shall pay the remainder. Buyer and Seller agree to sign any documents required by the lessor in the Fixture Leases to assume or assign the Fixture Leases.

(2) Prior to closing, Seller ❑ will ❑ will not remove the Leased Fixtures covered by the Fixture Leases that Buyer does not assume. Seller will repair any damage to the Property caused by any removal. Notice: Any Leased Fixture remaining in the Property are subject to the rights of the lessor under the Fixture Lease.

B. Delivery of Fixture Leases:

❑ (1) Buyer has received a copy of all Fixture Leases Buyer has agreed to assume.

❑ (2) Buyer has not received a copy of all Fixture Leases Buyer has agreed to assume. Seller shall provide a copy of the Fixture Leases within 5 days after the Effective Date. Buyer may terminate the contract within 7 days after the date the Buyer receives the Fixture Leases and the earnest money shall be refunded to Buyer.

❑ (3) Seller provides Buyer with notice of the following oral Fixture Lease(s) (or on the attached exhibit), identifying the name of the lessee(s), rental amount, and term: ________________
____.

C. At closing, there will be no liens or security interests against Leased Fixtures which will not be satisfied out of the sales proceeds except for Leased Fixtures covered by Fixture Leases Buyer agrees to assume.

Notice: Seller and Buyer should consult with the lessor and their attorneys regarding the assignment, assumption, or termination of any Fixture Leases.

______________________________ ______________________________
Buyer Seller

______________________________ ______________________________
Buyer Seller

TREC
TEXAS REAL ESTATE COMMISSION

PROMULGATED BY THE TEXAS REAL ESTATE COMMISSION (TREC) 11-07-2022

TREC
TEXAS REAL ESTATE COMMISSION

ADDENDUM REGARDING RESIDENTIAL LEASES

EQUAL HOUSING OPPORTUNITY

CONCERNING THE PROPERTY AT:______________________________________
(Street Address and City)

"Residential Lease" means any lease of the Property to a tenant including any addendum, amendment, or move-in condition form.

Seller may not execute any new Residential Lease or amend any Residential Lease without Buyer's written consent. Existing Residential Leases will have the following status at closing. (Check only A or B)

❑ A. Termination of Residential Leases: All Residential Leases must be terminated by closing. Seller shall deliver possession of the Property in accordance with Paragraph 10 of the contract with no tenant or other person in possession or having rights to occupy the Property. **[Notice: This paragraph will not amend or terminate any existing lease. Consult an attorney and refer to the Residential Leases for rights to terminate before agreeing to this provision.]**

❑ B. Assignment and Assumption of Residential Leases: Existing Residential Leases shall be assigned by Seller and assumed by Buyer at closing.

(1) Delivery of Residential Leases:

❑ (a) Buyer has received a copy of all Residential Leases.

❑ (b) Buyer has not received a copy of all Residential Leases. Seller shall provide a copy of the Residential Leases within 3 days after the Effective Date. Buyer may terminate the contract within ____days after the date the Buyer receives the Residential Leases and the earnest money shall be refunded to Buyer.

❑ (c) Seller provides Buyer with notice of the following oral Residential Lease(s) (or on the attached exhibit), identifying the name of the tenant(s), rental amount, and term:
____

(2) At closing, Seller shall transfer security deposits (as defined under §92.102, Property Code), if any, to Buyer. At closing, Buyer shall deliver to the tenant a signed statement acknowledging that the Buyer has acquired the Property and is responsible for the return of the security deposit, and specifying the exact dollar amount of the security deposit.

(3) Except as described below, and to Seller's knowledge for each Residential Lease:
(a) the Residential Lease is in full force and effect;
(b) no tenant is in default or in violation of the Residential Lease;
(c) no tenant has prepaid any rent;
(d) no tenant is entitled to any offset against rent;
(e) there are no outstanding tenant claims against Seller involving the Property;
(f) there are no pending disputes with any tenant or prior tenant; and
(g) there are no other agreements, options, or rights outside the Lease between Landlord and Tenant regarding the Property.

Explain if any of the above is not accurate (attach additional sheets if necessary): ______________
____
____
____

(4) Seller will promptly notify Buyer if Seller learns that any statement in Paragraph B(3) becomes untrue after the Effective Date. Seller shall cure the condition making the statement untrue within 7 days after providing the notice to Buyer. If the statement remains untrue beyond the 7-day period, Buyer may, as Buyer's sole remedy, terminate the contract within 5 days after the expiration of the 7-day period, by delivering notice to the Seller and the earnest money will be refunded to Buyer. If Buyer does not terminate the contract within the time required, Buyer waives the right to terminate. The Closing Date will be extended daily as necessary to afford the parties their rights and time to provide notices under this paragraph.

____________________ Buyer	____________________ Seller
____________________ Buyer	____________________ Seller

PROMULGATED BY THE TEXAS REAL ESTATE COMMISSION (TREC) 11-03-2025

(NOTICE: For use only when BUYER occupies the property for no more than 90 days PRIOR to the closing)

TREC
TEXAS REAL ESTATE COMMISSION

BUYER'S TEMPORARY RESIDENTIAL LEASE

EQUAL HOUSING OPPORTUNITY

1. **PARTIES:** The parties to this Lease are____ (Landlord) and ____(Tenant).

2. **LEASE:** Landlord leases to Tenant the Property described in the Contract between Landlord as Seller and Tenant as Buyer known as ____(address).

3. **TERM:** The term of this Lease commences ______________________________ and terminates as specified in Paragraph 18.

4. **RENTAL:** Rental will be $______________ per day. Upon commencement of this Lease, Tenant shall pay to Landlord the full amount of rental of $ _______________ for the anticipated term of the Lease (commencement date to the Closing Date specified in Paragraph 9 of the Contract). If the actual term of this Lease differs from the anticipated term, any additional rent or reimbursement will be paid at closing. No portion of the rental will be applied to payment of any items covered by the Contract.

5. **DEPOSIT:** Tenant has paid to Landlord $____________________ as a deposit to secure performance of this Lease by Tenant. If this Lease is terminated before the Closing Date, Landlord may use the deposit to satisfy Tenant's obligations under this Lease. Landlord shall refund to Tenant any unused portion of the deposit together with an itemized list of all deductions from the deposit within 30 days after Tenant (a) surrenders possession of the Property and (b) provides Landlord written notice of Tenant's forwarding address. If this Lease is terminated by the closing and funding of the sale of the Property, the deposit will be refunded to Tenant at closing and funding.
<u>NOTICE:</u> The deposit must be in addition to the earnest money under the Contract.

6. **UTILITIES:** Tenant shall pay all utility connections, deposits and charges except ____, which Landlord shall pay.

7. **USE OF PROPERTY:** Tenant may use the Property only for residential purposes. Tenant may not assign this Lease or sublet any part of the Property.

8. **PETS:** Tenant may not keep pets on the Property except ______________________________________.

9. **CONDITION OF PROPERTY:** Tenant accepts the Property in its present condition and state of repair, but Landlord shall make all repairs and improvements required by the Contract. If this Lease is terminated prior to closing, Tenant shall surrender possession of the Property to Landlord in its present condition, as improved by Landlord, except normal wear and tear and any casualty loss.

10. **ALTERATIONS:** Tenant may not: (a) make any holes or drive nails into the woodwork, floors, walls or ceilings (b) alter, paint or decorate the Property or (c) install improvements or fixtures without the prior written consent of Landlord. Any improvements or fixtures placed on the Property during the Lease become a part of the Property.

11. **SPECIAL PROVISIONS:** ____
____
____
____
____
____
____
____

12. **INSPECTIONS:** Landlord may enter at reasonable times to inspect, replace, repair or complete the improvements. Tenant shall provide Landlord door keys and access codes to allow access to the Property during the term of the Lease.

13. **LAWS:** Tenant shall comply with all applicable laws, restrictions, ordinances, rules and regulations with respect to the Property.

14. **REPAIRS AND MAINTENANCE:** <u>Except as otherwise provided in this Lease, Tenant shall bear all expense of repairing, replacing and maintaining the Property, including but not limited to the yard, trees, shrubs, and all equipment and appliances, unless otherwise required by the Texas Property Code. Tenant shall promptly repair at Tenant's expense any damage to the Property caused directly or indirectly by any act or omission of the Tenant or any person other than the Landlord, Landlord's agents or invitees.</u>

Initialed for identification by Landlord ________ and Tenant ________

TREC NO. 16-7

15. INDEMNITY: Tenant indemnifies Landlord from the claims of all third parties for injury or damage to the person or property of such third party arising from the use or occupancy of the Property by Tenant. This indemnification includes attorney's fees, costs and expenses incurred by Landlord.

16. INSURANCE: Landlord and Tenant shall each maintain such insurance on the contents and Property as each party may deem appropriate during the term of this Lease. NOTE: CONSULT YOUR INSURANCE AGENT; POSSESSION OF THE PROPERTY BY BUYER AS TENANT MAY CHANGE INSURANCE POLICY COVERAGE.

17. DEFAULT: If Tenant fails to perform or observe any provision of this Lease and fails, within 24 hours after notice by Landlord, to commence and diligently pursue to remedy such failure, Tenant will be in default.

18. TERMINATION: This Lease terminates upon (a) closing and funding of the sale under the Contract, (b) termination of the Contract prior to closing, (c) Tenant's default under this Lease, or (d) Tenant's default under the Contract, whichever occurs first. Upon termination other than by closing and funding of the sale, Tenant shall surrender possession of the property.

19. HOLDING OVER: Any possession by Tenant after termination creates a tenancy at sufferance and will not operate to renew or extend this Lease. Tenant shall pay $_______ per day during the period of any possession after termination as damages, in addition to any other remedies to which Landlord is entitled.

20. ATTORNEY'S FEES: The prevailing party in any legal proceeding brought under or with respect to this Lease is entitled to recover from the non-prevailing party all costs of such proceeding and reasonable attorney's fees.

21. SMOKE ALARMS: The Texas Property Code requires Landlord to install smoke alarms in certain locations within the Property at Landlord's expense. Tenant expressly waives Landlord's duty to inspect and repair smoke alarms.

22. SECURITY DEVICES: The requirements of the Texas Property Code relating to security devices do not apply to a residential lease for a term of 90 days or less.

23. CONSULT YOUR ATTORNEY: Real estate licensees cannot give legal advice. This Lease is intended to be legally binding. READ IT CAREFULLY. If you do not understand the effect of this Lease, consult your attorney BEFORE signing.

24. NOTICES: All notices from one party to the other must be in writing and are effective when mailed to, hand-delivered at, or transmitted by facsimile or electronic transmission as follows:

To Landlord: ______________________	**To Tenant:** ______________________
______________________	______________________
______________________	______________________
Telephone: ( ) ______________	Telephone: ( ) ______________
Facsimile: ( ) ______________	Facsimile: ( ) ______________
E-mail: ______________________	E-mail: ______________________

______________________ Landlord ______________________ Tenant

______________________ Landlord ______________________ Tenant

PROMULGATED BY THE TEXAS REAL ESTATE COMMISSION (TREC) 12-05-11

EQUAL HOUSING OPPORTUNITY

ENVIRONMENTAL ASSESSMENT, THREATENED OR ENDANGERED SPECIES, AND WETLANDS ADDENDUM

TO CONTRACT CONCERNING THE PROPERTY AT

____

(Address of Property)

❑ A. ENVIRONMENTAL ASSESSMENT: Buyer, at Buyer's expense, may obtain an environmental assessment report prepared by an environmental specialist.

❑ B. THREATENED OR ENDANGERED SPECIES: Buyer, at Buyer's expense, may obtain a report from a natural resources professional to determine if there are any threatened or endangered species or their habitats as defined by the Texas Parks and Wildlife Department or the U.S. Fish and Wildlife Service.

❑ C. WETLANDS: Buyer, at Buyer's expense, may obtain a report from an environmental specialist to determine if there are wetlands, as defined by federal or state law or regulation.

Within _____days after the effective date of the contract, Buyer may terminate the contract by furnishing Seller a copy of any report noted above that adversely affects the use of the Property and a notice of termination of the contract. Upon termination, the earnest money will be refunded to Buyer.

Buyer	Seller
Buyer	Seller

TREC TEXAS REAL ESTATE COMMISSION

This form has been approved by the Texas Real Estate Commission for use with similarly approved or promulgated contract forms. Such approval relates to this form only. TREC forms are intended for use only by trained real estate licensees. No representation is made as to the legal validity or adequacy of any provision in any specific transactions. It is not suitable for complex transactions. Texas Real Estate Commission, P.O. Box 12188, Austin, TX 78711-2188, 512-936-3000 (http://www.trec.texas.gov) TREC No. 28-2. This form replaces TREC No. 28-1.

PROMULGATED BY THE TEXAS REAL ESTATE COMMISSION (TREC) 11-07-2022

TREC
TEXAS REAL ESTATE COMMISSION

EQUAL HOUSING OPPORTUNITY

LOAN ASSUMPTION ADDENDUM
TO CONTRACT CONCERNING THE PROPERTY AT

____
(Address of Property)

A. **CREDIT DOCUMENTATION.** To establish Buyer's creditworthiness, Buyer shall deliver to Seller within _______ days after the Effective Date of this contract ❑ credit report ❑ verification of employment, including salary ❑ verification of funds on deposit in financial institutions ❑ current financial statement and ❑ ____
____.
Buyer hereby authorizes any credit reporting agency to furnish copies of Buyer's credit reports to Seller and the noteholder(s) of the loan(s) being assumed at Buyer's sole expense.

B. **BUYER'S CREDIT APPROVAL.** If the credit documentation described in Paragraph A is not delivered to Seller within the specified time, Seller may terminate this contract by notice to Buyer given at any time before all of the required credit documentation is furnished, and the earnest money will be paid to Seller. If the credit documentation is delivered, and Seller determines in Seller's sole discretion that Buyer's credit is unacceptable, Seller may terminate this contract by notice to Buyer within 7 days after expiration of the time for delivery or its actual delivery, whichever is later, and the earnest money will be refunded to Buyer. If Seller does not terminate this contract within the specified, Seller will be deemed to have approved Buyer's creditworthiness.

C. **ASSUMPTION.** At Closing, Buyer will assume in writing the following existing note(s) and all obligations imposed by the deed(s) of trust securing the notes assumed:

❑ (1) The unpaid principal balance of a first lien promissory note payable to__________________ ____________________________which unpaid balance at closing will be $ _______________. The total current monthly payment including principal, interest and any reserve deposits is $ _______________. Buyer's initial payment will be the first payment due after closing.

❑ (2) The unpaid principal balance of a second lien promissory note payable to _____________ ____________________________which unpaid balance at closing will be $ _______________. The total current monthly payment including principal, interest and any reserve deposits is $ _______________. Buyer's initial payment will be the first payment due after closing.

If the unpaid principal balance of any assumed loan as of the Closing Date varies from the loan balance stated above, the ❑ cash payable at closing ❑ Sales Price will be adjusted by the amount of any variance. If the total principal balance of all assumed loans varies in an amount greater than $__________ at closing, either party may terminate this contract and the earnest money will be refunded to Buyer unless the other party elects to pay the excess of the variance. Within 7 days after the Effective Date, Seller will deliver to Buyer copies of the note(s) to be assumed, the deed (s) of trust, and the most recent loan statement(s) from the lender.

D. **LOAN ASSUMPTION TERMS.** Buyer may terminate this contract and the earnest money will be refunded to Buyer if the noteholder requires:

(1) payment of an assumption fee in excess of $ _________in C(1) or $ ____________in C(2) and Seller declines to pay such excess, or
(2) an increase in the interest rate to more than ______% in C(1) or______% in C(2), or
(3) any other modification of the loan documents.

E. **CONSENT BY NOTEHOLDER.** If the noteholder fails to consent to the assumption of the loan, either Seller or Buyer may terminate this contract by notice to the other party and the earnest money will be refunded to the Buyer.

Initialed for identification by Buyer______________ and Seller___________ TREC NO. 41-3

____
(Address of Property)

F. SELLER'S LIENS. Unless Seller is released from liability on any assumed note, a vendor's lien and deed of trust to secure assumption will be required. The vendor's lien will automatically be released on delivery of an executed release by noteholder.

G. TAX AND INSURANCE ESCROW. If noteholder maintains an escrow account for ad valorem taxes, casualty insurance premiums or mortgage insurance premiums, Seller shall transfer the escrow account to Buyer without any deficiency. Buyer shall reimburse Seller for the amount in the transferred accounts.

H. AUTHORIZATION TO RELEASE INFORMATION:

(1) The lender(s) of note(s) being assumed are authorized to furnish to Seller or Buyer or their representatives information relating to the status of the consent to the assumption.

(2) Seller and Buyer authorize the lender(s) of note(s) being assumed, Title Company, and Escrow Agent to disclose and furnish a copy of the closing disclosures and settlement statements to the parties' respective brokers and sales agents provided under Broker Information.

NOTICE TO BUYER: If you are concerned about the possibility of future adjustments, monthly payments, interest rates or other terms, do not sign the contract without examining the notes and deeds of trust.

NOTICE TO SELLER: Your liability to pay the notes assumed by Buyer will continue unless you obtain a release of liability from the noteholders. If you are concerned about future liability, you should use the TREC Release of Liability Addendum.

DUE ON SALE NOTICE: Any note to be assumed or the deed of trust securing the note may contain a provision, commonly known as a "due on sale" clause, stating that the noteholder may declare the note to be immediately due and payable upon conveyance of an interest in the Property. If the noteholder fails to consent to the sale and assumption of the loan, the noteholder may have the right to declare the entire note to be immediately due and payable in full.

______________________________	______________________________
Buyer	Seller
______________________________	______________________________
Buyer	Seller

APPROVED BY THE TEXAS REAL ESTATE COMMISSION (TREC)
FOR VOLUNTARY USE

10-10-11

EQUAL HOUSING OPPORTUNITY

NON-REALTY ITEMS ADDENDUM

TO CONTRACT CONCERNING THE PROPERTY AT

____
(Address of Property)

A. For an additional sum of $_______________and other and good valuable consideration, Seller shall convey to Buyer at closing the following personal property (specify each item carefully, include description, model numbers, serial numbers, location, and other information):

____
____
____
____
____
____
____
____
____
____
____

B. Seller represents and warrants that Seller owns the personal property described in Paragraph A free and clear of all encumbrances.

C. Seller does not warrant or guarantee the condition or future performance of the personal property conveyed by this document.

______________________ Buyer	______________________ Seller
______________________ Buyer	______________________ Seller

This form has been approved by the Texas Real Estate Commission for voluntary use by its licensees. Copies of TREC rules governing real estate brokers, salesperson and real estate inspectors are available at nominal cost from TREC. Texas Real Estate Commission, P.O. Box 12188, Austin, TX 78711-2188, 512-936-3000 (http://www.trec.texas.gov).

PROMULGATED BY THE TEXAS REAL ESTATE COMMISSION (TREC) 11-07-2022

SELLER FINANCING ADDENDUM

TO CONTRACT CONCERNING THE PROPERTY AT

____

(Address of Property)

Agreements for Seller Financing can be complicated and may be subject to laws regulating loans. CONSULT AN ATTORNEY AND A FINANCIAL PROFESSIONAL BEFORE SIGNING. Seller may have accounting or reporting obligations concerning the Seller Financing. TREC rules prohibit real estate brokers and agents from giving legal advice. READ THIS ADDENDUM CAREFULLY.

A. CREDIT DOCUMENTATION. To establish Buyer's creditworthiness, Buyer shall deliver to Seller within_______days after the Effective Date of this contract, ❑ credit report ❑ verification of employment, including salary ❑ verification of funds on deposit in financial institutions ❑ current financial statement and ❑ ____. Buyer hereby authorizes any credit reporting agency to furnish copies of Buyer's credit reports to Seller at Buyer's sole expense.

B. BUYER'S CREDIT APPROVAL. If the credit documentation described in Paragraph A is not delivered within the specified time, Seller may terminate this contract by notice to Buyer given at any time before all of the required credit documentation is furnished, and the earnest money will be paid to Seller. If the credit documentation is delivered, and Seller determines in Seller's sole discretion that Buyer's credit is unacceptable, Seller may terminate this contract by notice to Buyer within 7 days after expiration of the time for delivery or its actual delivery, whichever is later, and the earnest money will be refunded to Buyer. If Seller does not terminate this contract, Seller will be deemed to have approved Buyer's creditworthiness.

C. PROMISSORY NOTE. The promissory note in the amount of $____________(Note), included in Paragraph 3B of the contract payable by Buyer to the order of Seller will bear interest at the rate of _____% per annum and be payable at the place designated by Seller. Buyer may prepay the Note in whole or in part at any time without penalty. Any prepayments are to be applied to the payment of the installments of principal last maturing and interest will immediately cease on the prepaid principal. The Note will contain a provision for payment of a late fee of 5% of any installment not paid within 10 days of the due date. Matured unpaid amounts will bear interest at the rate of 18% per annum or at the highest lawful rate, whichever is less. The Note will be payable as follows: (check one box only)

❑ (1) In one payment due ___________________________________ after the date of the Note with interest payable ❑ at maturity ❑ monthly ❑ quarterly (check one box only).

❑ (2) In monthly installments of $ ______________ ❑ including interest ❑plus interest (check one box only) beginning ____________________ after the date of the Note and continuing monthly thereafter for____________ months when the balance of the Note will be due and payable.

❑ (3) Interest only in monthly installments for the first ___________ month(s) and thereafter in installments of $________________ ❑ including interest ❑ plus interest (check one box only) beginning ___________________ after the date of the Note and continuing monthly thereafter for___________ months when the balance of the Note will be due and payable.

D. DEED OF TRUST. The deed of trust securing the Note will provide for the following:

(1) PROPERTY TRANSFERS: (check one box only)

❑ (a) Consent Not Required: The Property may be sold, conveyed or leased without the consent of Seller, provided any subsequent buyer assumes the Note.

(Address of Property)

☐ (b) Consent Required: If all or any part of the Property is sold, conveyed, leased for a period longer than 3 years, leased with an option to purchase, or otherwise sold (including any contract for deed), without Seller's prior written consent, which consent may be withheld in Seller's sole discretion, Seller may declare the balance of the Note to be immediately due and payable. The creation of a subordinate lien, any conveyance under threat or order of condemnation, any deed solely between buyers, or the passage of title by reason of the death of a buyer or by operation of law will not entitle Seller to exercise the remedies provided in this paragraph.

NOTE: *Under (a) or (b), Buyer's liability to pay the Note will continue unless Buyer obtains a release of liability from Seller.*

(2) CASUALTY INSURANCE: The deed of trust will provide that Buyer ☐ shall ☐ shall not obtain casualty insurance naming Seller as a mortgagee loss payee effective on the date of closing.

(3) TAX AND INSURANCE ESCROW: (check one box only)

☐ (a) Escrow Not Required: Buyer shall furnish Seller, before each year's ad valorem taxes become delinquent, evidence that all ad valorem taxes on the Property have been paid. Buyer shall annually furnish Seller evidence of any required paid-up casualty insurance.

☐ (b) Escrow Required: With each installment Buyer shall deposit in escrow with Seller a pro rata part of the estimated annual ad valorem taxes and any required casualty insurance premiums for the Property. Buyer shall pay any deficiency within 30 days after notice from Seller. Buyer's failure to pay the deficiency will be a default under the deed of trust. Buyer is not required to deposit any escrow payments for taxes and any required insurance that are deposited with a superior lienholder. Seller will provide Buyer with an annual accounting of the escrow account, use escrow deposits to pay taxes and any required insurance premiums in a timely manner if and to the extent funds are available in the escrow account, and hold the escrow deposit in a separate account. The escrow account ☐ will ☐ will not be serviced by a third-party servicer. ☐ Buyer ☐ Seller will pay the cost of escrow service.

(4) PRIOR LIENS: Any default under any lien superior to the lien securing the Note will be a default under the deed of trust securing the Note.

Buyer	Seller
Buyer	Seller

PROMULGATED BY THE TEXAS REAL ESTATE COMMISSION (TREC) 11-03-2025

(NOTICE: For use only when SELLER occupies the property for no more than 90 days AFTER the closing)

TREC
TEXAS REAL ESTATE COMMISSION

SELLER'S TEMPORARY RESIDENTIAL LEASE

EQUAL HOUSING OPPORTUNITY

1. **PARTIES:** The parties to this Lease are ____ (Landlord) and ____(Tenant).

2. **LEASE:** Landlord leases to Tenant the Property described in the Contract between Landlord as Buyer and Tenant as Seller known as ____(address).

3. **TERM:** The term of this Lease commences on the date the sale covered by the Contract is closed and funded and terminates ___________________, unless terminated earlier by reason of other provisions.

4. **RENTAL:** Tenant shall pay to Landlord as rental $___________ per day (excluding the day of closing and funding) with the full amount of rental for the term of the Lease to be paid at the time of funding of the sale. Tenant will not be entitled to a refund of rental if this Lease terminates early due to Tenant's default or voluntary surrender of the Property.

5. **DEPOSIT:** Tenant shall pay to Landlord at the time of funding of the sale $_____________ as a deposit to secure performance of this Lease by Tenant. Landlord may use the deposit to satisfy Tenant's obligations under this Lease. Landlord shall refund any unused portion of the deposit to Tenant with an itemized list of all deductions from the deposit within 30 days after Tenant (a) surrenders possession of the Property and (b) provides Landlord written notice of Tenant's forwarding address.

6. **UTILITIES:** Tenant shall pay all utility charges except ____________________________________ which Landlord shall pay.

7. **USE OF PROPERTY:** Tenant may use the Property only for residential purposes. Tenant may not assign this Lease or sublet any part of the Property.

8. **PETS:** Tenant may not keep pets on the Property except _______________________________________.

9. **CONDITION OF PROPERTY:** Tenant accepts the Property in its present condition and state of repair at the commencement of the Lease. Upon termination, Tenant shall surrender the Property to Landlord in the condition required under the Contract, except normal wear and tear and any casualty loss.

10. **ALTERATIONS:** Tenant may not alter the Property or install improvements or fixtures without the prior written consent of the Landlord. Any improvements or fixtures placed on the Property during the Lease become the Property of Landlord.

11. **SPECIAL PROVISIONS:** ____

12. **INSPECTIONS:** Landlord may enter at reasonable times to inspect the Property. Tenant shall provide Landlord door keys and access codes to allow access to the Property during the term of Lease.

13. **LAWS:** Tenant shall comply with all applicable laws, restrictions, ordinances, rules and regulations with respect to the Property.

14. **REPAIRS AND MAINTENANCE:** Except as otherwise provided in this Lease, Tenant shall bear all expense of repairing and maintaining the Property, including but not limited to the yard, trees and shrubs, unless otherwise required by the Texas Property Code. Tenant shall promptly repair at Tenant's expense any damage to the Property caused directly or indirectly by any act or omission of the Tenant or any person other than the Landlord, Landlord's agents or invitees.

15. INDEMNITY: Tenant indemnifies Landlord from the claims of all third parties for injury or damage to the person or property of such third party arising from the use or occupancy of the Property by Tenant. This indemnification includes attorney's fees, costs and expenses incurred by Landlord.

16. INSURANCE: Landlord and Tenant shall each maintain such insurance on the contents and Property as each party may deem appropriate during the term of this Lease. NOTE: CONSULT YOUR INSURANCE AGENT; POSSESSION OF THE PROPERTY BY SELLER AS TENANT MAY CHANGE INSURANCE POLICY COVERAGE.

17. DEFAULT: If Tenant fails to perform or observe any provision of this Lease and fails, within 24 hours after notice by Landlord, to commence and diligently pursue to remedy such failure, Tenant will be in default.

18. TERMINATION: This Lease terminates upon expiration of the term specified in Paragraph 3 or upon Tenant's default under this Lease.

19. HOLDING OVER: Tenant shall surrender possession of the Property upon termination of this Lease. Any possession by Tenant after termination creates a tenancy at sufferance and will not operate to renew or extend this Lease. Tenant shall pay $______ per day during the period of any possession after termination as damages, in addition to any other remedies to which Landlord is entitled.

20. ATTORNEY'S FEES: The prevailing party in any legal proceeding brought under or with respect to this Lease is entitled to recover from the non-prevailing party all costs of such proceeding and reasonable attorney's fees.

21. SMOKE ALARMS: The Texas Property Code requires Landlord to install smoke alarms in certain locations within the Property at Landlord's expense. Tenant expressly waives Landlord's duty to inspect and repair smoke alarms.

22. SECURITY DEVICES: The requirements of the Texas Property Code relating to security devices do not apply to a residential lease for a term of 90 days or less.

23. CONSULT YOUR ATTORNEY: Real estate licensees cannot give legal advice. This Lease is intended to be legally binding. READ IT CAREFULLY. If you do not understand the effect of this Lease, consult your attorney BEFORE signing.

24. NOTICES: All notices from one party to the other must be in writing and are effective when mailed to, hand-delivered at, or transmitted by facsimile or electronic transmission as follows:

To Landlord: ______________________	**To Tenant:** ______________________
______________________	______________________
______________________	______________________
Telephone: ( ) ______________	Telephone: ( ) ______________
Facsimile: ( ) ______________	Facsimile: ( ) ______________
E-mail: ______________	E-mail: ______________

______________________ Landlord	______________________ Tenant
______________________ Landlord	______________________ Tenant

PROMULGATED BY THE TEXAS REAL ESTATE COMMISSION (TREC) 02-19-2021

SHORT SALE ADDENDUM

ADDENDUM TO CONTRACT CONCERNING THE PROPERTY AT

____
(Street Address and City)

A. This contract involves a "short sale" of the Property. As used in this Addendum, "short sale" means that:

(1) Seller's net proceeds at closing will be insufficient to pay the balance of Seller's mortgage loan; and

(2) Seller requires:
(a) the consent of the lienholder to sell the Property pursuant to this contract; and
(b) the lienholder's agreement to:
(i) accept Seller's net proceeds in full satisfaction of Seller's liability under the mortgage loan; and
(ii) provide Seller an executed release of lien against the Property in a recordable format.

B. As used in this Addendum, "Seller's net proceeds" means the Sales Price less Seller's Expenses under Paragraph 12 of the contract and Seller's obligation to pay any brokerage fees.

C. The contract to which this Addendum is attached is binding upon execution by the parties and the earnest money and the Option Fee must be paid as provided in the contract. The contract is contingent on the satisfaction of Seller's requirements under Paragraph A(2) of this Addendum (Lienholder's Consent and Agreement). Seller shall apply promptly for and make every reasonable effort to obtain Lienholder's Consent and Agreement, and shall furnish all information and documents required by the lienholder. Except as provided by this Addendum, neither party is required to perform under the contract while it is contingent upon obtaining Lienholder's Consent and Agreement.

D. If Seller does not notify Buyer that Seller has obtained Lienholder's Consent and Agreement on or before ______________________________, this contract terminates and the earnest money will be refunded to Buyer. Seller must notify Buyer immediately if Lienholder's Consent and Agreement is obtained. For purposes of performance, the effective date of the contract changes to the date Seller provides Buyer notice of the Lienholder's Consent and Agreement (Amended Effective Date).

E. This contract will terminate and the earnest money will be refunded to Buyer if the Lienholder refuses or withdraws its Consent and Agreement prior to closing and funding. Seller shall promptly notify Buyer of any lienholder's refusal to provide or withdrawal of a Lienholder's Consent and Agreement.

F. If Buyer has the unrestricted right to terminate this contract, the time for giving notice of termination begins on the effective date of the contract, continues after the Amended Effective Date and ends upon the expiration of Buyer's unrestricted right to terminate the contract under Paragraph 5.

G. For the purposes of this Addendum, time is of the essence. Strict compliance with the times for performance stated in this Addendum is required.

H. Seller authorizes any lienholder to furnish to Buyer or Buyer's representatives information relating to the status of the request for a Lienholder's Consent and Agreement.

I. If there is more than one lienholder or loan secured by the Property, this Addendum applies to each lienholder.

______________________ Buyer	______________________ Seller
______________________ Buyer	______________________ Seller

TREC NO. 45-2

11-04-2024

PROMULGATED BY THE TEXAS REAL ESTATE COMMISSION (TREC)

THIRD PARTY FINANCING ADDENDUM

TO CONTRACT CONCERNING THE PROPERTY AT

____

(Street Address and City)

1. **TYPE OF FINANCING AND DUTY TO APPLY AND OBTAIN APPROVAL:** Buyer shall apply promptly for all financing described below and make every reasonable effort to obtain approval for the financing, including but not limited to furnishing all information and documents required by Buyer's lender. (Check applicable boxes):

❑ A. CONVENTIONAL FINANCING:

❑ (1) A first mortgage loan in the principal amount of $________________ (excluding any financed PMI premium), due in full in ______ year(s), with interest not to exceed _____% per annum for the first _______ year(s) of the loan with Origination Charges as shown on Buyer's Loan Estimate for the loan not to exceed _______% of the loan.

❑ (2) A second mortgage loan in the principal amount of $_______________ (excluding any financed PMI premium), due in full in __________ year(s), with interest not to exceed _____% per annum for the first ________ year(s) of the loan with Origination Charges as shown on Buyer's Loan Estimate for the loan not to exceed _________% of the loan.

❑ B. TEXAS VETERANS LOAN: A loan(s) from the Texas Veterans Land Board of $_______________ for a period in the total amount of _______ years at the interest rate established by the Texas Veterans Land Board.

❑ C. FHA INSURED FINANCING: A Section ________________ FHA insured loan of not less than $_________________(excluding any financed MIP), amortizable monthly for not less than _______ years, with interest not to exceed _______% per annum for the first _______ year(s) of the loan with Origination Charges as shown on Buyer's Loan Estimate for the loan not to exceed ______ % of the loan.

❑ D. VA GUARANTEED FINANCING: A VA guaranteed loan of not less than $_________________ (excluding any financed Funding Fee), amortizable monthly for not less than ______ years, with interest not to exceed ______% per annum for the first _____ year(s) of the loan with Origination Charges as shown on Buyer's Loan Estimate for the loan not to exceed _______% of the loan.

❑ E. USDA GUARANTEED FINANCING: A USDA-guaranteed loan of not less than $____________ (excluding any financed Funding Fee), amortizable monthly for not less than _______ years, with interest not to exceed _____% per annum for the first _______ year(s) of the loan with Origination Charges as shown on Buyer's Loan Estimate for the loan not to exceed _____% of the loan.

❑ F. REVERSE MORTGAGE FINANCING: A reverse mortgage loan (also known as a Home Equity Conversion Mortgage loan) in the original principal amount of $ _____________ (excluding any financed PMI premium or other costs), with interest not to exceed _____% per annum for the first _______ year(s) of the loan with Origination Charges as shown on Buyer's Loan Estimate for the loan not to exceed ____% of the loan. The reverse mortgage loan ❑will ❑ will not be an FHA insured loan.

❑ G. OTHER FINANCING: A loan not of a type described above from ____________________ (name of lender) in the principal amount of $___________ due in ______ year(s), with interest not to exceed ____% per annum for the first _____ year(s) of the loan with Origination Charges not to exceed ____% of the loan. Buyer ❑ does ❑ does not waive all rights to terminate the contract under Paragraph 2B of this addendum for the loan described in this paragraph.

2. **APPROVAL OF FINANCING**: Approval for the financing described above will be deemed to have been obtained when Buyer Approval and Property Approval are obtained. **Time is of the essence for this paragraph and strict compliance with the time for performance is required.**

Initialed for identification by Buyer____ _____ and Seller_____ _____ TREC NO. 40-11

____
(Address of Property)

A. BUYER APPROVAL *(Check one box only)*:

❑ This contract is subject to Buyer obtaining Buyer Approval. If Buyer cannot obtain Buyer Approval, Buyer may terminate this contract within _____ days after the Effective Date of the contract by giving Seller: (i) notice of termination; and (ii) a copy of a written statement from the lender setting forth the reason(s) for lender's determination. If Buyer terminates the contract under this provision, this contract will terminate and the earnest money will be refunded to Buyer. If Buyer does not terminate the contract under Paragraph 2A, the contract shall no longer be subject to the Buyer obtaining Buyer Approval. Buyer Approval will be deemed to have been obtained when (i) the terms of the loan(s) described above are available and (ii) lender determines that Buyer has satisfied all of lender's requirements related to Buyer's assets, income and credit history.

❑ This contract is not subject to Buyer obtaining Buyer Approval.

B. PROPERTY APPROVAL: If Buyer's lender determines that the Property does not satisfy lender's underwriting requirements for the loan (including but not limited to appraisal, insurability, and lender required repairs) Buyer may terminate this contract on or before the 3rd day before the Closing Date by giving Seller: (i) notice of termination; and (ii) a copy of a written statement from the lender setting forth the reason(s) for lender's determination. If Buyer terminates under this paragraph, the earnest money will be refunded to Buyer. If Buyer does not terminate under this paragraph, Property Approval is deemed to have been obtained.

3. **SECURITY**: If required by Buyer's lender, each note for the financing described above must be secured by vendor's and deed of trust liens.

4. **FHA/VA REQUIRED PROVISION**: If the financing described above involves FHA insured or VA financing, it is expressly agreed that, notwithstanding any other provision of this contract, the purchaser (Buyer) shall not be obligated to complete the purchase of the Property described herein or to incur any penalty by forfeiture of earnest money deposits or otherwise: (i) unless the Buyer has been given in accordance with HUD/FHA or VA requirements a written statement issued by the Federal Housing Commissioner, Department of Veterans Affairs, or a Direct Endorsement Lender setting forth the appraised value of the Property of not less than $__________________ or (ii) if the contract purchase price or cost exceeds the reasonable value of the Property established by the Department of Veterans Affairs. The 3-day notice of termination requirement in Paragraph 2B does not apply to this Paragraph 4.

A. The Buyer shall have the privilege and option of proceeding with consummation of the contract without regard to the amount of the appraised valuation or the reasonable value established by the Department of Veterans Affairs.

B. If FHA financing is involved, the appraised valuation is arrived at to determine the maximum mortgage the Department of Housing and Urban Development will insure. HUD does not warrant the value or the condition of the Property. The Buyer should satisfy himself/herself that the price and the condition of the Property are acceptable.

C. If VA financing is involved and if Buyer elects to complete the purchase at an amount in excess of the reasonable value established by the VA, Buyer shall pay such excess amount in cash from a source which Buyer agrees to disclose to the VA and which Buyer represents will not be from borrowed funds except as approved by VA. If VA reasonable value of the Property is less than the Sales Prices, Seller may reduce the Sales Price to an amount equal to the VA reasonable value and the sale will be closed at the lower Sales Price with proportionate adjustments to the down payment and the loan amount.

5. **AUTHORIZATION TO RELEASE INFORMATION**:

A. Buyer authorizes Buyer's lender to furnish to Seller or Buyer or their representatives information relating to the status of the approval for the financing.

B. Seller and Buyer authorize Buyer's lender, title company, and Escrow Agent to disclose and furnish a copy of the closing disclosures and settlement statements to the parties' respective brokers and sales agents provided under Broker Information.

______________________ Buyer	______________________ Seller
______________________ Buyer	______________________ Seller

RESALE CERTIFICATES

Property Owners Association and Condominium Resale Certificates

Condominium Resale Certificate (Form 32-5, effective 11/25/2024)

Subdivision Information, Including Resale Certificate for Property Subject to Mandatory Membership in a Property Owners' Association (Form 37-5, effective 02/10/2014)

PROMULGATED BY THE TEXAS REAL ESTATE COMMISSION (TREC) 11-04-2024

CONDOMINIUM RESALE CERTIFICATE

(Section 82.157, Texas Property Code)

Condominium Certificate concerning Condominium Unit _____, in Building _______, of _______________ ____________________________________,a condominium project, located at ____________________ ____(Address), City of ____________________________, County of ___________________________, Texas, on behalf of the condominium owners' association (the Association) by the Association's governing body (the Board).

A. The Declaration ❑does ❑does not contain a right of first refusal or other restraint that restricts the right to transfer the Unit. If a right of first refusal or other restraint exists, see Section _______of the Declaration.

B. The periodic common expense assessment for the Unit is $___________ per ________________.

C. There ❑ is ❑is not a common expense or special assessment due and unpaid by the Seller to the Association. The total unpaid amount is $_____________ and is for __________________________.

D. Other amounts ❑are ❑are not payable by Seller to the Association. The total unpaid amount is $________________and is for ____.

E. Capital expenditures approved by the Association for the next 12 months are $______________.

F. Reserves for capital expenditures are $______________; of this amount $___________________ has been designated for____.

G. The current operating budget and balance sheet of the Association is attached.

H. The amount of unsatisfied judgments against the Association is $ _________________________.

I. There ❑are ❑are not any suits pending against the Association. The nature of the suits is ____.

J. The Association ❑does ❑does not provide insurance coverage for the benefit of unit owners as per the attached summary from the Association's insurance agent.

K. The Board ❑has ❑has no knowledge that any alterations or improvements to the Unit or to the limited common elements assigned to that Unit violate the Declaration, by-laws, or Association rules. Known violations are:____ ____.

L. The Board ❑has ❑has not received notice from a governmental authority concerning violations of health or building codes with respect to the Unit, the limited common elements assigned to the Unit, or any other portion of the condominium. Notices received are: _______________________ ____.

M. The remaining term of any leasehold estate that affects the condominium is ________________ and the provisions governing an extension or a renewal of the lease are: __________________ ____ ____.

N. The Association's managing agent is ____
(Name of Agent)

____
(Mailing Address)

____________________________________ ____________________________________
(Phone) (Fax)

____
(E-mail Address)

TREC NO. 32-5

____
(Address of Property)

O. Association fees resulting from the transfer of the unit described above:

Description	Paid To	Amount
____________	____________	____________
____________	____________	____________
____________	____________	____________

P. Required contribution, if any, to the capital reserves account $______________.

REQUIRED ATTACHMENTS:
1. Operating Budget
2. Insurance Summary
3. Balance Sheet

NOTICE: The Certificate must be prepared no more than three months before the date it is delivered to Buyer.

____
Name of Association

By: ________________________________

Name: ________________________________

Title: ________________________________

Date: ________________________________

Mailing Address: ________________________________

E-mail: ________________________________

PROMULGATED BY THE TEXAS REAL ESTATE COMMISSION (TREC)

2-10-2014

TREC
TEXAS REAL ESTATE COMMISSION

EQUAL HOUSING OPPORTUNITY

SUBDIVISION INFORMATION, INCLUDING RESALE CERTIFICATE FOR PROPERTY SUBJECT TO MANDATORY MEMBERSHIP IN A PROPERTY OWNERS' ASSOCIATION

(Chapter 207, Texas Property Code)

Resale Certificate concerning the Property (including any common areas assigned to the Property) located at ____(Street Address), City of ________________________________, County of ______________, Texas, prepared by the property owners' association (Association).

A. The Property ❑is ❑ is not subject to a right of first refusal (other than a right of first refusal prohibited by statute) or other restraint contained in the restrictions or restrictive covenants that restricts the owner's right to transfer the owner's property.

B. The current regular assessment for the Property is $______________________ per _________.

C. A special assessment for the Property due after this resale certificate is delivered is $________ payable as follows____ for the following purpose:____.

D. The total of all amounts due and unpaid to the Association that are attributable to the Property is $ _______________ .

E. The capital expenditures approved by the Association for its current fiscal year are $ _______________.

F. The amount of reserves for capital expenditures is $_______________.

G. Unsatisfied judgments against the Association total $_______________.

H. Other than lawsuits relating to unpaid ad valorem taxes of an individual member of the association, there ❑ are ❑ are not any suits pending in which the Association is a party. The style and cause number of each pending suit is: ____________________.

I. The Association's board ❑has actual knowledge ❑has no actual knowledge of conditions on the Property in violation of the restrictions applying to the subdivision or the bylaws or rules of the Association. Known violations are: ____________________.

J. The Association ❑has ❑has not received notice from any governmental authority regarding health or building code violations with respect to the Property or any common areas or common facilities owned or leased by the Association. A summary or copy of each notice is attached.

K. The amount of any administrative transfer fee charged by the Association for a change of ownership of property in the subdivision is $__________. Describe all fees associated with the transfer of ownership (include a description of each fee, to whom each fee is payable and the amount of each fee).__________

____

____

TREC NO. 37-5

L. The Association's managing agent is ______________________________
(Name of Agent)

____
(Mailing Address)

______________________________ ______________________________
(Telephone Number) (Fax Number)

____
(E-mail Address)

M. The restrictions ❑ do ❑ do not allow foreclosure of the Association's lien on the Property for failure to pay assessments.
REQUIRED ATTACHMENTS:

1. Restrictions
2. Rules
3. Bylaws
4. Current Balance Sheet
5. Current Operating Budget
6. Certificate of Insurance concerning Property and Liability Insurance for Common Areas and Facilities
7. Any Governmental Notices of Health or Housing Code Violations

NOTICE: This Subdivision Information may change at any time.

____
Name of Association

By: ______________________________

Print Name: ______________________________

Title: ______________________________

Date: ______________________________

Mailing Address: ______________________________

E-mail: ______________________________

PROMULGATED NOTICES AND DISCLOSURES

Notices and Disclosures Used with a Promulgated Contract

Disclosure of Relationship with Residential Service Company (Form RSC-4, effective 06/11/2023)

Landlord's Floodplain and Flood Notice (Form 54-1, effective 11/26/2025)

Notice of Buyer's Termination of Contract (Form 38-8, effective 04/01/2025)

Notice of Seller's Termination of Contract (Form 50-0, effective 08/13/2018)

Notice to Prospective Buyer (Form 58-0, effective 09/03/2025)

Notice to Purchaser of Special Taxing or Assessment District (Form 59-0, effective 02/12/2024)

Seller's Disclosure about Groundwater and Surface Water Rights (Form 61-0, effective 07/01/2026)

Seller's Disclosure Notice (Form 55-1, effective 05/28/2026)

Seller's Notice to Buyer of Removal of Contingency Under Addendum for "Back-Up" Contract (Form 62-0, effective 05/28/2026)

PROMULGATED BY THE TEXAS REAL ESTATE COMMISSION (TREC) 05-16-2023

EQUAL HOUSING OPPORTUNITY

DISCLOSURE OF RELATIONSHIP WITH CONTRACT PROVIDER OR ADMINISTRATOR

RESIDENTIAL SERVICE CONTRACTS. A residential service contract is a product under which a residential service contract provider or administrator (Provider), for a fee, agrees to repair or replace certain equipment or items in a property. Co-payments typically apply to most service calls. Providers are licensed and regulated by the Texas Department of Licensing and Regulation. The extent of coverage and the cost of coverage will vary. Before buying a residential service contract, the buyer should read the contract and consider comparing it with the extent of coverage and costs from several other Providers. **YOU MAY CHOOSE ANY PROVIDER.**

THE PURCHASE OF A RESIDENTIAL SERVICE CONTRACT IS OPTIONAL. The TREC promulgated residential contract forms contain a paragraph in which the parties may negotiate whether the seller will reimburse the buyer the cost of a residential service contract. The choice of the Provider and extent of coverage lies with the buyer. **NEITHER A BROKER/SALES AGENT NOR A SELLER MAY CONDITION THE SALE OF A PROPERTY ON THE BUYER'S PURCHASE OF A RESIDENTIAL SERVICE CONTRACT.**

☐ Other Broker/Sales Agent will receive no compensation from a Provider.

☐ Other Broker/Sales Agent receives compensation from the following Provider:

____

____

for providing the following services:

____

____

☐ Listing Broker/Sales Agent will receive no compensation from a Provider.

☐ Listing Broker/Sales Agent receives compensation from the following Provider:

____

____

for providing the following services:

____

____

The compensation is not contingent upon a party to the real estate transaction purchasing a contract or services from the Provider.

The compensation is the fee for the services that Listing Broker or Other Broker, either directly or through an agent, provides to the company. As required by the Real Estate Settlement Procedures Act and HUD Regulation X, any fees paid to a settlement services provider are limited to the reasonable value of services actually rendered.

____
Other Broker's Name License No.

By: ______________________________

____
Listing Broker's Name License No.

By: ______________________________

The undersigned acknowledges receipt of this notice:

____
Buyer

____
Seller

____
Buyer

____
Seller

TREC

TEXAS REAL ESTATE COMMISSION

This form has been approved by the Texas Real Estate Commission (TREC) for use by license holders to disclose payments received from a residential contract provider or administrator. Texas Real Estate Commission, P.O. Box 12188, Austin, TX 78711-2188, (512) 936-3000 (http://www.trec.texas.gov) RSC-4.

RSC-4

11-03-2025

APPROVED BY THE TEXAS REAL ESTATE COMMISSION (TREC)

LANDLORD'S FLOODPLAIN AND FLOOD NOTICE

NOTICE: For Use With a Residential Lease. Not Required with a TREC Temporary Residential Lease

EQUAL HOUSING OPPORTUNITY

CONCERNING THE PROPERTY AT: ____
(Street Address and City)

A. Landlord ❑ is ❑ is not aware that the dwelling you are renting is located in a 100-year floodplain. If neither box is checked, you should assume the Property is in a 100-year floodplain. Even if the dwelling is not in a 100-year floodplain, the dwelling may still be susceptible to flooding. The Federal Emergency Management Agency (FEMA) maintains a flood map on its Internet website that is searchable by address, at no cost, to determine if a dwelling is located in a flood hazard area. Most tenant insurance policies do not cover damages or loss incurred in a flood. You should seek insurance coverage that would cover losses caused by a flood.

B. Landlord ❑ is ❑ is not aware that the dwelling you are renting has flooded at least once within the last five years.

C. For purposes of this notice:

(1) "100-year floodplain" means any area of land designated as a flood hazard area with a one percent or greater chance of flooding each year by the Federal Emergency Management Agency under the National Flood Insurance Act of 1968 (42 U.S.C. Section 4001 et seq.).

(2) "Flooding" means a general or temporary condition of partial or complete inundation of a dwelling caused by:
(a) the overflow of inland or tidal waters;
(b) the unusual and rapid accumulation of runoff or surface waters from any established water source such as a river, stream, or drainage ditch; or
(c) excessive rainfall.

(3) "Dwelling" means one or more rooms rented for use as a permanent residence under a single lease to one or more tenants.

Landlord	Date	Landlord	Date

The undersigned Tenant hereby acknowledges receipt of the foregoing notice.

Tenant	Date	Tenant	Date

This form was prepared by the Texas Real Estate Commission in accordance with Texas Property Code §92.0135 and is to be used in conjunction with a residential lease entered into or renewed on or after September 1, 2025. Texas Real Estate Commission, P.O. Box 12188, Austin, TX 78711-2188, 512-936-3000 (http://www.trec.texas.gov) TREC NO. 54-1. This form replaces 54-0.

02-10-2025

TREC
TEXAS REAL ESTATE COMMISSION

PROMULGATED BY THE TEXAS REAL ESTATE COMMISSION (TREC)

NOTICE OF BUYER'S TERMINATION OF CONTRACT

CONCERNING THE CONTRACT FOR THE SALE OF THE PROPERTY AT

EQUAL HOUSING OPPORTUNITY

____
(Street Address and City)

BETWEEN THE UNDERSIGNED BUYER AND ____________________________________

____ (SELLER)

Buyer notifies Seller that the contract is terminated pursuant to the following:

❑(1) The unrestricted right of Buyer to terminate the contract under Paragraph 5 of the contract.

❑(2) Buyer cannot obtain Buyer Approval in accordance with the Third Party Financing Addendum to the contract. Buyer has delivered to Seller lender's written statement setting forth the reason(s) for lender's determination.

❑(3) The Property does not satisfy Property Approval in accordance with the Third Party Financing Addendum to the contract. Buyer has delivered to Seller lender's written statement setting forth the reason(s) for lender's determination.

❑(4) Buyer elects to terminate under Paragraph A of the Addendum for Property Subject to Mandatory Membership in a Property Owners' Association.

❑(5) Buyer elects to terminate under Paragraph 7B(2) of the contract relating to the Seller's Disclosure Notice.

❑(6) Buyer elects to terminate under Paragraph (3) of the Addendum Concerning Right to Terminate Due to Lender's Appraisal. Buyer has delivered a copy of the Appraisal to Seller.

❑(7) Buyer elects to terminate under Paragraph 6.D. of the contract (6.C. for Residential Condominium Contract) because timely objections were not cured by the end of the Cure Period.

❑(8) Other *(identify the paragraph number of contract or the addendum)*: ________________

____

____

____

____

NOTE: This notice is not an election of remedies. Release of the earnest money is governed by the contract.

CONSULT AN ATTORNEY BEFORE SIGNING: TREC rules prohibit real estate license holders from giving legal advice. READ THIS FORM CAREFULLY.

Buyer	Date	Buyer	Date

TREC
TEXAS REAL ESTATE COMMISSION

This form has been approved by the Texas Real Estate Commission for use with similarly approved or promulgated contract forms. Such approval relates to this form only. TREC forms are intended for use only by trained real estate license holders. No representation is made as to the legal validity or adequacy of any provision in any specific transactions. It is not suitable for complex transactions. Texas Real Estate Commission, P.O. Box 12188, Austin, TX 78711-2188, (512) 936-3000 (http://www.trec.texas.gov) TREC No. 38-8. This form replaces TREC No. 38-7.

8-13-18

TREC
TEXAS REAL ESTATE COMMISSION

PROMULGATED BY THE TEXAS REAL ESTATE COMMISSION (TREC)

EQUAL HOUSING OPPORTUNITY

NOTICE OF SELLER'S TERMINATION OF CONTRACT

CONCERNING THE CONTRACT FOR THE SALE OF THE PROPERTY AT

____
(Street Address and City)

BETWEEN THE UNDERSIGNED SELLER AND ______________________________

____ (BUYER)

Seller notifies Buyer that the contract is terminated pursuant to the following:

☐ (1) Buyer failed to deliver the earnest money within the time required under Paragraph 5 of the contract and before the time Seller provided this notice to Buyer.

☐ (2) Other *(identify the paragraph number of contract or the addendum)*:

____
____
____
____
____
____

NOTE: This notice is not an election of remedies. Release of the earnest money is governed by the contract.

CONSULT AN ATTORNEY BEFORE SIGNING: TREC rules prohibit real estate license holders from giving legal advice. READ THIS FORM CAREFULLY.

Seller	Date	Seller	Date

TREC
TEXAS REAL ESTATE COMMISSION

APPROVED BY THE TEXAS REAL ESTATE COMMISSION

NOTICE TO PROSPECTIVE BUYER

As required by law, I advise you to have the abstract covering the property known as ____ ____ (Address) examined by an attorney of your own selection OR you should be furnished with or obtain a policy of title insurance.

If the property is situated in a Utility District, Chapter 49 of the Texas Water Code requires you to sign and acknowledge the statutory notice from the seller of the property relating to the tax rate, bonded indebtedness or standby fee of the District.

If the property is in a public improvement district, the seller must give you written notice as required by §5.014, Property Code.

DATED: ______________________ , __________ .

____
Brokerage Company Name

____
Broker or Sales Associate

I have received a copy of this **NOTICE TO PROSPECTIVE BUYER.**

____
Prospective Buyer

____
Prospective Buyer

This form has been approved by the Texas Real Estate Commission (TREC) for use when a contract of sale has not been promulgated by TREC. The form should be presented before an offer to purchase is signed by the prospective buyer. Texas Real Estate Commission, P.O. Box 12188, Austin, Texas 78711-2188, 512-936-3000 (http://www.trec.texas.gov). TREC No. 58-0 replaces TREC No. OP-C.

PROMULGATED BY THE TEXAS REAL ESTATE COMMISSION (TREC) 02-12-2024

TREC
TEXAS REAL ESTATE COMMISSION

NOTICE TO PURCHASER OF SPECIAL TAXING OR ASSESSMENT DISTRICT

EQUAL HOUSING OPPORTUNITY

NOTICE: Not for use for Public Improvement Districts (PIDs).

Section 49.453, Texas Water Code, requires each district to make the form of notice containing the information in this form available to the public on the district's website or otherwise. **If available, Seller should use the district's form instead of this form.** If the district does not have the form of notice on its website or does not publish a form of notice, Seller should obtain the information from the district and complete this form with the information from the district.

SELLER'S DISCLOSURE CONCERNING THE PROPERTY AT:

____
(Street Address and City)

1. **NAME OF SPECIAL DISTRICT:** The real property that you are about to purchase is located in the ______________ (insert name of district) and may be subject to district taxes or assessments.

2. **TAX RATE:** The district may, subject to voter approval, impose taxes and issue bonds. The district may impose an unlimited rate of tax in payment of such bonds. (Check only one box)

   ❑ The current rate of the district property tax is ______________ (insert current property tax rate) on each $100 of assessed valuation.

   ❑ The district has not yet imposed taxes. The projected rate of the district property tax is ______________ (insert projected property tax rate) on each $100 of assessed valuation.

3. **ASSESSMENTS:** The district may impose assessments and issue bonds and impose an assessment in payment of such bonds. (Check only one box)

   ❑ The rate of the district assessment is ______________ (insert current assessment amount) on each $100 of assessed valuation.

   ❑ The amount of the district assessment on the real property that you are about to purchase is ______________ (insert current assessment amount).

   ❑ The district has not yet imposed an assessment, but the projected ❑ rate ❑ amount of the assessment is ______________ (insert projected assessment rate or amount).

4. **BONDS:**

   A. The total amounts of bonds payable wholly or partly from ❑ property taxes ❑ assessments (❑ excluding refunding bonds that are separately approved by the voters ❑ excluding any bonds or any portions of bonds issued that are payable solely from revenues received or expected to be received under a contract with a governmental entity) approved by the voters are:

   (1) $ ______________ (insert amount) for water, sewer, and drainage facilities;

   (2) $ ______________ (insert amount) for road facilities;

   (3) $ ______________ (insert amount) for parks and recreational facilities; and

   (4) $ ______________ (insert amount) for ______________ (insert description of additional facilities, as applicable).

   B. The aggregate initial principal amounts of all such bonds issued are:

   (1) $ ______________ (insert amount) for water, sewer, and drainage facilities;

   (2) $ ______________ (insert amount) for road facilities;

   (3) $ ______________ (insert amount) for parks and recreational facilities; and

   (4) $ ______________ (insert amount) for ______________ (insert description of additional facilities, as applicable).

Initialed for identification by Buyer____ _____ and Seller_____ _____ TREC No. 59-0

____
(Address of Property)

5. **STANDBY FEES:** The district sought and obtained approval of the Texas Commission on Environmental Quality to adopt and impose a standby fee. The amount of the standby fee is $ ____________ (insert amount of standby fee). An unpaid standby fee is a personal obligation of the person that owned the property at the time of imposition and is secured by a lien on the property. Any person may request a certificate from the district stating the amount, if any, of unpaid standby fees on a tract of property in the district.

6. **LOCATION:** (Check only one box, if applicable)

   ❑ The district is located wholly or partly in the extraterritorial jurisdiction of the City of ____________ (insert name of municipality). Texas law governs the ability of a municipality to annex property in the municipality's extraterritorial jurisdiction and whether a district that is annexed by the municipality is dissolved.

   ❑ The district is located wholly or partly within the corporate boundaries of the City of ____________ (insert name of municipality). The municipality and the district overlap, but may not provide duplicate services or improvements. Property located in the municipality and the district is subject to taxation by the municipality and the district.

7. **STRATEGIC PARTNERSHIP AGREEMENT:** (Check box and complete, if applicable)

   ❑ The district has entered into a strategic partnership agreement with the City of ____________ (insert name of municipality). This agreement may address the timeframe, process, and procedures for the municipal annexation of the area of the district located in the municipality's extraterritorial jurisdiction.

8. **PURPOSE:** The purpose of the district is to provide the following facilities or services: (Check applicable boxes) ❑ water ❑ sewer ❑ drainage ❑ flood control ❑ firefighting ❑ road ❑ parks and recreational ❑ ____________ (insert other types of facilities or services, as applicable). The cost of district facilities is not included in the purchase price of your property.

PURCHASER IS ADVISED THAT THE INFORMATION SHOWN ON THIS FORM IS SUBJECT TO CHANGE BY THE DISTRICT AT ANY TIME. THE DISTRICT ANNUALLY ESTABLISHES TAX RATES. PURCHASER IS ADVISED TO CONTACT THE DISTRICT TO DETERMINE THE STATUS OF ANY CURRENT OR PROPOSED CHANGES TO THE INFORMATION SHOWN ON THE FORM.

______________________________ ______________________________
Signature of Seller Date Signature of Seller Date

The undersigned purchaser hereby acknowledges receipt of the foregoing notice at or before the execution of a binding contract for the purchase of the real property or at closing of purchase of the real property.

______________________________ ______________________________
Signature of Buyer Date Signature of Buyer Date

TREC
TEXAS REAL ESTATE COMMISSION

This form has been approved by the Texas Real Estate Commission for use with similarly approved or promulgated contract forms. Such approval relates to this form only. No representation is made as to the legal validity or adequacy of any provision in any specific transactions. Texas Real Estate Commission, P.O. Box 12188, Austin, TX 78711-2188, (512) 936-3000 (http://www.trec.texas.gov) TREC No. 59-0.

PROMULGATED BY THE TEXAS REAL ESTATE COMMISSION (TREC) 05-04-2026

TREC
TEXAS REAL ESTATE COMMISSION

SELLER'S DISCLOSURE ABOUT GROUNDWATER AND SURFACE WATER RIGHTS

EQUAL HOUSING OPPORTUNITY

THIS NOTICE IS A DISCLOSURE OF SELLER'S KNOWLEDGE ABOUT GROUNDWATER AND SURFACE WATER RIGHTS ON THE PROPERTY AS OF THE DATE SIGNED BY SELLER AND IS NOT A SUBSTITUTE FOR ANY INSPECTIONS OR WARRANTIES THE BUYER MAY WISH TO OBTAIN. IT IS NOT A WARRANTY OF ANY KIND BY SELLER OR SELLER'S AGENTS.

CONCERNING THE PROPERTY AT: ____
(Street Address and City)

1. Definitions. For the purposes of this form the following definitions, with notes, apply.

A. "**Groundwater**" means water percolating below the surface of the earth. Groundwater is usually found in subsurface reservoirs or aquifers and is accessed by Water Wells.
[Note: Unless severed from the surface estate, Groundwater is owned by the surface landowner who may be able to access the Groundwater by drilling a Water Well in compliance with the law and rules of the applicable Groundwater District, if any.]

B. "**Groundwater District**" means a local or regional Groundwater Conservation District, Underground Water Conservation District, Subsidence District, or other special district or authority that regulates the drilling or operation of Water Wells.
[Note: Not all land in Texas is subject to a Groundwater District.]

C. "**Surface Water**" means water in lakes, rivers, creeks, streams, and in the bays, estuaries, and arms of the Gulf of Mexico.

D. "**Surface Water Rights**" means a permit, certified filing, or certificate of adjudication administered by the Texas Commission on Environmental Quality (TCEQ) that authorizes the diversion, impoundment, or use of Surface Water.
[Note: Not all diversions, impoundments, or uses of Surface Water require a Surface Water Right.]

E. "**Water Well**" means an artificial excavation that is drilled or dug for the purpose of exploring for or producing Groundwater.
[Note: The drilling and operation of a Water Well may be regulated, restricted, or prohibited in a Groundwater District. Subdividing a property may impact rights related to drilling or operating a Water Well. A Water Well may be owned and operated by individuals, groups, cooperatives, associations, or other entities.]

2. Information Related to Groundwater and Water Wells. [Attach additional sheets as necessary.]

A. Is any portion of the Property located in a Groundwater District? ☐ Yes ☐ No ☐ Unknown
If yes, identify the district and its website: ____
____

B. Is Seller aware of one or more Water Wells on the Property? ☐ Yes ☐ No
If yes:
(1) The total number of Water Wells known to Seller is ________
(2) The number of Water Wells known to Seller that are currently in use is _________
(3) The number of Water Wells known to Seller that are not currently in use and have been capped, covered, plugged, or abandoned is _______
(4) Identify any registrations or permits (by number) from a Groundwater District for the Water Wells on the Property: ____
____

C. If the answer to 2B is yes, complete the following to the extent known.

☐ (1) All Water Wells on the Property are owned or operated solely by Seller for the sole benefit of the Property.

☐ (2) The following Water Wells: (i) are owned or operated by the person identified; (ii) benefit the identified beneficiary; and (iii) are governed by the identified agreements or understandings (attach additional sheets for each Water Well):
Water Well: ____
Owners/Operators: ____
Beneficiary: ____
Agreement or Understanding: ____
____

Initialed for identification by Buyer____ _____ and Seller_____ _____ TREC No. 61-0

____
(Address of Property)

D. Is Seller aware whether the Property receives water from a Water Well located on another property (not including water from a city, municipal utility district or other special district, water supply corporation, or private water company)? ❑ Yes ❑ No If yes, describe the Water Well and identify any agreements or understandings governing access to the water:______________________

E. Is Seller aware whether a Water Well on the Property relies in whole or in part on Groundwater rights owned or leased from land outside the boundaries of the Property? ❑ Yes ❑ No If yes, describe the Groundwater rights owned or leased:______________________

F. Is Seller aware whether any of the Groundwater rights to the Property have been severed, sold, or leased in whole or in part with or without the right to drill or operate a Water Well on the Property? ❑ Yes ❑ No If yes, describe the Groundwater rights severed, sold, or leased:______________________

3. Information Related to Surface Water. [Attach additional sheets as necessary.]

A. Does Seller own any Surface Water Right associated with the Property ❑ Yes ❑ No

If yes:

(1) Identify the applicable Surface Water Right by its permit, filing, or certification of adjudication number: ______________________

(2) If more than one person owns an interest in any Surface Water Right identified in 3A(1), identify each person and their respective ownership interest: ______________________

B. Is there a pond, lake, or water tank on the Property, whether currently with or without water? ❑ Yes ❑ No

Notices to Buyer and Seller:

(1) Statutes, rules, regulations, and court rulings concerning Groundwater, Water Wells, Groundwater rights, surface water, and Surface Water Rights (collectively, **Water Rights**) are multifaceted and may be complex.

(2) The Seller may not have complete knowledge or understanding of the Water Rights related to or affecting the Property.

(3) Water Rights that relate to the Property may be held by others. To determine the extent and application of Water Rights related to Property, consult an attorney who can examine the title to the Property and issues regarding Water Rights.

(4) Rules and regulations of Groundwater Districts regarding Water Wells differ from district to district and should be reviewed if the Property has an existing or potential future Water Well. Some Groundwater Districts have ad valorem taxing authority and others do not. Consult the local Appraisal District for applicable taxes and tax rates.

(5) If the parties need or intend to reserve, specifically except, or separately convey Water Rights related to the Property, each party should consult an attorney before signing a binding contract to purchase or sell the Property.

Seller	Date	Seller	Date
Buyer	Date	Buyer	Date

05-04-2026

TREC
TEXAS REAL ESTATE COMMISSION

APPROVED BY THE TEXAS REAL ESTATE COMMISSION (TREC)

EQUAL HOUSING OPPORTUNITY

SELLER'S DISCLOSURE NOTICE

CONCERNING THE PROPERTY AT ______________________________________
(Street Address and City)

THIS NOTICE IS A DISCLOSURE OF SELLER'S KNOWLEDGE OF THE CONDITION OF THE PROPERTY AS OF THE DATE SIGNED BY SELLER AND IS NOT A SUBSTITUTE FOR ANY INSPECTIONS OR WARRANTIES THE PURCHASER MAY WISH TO OBTAIN. IT IS NOT A WARRANTY OF ANY KIND BY SELLER OR SELLER'S AGENTS.

Seller ☐ is ☐ is not occupying the Property. If unoccupied, how long since Seller has occupied the Property? ________

1. The Property has the items checked below [Write Yes (Y), No (N), or Unknown (U)]:

____Range	____Oven	____Microwave
____Dishwasher	____Trash Compactor	____Disposal
____Washer/Dryer Hookups	____Window Screens	____Rain Gutters
____Security System	____Fire Detection Equipment	____Intercom System
	____Smoke Detector	
	____Smoke Detector-Hearing Impaired	
	____Carbon Monoxide Alarm	
	____Emergency Escape Ladder(s)	
____TV Antenna	____Cable TV Wiring	____Satellite Dish
____Ceiling Fan(s)	____Attic Fan(s)	____Exhaust Fan(s)
____Central A/C	____Central Heating	____Wall/Window Air Conditioning
____Plumbing System	____Septic System	____Public Sewer System
____Patio/Decking	____Outdoor Grill	____Fences
____Pool	____Sauna	____Spa ____Hot Tub
____Pool Equipment	____Pool Heater	____Automatic Lawn Sprinkler System
____Fireplace(s) & Chimney (Wood burning)		____Fireplace(s) & Chimney (Mock)
____Natural Gas Lines		____Gas Fixtures

____Liquid Propane Gas: ____LP Community (Captive) ____LP on Property

____Fuel Gas Piping: ____Black Iron Pipe ____Corrugated Stainless Steel Tubing ____Copper

Garage: ____Attached ____Not Attached ____Carport

Garage Door Opener(s): ____Electronic ____Control(s)

Water Heater: ____Gas ____Electric

Water Supply: ____City ____Well ____MUD ____Co-op

Roof Type: ______________________ Age: ______________ (approx.)

Are you (Seller) aware of any of the above items that are not in working condition, that have known defects, or that are in need of repair? ☐Yes ☐ No ☐ Unknown. If yes, then describe. (Attach additional sheets if necessary): ________

____

____

____

TREC No. 55-1

2. Does the property have working smoke detectors installed in accordance with the smoke detector requirements of Chapter 766, Health and Safety Code?* ☐ Yes ☐ No ☐ Unknown. If the answer to this question is no or unknown, explain (Attach additional sheets if necessary): ______________________________

____

____

____

* Chapter 766 of the Health and Safety Code requires one-family or two-family dwellings to have working smoke detectors installed in accordance with the requirements of the building code in effect in the area in which the dwelling is located, including performance, location, and power source requirements. If you do not know the building code requirements in effect in your area, you may check unknown above or contact your local building official for more information. A buyer may require a seller to install smoke detectors for the hearing impaired if: (1) the buyer or a member of the buyer's family who will reside in the dwelling is hearing impaired; (2) the buyer gives the seller written evidence of the hearing impairment from a licensed physician; and (3) within 10 days after the effective date, the buyer makes a written request for the seller to install smoke detectors for the hearing impaired and specifies the locations for the installation. The parties may agree who will bear the cost of installing the smoke detectors and which brand of smoke detectors to install.

3. Are you (Seller) aware of any known defects/malfunctions in any of the following? Write Yes (Y) if you are aware, write No (N) if you are not aware.

____Interior Walls	____Ceilings	____Floors
____Exterior Walls	____Doors	____Windows
____Roof	____Foundation/Slab(s)	____Sidewalks
____Walls/Fences	____Driveways	____Intercom System
____Plumbing/Sewers/Septics	____Electrical Systems	____Lighting Fixtures

____Other Structural Components (Describe): ______________________________

____

____

If the answer to any of the above is yes, explain. (Attach additional sheets if necessary): ______________________________

____

____

4. Are you (Seller) aware of any of the following conditions? Write Yes (Y) if you are aware, write No (N) if you are not aware.

____Active Termites (includes wood destroying insects)	____Previous Structural or Roof Repair
____Termite or Wood Rot Damage Needing Repair	____Hazardous or Toxic Waste
____Previous Termite Damage	____Asbestos Components
____Previous Termite Treatment	____Urea-formaldehyde Insulation
____Improper Drainage	____Radon Gas
____Water Damage Not Due to a Flood Event	____Lead Based Paint
____Landfill, Settling, Soil Movement, Fault Lines	____Aluminum Wiring
____Single Blockable Main Drain in Pool/Hot Tub/Spa*	____Previous Fires
	____Unplatted Easements
	____Subsurface Structure or Pits
	____Previous Use of Premises for Manufacture of Methamphetamine

If the answer to any of the above is yes, explain. (Attach additional sheets if necessary): ______________________________

____

____

* A single blockable main drain may cause a suction entrapment hazard for an individual.

5. Are you (Seller) aware of any item, equipment, or system in or on the Property that is in need of repair? ☐ Yes (if you are aware) ☐ No (if you are not aware). If yes, explain (attach additional sheets if necessary). ______________________

____

____

6. Are you (Seller) aware of any of the following conditions?* Write Yes (Y) if you are aware, write No (N) if you are not aware.

_____ Present flood insurance coverage

_____ Previous flooding due to a failure or breach of a reservoir or a controlled or emergency release of water from a reservoir

_____ Previous water penetration into a structure on the property due to a natural flood event

Write Yes (Y) if you are aware, and check wholly or partly as applicable, write No (N) if you are not aware.

_____ Located ○ wholly ○ partly in a 100-year floodplain (Special Flood Hazard Area-Zone A, V, A99, AE, AO, AH, VE, or AR)

_____ Located ○ wholly ○ partly in a 500-year floodplain (Moderate Flood Hazard Area-Zone X (shaded))

_____ Located ○ wholly ○ partly in a floodway

_____ Located ○ wholly ○ partly in a flood pool

_____ Located ○ wholly ○ partly in a reservoir

If the answer to any of the above is yes, explain (attach additional sheets if necessary): ______________________

____

*For purposes of this notice:

"100-year floodplain" means any area of land that:

(A) is identified on the flood insurance rate map as a special flood hazard area, which is designated as Zone A, V, A99, AE, AO, AH, VE, or AR on the map;

(B) has a one percent annual chance of flooding, which is considered to be a high risk of flooding; and

(C) may include a regulatory floodway, flood pool, or reservoir.

"500-year floodplain" means any area of land that:

(A) is identified on the flood insurance rate map as a moderate flood hazard area, which is designated on the map as Zone X (shaded); and

(B) has a two-tenths of one percent annual chance of flooding, which is considered to be a moderate risk of flooding.

"Flood pool" means the area adjacent to a reservoir that lies above the normal maximum operating level of the reservoir and that is subject to controlled inundation under the management of the United States Army Corps of Engineers.

"Flood insurance rate map" means the most recent flood hazard map published by the Federal Emergency Management Agency under the National Flood Insurance Act of 1968 (42 U.S.C. Section 4001 et seq.).

"Floodway" means an area that is identified on the flood insurance rate map as a regulatory floodway, which includes the channel of a river or other watercourse and the adjacent land areas that must be reserved for the discharge of a base flood, also referred to as a 100-year flood, without cumulatively increasing the water surface elevation of more than a designated height.

"Reservoir" means a water impoundment project operated by the United States Army Corps of Engineers that is intended to retain water or delay the runoff of water in a designated surface area of land.

7. Have you (Seller) ever filed a claim for flood damage to the property with any insurance provider, including the National Flood Insurance Program (NFIP)?* ☐ Yes ☐ No. If yes, explain (attach additional sheets as necessary): ______________________

____

*Homes in high risk flood zones with mortgages from federally regulated or insured lenders are required to have flood insurance. Even when not required, the Federal Emergency Management Agency (FEMA) encourages homeowners in high risk, moderate risk, and low risk flood zones to purchase flood insurance that covers the structure(s) and the personal property within the structure(s).

8. Have you (Seller) ever received assistance from FEMA or the U.S. Small Business Administration (SBA) for flood damage to the property? ☐ Yes ☐ No. If yes, explain (attach additional sheets as necessary): ______________________

____

9. Are you (Seller) aware of any of the following? Write Yes (Y) if you are aware, write No (N) if you are not aware.

_____ Room additions, structural modifications, or other alterations or repairs made without necessary permits or not in compliance with building codes in effect at that time.

_____ Homeowners' Association or maintenance fees or assessments.

_____ Any "common area" (facilities such as pools, tennis courts, walkways, or other areas) co-owned in undivided interest with others.

_____ Any notices of violations of deed restrictions or governmental ordinances affecting the condition or use of the Property.

_____ Any lawsuits directly or indirectly affecting the Property.

_____ Any condition on the Property which materially affects the physical health or safety of an individual.

_____ Any rainwater harvesting system located on the property that is larger than 500 gallons and that uses a public water supply as an auxiliary water source.

_____ Any portion of the property that is located in a groundwater conservation district or a subsidence district.

_____ Any conservation easements located on the Property.

"Conservation easement" means an easement (permanent or for a period of years) on the property that restricts the use of all or a part of the property to protect natural resources, wildlife habitat, open space, or historical sites.

_____ The Property is presently covered by insurance.

_____ The Property is presently covered by windstorm insurance.

_____ Seller has been unable to insure the Property for any reason.

_____ A private road on or adjoining the Property for which Seller is financially responsible for maintaining.

_____ Any aboveground or underground storage tanks on the Property. (If yes, see 30 Texas Administrative Code Chapter 334 for additional disclosure requirements.)

_____ Any aboveground storage tanks on the Property that hold 500 gallons or more and have stored petroleum products or other chemicals.

If the answer to any of the above is yes, explain. (Attach additional sheets if necessary): ______________________________

____

____

10. If the property is located in a coastal area that is seaward of the Gulf Intracoastal Waterway or within 1,000 feet of the mean high tide bordering the Gulf of Mexico, the property may be subject to the Open Beaches Act or the Dune Protection Act (Chapter 61 or 63, Natural Resources Code, respectively) and a beachfront construction certificate or dune protection permit maybe required for repairs or improvements. Contact the local government with ordinance authority over construction adjacent to public beaches for more information.

11. This property may be located near a military installation and may be affected by high noise or air installation compatible use zones or other operations. Information relating to high noise and compatible use zones is available in the most recent Air Installation Compatible Use Zone Study or Joint Land Use Study prepared for a military installation and may be accessed on the Internet website of the military installation and of the county and any municipality in which the military installation is located.

______________________________ ______________________________
Signature of Seller Date Signature of Seller Date

The undersigned purchaser hereby acknowledges receipt of the foregoing notice.

______________________________ ______________________________
Signature of Purchaser Date Signature of Purchaser Date

TREC
TEXAS REAL ESTATE COMMISSION

SELLER'S NOTICE TO BUYER OF REMOVAL OF CONTINGENCY UNDER ADDENDUM FOR "BACK-UP" CONTRACT

EQUAL HOUSING OPPORTUNITY

CONCERNING THE CONTRACT FOR THE SALE OF THE PROPERTY AT

____

(Street Address and City)

BETWEEN THE UNDERSIGNED SELLER AND ____________________________________(BUYER)

In accordance with Paragraph H of the Addendum for "Back-Up" Contract, Seller notifies Buyer that:

(1) the First Contract is terminated;
(2) the Back-Up Contract with Buyer is no longer subject to the contingency described in Paragraph G of the Addendum for "Back-Up" Contract; and
(3) the Amended Effective Date of the Back-Up Contract is ________________ (insert date when the notice is delivered in accordance with Paragraph 21 of the contract).

Seller	Date	Seller	Date

ADDITIONAL OPTION FEE RECEIPT

Receipt of $__________________ additional option fee in the form of ______________________ is acknowledged.

Escrow Agent	Date

ADDITIONAL EARNEST MONEY RECEIPT

Receipt of $__________________ additional earnest money in the form of ___________________ is acknowledged.

Escrow Agent	Date

REQUIRED DISCLOSURES
Statutory Notice Provided to Consumers

Information About Brokerage Services (Form IABS 1-2, effective 01/01/2026)

11-03-2025

Information About Brokerage Services

Texas law requires all real estate license holders to give the following information about brokerage services to prospective buyers, tenants, sellers and landlords.

TYPES OF REAL ESTATE LICENSE HOLDERS:

- **A BROKER** is responsible for all brokerage activities, including acts performed by sales agents sponsored by the broker.
- **A SALES AGENT** must be sponsored by a broker and works with clients on behalf of the broker.

A BROKER'S MINIMUM DUTIES REQUIRED BY LAW (A client is the person or party that the broker represents):

- Put the interests of the client above all others, including the broker's own interests;
- Inform the client of any material information about the property or transaction received by the broker;
- Answer the client's questions and present any offer to or counter-offer from the client; and
- Treat all parties to a real estate transaction honestly and fairly.

WRITTEN AGREEMENTS ARE REQUIRED IN CERTAIN SITUATIONS: A license holder who performs brokerage activity for a prospective buyer of residential property must enter into a written agreement with the buyer before showing any residential property to the buyer or if no residential property will be shown, before presenting an offer on behalf of the buyer. This written agreement must contain specific information required by Texas law. For more information on these requirements, see section 1101.563 of the Texas Occupations Code. **Even if a written agreement is not required, to avoid disputes, all agreements between you and a broker should be in writing and clearly establish: (i) the broker's duties and responsibilities to you and your obligations under the agreement; and (ii) the amount or rate of compensation the broker will receive and how this amount is determined.**

A LICENSE HOLDER CAN REPRESENT A PARTY IN A REAL ESTATE TRANSACTION:

AS AGENT FOR OWNER (SELLER/LANDLORD): The broker becomes the property owner's agent through an agreement with the owner, usually in a written listing to sell or property management agreement. An owner's agent must perform the broker's minimum duties above and must inform the owner of any material information about the property or transaction known by the agent, including information disclosed to the agent by the buyer or buyer's agent. **An owner's agent fees are not set by law and are fully negotiable.**

AS AGENT FOR BUYER/TENANT: The broker becomes the buyer/tenant's agent by agreeing to represent the buyer, usually through a written representation agreement. A buyer's agent must perform the broker's minimum duties above and must inform the buyer of any material information about the property or transaction known by the agent, including information disclosed to the agent by the seller or seller's agent. **A buyer/tenant's agent fees are not set by law and are fully negotiable.**

AS AGENT FOR BOTH - INTERMEDIARY: To act as an intermediary between the parties the broker must first obtain the written agreement of *each party* to the transaction. The written agreement must state who will pay the broker and, in conspicuous bold or underlined print, set forth the broker's obligations as an intermediary. A broker who acts as an intermediary:

- Must treat all parties to the transaction impartially and fairly;
- May, with the parties' written consent, appoint a different license holder associated with the broker to each party (owner and buyer) to communicate with, provide opinions and advice to, and carry out the instructions of each party to the transaction.
- Must not, unless specifically authorized in writing to do so by the party, disclose:
  - that the owner will accept a price less than the written asking price;
  - that the buyer/tenant will pay a price greater than the price submitted in a written offer; and
  - any confidential information or any other information that a party specifically instructs the broker in writing not to disclose, unless required to do so by law.

A LICENSE HOLDER CAN SHOW PROPERTY TO A BUYER/TENANT WITHOUT REPRESENTING THE BUYER/TENANT IF:

- The broker has not agreed with the buyer/tenant, either orally or in writing, to represent the buyer/tenant;
- The broker is not otherwise acting as the buyer/tenant's agent at the time of showing the property;
- The broker does not provide the buyer/tenant opinions or advice regarding the property or real estate transactions generally; and
- The broker does not perform any other act of real estate brokerage for the buyer/tenant.

Before showing a residential property to an unrepresented prospective buyer, a license holder must enter into a written agreement that contains the information required by section 1101.563 of the Texas Occupations Code. The agreement may not be exclusive and must be limited to no more than 14 days.

LICENSE HOLDER CONTACT INFORMATION: This notice is being provided for information purposes. It does not create an obligation for you to use the broker's services. Please acknowledge receipt of this notice below and retain a copy for your records.

Name of Sponsoring Broker (Licensed Individual or Business Entity)	License No.	Email	Phone
Name of Designated Broker of Licensed Business Entity, if applicable	License No.	Email	Phone
Name of Licensed Supervisor of Sales Agent/Associate, if applicable	License No.	Email	Phone
Name of Sales Agent/Associate	License No.	Email	Phone

Buyer/Tenant/Seller/Landlord Initials ______ ______ Date ______

www.ingramcontent.com/pod-product-compliance
Ingram Content Group UK Ltd.
Pitfield, Milton Keynes, MK11 3LW, UK
UKHW051510290926
15471UKWH00008B/1531

9 781965 482599